Building Red America

Building Red America

*The New Conservative Coalition
and the
Drive for Permanent Power*

THOMAS B. EDSALL

BASIC
BOOKS

A Member of the Perseus Books Group
New York

Published by Basic Books
A Member of the Perseus Books Group

Books published by Basic Books are available at special discounts for bulk purchases in the United States by corporations, institutions, and other organizations. For more information, please contact the Special Markets Department at the Perseus Books Group, 11 Cambridge Center, Cambridge MA 02142, or call (617) 252-5298 or (800) 255-1514, or e-mail special.markets@perseusbooks.com.

Editorial production by Word Craft Publishing Services.

Designed and typeset by Eric Rosenbloom, Kirby Mountain Composition.

A catalog-in-publication data record for this book is available from the Library of Congress.

ISBN-10: 0-465-01815-7
ISBN-13: 978-0-465-01815-4

06 07 08 09 / 10 9 8 7 6 5 4 3 2 1

To my wife, Mary,
and to my daughter, Lexa, her husband, Bob, and my two
grandchildren, Tommy and Lydia, for whom I have worked
and who have made my work worthwhile.

Contents

Preface

This book sets the stage for presidential and congressional elections over the next decade and beyond. Some of the major points that *Building Red America* explores and develops are:

- More than in the past, the Republican Party has become a coalition of the dominant, while the Democratic Party has become, in large part, an alliance of the socially and economically subdominant and those who identify with them.

- While there has been a growing recognition of the role of civil rights and of issues directly related to race in shaping partisan identity and voting behavior, much less thought has been given to the pivotal role in American politics of the sexual and women's rights revolutions and the effective use by the Republican Party of reaction to these insurgencies.

- The conservative movement has successfully merged explicit and concealed biases against minorities, homosexuals, "illegal" immigrants, and "radical" feminists with ideological opposition to interventionist government and higher taxes.

- Insufficient attention has been paid by supporters of the Democratic Party to the business and money revolutions of the past quarter century and to the impact on the American progressive movement of the failure of non-market economies in Europe and elsewhere.

- The Democratic Party has substantial vulnerabilities. It is no longer a populist coalition but is now controlled by a well-educated, relatively affluent, socially liberal elite that sets much of the party's program. At the same time, the rank and file of the party—the majority of its voters—are women and men from the bottom half of the economic order. There is a wide gulf separating the culturally liberal agenda of the party's leadership elite and the pressing material needs of the party's disadvantaged, disproportionately African American and Hispanic constituents. This disconnect has led to short-lived and transient Democratic victories while seriously obstructing the ability of the party to forge and maintain a powerful, resilient biracial, multiethnic coalition.

- Although the Republican Party has dominated American politics over the past forty years, it has not achieved a political realignment. Instead, the GOP has developed the capacity to eke out victory by slim margins in a majority of closely contested elections, losing intermittently but winning more than half the time. It is likely to continue this pattern for the foreseeable future. Conservatives have, furthermore, created a political arena in which winning Democrats are likely to find themselves forced to move to the right.

- When contemporary Republicans win office, their agenda is not moderate. Their effort has been to dismantle the welfare state, a structure built up over the last two-thirds of the twentieth century.

- The GOP has succeeded in institutionalizing a powerful, well-funded, durable infrastructure protecting conservative legislation and regulatory policies to secure ground it has gained, even when Democrats intermittently wrest control of one or more of the branches of government. To quote directly from the first chapter of the book: "In victory and defeat, the conservative Republican Party is certain to continue to press its agenda of weaning individuals from 'dependency' on the state. When out of power, the conservative movement has the resources and the managerial expertise to protect and preserve its ideological and institutional edifice intact. When the movement regains a base of elected power, conservatism is primed and ready to capitalize on prior successes, its agenda ever more aggressive and far reaching."

➤ ◄

The argument made over the following eight chapters is by no means summarized in this preface. The rise of contemporary conservatism in America and the inevitable reconfiguration of both political parties is an ongoing process. This is the fourth book I have written on the subject, and I suspect that it will not be the last.

Acknowledgments

The first of those I want to thank is Donald Lamm, formerly the CEO of W.W. Norton, my editor for over twenty years and now my agent. Don published three of my previous books, allowing me as a writer the most valuable gift: a free hand to write the truth as I see it. His expertise, imagination, and friendship have been invaluable. Don, working in partnership with Christy Fletcher, placed this book in the skilled hands of my editor at Basic Books, William Frucht. Bill Frucht has not only won my respect, but working with him has been an unalloyed pleasure.

I would like to acknowledge here my father's brother, John Tileston Edsall, professor of biochemistry at Harvard for over half a century, who gave close readings to all of my previous books. He died at the age of ninety-nine in 2001. Thanks also to my father-in-law, political scientist Karl W. Deutsch, who had unshakable faith in me.

To Seymour Martin Lipset, comrade and mentor, whose understanding of American politics is unparalleled, I owe more than I can say.

I have been privileged to have worked for some great editors: Martin Peretz at the *New Republic*, Charlie Peters at the *Washington Monthly*, Taylor Branch and Lewis Lapham at *Harpers*, Bob Silvers at the *New York Review of Books*, Jack Beatty and Scott Stossel at the *Atlantic*, and Irving Howe at *Dissent*. Ben Bradlee hired me onto the *Washington Post* and gave me carte blanche to chase the money trail during his great years there.

Thanks to David Brady at Stanford and to the Hoover Institution for generous support; also to the Woodrow Wilson Center in Washington DC, which gave me a fellowship for the year 1996–1997.

Bob Barnett of Williams and Connally has provided me with extraordinary service—my debt to him is immense.

Among my colleagues at the *Washington Post*, I would like to thank Frank Ahrens, Henry Allen, Chuck Babington, Peter Baker, Dan Balz, Peter Behr, Jeff Birnbaum, Dave Broder, Lou Cannon, Bill Casey, Sarah Cohen, Ceci Connolly, Alice Crites, E. J. Dionne, Juliet Eilperin, Michael Fletcher, Mike Getler, Amy Goldstein, Jim Grimaldi, Guy Gugliotta, John Harris, Ken Ikenberry, Haynes Johnson, Al Kamen, Colby King, Jonathan Krim, Chuck Lane, Christopher Lee, Jeff Leen, Madonna Leibling, Mark Leibovich, Bob Lyford, Ruth Marcus, Peter Masley, Kevin Merida, Larry Meyer, Harold Meyerson, Dana Milbank, Morton Mintz, Shailagh Murray, Terry Neal, Steve Pearlstein, Peter Perl, Don Pohlman, Keith Richburg, Hanna Rosin, Jim Rowe, Susan Schmidt, David Segal, Lucy Shackelford, Jeff Smith, Mark Stencel, Frank Swoboda, Jim VandeHei, David von Drehle, Ed Walsh, and Derek Willis.

Valued journalists elsewhere include Larry Barrett, Peter Beinart, Rick Berke, Peter Berkowitz, Sidney Blumenthal, John Breshnahan, Adam Clymer, Charles Cook, Howard Fineman, Frank Foer, Phil Gailey, Jack Germond, Mark Halperin, Bob Healy, Al Hunt, Mickey Kaus, Michael Kinsley, Bill Kristol, Bob Kuttner, Jim Mann, John Mashek, Dick Meyer, Cullen Murphy, Adam Nagourney, David Plotz, David Rogers. Jeff and Christine Rosen, David Rosenbaum, Kit Seeyle, Jim Sleeper, Paul Starr, Stuart Taylor, Chuck Todd, Martin and Susan Tolchin, Mike Tomasky, Robin Toner, Jim Warren, Curtis Wilkie, Juan Williams, and Jules Witcover.

I am deeply indebted to John Judis of the *New Republic* as a writer, thinker, and colleague.

My thanks to Bob Merry of the *Congressional Quarterly* and John Fox Sullivan of the *National Journal*.

In the world of politics, Howard Berman (D-California) has been a friend for over forty years, since we served in V.I.S.T.A. together. Also, gratitude to Devorah Adler, Lee Atwater, Whit Ayres, Jenny Backus, Charlie Baker, Nick Baldick, Jan Baran, Robert Bauer, Charlie Black, Donna Brazile, Matt Brooks, Jano Cabrera, David Carmen, Bill Carrick, Alex Castellanos, Tommy D'Alessandro, Tom Davis, Matthew Dowd, Jim Duffy, Jim Dyke, Steve Elmendorf, Rahm Emanuel, Robert Embry, Tony Fabrizio, Mark Farinella, Will Feltus, Al From, Alex Gage, Jerry L. Gallegos, Bill Galston, Geoff Garin, Mark Gersh, Ed Gillespie, Ben Ginsberg, Gina Glantz, Stan and Anna Greenberg, Marcia Hale, Paul Hancock, Peter Hart,

Harrison Hickman, Harold Ickes, David Israelite, Jim Jordan, Bruce Josten, Elaine Kamarck, Ron Kaufman, David Keene, Tom Korologos, Irv Kovens, Kam Kuwata, Celinda Lake, Frank Luntz, David Lyles, Will Marshall, Terry McAuliffe, Bill McInturff, Michael Meehan, Ken Mehlman, Mark Mellman, Neil Newhouse, Grover Norquist, Larry O'Brien, Ralph Reed, Will Robinson, Buddy Roemer, Simon Rosenberg, Steve Rosenthal, Karl Rove, William Donald Schaefer, Peter Secchia, Rob Shapiro, Craig Shirley, David Sirota, Doug Sosnick, Rob Stein, Andy Stern, Roy Temple, Michael Toner, Richard Viguerie, Dirk Von Dongen, Michael Whouley, and John Yoo.

Among the experts in campaign finance, independent polling, and demographics upon whom I have depended over the years are Fred Wertheimer, Kent Cooper, Larry Noble, Andy Kohut, Mark Gersh, Curtis Gans, and Michael Malbin.

Many scholars have illuminated politics for me, including Alan Abramowitz, Stephen Ansolabehere, Larry M. Bartels, Peter Berkowitz, Earl Black, Merle Black, Karlyn Bowman, Stanley Brubaker, David Buss, Ted Carmines, Steve Erie, Morris Fiorina, Richard Freeman, Robert George, Todd Gitlin, John Green, Jim Guth, David Howell, Gary Jacobson, Matthew Lavendusky, Geoff Layman, Nicholas Lemann, Frank Levy, David Lublin, Sandy Maisel, Tom Mann, Pietro Nivola, Peter Orszag, Carl Pinkele, Sam Popkin, Fred Siegel, Jeff Stonecash, Ruy Teixeira, Marty Wattenberg, and, especially, two of my professors at Boston University, Murray Levin and Howard Zinn.

For help in the final preparation of the manuscript, my thanks to Judy Ng, who lent her talents to the logistics of producing this book on an expedited schedule. Thanks also to Jeffrey Quackenbush, Jane McGraw at Word Craft Publishing Services, and Kate Waldeck and Tom Brazier for their stellar support at Basic Books.

➤ ◄

I met Joe Foote when he was at Harvard Law School. Joe took his legal training into journalism and introduced me to the profession that has become my life's work. Joe read in detail the complete manuscript of this book and provided superb advice.

William F. Schmick Jr., my editor at the *Baltimore Sun*, sent me to Washington and gave me a great ride. Mark London—lawyer and writer—has been an adviser for over three decades. Katherine Payne Moseley spent many hours working together with me and my wife between 1999 and 2001. Mark Kleiman, professor of public policy at UCLA, has provided wise counsel.

Many of the people listed above have been competitors at the poker table, as well as at tennis and squash. Peter Silberman was not only my editor for some of the *Post*'s most glorious years but my poker partner for two and a half decades. Other close friends include Jim Jaffe and Leslie Sewell, Carla Anne Robbins and Guy Gugliotta, Eric Pfeufer and Jean Herman, Bill Fritzmeier, Judith Milliken, Abigail Trafford, Bob Dowling, Adam and Gabrielle Spiegel, Jeff Jones, Fred Hill, Gilbert Lewthwaite, Peter Reuter and Carolyn Isber, Richard Chused and Elizabeth Langer, James Pendleton Jordan—former Howard Baker staffer and expert on Republican politics—Jonathan Kempner and Lise von Susteren, Aviva Kempner, Peter Sherman, and Tom Meehan.

The support of Beatrice Johnson, Dale Underwood, Rosie Aruta, and Sarah Boutot has been essential.

➤ ◄

I am indebted to Henry Pitt, Robert Montgomery, Charles Angell, Mark Talamini, Kurtis Campbell, Anthony Tufaro, and Vincent Greco.

➤ ◄

My gratitude for the warm and loving family that has stood behind me and given me joy: most of all, to my devoted wife, Mary, my beloved daughter, Alexandra Tileston Victor Edsall, her two children, Thomas Edsall Victor and Lydia Edsall Victor, my exceptional son-in-law, Bob Victor, his parents, Alan and Constance Victor, my sister-in-law Margaret Carroll, her two children, Sam and Sophia Carroll, and my nephew John Kamin. Thanks also to my cousins David Tileston Edsall and Nicholas Cranford Edsall and, finally, to the memory of my mother and father, Katherine Byrne Edsall and Richard Linn Edsall.

1 Democratic Party Weaknesses Have Magnified Republican Party Advantages

The two major American political parties are close to parity in numbers of voters, but the Republican Party holds a set of advantages, some substantial and some marginal. Although these advantages do not guarantee victory in any individual election, cumulatively they have given the GOP an edge—an edge the GOP has maintained for almost four decades.

First, the GOP is the party of the socially and economically dominant and of those who identify with the dominant. It is the party of the affluent, of CEOs, of the managerial elite, of successful entrepreneurs, of viable small businesses. It is the party of those blue- and white-collar workers with a record of holding their own in market competition, the party of more stable families, and of those belonging to ascendant rather than to waning religious communities. In 2004, 87.5 percent of citizens who voted Republican in the presidential election were white.

The Democratic Party, conversely, is the party of the so-called "subdominant" and of those who identify with the subdominant, including those upper-income voters who have taken the side of the insurgents in the sexual, women's rights, and civil rights revolutions. Roughly two-thirds of the Democratic Party's adherents are Americans who struggle to survive in an increasingly brutal competitive environment. The party is also the representative of organized labor and of the leadership of old-line religious denominations—institutions in decline.

In a struggle between two numerically equal forces, the side more broadly skilled in economic combat, whose constituents control more resources; the side more accustomed to the rigors of the market, more practiced in the arts of commerce and marketing; the side with greater access to corporate power; the side more adept at risk management; the side with the means to repeatedly assemble and sustain long-lasting, powerful coalitions; the side that has revealed ruthless proficiency in winning and in shaping American institutions to its purposes; the side that has behind it most of those at the helm of the financial, technological, commercial, and information revolutions—this side has had a substantial long-term advantage.

This book argues that, unless the Democratic Party finds a way to defeat Republican "wedge issue" strategies, radically improves its organizational foundations, resolves its internal divisions on national security, formulates a compelling position on the use of force, addresses the schisms generated by its stands on moral, racial, and cultural issues, develops the capacity to turn Republican positions on sociocultural matters into a liability, devises an economic program capable of generating—and generating belief in—wealth, broadens its voter base, recruits candidates who sufficiently embody (or can be portrayed to embody) credible military leadership and mainstream populist values, and develops a strategy to hold together a biracial, multiethnic coalition—or unless the population of the disadvantaged swells—the odds are that the Republican Party will continue to maintain, over the long term, a thin but durable margin of victory.

In order to reverse the rightward drift of the electorate, Democrats will have to grapple with voters who hold "illiberal" views, as expressed by a Republican voter from Memphis, Tennessee:

> Gun activists are sick of having to get a license, and a stamp on that license, there are people who want government to stop forcing integration down their throats, there are people who want government to stop pushing that men and women are the same. There are people who want the government to keep its hands off their wallets, who are sick of getting a surly bureaucrat on the phone, sick of getting a busy signal at Social Security, sick of getting wrong answers from the IRS, sick of waiting in line at the Post Office, sick of wasting a day at the DMV, sick of vagrants in the public library, sick of incompetent schools,

overcrowded classrooms, dirty lavatories, and teachers who can't spell, sick of police who are more like criminals than law enforcement officers, sick of waiting on hold when they call 911, sick of their garbage being spilled, sick of burned-out streetlights, potholes, road work that goes on for months, traffic jams that double their commute time, paychecks going to taxes for services they don't believe will be there when they need them—sick of the whole damn thing.

It is this kind of worldview that Grover Norquist, president of Americans for Tax Reform, has capitalized on in building his "leave us alone coalition," which has successfully demonized government and forged an alliance of economic conservatives, libertarians, and social conservatives in support of the Republican Party.

For Democrats, although an aggressive attempt to exploit Republican vulnerabilities on corruption is necessary (lobbyist Jack Abramoff, Republican Majority Leader Tom DeLay, Ohio Representative Bob Ney, California Representative Duke Cunningham, etc.), by itself a focus on corruption can produce only short-term gains. Nor is the quagmire in Iraq enough to guarantee Democrats a reliable progressive coalition. The last years of the Vietnam War hurt the GOP but by no means killed it. Watergate was a more serious scandal than allegations in 2006 of corruption affecting the GOP. Watergate, and America's defeat under Republican leadership in Vietnam, produced major congressional victories for the Democrats in 1974 and gave them the presidency in 1976. All those gains and more were swept away in 1980 with Ronald Reagan's victory and the Republican takeover of the Senate.

Despite the post-Watergate, post-Vietnam Democratic victory of 1976, the Republican Party went on to control the White House for twenty of the next twenty-eight years, the Senate for eighteen of the next twenty-six years, and the House for twelve of the next twenty-six years.

Furthermore, when Democrats have seized the reins of power, episodically over the last forty years, they have been hampered by their weakened condition, unable, for example, to shape the legislative process during the first two years (1992–1994) of Bill Clinton's term, a time in which the Democratic Party technically commanded the legislative and executive branches of government.

⊱ ⊰

As of mid-2006, the Republican Party is in charge of all three branches of the federal government: it controls twenty-eight of the fifty governorships and twenty state legislatures to the Democrats' nineteen (ten are split, and Nebraska is unicameral). In addition, Republicans have appointed more judges to the current federal bench than Democrats: 362 Republican to 291 Democratic appointees on the federal district courts, 97 Republican to 66 Democratic appointees on the federal appeals courts, and 7 Republican to 2 Democratic appointees on the U.S. Supreme Court.

While Republicans will lose individual elections—as they lost the Senate for the eight years between 1986 and 1994 and the White House, with the help of Ross Perot, in 1992 and 1996[1]—their track record and the trend lines over the past four decades suggest that, in America today, the GOP has bested the Democratic Party in the symbolic manipulation of controversial sociocultural issues touching upon national security, patriotism, race, sex, and religion. The Republican Party has both capitalized upon and driven political polarization, speaking to genuine cultural needs and at the same time ruthlessly deploying deeply divisive social/cultural "wedge issues" so that the GOP has come to set the national agenda.

THE REPUBLICAN STRENGTH IN INTER-PARTY COMPETITION

Republican advantages in inter-party competition include a business ethos that concentrates heavily on long- and short-range cal-

---

[1]Ross Perot in the 1992 presidential election won 19 percent of the popular vote and in 1996 won 9 percent. In 1992 Clinton won 43 percent of the popular vote, and in 1996 he won 49.2 percent—in neither case did he carry a majority. Perot ran more strongly among Republican demographic groups than he did among Democrats: Perot in 1992 won 22 percent of the white vote and 19 percent of the white female vote, but only 7 percent of the black vote. Perot's 21 percent margin among white Protestants was twice as high as his 9 percent margin among Jewish voters (a Democratic constituency). Perot's margins were highest in suburban, small town, and rural communities and lowest in big cities, generally bastions of Democratic support. "Presidential Elections, 1972–2004," *Washington Post* exit poll data, compiled by *Washington Post* reporter Dan Balz.

culations to keep and expand market share and its success, to date, in preventing a second terrorist attack. Republican planners and operatives from Ray Bliss to Lee Atwater to Haley Barbour to Karl Rove have a record of strategizing both in terms of candidates and multi-year party interests. In the arena of party-building, the Democrats have no counterparts to these men. The conservative movement itself—independent of the GOP—has been resilient. This movement continues, even as individual Republican office-holders and strategists come and go—notably, Nixon, Atwater, and Reagan.

Over the past forty years, the Republican Party and the conservative movement have together created a juggernaut—a loosely connected but highly coordinated network of individuals and organizations—with a shared stake in a strong, centralized political machine. This machine includes the national party itself, a collection of campaign contributors large and small, a majority of the country's business and trade associations, the bulk of the corporate lobbying community, and an interlocking alliance of muscular conservative "values" organizations and churches (The Family Research Council, The Coalition for Traditional Values, Focus on the Family, the Southern Baptist Convention, thriving Pentecostal, evangelical, and right-leaning Catholic communities, and so forth). It includes a powerful array of conservative foundations with focused social and economic agendas (Scaife, Bradley, Olin, Koch, Smith Richardson, Carthage, Earhart, etc.), as well as prosperous right-of-center think tanks such as the American Enterprise Institute, the Cato Institute, the Free Congress Foundation, the Heritage Foundation, and the Manhattan Institute. This interlocking alliance—a "new conservative labyrinth"—has proven deft at redefining key American concepts of social justice, at marketing conservative ideologies in both domestic and international affairs, and at successfully integrating these redefined ideals—in the eyes of many voters—with goals of economic efficiency.

The Republican Party has secured and formalized a stronger compact with corporate America than at any time since the 1920s. This web of corporate power, party organizations, research and policy institutions, philanthropic foundations, religious groups, interest groups such as the National Rifle Association (NRA), and lobbyists supports and finances not only the party but its intellectual

champions, its public relations initiatives, its candidates, and its officeholders. It serves as a system for the cultivation and nurturance
of political talent, providing opportunities, jobs, and the chance to
get rich to those committed to the GOP and to the conservative
cause.

This network acts as a powerful force buttressing the Republican legislative and regulatory agenda. It focuses on the dissem-
ination of conservative ideas—social, moral, cultural, military,
geopolitical, and economic—and it remains constantly on the look-
out for ways to splinter, weaken, and demonize the left coalition and
the intellectual and moral convictions of the Democratic Party. This
conservative confederation has succeeded in permanently tainting
the core doctrinal underpinnings of the Democratic alliance: the
ideologies of modern racial, social, and economic liberalism.

The Republican Party and its allies in the business community,
in the conservative movement, in the foreign policy community,
and on the religious right have set up an astonishingly ambitious
goal: to remake America—as well as America's role in the world.
What gives this endeavor its grandiose aspect is that the GOP is
working with the slimmest of political margins. The Republican
program is not the expression of a broad public agreement. It is the
agenda of a conservative elite expert in capturing the support of a
slender majority of the electorate and seizing control of the nation's
political machinery.

The potential vulnerability and tenuousness of the Republican
coalition has forced the GOP to adopt a strategy of consciously
building a Republican voting majority, a loyal base secured by elab-
orate institutional scaffolding, engineered to remain intact through
inevitable periods of defeat. The building of a political stronghold
at a time of heightened political competition requires aggressive
polarizing strategies—many touching upon issues of race, rights,
and sex—designed to strengthen and reward allies and to weaken
and deplete the resources of adversaries. Such stratagems explicitly
reject the politics of consensus and exploit the conception of the
American electorate as made up of two warring camps, one on
the right and one on the left.

First and foremost, Republican political strategy requires the
concentration of as much power as possible in the executive

branch—in the hands of the president and of his closest allies and operatives. The Bush administration has set about achieving this goal with determination. The administration's refusal to give Congress information about the meetings between executives from major oil companies and Vice-President Richard Cheney's secret energy task force, its assertion of the right to wage unilateral, preemptive war, and its strenuous defense of presidential authority to order secret surveillance, interrogations, imprisonments, and warrantless wiretapping have all been part of a drive to concentrate power in the White House. So, too, have been the appointments to the Supreme Court of John Roberts and Samuel Alito, both strong supporters of executive prerogative.

Business Firmly in the Republican Corner

Corporate America has lined up behind the broader goals of the Republican Party. Virtually every major industrial and commercial sector now sees itself as more advantaged by Republican policies than by Democratic policies. This allegiance to the GOP is graphically evident in the pattern of campaign contributions, but the depth of the commitment is even better reflected in the willingness of the CEOs and chairmen of businesses large and small to devote substantial personal time and energy to the Bush campaign, competing to win such honorifics as "Pioneers," "Rangers," and "Super Rangers."

With American business firmly in its corner—including such major trade associations as the Business Roundtable, the U.S. Chamber of Commerce, the National Association of Manufacturers, and the National Federation of Independent Business—the Republican Party has not only substantial business acumen behind it but has added credibility in debates over tax and spending, as well as financial backing for its cultural and moral agenda. Again, even though the Democrats may return temporarily to power and business interests may be forced to allocate campaign contributions in a more bipartisan manner, the long-term strategic interests of the American corporate community dictate its enduring alliance with, and strong financial support for, the GOP and for the larger conservative movement.

Leveraging Anger

In the political arena, the Republican Party has successfully enlisted support for its program by tapping and exploiting the anger and cultural anxiety of middle- and lower-income white Americans. The GOP has courted those white voters whose interests are overwhelmingly focused on tempering, if not altogether rolling back, the civil rights movement, on forcibly stemming the tide of migrants from developing countries, on seeking to decelerate or reverse libertarian cultural trends, and on re-establishing what they see as a "decent and honorable" society. To this end, the GOP and its allies in the conservative movement have focused on hot-button appeals concerning moral values such as "the homosexual lifestyle," the "rights of the unborn," or "illegal" immigration.

The votes of these middle- and working-class, culturally conservative whites have been deployed for noncultural objectives as well—to provide backing for the Republican economic agenda, especially for tax cuts directed at business interests and the wealthy, for policies favoring powerful energy interests, and for a reduction in regulations and other burdens on corporations and the affluent. Middle- and working-class white voters have supported the Republican emphasis on cutting government spending on social welfare programs—despite the fact that these programs are of potential benefit to themselves—in part because these tax dollars provide proportionally larger benefits to racial and ethnic minorities, who make up a larger proportion of the poor, often conceptualized by social moderates and conservatives as the "undeserving" poor.

Coded Rhetoric

The Republican Party has assembled a coalition of supporters who can be reached by code words or coded phrases that signal the reliability of a candidate to voters who have conservative values, interests, and "anger points."[2] A candidate affirming his or her support for "family values" or for the physical display of religious symbols such as the Ten Commandments in public areas, using the noun

---

[2]For more on "anger points" see chapter 2.

"Democrat" as an adjective (as in "Democrat senator praises bin Laden"), or simply describing himself or herself as a conservative is indicating, in the symbolic language of politics, opposition to taxes, to "big government," to gay marriage, to affirmative action, and to key court-ordered remedies for racial segregation, while supporting deregulation, religious expression in the public sphere—including prayer in the schools—the overturn of *Roe v. Wade*, lower taxes, and abstinence education.

Words and phrases such as "the culture of life," "frivolous lawsuits," "activist judges," "class action reform," "gun liability," "the death tax," "make tax relief permanent," "ownership society," "liberal," "school prayer," "marriage between a man and a woman," responsibility, and even "Harvard" signal support, to those sensitive to such cues, for a larger conservative package. While Republicans have used modern technology to discover the anger points that mobilize individual voters, the party has also developed an encompassing rhetoric to signal sympathy to those constituencies it is most interested in getting to the polls.

The roots of contemporary conservative rhetoric go directly back to the issue of race in the early 1960s. Alabama Governor George Corley Wallace, the southern Democrat who ran for president as a segregationist independent in 1968, laid much of the groundwork for the development of contemporary Republican conservative populism, driven by opposition to the civil rights movement in the 1960s, and expanding steadily to encompass opposition to abortion, welfare, crime, homosexuality, "radical" feminism, and aspects of the sexual revolution.

Wallace's 1963 gubernatorial inaugural speech is most famous for its direct appeal to racial hatred—"I say . . . segregation today, . . . segregation tomorrow, . . . segregation forever"—but what is more striking, in retrospect, is how Wallace captured and articulated forty years ago key elements of the language and imagery routinely invoked today in the speech of mainstream Republican candidates and officeholders. Many of the ideas and phrases in Wallace's 1963 inaugural address are regularly referred to or paraphrased by Republican politicians in the contemporary North and South.

After his famous "segregation forever" line, Wallace hit a number of familiar notes, by now so often used by Republicans on the stump that their origins have become invisible:

> We are faced with an idea that if a centralized government [federal judges] assumes enough authority, enough power over its people, that it can provide a utopian life. . . . It is a government that . . . buys its power from us, . . . credit without responsibilities to the debtors, . . . our children. . . .Governments do not produce wealth; . . . people produce wealth. . . . As the government must restrict and penalize and tax incentive and endeavor and must increase its expenditures, . . . then this government must assume more and more police powers and we find we are become government-fearing people, . . . not God-fearing people. . . . Government has become our god. . . . Pseudo-liberal spokesmen and some Harvard advocates have never examined the logic of its substitution of what it calls "human rights" for individual rights. . . . Progressives tell us that our Constitution was written for "horse and buggy" days. . . . So were the Ten Commandments. . . . Power politics that led a group of men on the Supreme Court . . . to issue an edict, based not on legal precedent, . . .which said our Constitution is outdated and must be changed . . . led this same group of men to . . . [forbid] little school children to say a prayer, . . . [to remove] the words "in God we trust." . . . We have placed this sign, "In God We Trust," upon our State Capitol on this Inauguration Day as physical evidence of determination to renew the faith of our fathers. . . . Such physical evidence is evidently a direct violation of the logic of that Supreme Court in Washington D.C., and if they or their spokesmen in this state wish to term this defiance, . . . I say . . . then let them make the most of it.

Even as many voters today have their attention focused not only on racial matters but on a host of other issues—taxes, religion, federal judges, liberals, prayer, centralized government, and so on—in political terms, racially coded rhetoric has served over the past four decades to bring together—to "bundle"—and to unify key Republican messages.

REPUBLICAN GOALS

Perhaps the first and central policy goal of the GOP, whether in the majority or the minority, has been to break the trust, originally forged by Franklin Roosevelt during the Great Depression, between the government and millions of its less advantaged citizens. It was this alliance that became the basis of the New Deal Coalition. The Republican Party has had the consistent aim of replacing this collective project with an entirely different ethos, one of individualism. This ethos dictates that the provision of key goods such as health care, retirement security, and protection from natural or other catastrophes is no longer a public responsibility, the province of government, but rather a matter of personal duty with responsibility for basic survival needs falling on the individual instead of the state. In the Republican view, risks are to be shifted as much as possible from government to the lone citizen.

The function of government, in the view of the GOP and its advocates, is limited to facilitating "the ownership society," the ability of the individual to contract with private sector institutions—banks, brokerage houses, investment advisors, financial planners, insurance firms, physicians, nursing homes, pharmaceutical suppliers, hospitals, disaster and risk management firms, conservative churches, and "faith-based" charities—for essential services. Insofar as politics is a form of competition for limited resources, these policies continue to shift government resources, tangible and intangible, away from racial and ethnic minorities—an objective not only of the opponents of racial integration but also one that is, intentionally or not, to the advantage of those who are already dominant and who happen to be white.

Conservatives have been helped inestimably in their anti-government project by the daily inefficiencies of government, as expressed by the angry Memphis voter quoted above. The monopoly nature of government guarantees that public services will often lag in quality behind those delivered in the competitive private sector. Americans are used to—and require—a high level of quality in the services they purchase; this expectation works to the disadvantage of those who support government and to the advantage of those who do not.

The second major goal of the contemporary Republican Party and of the conservative movement has been the easing of regulations and the reduction of labor and social welfare costs viewed as inimical to the interests of American business. Republican supporters from the corporate community seek government help in shedding burdensome, legislatively mandated obligations in order to strengthen firms facing competitors from China, India, former Soviet bloc countries in Europe, and Latin America. Some of these labor and regulatory costs were imposed through initiatives dating back to the Roosevelt administration, especially the National Labor Relations Act, but many were enacted into law in the 1960s and 1970s: the Age Discrimination in Employment Act of 1967, regulations enacted by the Occupational Safety and Health Administration (1970) and the Environmental Protection Agency (1970), the Clean Air Act (1970), the Clean Water Act (1972), the Employee Retirement Income Security Act of 1974 (ERISA), consumer protection legislation, the expansion of programs directed at the poor, such as food stamps, and regulations supporting, enforcing, and expanding provisions of the Civil Rights and Voting Rights acts of 1964 and 1965.

The third goal of the GOP has been to demonstrate military leadership, to revive and reassert the nation's armed strength to maintain a dominant global presence, and to forestall other countries from eroding American power or diminishing American access to energy and other resources. The result has been the adoption by the Bush administration of an explicit policy declaring the right of the United States unilaterally to initiate preemptive war. As the White House put it in a document released by the National Security Council in September 2002:

> The United States has long maintained the option of preemptive actions to counter a sufficient threat to our national security. The greater the threat, the greater is the risk of inaction—and the more compelling the case for taking anticipatory action to defend ourselves, even if uncertainty remains as to the time and place of the enemy's attack. To forestall or prevent such hostile acts by our adversaries, the United States will, if necessary, act preemptively.

The fourth goal of the contemporary GOP has been to approximate a restoration of traditional morality and traditional family structures that characterized American culture before the oral contraceptive pill became widely available in the mid-1960s and before surgical abortion became legal and safe in 1973, developments that spurred the far-reaching sexual revolution, which came to include both homosexual and heterosexual participants. In many respects, the conservative morality agenda carries the highest political risks, both in its potential to mobilize the left and to divide the right.

ATTACKING DEMOCRATIC IDEOLOGIES

Pursuit of all four of these Republican goals requires a sustained effort to attack and marginalize powerful ideological currents within the Democratic Party:

1. the commitment to government intervention to redistribute wealth;

2. the aggressive use of the regulatory state to protect the environment and the workplace;

3. the commitment to defend and expand rights for, and to redress past discrimination against, racial and ethnic minorities;

4. affirmative support for expanded opportunities for women—particularly for working women and single mothers;

5. the commitment to offer government-mandated protections to once-stigmatized groups such as homosexuals;

6. the pledge to maximize rights, and to redistribute them if necessary, regarding sexual privacy, self-potentiation, and "expressive individualism";

7. an aversion to the use of coercive measures in law enforcement, including opposition to police brutality, capital punishment, and harsh sentencing guidelines; and

8. a reluctance to use the instruments of war and military action to resolve resource competitions and other conflict—evolving from liberal opposition, in the aftermath of World War II, to the development of atomic weapons and to the escalating nuclear arms race.

During the Vietnam War, with its universal draft, antiwar sentiment became a hallmark of the new Democratic left. This sentiment became institutionalized within the party, as antiwar activists assumed leadership positions following the McGovern commission reforms after the 1968 election.

All of these Democratic Party issue positions—which create clear opportunities for the GOP—have been reinforced by the gender gap that first appeared in 1980. The gender gap was created by the departure of men from the Democratic Party, not, as often claimed, by the movement of women to the Democratic Party. By 2004, the gap led to a majority female Democratic Party (54 percent female and 46 percent male) and a majority male Republican Party. Gender gap trends from 1996 to 2004 suggest that male allegiance to the Democratic Party has continued to weaken: Clinton carried women by sixteen percentage points and lost men by one; Gore carried women by eleven points and lost men by eleven—a ten-point negative swing among men and a five-point negative swing among women. Kerry lost men by the same margin as Gore and carried women only by three points, an eight-point drop.

According to National Election Studies (NES) data, women are far more opposed to the use of force than are men. Political scientists Benjamin I. Page and Robert Y. Shapiro of Northwestern University and Columbia University, in their study of public attitudes, *The Rational Public*, stated, "In practically all realms of foreign and domestic policy, women are less belligerent than men. They are more supportive of arms control and peaceful foreign relations; they are more likely to oppose weapons buildups or the use of force. They much more frequently favor gun control and oppose capital punishment." Equally important, Page and Shapiro found that "more women than men have favored policies which aid the poor, the unemployed, the sick, and others in need. This kind of difference has also applied to key policies concerning consumer protection, personal safety, and protection of the environment, with more women than men favoring regulation."

The gender gap—both the preference of women for the Democratic Party and the flight of men to the GOP—has been reinforced by the emergence of women in powerful positions in the Democratic Party. Among them are House Democratic Leader Nancy Pelosi (California) and Senator Hillary Clinton (New York), a potential candidate for the Democratic presidential nomination in 2008. Emily's List, the Feminist Majority, the National Women's

Caucus, NOW, and NARAL are currently among the most influential interest groups within the Democratic Party, providing ammunition for those who characterize the Democrats as the "Mommy" or "Nanny" party and who feel that only the GOP is genuinely hospitable to men.

Liberal Institutions Are Easy Targets for Republican Attack

While the Democratic Party has an extensive network of defenders in the advocacy community on the left, these center-left groups operate on uncertain terrain. They have to date been less aggressive, less innovative, less resourceful and entrepreneurial, less hard-nosed in their media tactics, less effective in influencing the outcome of policy debates, and less systematically focused on the political dimension of their goals than their conservative counterparts. Though these progressive groups have achieved successes (for example, defeating the 1987 Bork nomination to the Supreme Court), they now operate with a far more unreliable base of support than similar Republican associations.

Democratic institutions have precipitously faded in political influence by failing to leverage their dollars as efficiently as Republicans and by seeking policy goals (for example, protecting the free speech rights of cable TV and Internet pornographers) that often incite moral opposition among a critical mass of voters. Liberal institutions have proven susceptible to Republican attack and have lost ground as donors and adherents have become discouraged, turning their attention to new causes. America Coming Together (ACT), The Media Fund, the Institute for Policy Studies, Common Cause, the Industrial Areas Foundation, Operation PUSH, the NAACP, and the mainline denominations of the National Council of Churches (NCC) are only a few examples.

Other left organizations—People for the American Way, Americans United for Separation of Church and State, the Human Rights Campaign, and the ACLU—have retained supporters but pursue policy initiatives that, in the eyes of critics, cost Democrats more votes than they recruit. In general, the left establishment has placed a far higher priority on specific, narrow legislative and policy goals, on grassroots demonstration projects, on ad hoc victories, and on culturally inflammatory initiatives that expend moral capital rather than on building political power through Democratic Party victories.

Many organizations on the right, in contrast, see the future of the Republican Party and their own policy agendas as inextricably intertwined, with success or failure linked directly to the victory or defeat of Republican candidates.

Democratic Supporters Are Split into Two Factions

The long-term liabilities of the Democratic Party are deeply rooted in the history of the past half-century. In the more than forty years since 1964, political liberalism has undergone a major conceptual transformation, and its supporters have divided into two major factions.

The *larger* of these two major factions, the one making up just over 60 percent of all Democratic voters, is composed of an alliance of the socially and economically disadvantaged. They are joined by the shared goal of seeking government help in meeting essential material needs, income transfers, a haven from market pressures, and at times protection from majoritarian cultural norms. During the 1930s and 1940s, this relatively disadvantaged component of the Democratic Party was dominated by the traditional working class: skilled and unskilled private sector workers, many of whom were just beginning to form unions. Globalization and deindustrialization have decimated the ranks of this Democratic constituency.

Currently, the lower-income, "downscale" wing of the Democratic Party includes, but is not limited to, a number of overlapping groups:

- The victims of economic competition—poorly paid workers and workers in downsizing sectors.

- The unemployed and the unemployable. Only 45 percent of those of voting age in the bottom third of the income distribution are employed, compared to 80 percent of those in the top third. The low-income unemployed include the elderly, unmarried mothers at home with children, students, and the disabled.

- Union members, older white Southerners, and public employees who are committed to the Democratic Party for either historical reasons or because they believe that the party does in fact represent their interests better than the GOP.

- Ethnic and racial minorities—roughly 90 percent of African Americans, about two-thirds of Hispanic voters, a significant proportion of Muslims, and Southeast Asians—all of whom have been historically barred from social and economic participation.

- Those seeking support from the government as they struggle to deal with the aftermath of the sociocultural revolutions of the past forty years, revolutions that have led to an explosive growth in childbearing by unmarried women (which reached a record high of 35.7 percent in 2004 for the entire United States and 69.2 percent in 2004 among African Americans, according to the CDC's National Center for Health Statistics) and divorce rates approaching 50 percent, leaving many single mothers and children in need of taxpayer-provided help to finance the basic necessities of life.

- A population of well over 7 million Americans entangled in the criminal justice system—those with police records themselves or with family members or friends in prison, on probation, or on parole—costing federal, state, and local governments a total of $159 billion in 1999. This group includes a large population struggling with substance abuse, reliant upon government-sponsored counseling and treatment resources.

- A growing American population, heterosexual and homosexual, who are HIV positive—1,039,000 to 1,185,000 people at the end of 2004—or have AIDS—415,193 in 2004—for a total of 1.5 million people or more affected, many impoverished and dependent on government-supported drug therapy, needle-exchange programs, and medical care. Family members and friends swell the numbers of this group.

The *smaller* of the two major factions, "upscale Democrats," makes up close to 40 percent of the Democratic vote and is composed of relatively well-educated, well-off, culturally liberal professionals ("information workers," "symbol analysts," "creatives," knowledge workers, etc.). These voters have joined the Democratic Party over the past four decades, helping to compensate for the defection of middle- and lower-income whites (disproportionately male) to the GOP. From 1960 to the present, the percentage of Democratic presidential voters employed in the professions has doubled. Democratic professionals include academics, artists, designers, editors, human relations managers, lawyers, librarians, mathematicians, nurses, personnel specialists, psychologists, scientists, social workers, teachers, and therapists. While this upscale group, according to the Pew Research Center, makes up almost 40 percent of all Democratic voters, it makes up only 19 percent of all registered voters.

A solid 83 percent of these better-off Democratic voters are white. Upper-income Democratic voters have the highest education level of any Pew typology group—Democrat or Republican. Females make up 54 percent, 41 percent are college graduates, and 26 percent have some postgraduate education. They stand apart from the rest of the population in that 43 percent seldom or never attend religious services. More than one-third have never married (36 percent), 42 percent reside in urban areas, 41 percent earn at least $75,000 a year, and 77 percent do not have a gun in the home. Only 6 percent watch FOX television, whereas 37 percent go online for news. A striking 92 percent believe homosexuality should be accepted as a way of life by society, and 80 percent support gay marriage. Only 7 percent believe peace is achieved through a strong military. Fully 88 percent are persuaded that it is not necessary to believe in God to have good values.

Although this well-educated, culturally libertarian, relatively affluent progressive elite forms a minority of the Democratic electorate and a substantially smaller minority of the national electorate, it is this activist stratum that sets the agenda for the Democratic Party and that provides the majority of delegates to the national Democratic conventions, where party platforms and party rules are written. In this upscale faction are many voters who share with some—but by no means all—lower-income Democrats an oppositional stance and even animosity toward "repressive" or "conformist" mainstream social and sexual cultural norms.

The power of this wing of the Democratic Party is reflected in the centrality of a single issue—abortion rights—in weighing the credentials of nominees to the federal bench. As Democrats review the records of Republican candidates for the Supreme Court, or for appeals courts, abortion supersedes all other issues, eclipsing questions of judicial views on wages, collective bargaining, employee benefits, workplace safety, job security, disability rights, trade agreements, immigration, tenant-landlord relations, employment discrimination, and eligibility criteria for the Earned Income Tax Credit.

"Discipline versus Therapy"

The leadership of the contemporary Democratic Party pits this socially progressive, upper-echelon, activist "post-materialist" cadre against many of the most economically pressed within the party— who would arguably be better served by income transfers or public works spending than by battles as to whether the words "under God" should be included in the Pledge of Allegiance. The Democratic Party's progressive elite is pitted, as well, against middle- and lower-income white citizens who now vote Republican and who adhere to values oriented toward "discipline" rather than "nurturance"—or, to use another formulation, toward "discipline versus therapy." These Republican voters believe that what they term "irresponsible behavior" is the cause of a broad spectrum of social ills, including the demand for abortion.

As Michael Stephens, twenty-nine, the Youth Director of the First United Methodist Church in Alpharetta, Georgia, puts it:

> If someone has sex and gets pregnant and all of a sudden says, "I want to get it out," I do not agree with that at all. Just to get rid of it because you don't want it, there are families that want children. Taking a life, you cannot do that. Even with rape, if you don't want the baby, you give it up for adoption.

From abortion to single motherhood to homelessness to dependence on government "handouts," many Republican voters— both members of the Christian right and those intensely hostile to the Christian right—along with millions of independent voters, sound the theme of responsibility or of "behaving responsibly."

Such voters are convinced, fairly or unfairly, that liberal Democratic ideology and policies undermine this standard.

In this view, Democratic leadership elites are adversaries of those Americans who are uneasy with a "permissive lifestyle," offended by a coarsening of the popular culture, and wary of secularization, of current rates of immigration (legal and illegal), of multiculturalism, of the liberal embrace of "diversity," of nontraditional gender roles, of what is characterized as "the gay lifestyle," and of those seen as disruptive of conventional sexual mores. Such voters resent what they view as a tax-subsidized government dole to those who evade "personal responsibility."

It would be a mistake, however, to oversimplify the views of social conservatives. Voters in this pool do not have a monolithic view; their concerns vary, and these concerns are all grist for the Republican mill. A retired state policeman in Georgia sees the Democratic leadership in Washington this way:

> I think Kennedy, he should be in prison really because of Chappaquiddick. He should be there, no doubt about that. How can they have someone like that who has no credibility be able to ask questions of a man who is as honorable as Alito [the 2006 Alito hearings before the Senate Judiciary Committee for a seat on the US Supreme Court]. I think he is a shame and a disgrace. . . . The Democratic party, they have gone too far left. . . . Gay marriage? They can do what they want to do, I have no problems with homosexuals. However I do have problems with adoptions. I'm not saying they are going to change that child's mind, and all. But it's on the child in school and the future. It puts a burden on the child.

Another Georgia voter, David Loudenflager, has a different but compatible perspective:

> I worked 32 years for the Arrow Shirt Company. They got bought out and downsized, then I went to work for Proctor and Gamble. . . . The Democratic Party is too much special interests. Give away everything. The gays hold a demonstration, they are right there with them. Any feminists, they are right there with them. I just think the Republican Party is more accountable, more responsible. You can't be all things to all people. "Vote for me, I'm going to get you anything you want. Tell

me what you want, I'll go get it." You don't have to be account-
able that way. But the Christian Coalition, I don't like them.
Again, it's just a matter of another special interest group, as far
as I'm concerned. All these people running around telling you
how good they are, and how right they are. You better be care-
ful and hold on to your wallet. That's right, that's how I feel.

Security: A Threshold Matter for Many Voters

Nothing has been more important to the continuing strength of the
Republican Party since the beginning of the twenty-first century than
the terrorist attacks of September 11, 2001. Events on that day tapped
voter fears that played directly to built-in Republican strengths while
reviving the Democratic vulnerabilities on military and national security issues that have plagued the party since the 1960s.

The 9/11 attacks turned national security into a top tier issue.
Even worse for the Democrats, security became a "threshold" matter for many voters, especially for women with children, who had
been a key Democratic target constituency throughout the 1990s.
To be considered eligible for public office after 9/11, a candidate
had to cross a security threshold. Because the Democratic Party became the party of antiwar activists during the Vietnam War—particularly with the nomination of George McGovern—and because
the party became increasingly hostile to defense spending, the security threshold has been a major stumbling block for the party's
candidates. Voters have consistently identified the GOP as better
equipped to deal with foreign threats and military issues.

Republican strength on the issues of terrorism and security
proved to be crucial assets in the 2002 and 2004 elections. In both
contests, the GOP made sure these issues were front and center. At
a January 17, 2002, meeting of the Republican National Committee
(RNC) in Austin, Texas, Rove declared, "We can go to the country
on this issue because they trust the Republican Party to do a better
job of protecting and strengthening America's military might and
thereby protecting America." Rove then added, "The second place
we should go to the country is on protecting the homeland. We can
go to the country confidently on this issue because Americans trust
the Republican Party to do a better job of keeping our communities
and families safe."

In the November 2002 elections, the Republican margin in the House grew from nine to twenty-five seats and, in 2004, to thirty seats. In the Senate, the GOP picked up two seats to regain a fifty-one-vote majority in 2002 and strengthened that to fifty-five seats in 2004. Bush legitimated his presidency in 2004, winning re-election by an absolute majority, 50.73 percent, and defeating John F. Kerry by a solid 3,012,166 votes.

In a January 20, 2006, speech to the RNC, Rove once again made clear that the issue of security would be central to future elections:

> America is at war—and so our national security is at the fore-front of the minds of Americans. President Bush has established a remarkable record. He is winning the war against terrorism, promoting liberty in regions of the world that have never known it, and protecting America against attacks. The United States faces a ruthless enemy—and we need a commander-in-chief and a Congress who understand the nature of the threat and the gravity of this moment.
>
> President Bush and the Republican Party do. Unfortunately, the same cannot be said for many Democrats. . . . [W]e now hear a loud chorus of Democrats who want us to cut-and-run in Iraq. . . . To retreat before victory has been won would be a reckless act—and this President will not allow it. . . .
>
> The Patriot Act tore down the wall that prohibited law enforcement and intelligence authorities from sharing information about terrorist threats. And the Patriot Act allowed federal investigators to pursue terrorists with tools they already used against other criminals. . . . In 2001 Congress passed this law with a large, bipartisan majority—including a vote of 98–1 in the Senate. The Patriot Act has protected the United States from attack and saved American lives—and yet the Democrat leader in the Senate, Harry Reid, recently boasted that Democrats had "killed the Patriot Act." Republicans want to renew the Patriot Act—and Democrat leaders take special delight in trying to kill it.

Just as the Democratic Party has suffered from a "values barrier" or a "values gap" in assembling a governing coalition, it has faced a deepening national security gap since 9/11—a gap that is profoundly damaging to Democratic prospects. The 2004 Swift Boat Veterans for Truth attacks on Kerry's record in Vietnam would not have struck home had his party not been vulnerable on the issue.[3] Bush has been able to shrug off allegations concerning his controversial record of service in the Texas Air National Guard during the Vietnam War, and Cheney has been similarly immune on his avoidance of military service, because both men are insulated by the strength of their party on military issues.

As the elections of 2006 and 2008 approach, the Bush administration has begun laying the groundwork to make sure that the public recognizes the ongoing importance of national security and the threats posed by terrorism to the United States. Bush and the Pentagon began, at the start of 2006, to refer to the war on terror as "the long war," one that, like the Cold War, might be expected to continue for decades. "Our own generation is in a long war against a determined enemy," Bush declared in his 2006 State of the Union address.

The next day, at a press briefing, Defense Secretary Donald Rumsfeld continued the theme: "The truth is that just as the Cold War lasted a long time, this war is something that is not going to go away. It's not going to be settled with a signing ceremony on the USS *Missouri*. It is of a different nature." The purpose of the Pentagon briefing was to outline the contents of the Quadrennial Defense Review (QDR), which attempts to project security issues for the next twenty years. The opening sentence of the 2006 QDR reads: "The United States is a nation engaged in what will be a long war."

Among the greatest advantages to the GOP has been the absence to date of a second terrorist attack on American ground. The ability of the current Bush administration to safeguard its home terrain not only strengthens the position of the Republican Party but also highlights the dangers to the Democratic Party of its positions stressing civil liberties over national security. This issue colors debate on a range of divisive security-related issues, from the Patriot Act to warrantless wiretapping by the National Security Agency and other intelligence surveillance practices and methods. Any weakness on national defense that dogs the Democratic Party is substantially amplified in the context of a "long war."

---

[3]For more detail on the Swift Boat Veterans campaign against Kerry, see chapter 4.

Furthermore, sharply divided opinion—indeed, a chasm—within the Democratic coalition (antiwar Democratic National Committee Chair Howard Dean and Representatives Nancy Pelosi and Jack Murtha, for example, on one side, and prowar Democrats like Senator Joseph Lieberman, on the other) has hindered the ability of the Democratic Party and of the broader left to capitalize on whatever public support there might be among voters for opposing the war in Iraq.

Declining Credibility of Democratic Solutions

On another front, the ability of the Democratic Party to mount an effective long-term campaign against the Republican Party has been undermined by the declining credibility of non-market solutions to economic problems and by the decreasing confidence in the ability of central governments to make key decisions on economic growth, production, wages, and related matters. Among the obstacles facing the American party of the left are the failures of the Soviet Union and of socialist or communist economies around the world, the history of underperformance of social market and welfare states in Europe, the perceived shortcomings of government interventions in the U.S. economy after the high rates of growth in the first two decades after World War II (the failure of Nixon's wage and price controls in the 1970s, for example), and the disappointing results of domestic attempts to eliminate poverty at home—"enterprise zones," the War on Poverty, Job Corps, Community Action, Trade Adjustment Assistance programs, and so forth.

These developments have sapped the confidence of the left in the efficacy of government-imposed restraints on business and in the value of the state as a regulator. They have demoralized backers of a redistributive agenda, and they have undermined the ability of Democrats to press the case for active government intervention in managing an economy generating enterprise, competitively viable, capable of reducing inequality among its citizens, and creating new wealth.

The failures of social democracies and of socialist regimes overseas, as well as the history of intractable stagflation in the Carter era, have made it difficult to press the case for the Democratic Party's longtime goal of economic redistribution or for the party's ability to raise standards of living or to generate prosperity (the Clinton years still viewed by many as the exception, not the rule). The failures of centralized economic planning have deprived the left of its greatest historical advantage: the plausible alternative the movement once presented to conservative doctrines of free market capitalism and the promise of the Democratic Party of the past that it knew how to make Americans better off in the future.

International competition has forced Democrats to confront another harsh reality that is undermining its formerly successful alliance with organized labor. American legislative and regulatory initiatives to protect domestic workers and industries, to strengthen worker rights, and to boost worker pay and benefits can no longer withstand the pressures of hypercompetition. High wages and generous benefits are now seen as driving companies overseas or out of business, thus resulting, for many American employees, in more harm than good. For instance, General Motors, Ford, and Delphi in 2005 and 2006 were forced to eliminate 84,000 jobs as a result of low-wage global competition.

➤ ◄

Another brutal reality is just around the corner: the nation's Social Security, Medicare, Medicaid, and pension systems all face the prospect of fiscal shortfall. According to an estimate by Douglas Holtz-Eakin, the director in 2005 of the Congressional Budget Office,

> people get older one year at a time. Then you layer on historical trends in health-care spending. If you take demography plus history as your guide, Medicare and Medicaid are as big in 2050 as the entire federal government is today. . . . There's a point where, for some politician, it will be better to fix it than to let it happen. I don't know when that is. But given how fast health-care costs are going up, that phenomenon will be a driving one.

The Democrats have been skillful in opposing Republican legislative initiatives to cut back such safety net features. In the long run, however, the Democratic Party, the architect of the American welfare state, will have to produce credible fiscal solutions to the social insurance crisis if it is to remain viable as a major political party.

THE MODERN GOP CAPITALIZES ON DEMOCRATIC WEAKNESSES DESPITE ITS OWN VULNERABILITIES

The weaknesses of the Democratic Party have magnified the advantages of the Republican Party. The ability of the GOP in recent decades to manipulate and exploit the vulnerabilities of the left demonstrates the adroitness that the GOP has shown in capitalizing on any margin in its favor. Going into the 2006 election, which appears at this writing certain to deal a setback to the GOP, the fact that the GOP has achieved victory after victory in spite of its many vulnerabilities speaks to the skill of the party and its supporters in preventing key issues, historically favorable to Democrats, from gaining traction.

The GOP has survived an era of accelerating income inequality and declining social mobility, trends that have become more widespread in recent years and have in the past benefited Democrats. From 1980 to 2004, the share of household income going to those in the bottom 60 percent of the income distribution has fallen from 30.8 percent to 26.8 percent. The share of income going to the top 0.1 percent of the population has grown the fastest of all, more than doubling to 7.4 percent. Republican success has defied the threat traditionally posed by these trends, as the disparity in resources between those at the very top and those in the bottom three quintiles of the income distribution has continued to grow.

The GOP has, in addition, survived the repeated propensity of the leaders of the Republican Party to go too far. Examples of Republican overreaching are legion, running from the nomination of arch-conservative Barry Goldwater in 1964, to Watergate, to repeated bids to eliminate or radically scale back Medicare and Social Security, to political scandals surrounding the lobbying and legislative process in Washington, to George W. Bush's military assault on Iraq.

The GOP has eked out a succession of election victories despite widespread public opposition to the religious right, which is made up of white, culturally conservative, evangelical born-again Christians. Such voters together produce roughly a third of the ballots cast for Republican presidential candidates on election day. This wing of the GOP, while tapping genuine cultural anxieties in the American mainstream, is far to the right of most Americans. It is among the best organized of the constituent GOP interest groups and delivers a disproportionate share of Republican grassroots activists, controlling the public agenda on a number of incendiary issues and wielding immense power within the Republican coalition.

The religious right has forced the GOP to take aggressive and intrusive stands on issues that many Americans view as matters of personal privacy: supporting traditional gender roles at a time when a large majority of women work outside the home and are rising rapidly through the ranks; espousing traditional marriage, even as almost 50 percent of marital unions end in divorce; supporting prohibitions on embryonic stem cell research when there is increasing scientific consensus regarding the importance of such work; and supporting state intervention into the kinds of end-of-life questions that surrounded the Terry Schiavo case.

As Republicans gain an ever-more powerful majority on the Supreme Court, party leaders have continued to stand behind the platform position of the Republican Party on abortion: a total ban, with no exceptions for the life or health of the mother. The 2004 GOP platform reads: "We say the unborn child has a fundamental individual right to life which cannot be infringed." This position tests the loyalty of the party's large constituency of socially moderate married women and undermines its efforts to create a permanent Republican majority.

In addition, the Christian right takes a hard and fast position on an issue about which many Americans feel uncomfortable: that homosexual acts are a sin, that the sexual orientation of people can be changed through prayer, counseling, and so-called conversion therapy, that homosexuality is preventable and treatable, that most gays and lesbians can leave the "gay lifestyle" and "walk away from homosexuality," and that a "relationship with Jesus Christ and a life of prayer are the keys to changing homosexual desires and fostering the development of healthy, nonsexual intimate relationships." While gay rights are the cultural-moral issue on which Americans display the least tolerance, the social issue that is the most polarizing in today's political debate, and the issue on which Republican and Democratic activists disagree most strongly, according to Boston University sociologist Alan Wolfe, Americans are highly individualistic, and it is difficult to amass a majority political consensus behind measures that forcibly restrict the freedom of private behavior. Moreover, substantial numbers—although not a majority—of Americans have shifted their views on homosexuality in recent years under the influence of more liberal Christians, mental health professionals, scientists, geneticists, and academic researchers in the field of human sexuality. According to Pew data, "young people, especially those in their late teens and twenties, are more supportive of gay marriage than are older Americans."

Further complicating Republican maneuvering on this ground is the degree to which discourse about gay rights is conducted in rhetoric that takes on a substantial symbolic role. The attack on homosexuality now stands in for an attack on virtually all sexual behavior not confined to procreative acts within the confines of life-long monogamous marriage. The issue of gay rights has become the medium through which cultural conservatives take aim at the entire sexual revolution.

How Conservatives Attack Liberal Institutions and Protect Their Own

The conservative attack on the core beliefs of the left has been paralleled by an assault on the institutions that underpin them. These associations include labor unions—with a special emphasis on public employee and teachers' unions—the plaintiffs' or trial lawyers' bar, the media, mainstream liberal churches and religious organizations—especially those that permit the ordination of gay clergy—the traditional philanthropic community—notably foundations such as Rockefeller, Ford, Carnegie, and MacArthur that have underwritten much of the socially progressive agenda of the past half-century—major research universities, and the rights movements, including organizations that uphold and protect women's rights, civil rights, criminal defendants' rights, the rights of the deinstitutionalized mentally ill, and so on.

Leaders of the Republican Party used the 9/11 terrorist attack, for example, to justify an assault on public employee unions, weakening or eliminating bargained protections of government employees by arguing that, in times of danger, management requires the ability to exercise authority over a flexible workforce. Command of congressional majorities empowered Republicans to pass tort reform legislation in 2005, weakening the ability of trial lawyers to bring class action suits—suits that, in their broadest form, have brought significant protection to consumers, patients, employees, investors, victims of discrimination, and others.[4]

The Republican leadership has promoted the interests of credit card companies, banks, and other lenders—all supporters of the GOP—through 2005 legislation limiting debtor protection in bankruptcy proceedings. The energy sector, financial services, insurance, and real estate have all been major beneficiaries of this legislation and of executive branch administrative decisions over the past five years. In the case of both Social Security and health care legislation, the goal of the Republican Party is to create systems of individual, tax-subsidized accounts to eliminate as much as possible the role of government or of the employer as sources of protection and security in times of calamity.

On a broader scale, the conservative movement has conducted an unremitting, and in many respects successful, campaign to portray contemporary liberalism as violating the American ethic. Conservatives redefine civil rights and civil liberties associations as "special interests" seeking exceptional rights for specific minorities—including unpopular groups ranging from criminal defendants to pedophiles, death row inmates, drug users, and the homeless—rather than seeking equal opportunities for all members of society. The right has capitalized on the advocacy by the left of race and gender preferences, of sexual harassment rules restricting "free speech" in the workplace, of prisoner's rights and the rights of those convicted of capital crimes, as well as of liberalized law enforcement policies designed to protect vulnerable groups that at times stir public apprehension. The conservative movement paints contemporary liberalism—in the eyes of as wide a public as possible—as opposed to all the cardinal American virtues: moral probity, responsibility, foresight, prudence, patriotism, diligence, self-restraint, temperance, justice, and reward based on merit and performance.

---

[4]For more on class action and tort reform, see chapter 4.

COMPASSIONATE CONSERVATISM LESSENS THE LIABILITIES OF THE GOP

Part of the genius of the contemporary conservative movement has been its use of the concept of "compassionate conservatism" to lessen the liabilities of a Republican Party committed to paring back the welfare state and to minimizing the tax burden on the most wealthy. Similarly, the GOP—a party whose supporters are more than 87 percent white—arranged to present an extraordinary display of multiculturalism at its national conventions in 2000 and 2004, with a heavily African American and Hispanic line-up of speakers and performers designed to attract maximum attention during prime time televised proceedings. Along parallel lines, the Bush administration has been attentive to rebutting any possible charges of racism, appointing African Americans, Asian Americans, and Hispanics to some of the most visible positions in the federal government, including Colin Powell and Condoleeza Rice as secretaries of state, Alberto Gonzalez as attorney general, and Elaine Chao as secretary of labor.

Public proclamations of compassionate conservatism have helped override a potentially less popular face of the contemporary Republican Party, a party that strongly supports harsh anticrime measures such as capital punishment and long prison terms. The GOP is militant about counteracting negative stereotyping of conservatives, carefully avoiding any display of the kind of "contempt for the weak" that has proven detrimental to conservative movements in the past. Thus, the GOP uses "compassionate conservative" rhetoric to negate the kind of damage that Bush might have courted in an unguarded moment.

Tucker Carlson, the conservative writer and television host, captured the harsh face of conservatism—including its contempt for the weak—that Bush and other Republicans seek to suppress. In an article for the now-defunct *Talk* magazine, Carlson recounted how, during his first presidential campaign, George Bush mocked Texas death row inmate Karla Fay Tucker's plea for clemency. Under Bush's governorship, Karla Tucker, a converted Christian evangelical, became the only woman put to death in Texas since the Civil War. Bush told Carlson that he had watched a television interview with Karla Tucker, and that she had been asked "real difficult questions, like, 'What would you say to Governor Bush?'" Carlson asked Bush how she had answered. "'Please,' Bush whimper[ed], his lips pursed in mock desperation, 'don't kill me,'" Carlson wrote. This revealing moment contrasts with the carefully crafted "empathetic conservative" campaign style Bush has used to great effect to court a mass public and to broaden the appeal of the party.

GOP Scores Successes over the Past Decades

The GOP has successfully played both offense and defense in overcoming possible objections to or queasiness about conservative policies among enough mainstream voters to win the White House. This success extends back across the past four decades. Furthermore, even when in the minority, the Republican Party repeatedly prevailed in blocking Democratic initiatives. The presidency of Jimmy Carter, when Democrats held solid majorities in the House and Senate, was marked by the defeat of liberal tax legislation, a consumer protection bill, labor law reform, campaign finance reform, and legislation to make Martin Luther King Jr.'s birthday a holiday (the bill passed in 1983 under Ronald Reagan). Similarly, the first two years of the administration of Bill Clinton, when Democrats controlled the House and Senate, saw the defeat of his first legislative proposal, an economic stimulus bill, and the centerpiece of his agenda, universal health care.

The commitment of the Republican Party to a take-no-prisoners approach was reflected in a 1993 strategy memo by Bill Kristol, then chair of the Project for the Republican Future. Kristol called for the "unqualified political defeat" of the Clinton health plan: "Any Republican urge to negotiate a 'least bad' compromise with the Democrats, and thereby gain momentary public credit for helping the president 'do something' about health care, should also be resisted. . . . The plan should not be amended; it should be erased." In Kristol's view, the Clinton health plan "is liberalism's invasion of Afghanistan: It's their overreaching grasp for everything. If it can be beaten, it unravels other things. We have to beat the Clinton plan period, no ifs, ands or buts."

The mainstream media, an institution that was just a generation ago powerful enough to bring down a Republican president, has been successfully redefined by conservative interest groups as partisan and biased toward the left. This characterization has, in turn, taken the sting out of news reports critical of conservative initiatives and policies. The right has made the most of the traditionally liberal leanings of the national press and of the decisively pro-Democratic voting patterns of reporters and editors to weaken significantly the power of the establishment media—the national newspapers, network and public television, and major magazines—to influence public opinion.

At the same time, the polarization of the electorate has created an ideal marketplace for the emergence of new powerful, conservative media, including the FOX network, television hosts such as Bill O'Reilly and Sean Hannity, radio talk show hosts along the lines of Rush Limbaugh, Laura Ingraham, and others, Christian radio, conservative blogs, and a now-extensive conservative book publishing industry. Penguin and Random House have recently, for example, launched conservative imprints, joining the right-wing house Regnery, which has itself published twenty-nine bestsellers (*Bias*, *Slander*, *Shut Up and Sing*, and so forth) over the past ten years.

Under the current Bush administration, corporate America has been the recipient of massive tax cuts. The business community, in addition, has seen the rolling back of environmental and workplace regulations governing the extractive industries—from mining to off-shore drilling. Republican administrations have reliably appointed industry representatives to government positions overseeing energy, clean air, and clean water policies, financial practices, labor relations, agriculture, trade, health care, and transportation. Since George W. Bush took office in 2001, the tax, legislative, and regulatory agendas of his administration and those of the U.S. Chamber of Commerce have—with only minimal exceptions—been identical.

The Christian right has been instrumental in shaping administration policy on abortion, sex education, stem cell research, and judicial nominations. Leaders of the abstinence education and "pro-life" movements have been appointed to posts such as deputy assistant secretary of population affairs at the Department of Health and Human Services, co-chair of the Presidential Advisory Council on HIV and AIDS, and the Food and Drug Administration's Reproductive Health Drugs Advisory Committee. Internships throughout the executive branch and Congress—key to grooming a generation of future leaders—have gone to students from Christian schools such as Patrick Henry and Hillsdale colleges.

A central priority of the conservative movement since Ronald Reagan took office in 1980 has been the carefully planned restructuring of the federal courts to ensure a critical mass of judges who will support the larger conservative agenda. George W. Bush has been explicit in seeking to achieve a philosophical and ideological conversion of the nation's legal system, declaring repeatedly on the campaign trail that he intended to pick judges in the mold of Antonin Scalia and Clarence Thomas, the two most conservative members of the Supreme Court over the past fifteen years. The securing of conservative majorities in all but one federal circuit—the Second—and a Supreme Court now tilted to the right ensures that, when the Republican Party suffers political defeat, the judiciary will act as a brake on Democratic initiatives.

In addition, the conservative movement has built an array of institutions—from the Heritage Foundation and the Cato Institute to a network of legal foundations including the Federalist Society, the National Legal and Policy Center, the Pacific Legal Foundation, the Institute for Justice, the Washington Legal Foundation, and the Center for Individual Rights—all committed to advancing the agenda of the right when the GOP is in control of the political machinery and to protecting conservative legislation and regulatory policies when Democrats wrest control. It was the conservative Landmark Foundation and the Rutherford Institute, armed with Scaife and Bradley money, that backed the Paula Jones campaign, initiated in 1994, which charged Bill Clinton with sexual harassment, and that backed as well the prolonged Whitewater investigation against Clinton and his wife. The impeachment proceedings against Clinton, instigated in 1998 by the Republican leadership of the House, failed to remove Clinton from office but played to key Democratic weaknesses on "moral values" issues, shrinking Gore's vote count and leading to his electoral college defeat in 2000. Similarly, though no convictions were obtained in the Paula Jones case, many years of litigation did considerable damage to Democratic prospects.

THE LARGER GOAL OF THE RIGHT: ERODING THE POPULAR CONSENSUS BEHIND THE MAJOR EGALITARIAN MOVEMENTS OF THE TWENTIETH CENTURY

The larger goal behind all these efforts of the right has been to lock conservative policies in place and to erect high barriers to the restoration of liberal governance. The Republican aim has been to win the executive branch, to maintain a working majority in the Congress, to control the federal bench whenever possible, and when those goals are not possible to preclude passage of legislation or policy initiatives facilitating redistribution of income or wealth, higher taxes, or the revival of social welfare programs.

Both the administration and Republican leaders of the House and Senate used the 2005 demand for federal assistance in the aftermath of Hurricane Katrina—which devastated the homes of over a million residents of the Gulf region—to press further their conservative agendas. Bush quickly ordered the suspension of two federal policies that would normally have governed the award of contracts to repair the devastation: the pro-union prevailing wage law known as Davis-Bacon, and the requirement that contractors comply with federal affirmative action race and gender requirements. Federal spending on Katrina disaster relief was, in turn, used by Republican leaders to justify substantial cuts, over the next ten years, in domestic social spending, including a $26.4 billion cut in Medicaid (for the elderly and the poor), a $22.4 billion cut in Medicare, and a $11.9 billion cut in student loan programs. Liberals, who had thought Katrina would revive support for the social welfare functions of government, were stunned. "We've gone from a situation in which we might have a long-overdue debate on deep poverty to the possibility, perhaps even the likelihood, that low-income people will be asked to bear the costs. I would find it unimaginable if it wasn't actually happening," said Robert Greenstein, director of the Center on Budget and Policy Priorities.

➤ ◄

Although the contemporary conservative movement has won policy victory after policy victory, these gains have been achieved in a slow, step-by-step process, not through a political realignment. Although the incremental achievements of contemporary conservatism are less dramatic than the quick assault on states rights after the 1828 election of Andrew Jackson, the achievements of the Reagan and George W. Bush administrations and the achievements of the Jackson administration are comparably encompassing. Politically, however, the major difference between the two is that the Republican Party of today has never won the kind of popular mandate that propelled Jackson into office. Rather, contemporary conservative strategy has been to use victories based on tiny margins to force a major redistribution of public and private sector power, without clear majoritarian public support.

From 1825 to 1829, the number of Jackson loyalists in the 213-member House grew from 72, or just 34 percent of the total, to 136, a solid 64 percent majority. Similarly, the pre–Great Depression Republican House majority of 270 to 164 was reversed to become, by 1933, a 313 to 117 Democratic majority during the New Deal realignment. In stark contrast, Republican control of the House since the election of 1994 has wavered between a 9-vote majority and, at the top, a 30-vote majority—insignificant in comparison to the 196-vote Democratic advantage in 1933.

In this light, the considerable accomplishments of today's Republican Party stand out all the more. The GOP has achieved a gradual erosion of the popular consensus behind the major progressive and social-egalitarian movements of the twentieth century, a popular consensus that held through the Progressive era at the start of the century, through the years of the Depression and the trade union organizing movements, and through the human rights, women's rights, and civil rights movements of the 1960s. The determination and intensity of the conservative movement to undo the progressive agenda have been reflected in the resolute conversion of large and small functions of government to ensure the representation of interests and groups on the right, while diminishing the role of government service to racial, ethnic, and sexual-orientation minorities, single mothers, and other Democratic constituencies.

This drive to undo the past achievements of Democratic administrations has pushed deep into the federal bureaucracy. It has included, for example, the establishment of Centers for Faith-Based and Community Initiatives directives in ten cabinet-level departments that steer federal funding away from traditionally secular, nonprofit public service agencies and toward new religiously connected entities. It has also meant the appointment of representatives from interests such as oil and gas exploration, electric utilities, and nuclear power facilities to oversee regulation of these industries; a shift within the Justice Department away from enforcing prohibitions against racial discrimination in favor of enforcing religious discrimination laws benefiting fundamentalist and evangelical Christians; the shaping of the culture of Washington to permit semi-official lobbyist councils to write legislation, to advise key House and Senate committee chairmen, to play crucial roles in congressional leadership contests, and to run the national Republican conventions; and the purposeful conversion of the National Labor Relations Board from a guarantor of union organizing rights into an adversary of organized labor.

By its very nature, the Republican agenda precludes a political strategy of consensus or moderation. First and foremost, the conservative agenda is not moderate. It is an attempt to dismantle the welfare state, a structure built up over the last two-thirds of the twentieth century. Second, the conservative agenda does not have the decisive support of the people. In a two-party democracy such as the United States, the achievement of a radical change in the direction of government without the support of a clear majority of voters has required the strategic division of the electorate into two separate camps, a commitment to aggressively capitalize on all Republican victories, and purposeful polarization to force the electorate to pick between extremes. When Republicans have won—even without a majority of the popular vote—they have claimed that their election sanctioned the adoption of policies more extreme than voters favor when they have more ideologically varied choices.

➤ ◁

For nearly forty years, Democrats and liberals have been stunned by the ability of the Republican Party repeatedly to win the White House—as they were in 1994 by the GOP takeover the House and Senate. Liberals have been equally stunned by the short-lived and transient nature of Democratic victories. What most disturbs leaders and supporters of the center-left coalition has been the success of the conservative movement in accessing and manipulating concealed biases against minorities and homosexuals to persuade middle- and working-class whites to vote against their own economic interests.

Questions about the success of these tactics have marked several recent political books, including Tom Frank's *What's the Matter with Kansas? How Conservatives Won the Heart of America* and political scientists Jacob S. Hacker and Paul Pierson's *Off Center: The Republican Revolution and the Erosion of American Democracy*. These are important analyses of American politics and mandatory reading for those interested in partisan competition. *New York Times* political analyst Matt Bai has, however, labeled these works a "new genre of comfort books for liberals."

The Frank and Hacker-Pierson analyses focus on the substantial distance of the modern GOP from the center—on what the authors characterize as disregard by GOP elites of the views of "average American voters." An additional point is worth considering, however: that the success demonstrated by using moral/cultural issues and "traditional values" as a means of recruiting and retaining votes for the Republican party suggests that the so-called social issues driving white voters to the GOP may in fact have meaningful economic implications for conservative voters. Just as there are tangible benefits for white voters who support the GOP in opposing affirmative action in hiring, promotion, and college-admissions policies, there can be economic implications for voters of all backgrounds who support conservative cultural positions in other arenas. Marriage is viewed by some as a pocketbook issue, for example, as married men earn more than unmarried men, and as married women have access to larger incomes than their unmarried counterparts. University of Chicago sociologist Linda Waite has found that "improved financial resources are a key avenue through which marriage improves well-being and life chances for both men and women. . . . Married people have more than twice as much money, on average, as unmarried people." A RAND Corporation study reports that "married couples not only save more while enjoying some economies of scale, but married men also earn up to 26 percent more than single men." Insofar as conservative social policies create disincentives to family breakdown, Carol Aneshensel of UCLA and

Jo Phelan of Columbia University point out that "marital dissolution typically results in reduced economic resources, particularly for women."

Traditional values of family, neighborhood, church, school, and the workplace are, to millions of voters, "money in the bank"—they are what holds people together, providing security against a rainy day, making possible credit based on trust and familial cooperation in entrepreneurial endeavors. Such values are often seen as crucially important by voters because they are seen to give individuals the backing and the fortitude to meet their obligations and to fulfill their ambitions even in the face of setbacks. From this perspective, the liberal culture—the Democratic liberal culture—appears dangerous, encouraging social chaos, eroding kinship networks, and facilitating community breakdown.

For many American voters—more than Democrats are willing to acknowledge—perceived social chaos is a strong political motivator. The violent, sexualized content of popular music, television, and movies and the adoption of sex education curricula featuring condom demonstration appear to assume and effectively sanction sexual activity among young teenagers. Court rulings permitting juvenile abortions without parental consultation are viewed by some as part of a hazardous and disorderly environment—indeed, a sexually anarchic environment.

Free speech and First Amendment litigation have ensured that any child with use of a computer can access graphic pornography— gay and straight. Ninth-grade students can join an after-school club focused on gay rights or sign up for an email list of coming-out stories. While such access can be immensely helpful to gay youngsters needing guidance and support, it strikes terror into the hearts of parents who do not believe that homosexuality is a given but, rather, that it is a choice, and a choice influenced by mass culture. This belief is widespread in culturally conservative, "red" America. Many voters, particularly those without college degrees, consider such matters a far more serious problem than the rate of taxation on corporate dividends or the rolling back of regulations on carbon dioxide emissions.

On another front in the culture wars, Republicans have capitalized on the thinly veiled resentment on the part of white voters, across the income spectrum, of hiring, promotion, and admissions preferences given to African Americans, Hispanics, and other minorities. The GOP has also benefited from males resentful of being displaced from center stage—sexually, professionally, and personally—by the women's liberation movement and from male objections to gender preferences (demonized as affirmative action "quotas") in hiring and promotion.

Maneuvering through the Minefields of the Rights Revolutions

It is by maneuvering through the minefields of the rights revolutions of the 1960s and 1970s that the Republican Party has repeatedly won the White House, controlled the Senate from 1981 to 1987 and from 1995 onward, and the House since 1995. The civil rights revolution and issues of race have provided powerful tools to the GOP ever since voter backlash against passage of the Civil Rights Act of 1964 and the Voting Rights Act of 1965.

The issue of race has been central to the rise of the right over the entire span of the past forty years. So, too, have the women's rights and the sexual revolutions armed the "conservative majority." The political impact of these last two revolutions, which changed the social order at least as much as the civil rights revolution, has not been sufficiently appreciated. The sexual revolution, stemming from new technologies (contraception, antibiotics, surgical abortion, fertility treatments), and the women's rights revolution (also directly correlated with advances in reproductive technologies) created opportunities for social backlash and for conservative Republican strategists to grasp the technique of using "wedge issues" for political gain.

The Republican Party has capitalized on the disruption and upheaval that emerged over the past forty years as millions of women left homemaking for work, including most mothers, as women discarded norms of premarital chastity (no matter that such norms had arguably been honored more in the breach), as the growth of the female workforce created a thicket of rules governing sexual harassment, as gender-based affirmative action was perceived by men as unfairly catapulting women over their heads, and as prohibitions regarding a "hostile workplace environment" created, for many men, a sense of Orwellian surveillance. These issues will be explored in more detail in chapter 5.

Demographic Balkanization

On a different front, University of Michigan demographer William Frey has produced extensive research showing that immigration from abroad, in tandem with population movements within the United States, is producing "two Americas," a demographic balkanization that "will continue and become more entrenched over the decades ahead." Frey has documented the emergence of Democratic multiracial and multiethnic communities on the two coasts and in some major Midwestern cities. At the same time, Republican-leaning whites, especially those who are working or middle class and more socially conservative, have moved out of these bi-coastal and urban metropolitan areas to less densely populated but more Republican regions, many of them inland. With "the nation gaining an immigrant every 31 seconds, on average," according to Census Bureau data reported in the *New York Times*, the political ramifications of this movement are considerable.

➣ ◃

The American electorate has in many ways separated not only into two political parties but also into two separate partisan cultures, each with its own community institutions, television and consumer habits, patterns of religious observance, and racial diversity or homogeneity. Viewers of the *CBS Evening News* in 2004 were, for example, substantially more Democratic than Republican, and viewers of the CBS Sunday program *Face the Nation* were even more Democratic. Conversely, viewers of *FOX Sunday News* were overwhelmingly Republican. In entertainment television, *JAG*, *Navy NCIS*, and *The Simpsons* have had more Republican than Democratic watchers, whereas *West Wing* and UPN's *Girlfriends* have been solidly Democratic. Jaguar and Land Rover owners are reliably Republicans, whereas Volvo, Subaru, and Hyundai owners are predominately Democratic.

Religion and gun ownership have, in turn, become powerful predictors of voting behavior; those who worship once or more a week and those who own guns are very likely to vote for Republican candidates, while nonbelievers, those who worship only infrequently, and voters from households without guns are more likely to vote Democratic. In other words, Republicans and Democrats are separated by differences on a broad range of choices over consumer goods, religious participation, entertainment, and leisure time activities. The Republican Party much more than the Democratic Party, as will be seen in chapter 2, has recognized these trends and has incorporated them into highly quantified, technologically sophisticated political strategies that have added to the long-term GOP edge.

Republican Troops Are Committed to the Pursuit of Their Quarry

Perhaps the most striking characteristic of contemporary American conservatism is that it has not only survived repeated reversals of fortune but that it has also consistently emerged strengthened and more aggressive in its policies. One important reason for the resilience of this movement is that it is agenda-driven, sustained by the continuing support of constituent groups for its two central goals, each vigorously supported by its own universe of adherents.

First, the GOP has in its sights the sociocultural goal of unraveling or reversing the rights revolutions of the 1960s—often cast in terms of such issues as pro-life, partial birth abortion, gay marriage, welfare, responsibility, crime, drug abuse, lenient judges ruling from the bench, lawsuit abuse, failing schools, school prayer, and family collapse. Second, the GOP—propped up by popular support garnered through its advocacy of moral, cultural, and racial goals—has set economic policy goals: reducing long-term demands on the state, lowering taxes on businesses and individuals, reducing demands on business to provide social insurance (health care, pensions, job security), increasing efficiency and profitability, securing property rights, expanding free trade, eliminating the power of labor unions, and shrinking market regulation.

The interlocking strength of constituencies behind each of these goals—one cultural/racial/moral and the other economic—has equipped conservatism to absorb defeat in any single area and to adopt new tactics. Republican troops are prepared, even in the face of adversity and periodic election losses, to remain committed to the pursuit of their quarry. In this respect, conservative Republicanism stands in contrast to contemporary liberalism and to the Democratic Party, which are fighting less for an agenda to be enacted than to ward off assaults on gains once made.

The contemporary left does not have a clearly articulated, politically robust agenda to address looming public policy problems. They do not at present have tax, regulatory, or other economic proposals capable of permanently recruiting a decisively large group of additional voters to the Democratic coalition. Nor have progressives yet unveiled innovative urban policies, credibly focused on revitalization of blighted cores in cities like Baltimore, Cleveland, or Detroit, nor have they made public a plan to address increasing indebtedness on the part of the state or of individuals.

Liberals have not to date presented plausible proposals to pull the remaining 20 percent of the nation out of poverty. They do not have a persuasive proposition to reverse the decline of organized labor, nor a proposal to meet the costly needs of an aging society that is going to make vastly expanded demands on scarce government resources. The left has no solution to the contagion of conflicts across the Mideast, a blueprint for attacking the proliferation of weapons of mass destruction in countries around the globe, or a viable program to provide for the nation's future energy needs. Instead, the most important objective of Democratic liberalism has been to stop Republican conservatism. Democrats, already in retreat and on the defensive for nearly forty years, have built-in difficulties converting episodic victories into sustained domination of the national agenda.

As liberalism has lost its power to block the conservative agenda, conservatives have patiently but aggressively expanded the scope of their challenges to the liberal state. From the 1978 cut in the capital gains tax rate, to Ronald Reagan's 1981 tax cuts, to the four tax cuts during George W. Bush's first term, Republicans have continuously raised the stakes in the debate over financing the federal government. The tax bills passed by a Republican Congress between 2001 and 2004 reduced the obligations of the affluent in ways that would have been inconceivable under Nixon, Reagan, or Bush's father. The tax cuts have, in turn, served a second key purpose: to "starve the beast," the conservative strategy of restricting federal revenues to prevent future Democratic majorities from reviving spending policies.

Similarly, the enactment of pro-business bankruptcy and class action legislation in 2005, at the start of George W. Bush's second term, was the result of decades of work—a lobbying effort that cost

American companies well over $100 million—in a sustained offensive to win what might initially have appeared to be an impossible goal. Along the same lines, by proposing to partially privatize Social Security (a position first advocated in 1964 by Barry Goldwater), George W. Bush demonstrated a willingness to absorb a short-term defeat to put the issue squarely into the public arena and to show that a Republican president could touch the "third rail" of American politics—challenging a mainstay of the New Deal and a program of great importance to millions of Americans.

The steady movement of American domestic and foreign policy toward the right has demonstrated the vulnerabilities of modern liberalism. These policy shifts have enfeebled key institutions of the left, which have found themselves restricted to throwing up temporary impediments and powerless to definitively turn around the debate. At the same time, these rightward policies have enriched, made confident, and rewarded the GOP's corporate donor base, the religious right, loyalists in Washington's K Street lobbying community (which, despite the rash of scandals in 2005 and 2006, faces essentially cosmetic reform), business generally, and heavily regulated industries in particular.

Building an Investor Class

The strategy of the GOP to create a resilient conservative majority is no secret. Key strategists and operatives openly discuss their plans: "The dividend tax cut, expanding IRAs, and private Social Security Accounts are all examples of President Bush and Karl Rove understanding that the more people we can lure into the investor class with private pools of private capital, the better it is for Republicans and Republican issues," notes Stephen Moore, formerly president of the Club for Growth and now president of the Free Enterprise Fund, both key institutions within the conservative movement. If the Bush agenda is enacted, "there will be a continued growth of the percentage of Americans who consider themselves Republican, both in terms of self-identified party ID, and in terms of their economic interests," argues Grover Norquist, president of Americans for Tax Reform, a major conservative interest group.

Bush's success in winning cuts in taxes on dividend and capital gains income was, according to Norquist, a key political victory:

"The President got out ahead and laid claim to the growing in-vestor class." For this investor class, taxation is perceived as taking from the "haves" and giving to the "have nots." "If you don't need something from the government, why would you be a Democrat?" asks Norquist.

Pollster Scott Rasmussen argues:

> There's a simple reason that Social Security reform is on the nation's agenda at this time—the New Deal generation has re-cently left this earth. Among all Americans alive in 2004, less than one-half of one percent were adults when Social Security was signed into law. Just 9% were alive at all. . . . The political viability [of privatization] can be seen in the results of Election 2004. Despite the Kerry campaign's best efforts to demonize the President's position on Social Security, most voters over 65 cast their vote for George W. Bush. Kerry went to Florida rais-ing alarms about secret plans for "privatization." Florida went decisively for Bush.

Rasmussen contends that there have been major changes in the composition of the nation's workforce, and "these changes mean that the workforce today is a lot closer to George W. Bush's goal of an 'ownership society' than it is to Franklin D. Roosevelt's New Deal."

Pollster John Zogby makes a parallel case for the growth of a stock-owning class of voters as the ideal GOP target constituency:

> What sways the investor class to vote Republican is the fact that it does not see itself as a disadvantaged group, and does not see government as the solution to its problems. . . . The Democratic party, however, has traditionally appealed to mi-nority groups such as liberals, women's rights advocates, gay people and union groups that see government as a solution to social problems.

Zogby counts self-identified investors as making up 46 percent of the total vote in 2004. According to his data, this group voted 61 to 39 percent for Bush, whereas noninvestors voted 57 to 42 per-cent for Kerry. Looking at all voters with annual incomes between $50,000 and $75,000, Zogby found that investors in this income bracket voted for Bush 64 to 36 percent, while noninvestors voted for Kerry 55 to 45 percent. In that context, for the party seeking a

Republican realignment, privatized social security accounts are something worth fighting for.

The Partnership between the GOP, Business, and Moral/Cultural/Racial Interests

The conservative movement has created a powerful, synergistic system that rewards supporters and expands the base of those whose futures are irrevocably tied to its agenda. Corporate America and the Republican Party, exercising the power of the state, have been fused in a mutually rewarding partnership. The corporate side of the partnership provides the money to win elections and receives the economic fruits of victory through lessened oversight, tax cuts, and other beneficial legislation and regulation. The political party is guaranteed a reliable source of campaign money, a powerful network of corporate-financed lobbyists and "grassroots" activists to produce legislative victories, and a supply of well-paid lobbying and trade association jobs after a politician's service as an elected official, a campaign operative, or a congressional aide has been completed.

For social conservatives, the rewards are far less lavish but not without significance. The Republican Party has expressed platform support for the drive to end abortion and has backed the effort to pass a constitutional amendment to ban same sex marriage. The GOP and the conservative movement have opposed race-based affirmative action, winning a number of key court cases. The Bush administration has put government money into abstinence education, has begun efforts, by increasing fines and threatening to impose FCC rules and "persuading" the entertainment industry, to regulate "indecent content" on cable television, and has opened the federal grant process to religious organizations. More broadly, the Republican Party has avidly recruited white, born-again Protestants and conservative Catholics into its ranks and into positions of policymaking authority, granting conservative Christian voters the recognition and legitimacy often denied them by liberal America.

The creation of this partnership between the Republican Party, business, and moral/cultural and racially motivated interests has required aggressive action on all sides. Corporate America has traditionally been uncomfortable with overt public alliances with one political party over the other, fearing retaliation when the tables are turned. Ideologically committed, socially conservative Republicans are, for their part, wary of what they see as insufficient commitment to moral absolutes and a laissez faire tendency toward cultural issues characteristic of those in the business of making money.

Social-cultural issues aside, the partnership between the Republican Party and business has been achieved, to some extent, by a combination of powerful incentives and disincentives—brute force backed up by threats, on the one hand, and rewards so alluring they cannot be resisted, on the other. Consider the rewards offered to the lobbying community by former House Majority Leader Tom DeLay, Grover Norquist, and the other Republican strategists who initiated the "K Street Project" in 1995. This project was launched to compel the hiring of Republican Party loyalists to top posts in the lobbying firms and trade associations that line downtown Washington, especially K Street. The project created a commanding base of support for the Republican agenda, a base that has and will continue to survive episodic scandal. The House Republican leadership, in a program copied by the Senate GOP, assembled what amounts to a working army—shock troops of 1,200 business and trade association lobbyists committed to the party's entire leadership program, not just to the specific interests and concerns of their individual clients (for example, a change in the equipment depreciation schedule for General Motors or elimination of the 4.3 cents per gallon diesel fuel tax for Burlington Northern). These lobbyists are willing to work to pass the whole Republican budget, an entire energy bill, or a broad class action bill, even if their clients are not paying for the work. In the wake of DeLay's decision to step down and the growing number of convictions in the corruption investigation surrounding lobbyist Jack Abramoff, the Republican House leadership has been able to continue to depend on its army of K Street supporters to twist arms to win legislative fights and to hold fundraisers night after night.

The lobbying community reaps multimillion-dollar rewards. Annual client retainers of $200,000 on up for lobbyists with access to a leader (the Speaker, majority leader, majority whip) or committee chairman are routine. In fact, heavily regulated companies hire multiple lobbyists to ensure access at every level during the legislative process, as a bill moves step-by-step through a House committee to the full House, to a Senate committee, to the full Senate, and

then to a leadership-appointed House-Senate conference committee. Republican staffers and political operatives who have paid their
dues, worked hard, and played by the rules can move over to the
private sector, often to K Street, by their early or mid-thirties and
earn salaries well into six figures, sometimes into seven figures.

Although as of early 2006 DeLay and other members of the
House leadership had finally pushed the symbiotic relationship
between lobbyists and elected officials too far, the links between
corporate lobbyists, representatives, and senators will outlast prosecutorial zeal and—no matter what short-term reform measures are
passed—will be increasingly integrated into the daily operations of
Capitol Hill. Not only does lobbying enjoy its constitutionally
protected right under the First Amendment to petition the government, but as legislation becomes ever more voluminous and com-
plex, Congress requires the detailed expertise that industry lobbyists
transmit to bill-writing staff. Most important, corporate America is
not going to sit idly by while Congress and the executive branch
make, or do not make, decisions that determine profits and losses.

For members of the House who are defeated or step down and
move into the lobbying universe, salaries are high. After giving up
his seat in disgrace in 1999, when disclosures of extramarital affairs
(in the midst of the Clinton impeachment scandal) ended his bid to
become Speaker, Republican Bob Livingston set up the Livingston
Group. By 2004, the Livingston Group had $7.42 million in billings
for lobbying work, not including payments for other services such
as providing "access to venture capital and product tie-in referrals,
and public affairs counsel in the areas of coalition building and
strategic communications," according to the firm's Web site.

These benefits pale in comparison to those flowing to two additional, overlapping constituencies: the very rich and heirs to large
estates, and companies, principally on Wall Street, specializing in
the purchase and sale of stocks, bonds, and other forms of investment. The tax cuts enacted by the Bush administration during its
first term enriched each of these constituencies by billions of dollars. Elimination of the estate tax promises to give beneficiaries of
each of the annual 830 estates valued at $20 million or more an
average of $11.7 million in excess of what they would have gotten
under the law as of 2004. If Republican efforts to permanently
eliminate the estate tax ("death tax") are successful, there will, over

the long run, be a vast increase in the concentration of wealth at the top.

Along similar lines, the Bush administration income tax cuts will result, by 2010, in an annual average savings of $166,264 for those in the top 0.5 percent of the income distribution. For those in the bottom 20 percent, the annual break will amount to $23; for those in the second quintile, $364; for those in the middle quintile, $1,079; and the top quintile, $3,623. The Republican drive for "tort reform legislation" has not only produced billions of dollars in savings for business but has also provided a common agenda for the business community and for social conservatives, a topic that will be taken up in detail in chapter 4.

The corporate recipients of this largess have, in turn, become vital players in Republican presidential and congressional fundraising. In the 2004 election, the top Bush fundraisers—the elite "Rangers," men and women who raised at least $200,000 each— were dominated by the CEOs and chairmen of Wall Street firms that year: E. Stanley O'Neal, chairman, CEO, and president of Merrill Lynch & Co.; Joseph J. Grano, chairman and CEO, UBS Wealth Management USA; John Mack, CEO, Credit Suisse First Boston; and Philip J. Purcell, CEO, Morgan Stanley, among others.

GOP SUCCESS: A REMARKABLE COLLECTIVE ACHIEVEMENT

The conservative Republican drive to remake America has been an incremental, long-range endeavor. Although specific events in the steady record of success after success may not appear individually significant, each has marked the clearing of a substantial hurdle. Taken together, these events constitute a remarkable collective achievement.

In 1964, the leaders of the conservative movement took over the presidential and nominating wing of the Republican Party, converting what had been the voice of the Northeastern and Midwestern GOP establishment into a counterinsurgency led by southern and western elites, battling both the civil rights movement and the crowning achievement of twentieth century liberalism, the welfare state. In 1972, the conservative movement expanded its reach and acquired majority status by incorporating supporters of the independent George Wallace campaign and millions of northern white working-class voters who felt their jobs, neighborhoods, unions, and schools were threatened by newly enfranchised African Americans. In 1980, the campaign of Ronald Reagan demonstrated that it was possible for a presidential candidate to voice explicitly conservative goals and win, carrying with him a Republican majority in the U.S. Senate and a working conservative majority in the U.S. House.

The 1994 Republican takeover of the House marked the fall of the last secure bastion of Democratic liberalism within the federal government, putting the leadership of "the people's house" into the hands of avowedly ideological conservatives. The presidency of George W. Bush has completed the process of returning to the Republican fold the establishment/Wall Street wing of the party that had been wary of the hard-right tilt of the GOP since it became the party of racial and moral reaction in the 1960s. Most importantly, Republican administrations, from Ronald Reagan through the George W. Bush years, have demonstrated that the structural fasteners, the "nuts and bolts," that have joined the Democratic Party to its constituencies—welfare, food stamps, affirmative action, Medicaid, Medicare, Social Security—are no longer secure.

In victory and defeat, the conservative Republican Party is certain to continue to press its agenda of weaning individuals from "dependency" on the state. When out of power, the conservative movement has the resources and the managerial expertise to protect and preserve its ideological and institutional edifice intact. When the movement regains a base of elected power, conservatism is primed and ready to capitalize on prior successes, its agenda ever more aggressive and far reaching.

2 Anger Points: Polarization as a Republican Strategy

Before the Supreme Court decided the outcome of the presidential election of 2000, Matt Dowd, the former Democrat who had become George W. Bush's chief pollster, sent a memo to the architect of Bush's political career, Karl Rove, declaring, in effect, that the center of the electorate had collapsed. The memo, based on a detailed historical examination of poll data from the previous five decades, set the stage for President-elect Bush to abandon the themes that had guided him as Texas governor and as a candidate for president. Dowd's analysis destroyed the rationale for Bush to govern as "a uniter, not a divider." The memo freed Bush to discard centrist strategies and to promote instead polarizing policies designed explicitly to appeal to the conservative Republican core.

Dowd had been examining polling data from the weeks before, during, and after the 2000 election and had reached a startling conclusion: the percentage of "true swing" voters had shrunk to a tiny fraction of the electorate. For decades, swing, or middle-ground, voters had shaped election strategies. Campaigns had been structured on the belief that winning a majority of their votes was crucial on election day. George W. Bush himself had campaigned throughout 1999 and 2000 on the assumption that the middle would determine the outcome. Under Rove's guidance in 1999–2000, Bush had pointedly abandoned the divisive and hard-edged conservatism of Newt Gingrich for his own "compassionate conservatism."

Even Karl Rove, who became known as the leading advocate of polarization, had voiced very different views before reading the Dowd memo. In 2000, Rove had rejected the GOP's southern strat-

egy and the calculated use of racially divisive issues or of issues focusing on patriotism, crime, welfare, and so on—approaches that
had produced winners from Richard Nixon to Bush's father in 1988.
These strategies Rove dismissed as "an old paradigm. . . . People are
more attracted today by a positive agenda than by wedge issues."
Instead, the new, post–Cold War political environment called for a
more consensual approach: "We are at a point where each party's
agenda has been somewhat achieved, and the parties are being seen
as increasingly irrelevant to the times," the Rove of 2000 said in an
interview. "If you have knocked down the Berlin Wall and the Evil
Empire has disappeared, it makes it a little bit difficult to run on a
platform of 1956 or 1960."

While running for president in 1999–2000, Bush had explicitly
reached out to the center-left, a strategy antithetical to that of his
2004 campaign. On September 29, 1999, for example, Bush had
sharply criticized the Republican Congress for reducing tax credits
for the working poor: "I'm concerned about the earned income-tax
credit. I'm concerned for someone who is moving from near-
poverty to middle class. I don't think they [House Republican lead-
ers] ought to balance their budget on the backs of the poor."

Bush had stressed the importance of education, a traditionally
Democratic issue avoided by Republicans, and proposed a costly
prescription drug benefit for seniors. In addition, Bush had reached
out to the homosexual community, holding a press conference in
April 2000 with a dozen gay Republicans and announcing, "These
are people from our neighborhoods, people with whom all of us
went to school, people who generally care about America. . . . And
I'm mindful that we're all God's children." Rove was then operating
on the theory that partisanship and political parties were less and
less important to voters and that consensus-building campaigning
was crucial to victory. In 2000, this approach resulted in a 543,895-
vote loss for Bush—50,456,002 to 50,999,897—a loss of the popular vote converted to victory only by a 5 to 4 decision in favor of
Bush by a Republican-appointed Supreme Court majority.

After examining the election results and survey data gathered
in the immediate aftermath of the 2000 election, Dowd reached
the conclusion that the center was literally disappearing and that
strategies based on winning the center were no longer optimal.
Self-described "independent" voters "are independent in name

only," Dowd noted. "Seventy-five percent of independents vote straight ticket" for one party or the other. Once these "false" independents were correctly classified as Democratic or Republican, a very different trend emerged: in the twenty years from 1980 to 2000, the percentage of true swing voters—those who were not virtually certain to vote Democratic or Republican—had fallen from a very substantial 24 percent of the electorate to just 6 percent.

The Dowd memo allowed Republican leaders and strategists to return to the kinds of wedge issues and polarizing tactics that had worked so effectively in the decades following the 1960s, once again tapping the party's genius in developing themes that create coherence among angry constituencies on the right. "There are twice as many angry conservatives in this country as there are angry liberals," notes Democratic direct mail specialist Hal Malchow. "Liberals by their very nature don't get as angry as conservatives do."

WEDGE ISSUES:
POINTS OF INTERSECTION AND THE
MORAL HIGH GROUND

Karl Rove's father abandoned the family soon after Rove's birth on Christmas Day, 1950. Rove's mother remarried, but in 1969, when Rove was nineteen and living in Salt Lake City, Rove recalled that his stepfather returned from a business trip to find "this fellow sitting there on the couch drinking beer [who] didn't rouse himself up to say hello and so forth. Later my mother and father exchanged words and my [step]father got in the car" and took off, never to return. Eleven years later, in 1980, Rove's mother "drove out into the desert, did the classic, drove out to the desert north of Reno and filled the car with carbon monoxide and then left all of her children a letter saying, 'don't blame yourselves for this,' which is, as they say, sort of the classic fuck you gesture."

➤ ◄

Karl Rove intuitively recognized the potential importance for the evolving Republican electorate of the widespread hunger among middle Americans for a less chaotic social order, for a return to a time of more stable families, of more familiar gender roles, of greater community coherence, of more reliable, long-term human affiliations. He saw as well the rage of many voters at the loss of respected institutions and values. It was Rove's genius to envision the compatibility of this yearning with a compendium of emotionally charged issues that could be deployed individually or in interconnected sequences to mobilize, on behalf of the Republican Party, a body of loyal political supporters.

➤ ◄

For nearly four decades, the conservative movement and the Republican Party had found ways to tap the anger and resentment of middle- and working-class white Americans, framing wedge issues to force liberal and Democratic opponents out of the political mainstream while holding the moral high ground in the eyes of a slim but recurrent voting majority. Gay marriage is easier to attack than divorce, adultery, or civil rights for blacks.

On the surface, issues that politically galvanize the right appear diffuse—arguments against abortion, "the gay lifestyle," the erosion of the two-parent family, "radical" feminism, pornography, sex education, embryonic stem cell research, affirmative action, immigration, "activist" judges, gun control, the antiwar movement, women in combat, flag burning, high taxes, and big government as well as advocacy for school prayer, the display of religious symbols, school vouchers, and keeping God in the Pledge of Allegiance. In fact, these issues have significant points of intersection. For example, the extent to which a large number of wedge—that is, polarizing— issues touch upon the subject of sexuality suggests the profound hold that disputed visions of this topic, and of reproductive matters in general, have on voters and on political actors.

A central achievement of Rove and of other Republican strategists has been to fuse these issues, to establish associations between them, linking them to provide the connections necessary to assemble a larger, coherent conservative vision. From this perspective, for example, taxes are used to finance welfare and Great Society programs that shift public resources so as to encourage family dissolution. African Americans, immigrants, and their children are deeply affected by such government policies, but in the Republican view, no family is immune. Lax law enforcement, government permissiveness, no-fault divorce, sex education, and pornography together foster fragile families, father absence, and out-of-wedlock childbirth, which in turn drive crime, drug abuse, and urban and suburban chaos. In the eyes of the cultural right, the sexual revolution, sex education, the women's rights revolution, the blurring of gender roles, "partial birth" abortion, and the "gay agenda" all merge to usurp the status of those who were traditionally dominant, to upend authority, including paternal authority, and to corrode the lives of children and of orderly, decent communities.

The breakdown of the "nuclear" family, from this standpoint, not only fosters moral decay but also leads to the overturning of established hierarchy and directly attacks the advantages of those who have been historically powerful. For such voters, all of these developments take place against a racially charged backdrop of immigration and of other demographic trends that, according to the U.S. Census Bureau, predict that white Americans will comprise just 50.1 percent of the total population in 2050.

For many conservatives, tax policy generates the revenue stream that funds coercive, invasive government, that provides the means for an activist judicial system, that validates new "rights" and hands down decisions that erode legal constraints on cultural production, and that undermines standards of decency, promoting secularism, devastating communities, and enabling the emergence of an increasingly capacious, deregulated sphere for immoral private action. In this apocalyptic version of events, contemporary sociocultural trends lead to endemic anarchy—social, sexual, and moral—threatening the future of the American people themselves.

An extreme version of this view was captured on September 14, 2001—three days after the 9/11 terrorist attacks on the United States—when the Reverend Jerry Falwell, founder of the Moral Majority, and televangelist Pat Robertson, founder of the Christian Coalition, appeared together on the Christian Broadcasting Network's *700 Club*. They exchanged the following remarks:

> JERRY FALWELL: . . . throwing God out successfully with the help of the federal court system, throwing God out of the public square, out of the schools. The abortionists have got to bear some burden for this because God will not be mocked. And when we destroy 40 million little innocent babies, we make God

mad. I really believe that the pagans, and the abortionists, and the feminists, and the gays and the lesbians who are actively trying to make that an alternative lifestyle, the ACLU, People for the American Way—all of them who have tried to secularize America—I point the finger in their face and say "you helped this happen."

PAT ROBERTSON: Well, I totally concur, and the problem is we have adopted that agenda at the highest levels of our government. And so we're responsible as a free society for what the top people do. And, the top people, of course, is the court system.

JERRY FALWELL: Pat, did you notice yesterday the ACLU, and all the Christ-haters, People for the American Way, NOW, etc. were totally disregarded by the Democrats and the Republicans in both houses of Congress as they went out on the steps and called out on to God in prayer and sang "God Bless America" and said "let the ACLU be hanged?" In other words, when the nation is on its knees, the only normal and natural and spiritual thing to do is what we ought to be doing all the time—calling upon God.

Volatile Issues Can Be "Bundled" Together with the Interests of Those Who Are Indifferent to Cultural Retrenchment

Conservatives see a unifying theme behind Ronald Reagan's critique of "welfare queens," George H. W. Bush's focus on black murderer-rapist Willie Horton, gays in the military, Clinton's "dishonoring" of the Oval Office, Howard Dean's action as governor of Vermont legalizing same-sex civil unions (establishing hospital visitation, inheritance, and health insurance for gay and lesbian couples), and George W. Bush's call for a constitutional amendment to prohibit gay marriage. Each of these intensely volatile issues can be and have been "bundled" or made to dovetail with the interests of those indifferent to cultural retrenchment, whose focus is on economic issues and national defense. These latter voters include affluent "wing-tip" Republicans, overseers of the corporate sector, neoconservatives, and free market and social libertarians. For this class of Republicans, the objective of political power is to foster conditions favoring free enterprise, to guard America's global standing, to reduce spending on social programs that increase tax burdens, to support pro-competitive deregulation, and to shrink the depth, width, and breadth of the redistributive state. Both economic and social conservatives share an intense hostility to oppressive regulation that seeks either to constrain the market or to stifle moral and religious expression in the public square. Consequently, sex, race, power, religion, and the interests of the business class have been harnessed in recent decades by the Republican Party to pull together and steer American politics to the right.

The Unlikely Subject of Homosexuality

Polarizing tactics that touch on core issues of human sexual and reproductive behavior cut close to the bone and have helped, over the past forty years, to drive a process of partisan self-sorting. This process started at the top, among elites, and then worked its way deep into the American voting population. First, elected officials and party activists became increasingly ideological, particularly on sociocultural grounds—liberal if they are Democrats and conservative if they are Republicans. Voters, in turn, increasingly aligned themselves with the more ideologically compatible party, reducing the number of racially or morally conservative Democrats and the number of racially or morally liberal Republicans. Cultural liberals now cluster within the center-left Democratic coalition, and a parallel group of racial and social conservatives clusters within the center-right GOP.

The politics of race have lost some force over the past decade—in part due to the stigmatization of overt racial prejudice, in part due to the upward mobility of many African Americans and Hispanics, in part due to the declining salience of busing and to the acceptance in many quarters of the de facto re-segregation of public schools, and in part due to conservative success in staying the helping hand once extended by government to blacks. In place of the politics of race or ethnicity, much of the recent polarization of the electorate has been driven by—or coded into—topics related to sexuality, such as abortion and gay rights.

➤ ◄

Homosexuality has gained political and partisan significance since 1969, when patrons of the Stonewall bar in New York City fought off a police raid, giving birth to the modern gay liberation movement. Between 1969 and the present, gay rights activists emerged from their status as a "largely closeted, fragmented and shunned community" to shape a visible gay culture, creating not only theater, literature, art, and film but also an organized social, legal, and political presence, establishing lesbian, gay, bisexual, and transgender advocacy organizations (LGBT rights groups) such as Act UP!, the Gay and Lesbian Alliance against Defamation, Parents and Friends of Lesbians and Gays, the Lambda Legal Defense Fund, Log Cabin Republicans, Stonewall Democrats, and the Human Rights Campaign. The gay rights community has achieved significant gains over the past quarter century, including domestic partnership benefits, legislation banning discrimination against gays, equal employment opportunities, the right to be adoptive and natural parents, protections for children of LGBT couples, the lifting of some military restrictions on gay soldiers, and the legal right to form civil unions in at least one state.

The acceptance that the gay community was struggling for was complicated, but not derailed, by the rise of AIDS. With 1.5 million people in the United States living with HIV or AIDS, and with more than a half million dead, public awareness of the disease increased. Of those affected, U.S. Centers for Disease Control (CDC) data as of 2004 show that 35 percent were white, 43 percent were black, 20 percent were Hispanic, and 1 percent was of other race/ethnicity. Of the adults and adolescents with AIDS, 77 percent were men. Of these men, 58 percent were men who had sex with men (MSM), 21 percent were injection drug users (IDU), 11 percent were exposed through heterosexual contact, and 8 percent were both MSM and IDU. Of the 93,566 women with AIDS, 64 percent were exposed through heterosexual contact, and 34 percent were exposed through injection drug use. Because of mounting numbers, the costs of the epidemic to the government have been substantial. The administration's FY2006 federal budget request to Congress in February 2005 totaled an estimated $21 billion for HIV and AIDS.

While Congress has heavily funded HIV/AIDS programs, both domestically and internationally, the cultural struggle has intensified.

On April 27, 2000, Vermont Governor Howard Dean signed the state's landmark civil union bill "enshrining in law the concept that committed couples deserve the same rights and benefits regardless of sexual orientation." Dean said afterward that he was proud to be the governor who expanded the civil rights of gays and lesbians but that the law he signed can only go so far: "We now have to change the hearts and minds of Vermonters so that they will truly accept gay and lesbian people as neighbors and equals in every way."

Federal action soon followed. On June 26, 2003, thirty-four years after Stonewall, the U.S. Supreme Court, in *Lawrence et al. v. Texas*, handed down a decision legalizing private homosexual acts between consenting adults. The Court wrote, "The liberty protected by the Constitution allows homosexual persons the right to choose to enter upon relationships in the confines of their homes and their own private lives and still retain their dignity as free persons."

In an unprecedented confluence of events, *Lawrence* was decided on the heels of a wave of scandal that rocked the Catholic Church. A study prepared for the U.S. Conference of Catholic Bishops found that, across the United States, there were "more than 11,000 abuse accusations against priests, of which 6,700 were substantiated, 1,000 were unsubstantiated, and the remainder was not investigated because the alleged perpetrators had died." Seventy-eight percent of the overwhelmingly male victims were between the ages of eleven and seventeen, while nearly 6 percent were seven or younger. The scandal filled headlines throughout 2002, 2003, and 2004. In his annual letter to priests before Easter 2002, the Pope denounced the "sins of our brothers" that "brought scandal upon the Church and made the laity suspicious of even the finest priests," saying that these men had succumbed to "the most grievous form of evil at work in the world."

Public opinion, which for several decades had been moving in an increasingly liberal direction on the subject of gay rights, abruptly shifted rightward, particularly after the Supreme Court ruling in *Lawrence*. The Pew Center for the People and the Press and Gallup, both of which had been documenting increasing tolerance for homosexuality, reported sharp drops in backing for gay marriage. In midsummer 2003, support for gay marriage had reached a high of 38 percent, and opposition to it a low of 53 percent in Pew surveys. By November 2003, support fell eight points to 30 percent, and opposition grew by nine points to 62 percent.

In short, the point spread against gay marriage more than doubled, from fifteen percentage points to a massive thirty-two points. The July 29, 2003, Gallup-*USA Today* poll found a sharp drop in public tolerance for homosexual relations. In May 2003, a strong sixty to thirty-five majority agreed that "homosexual relations between consenting adults should be legal." By July 2003, only 48 percent agreed, and 49 percent disagreed, the lowest levels since the mid-1990s.

The issue gained new traction on November 18, 2003, when the Massachusetts Supreme Judicial Court ruled in *Goodridge v. Department of Public Health* that

> barring an individual from the protections, benefits, and obligations of civil marriage solely because that person would marry a person of the same sex violates the Massachusetts Constitution. . . . It is the exclusive and permanent commitment of the marriage partners to one another, not the begetting of children, that is the sine qua non of marriage.

In the next nine months, more than 6,100 same-sex couples were married in Massachusetts—one out of six marriage licenses issued in the state.

In February 2004, the Democratic mayor of San Francisco turned the issue into a media extravaganza, televised nightly, after he ordered city officials to marry gay and lesbian couples—in violation of a measure California voters had approved in 2000 that defined marriage as a union between a man and a woman.

A Political Goldmine: "Gay Marriage Has Surpassed Other Major Social Issues Like Abortion and Gun Control in Its Influence on Voters"

On February 24, 2004, with just a little over nine months until the presidential election, Republican strategists—both responding to and driving a backlash—saw a potential political goldmine, and Bush stepped into the controversy to declare his support for a constitutional amendment for the "protection of marriage":

The union of a man and woman is the most enduring human institution, honoring—honored and encouraged in all cultures and by every religious faith. Ages of experience have taught humanity that the commitment of a husband and wife to love and to serve one another promotes the welfare of children and the stability of society. Marriage cannot be severed from its cultural, religious and natural roots without weakening the good influence of society. Government, by recognizing and protecting marriage, serves the interests of all. Today, I call upon the Congress to promptly pass and to send to the states for ratification an amendment to our Constitution defining and protecting marriage as a union of a man and woman as husband and wife.

From a Republican strategic vantage point, Bush's support for the amendment was a clear winner. First, gay marriage had risen to the top of the social issue agenda. According to the Pew Research Center:

Gay marriage has surpassed other major social issues like abortion and gun control in its influence on voters. Four-in-ten voters say they would not vote for a candidate who disagrees with them on gay marriage, even if they agree with the candidate on most other issues. By comparison, 34% say they would not support a candidate who disagrees with them on abortion and 32% expressed that opinion about a candidate's stance on gun control.

Second, and more important, there were substantial gains but few costs to taking a stand in opposition to gay marriage, according to the Pew poll data:

For the most part, gay marriage is a make-or-break voting issue only to the opponents of that idea; supporters of gay marriage generally say a candidate's stance would not affect their vote. Moreover, even among gay marriage opponents, the issue has a disproportionate impact on some groups—notably conservative Republicans, evangelical Christians and voters age 65 and older.

Thus, taking up the cause of the constitutional amendment outlawing homosexual marriage fit perfectly into the Republican base-building, polarizing strategy.

In a move designed to increase turnout, Republicans and conservatives succeeded in putting same-sex marriage ban referendums on the ballot in eleven states in November 2004, including in battleground states such as Michigan, Ohio, and Oregon. The referendums passed by decisive margins in every state. Arguably, the Ohio referendum contributed to Bush's 51 to 49 percent victory in that state—whose electoral votes put him over the top—and thus to his victory in the election. Political scientist Daniel A. Smith of the University of Florida writes, "Holding constant an array of demographic, economic, and partisan factors, Bush's level of support across Ohio was positively tied to a county's support for the gay marriage ban."

THE PARTIES COME TO FUNCTION AS POLITICAL BRAND NAMES

The partisan self-sorting of voters into the ideologically more compatible party—social/racial conservatives finding a home in the GOP and social/racial liberals in the Democratic fold—has captured the imagination of political scientists who specialize in voting behavior. Stanford political scientist Matt Levendusky writes:

> [T]hroughout the electorate, there has been a fundamental change in the relationship between partisanship and ideology. A generation ago, for most members of the mass electorate, party ID and ideology were only weakly related. Now, for a sizeable portion of the U.S. electorate, party and ideology are deeply inter-twined. . . . The national parties have drifted further from one another over the past thirty years, and became more ideologically distinct, which means that the parties now send a more unified and homogenous ideological signal. As voters see this purer signal from each party, they can more easily see what policy positions make someone a Democrat or a Republican. The parties come to function as political "brand names."

Along similar lines, Dowd argues that "issues don't matter in presidential campaigns, it's your 'brand' values that matter. Voters see their issue through that brand and how they judge that issue is seen through the brand." To understand this phenomenon requires looking at politics as brand marketing. Dowd adds:

> That is why the [Toyota hybrid] Prius is doing so well. It has nothing to do with gas mileage, it has to do with the statement it makes: "This is a car that represents caring for people or caring for the environment, therefore I am going to drive it and it sends a statement to my friends and neighbors."

Thomas Carsey and Geoffrey Layman, political scientists from Florida State University and the University of Maryland, after extensive analysis of poll data, conclude that "our results demonstrate that party identification indeed serves as a perceptual screen that shapes attitudes toward policy issues." Voters are increasingly evaluating issues and debates by looking through Republican and Democratic lenses. The result is that voters judge issues less on the merits than on how fellow partisans either support or oppose issue positions. Conservative Christian voters, for example, strongly support Republican tax cuts and Republican calls for military intervention in the Middle East. Well-educated liberals, in turn, often oppose school vouchers and charter schools because these are initiatives from the Republican right.

The growing partisanship of the electorate has striking consequences when voters attempt to evaluate public policies. A pre-election report, "The Separate Realities of Bush and Kerry Supporters," based on a survey of 2,725 adults in September and October 2004 and conducted by the Center on Policy Attitudes at the University of Maryland's Center for International and Security Studies, found high levels of factual misinformation on the justifications for the war in Iraq. The misinformation was heavily concentrated among Bush supporters. The survey found that, "despite the report of the 9/11 Commission saying there is no evidence Iraq was providing significant support to al Qaeda, 75 percent of Bush supporters believe Iraq was providing substantial support to al Qaeda (compared to 30 percent of Kerry supporters), with 20 percent believing that Iraq was directly involved in 9/11." In fact, 56 percent of Bush supporters believed that the 9/11 Commission reported that Iraq was either directly involved in the attacks on the World Trade Center and Pentagon or that Iraq had given substantial support to al Qaeda—precisely the opposite of what the commission, in fact, had found.

➤ ◄

Truth and falsehood, right and wrong, good and bad, are now judged differently depending on the partisanship of the person making the judgment and the credibility he or she is willing to grant to the source of information. This makes it much easier for a Republican, for example, to discount as purely partisan unfavorable news coming from the *New York Times*, NPR, or CBS. A Democrat can similarly discount a negative story from *FOX News*, members of the National Association of Religious Broadcasters, or Rush Limbaugh. Each side is prone to distort reality, rejecting information that is out of line with prior ideological commitments—a development that makes the possibility of reaching agreement or consensus in a dispute highly unlikely.

Under Dowd's guidance, as it began to explore the character of the changing electorate, the GOP found the nation dividing into two distinct groups—groups echoing in many ways demographer William Frey's two Americas. Most importantly, these two ideological universes, with their differing cultural agendas, were increasingly divergent in their sources of information, feeding from two separate information streams. These divergent information sources continuously reinforced polarized worldviews.

A congressional redistricting process designed to produce secure seats has further divided the nation. In addition, as people relocate, they are increasingly choosing, when possible, to live in politically congenial communities; hunting and fishing, country-club, or church-going Republicans move to areas with like-minded neighbors, generally in "red" America, just as Starbucks-drinking, Birkenstock-wearing, independent-film, and alternative-rock Democrats prefer "blue" neighborhoods. Middle-class blacks have now established homogeneous "blue" suburban enclaves, and gay neighborhoods in densely populated, gentrified downtowns add another dimension to Democratic America. At a different socioeconomic level, low-income African Americans and other minorities not only chose like-minded neighbors but are also often forced by housing

costs and discrimination to live in fraying ethnic or racial enclaves—also blue. Similarly, large numbers of working- to middle-
class whites, labeled by writer Ross Douthat "Sam's Club Republicans"—those with annual incomes ranging from $30,000 to
$50,000—live in those broad swaths of lower-income rural, subur-
ban, and exurban America that are distinctively red.

POLARIZING STRATEGIES: MAKE SURE YOUR BASE IS BIGGER THAN THEIRS

Dowd's determination to deploy polarizing strategies for the 2004
election, recognizing that the importance of the center could be
downgraded—and that the month-long, post-election fight over
the contested 2000 Florida election results had served to intensify
voter partisanship—set off a strong reaction in the world of Republican election and policymaking calculus. The implications of
Dowd's 2000 post-election memo resonated immediately with Rove
and the rest of the Republican hierarchy.

The conclusions drawn from the Dowd memo shaped every aspect of the first Bush administration, from tax and regulatory policy
to stands on stem cell research, abortion, and gay marriage. In the
political arena, the memo soon led to a major restructuring of the
2004 presidential Republican campaign, to the emergence of new
target constituencies, and to the creation of increasingly sophisticated, high-tech means of reaching key voters through micro-
targeting—using statistical methods and computer technologies,
initially developed for commercial marketing operations but now
adapted to political purposes, to comb through a comprehensive
database of the U.S. electorate to locate, and if possible to turn out,
every likely Republican voter.

Dowd's most important strategic finding was that "you can lose
the swing voters and still win the election, if you make sure your
base is bigger than theirs." In fact, he was proved correct. Bush won
decisively in 2004 despite actually losing ground among the small
fraction of "independent" and "apolitical" voters compared with
2000, when he did better among swing voters but lost the overall
popular vote. Among independent, apolitical, and swing voters,

Bush's percentage fell from 55 to 42 percent, while Gore received 45 percent and Kerry 58 percent, according to National Election Studies surveys.

JETTISON THE NOTION OF HEALING THE BREACH

One of the first consequences of Dowd's insight was the Bush administration's decision to jettison the notion of healing the growing cultural breach between the two Americas. Political observers of all stripes had expected Bush at the beginning of 2001 to approach the presidency in a conciliatory manner. He had won the White House as a result of the 5 to 4 Supreme Court decision in *Gore v. Bush* after losing the popular vote and had no claim to a popular mandate. As the governor of Texas, Bush had run a bipartisan administration, notable for its cooperation with Democratic leaders in the legislature. Once in the White House, however, Bush rejected conciliation from day one. His presidency and his re-election strategies, working to reinforce each other, were geared to the conclusions reached in the Dowd memo: it was more important to strengthen and enlarge the reliably loyal socially and economically conservative base than it was to reach out to the tiny fraction of voters who could legitimately be described as independent and centrist and whose votes were erratic under the best of circumstances. In fact, reaching out to the center could lead to losing more votes among dissatisfied voters and interests on the right than would be gained from the middle. Corporate interests, affluent "country-clubbers," and the sector stretching from moderate-, lower-, and middle-income social-racial conservatives to the religious right already formed a powerful "iron triangle" at the core of the conservative Republican coalition, with each leg of the triangle receiving solid support from the other two.

Business interests and the interests of the affluent were highly congruent. Republican Pioneers—the 212 affluent investors, oil men, developers, and corporate CEOs who each raised at least $100,000 for the 2000 Bush campaign—had been crucial to Bush's victory. No other group in America would profit more from

Bush's 2001 tax cut. At least sixty-one of Bush's major fundraisers directly benefited in their business enterprises from the administration's 2003 Medicare prescription drug bill and the giant 2004 energy bill.

Conservatism's new allegiance to Israel was also used to build a Republican outreach to strongly pro-Israel Jewish voters and donors worried about growing criticism of the Jewish state by liberal Democrats. Bush won 25 percent of the Jewish vote in 2004. Republican allegiance to Israel fueled, as well, the fragmenting of Jewish support for Democrats. A majority of Jewish voters, 59 percent, supported the war against Iraq in early 2003. By early 2005, however, 70 percent of American Jews were opposed to the war in Iraq.

Members of the growing "investor class" (many with moderate incomes), who entered the stock market during the boom of the 1990s and who benefited directly as their pension and retirement investments in mutual funds, IRAs, and 401k accounts swelled, could also be swayed to support the GOP via lowered dividend, capital gains, and estate taxes. Wall Street, which had begun to tilt toward the Democratic Party during the Clinton administration as Robert Rubin, Larry Summers, and Alan Greenspan presided over record stock market growth, was an inviting Republican target. The financial services industry could be brought back into the fold by means of sharp reductions in taxes on investment income, encouraging clients to shift stocks and other assets to capitalize on the Bush tax breaks, with each transaction producing new commissions for investment banks and brokerage houses.

Governing Explicitly with the Purpose of Building Core Constituencies

The Bush administration adopted a governing policy explicitly in line with the purpose of building core constituencies for the Republican Party and undermining support for adversaries. This strategy served to open the door to new policy initiatives. Ever since the presidency of Dwight Eisenhower, for example, Republican leaders had been reluctant to take on Social Security. On November 8, 1954, in a letter to his brother, Edgar, President Eisenhower laid out what became the Republican "third rail" approach to Social Security, a stand that held for fifty years:

> Should any political party attempt to abolish social security, unemployment insurance, and eliminate labor laws and farm programs, you would not hear of that party again in our political history. There is a tiny splinter group, of course, that believes you can do these things. Among them are H. L. Hunt (you possibly know his background), a few other Texas oil millionaires, and an occasional politician or business man from other areas. Their number is negligible and they are stupid.

By 2005, Social Security, although still a sensitive and volatile issue, was no longer lethal. Despite the increased risks that private accounts pose for middle-income voters—including many Republicans—the administration set out on a relentless marketing mission, stressing the potential payoff to retirees in a boom market. Partial privatization could not get through the Congress in 2005—weak stock market performance in the years following 2000 was still fresh in memory—but cutting guaranteed Social Security benefits was now an issue that could be raised, debated, and placed in the political arena.

Other issues that had been untouchable in the past could also be broached. In 1982, Ronald Reagan buckled under press and interest-group criticism when his administration rescinded major corporate tax cuts enacted the year before and, again, when it backed off from aggressively pro-development environmental policies. Bush, facing much the same criticism, in contrast pressed forward with his tax and environmental policies, effectively asserting through most of his tenure his freedom from any obligation to accommodate critics in the center or on the left.

The decision to give up a commitment to be leader and representative of all of the people frees a Republican president from many of the traditional obligations of holding public office. Instead of being responsive, in varying degrees, to the entire spectrum of the voting public, a Republican in the White House seeking to promote polarization needs only to be assiduously attentive to key sectors within his own coalition.

➤ ◄

While polarization has worked exceptionally well for Republicans, a parallel strategy—of addressing the concerns of the partisan base rather than of the center—has not proven to be a viable option for Democrats. Roughly 40 percent of the population describes itself as "conservative," according to National Election Studies data, whereas only 20 to 25 percent is made up of self-described "liberals." A base strategy for the Republicans is to invest heavily in getting conservative nonvoters and/or intermittently conservative voters registered and to the polls. There are many more unreliable or nonvoting conservatives than liberals—almost twice as many—giving the GOP a much larger pool to draw upon.

Because the number of hard-core liberal adherents is so much smaller, Democrats are far more dependent on winning the votes of self-described moderates. Democratic election strategy thus depends on first winning a large percentage of reliably voting centrists, alienated by hard left appeals, and then building turnout among nonvoting moderates. In effect, the moderate voter is much more important to the Democratic Party than to the Republican Party. Political scientists and Democratic Party activists William Galston and Elaine Kamarck of the University of Maryland and Harvard, respectively, have made this argument effectively in their 2005 study, "The Politics of Polarization."

Substantial Benefits Accrue to the Majority Party from Intensely Polarized Politics and Policies

Before the 2000 election, Republican leaders in the House of Representatives had raised lonely voices advocating the gearing of policy and politics to the conservative base—a strategy of purposeful polarization. The House, more than the executive branch or Senate, is inherently receptive to ideologically driven approaches. Partisan gerrymandering to assure incumbents safe districts combined with population shifts—in which conservative voters move out of Democratic districts into Republican districts and liberals move into more Democratic districts—have altered the political pressures and incentives affecting incumbents. Members of the House are now, in many cases, more fearful of a primary challenge from an ideologically committed member of their own party than they are of a general election challenger from the other party.

A Republican elected from a majority-white district in South Carolina, for example, will do all he or she can to stay within the good graces of the Chamber of Commerce and the religious right to insulate himself or herself from accusations of accommodating liberals. Conversely, a Detroit Democrat will look to the NAACP, the AFL-CIO, and NARAL to determine which way to vote to undercut any insurgent challenge from the left. The result is that legislative decisions requiring clear-cut ideological choices, as opposed to bipartisan compromise, are often welcomed by members of both parties, as Republicans seek to protect their right flank and Democrats, their left flank. In this atmosphere, compromise does not enhance job security but only serves to create political uncertainty and potential danger.

Substantial benefits flow to the majority party from intensely polarized politics and policies. First, legislation can be explicitly written to reward supporters and to penalize opponents—the case in the four Bush tax cut bills, the 2005 energy bill, the 2004 bankruptcy bill, the 2005 class action bill, and the 2003 Partial Birth Abortion Ban Act. While retaining rhetorical pretences—"I'm a uniter, not a divider"—policies of serving the general good can, within broad limits, be abandoned.

Second, without pressure to accommodate the center, Republicans in the majority have been, with little cost, relatively unresponsive to criticism. Conservative voters who find the Christian right overly moralistic, for example, rarely vote Democratic on election day despite the power and prominence of evangelicals within the Republican coalition. Adverse newspaper and television coverage similarly fails to draw conservatives into the Democratic camp and is dismissed by core Republican voters as an attempt by the liberal media to undermine the conservative GOP agenda.

The ability to dismiss criticism of controversial political actions as merely partisan has allowed the Republican Party, both in Congress and in the executive branch, to break through traditional ethical boundaries. The distinction between elected leaders and the business and trade association lobbying community has, for all practical purposes, been abandoned, with lobbyists running the campaigns of House and Senate members for leadership posts, and with committee chairs and recognized cabals of lobbyists writing legislation as they become a formal part of the House whip operation. In the aftermath of the Abramoff lobbying scandal, there will undoubtedly be some regulatory reform, as there was after Watergate, but in an economy where billions of dollars are riding on congressional and executive branch decisions every day, such reforms are likely to have only a short-term impact.

The disappearance of the center has effectively eliminated any legitimate, nonpartisan mechanism—one that commands the respect of the general public—for arbitrating or evaluating the actions of elected officials. The media has been dismissed by many Americans as being in the service of either the left or the right. Environmental, civil rights, traditional good government, reform, gay, and women's rights groups are viewed as allies of the Democratic Party. Scholars from the major research universities—once an unassailable source of authority—are now viewed as representing liberal perspectives. And Senator John McCain, Republican of Arizona, is the sole member of the House or Senate who, at the moment, even approximates the kind of credibility with a broad cross-section of public that once characterized officeholders in both branches on both sides of the aisle—even though McCain has a lifetime rating of 83 out of 100 from the American Conservative Union.

Preaching to the Converted Turned Out to Be Increasingly Valuable

These trends toward polarization all played out in powerful ways during the Bush 2004 re-election campaign. Matt Dowd's 2000 memo and his role as senior adviser to the RNC and as chief campaign strategist and director of polling and media planning for the 2004 Bush-Cheney campaign opened the door to a fundamental transformation of campaign strategy. Because most people had already made up their minds about whether they were on Bush's side, the basic function of the campaign became to activate voters' "anger points," to mobilize the conservative base, to register supporters who were not registered, and to make sure that ballots were cast by all "unreliable" or "casual" registered voters who could be identified by Dowd and his team as Bush supporters. As a corollary strategy, the Bush campaign aimed at increasing defection and abstention among Democratic voters, sapping support for Kerry and undermining the Democrats' national security credibility—for example, by means of the "Swift Boat Veterans" attack on Kerry's war record.

Instead of putting 80 percent of campaign cash and staff into persuading the undecided—the traditional amount—only 50 percent went to that task in the 2004 Bush campaign. Undecided voters remained important but no longer the overwhelmingly dominant priority. The amount of money going to voter registration, mobilization, and turnout of the already-committed increased by 150 percent, from 20 percent of available resources to 50 percent.

The kind of spending that in the past would have been minimized or rejected—preaching to the converted by means of ads and appearances on the Rush Limbaugh show, events mobilizing white evangelical churches, a focus on direct mail to hunting and fishing club members—turned out to be crucially valuable. Getting a non-voting Southern Baptist, a Limbaugh-listener, or an O'Reilly or Sean Hannity fan registered and to the polls produced a virtually certain Bush vote, while costly television commercials designed to persuade the unpersuaded were found to be increasingly wasteful, for less and less of the viewing audience was undecided. At the same time, the partisan inclination of any individual, whether registered to vote or not, became subject to increasingly accurate predictive tests. The available data on which to base such predictions had, by 2004, grown geometrically, and computing speed and new information technologies permitted the manipulation and application of such data within hours or even minutes.

The 2004 Bush campaign decided to capitalize on one of the most politically important demographic trends in America: that voters and potential voters have been slowly but steadily separating themselves increasingly into two separate clusters reflecting not only political values but cultural preferences, consumer choices, religious convictions, television viewing habits, and leisure activities. "People's lifestyle choices—where they live and who they associate with—are leading people, and their political affiliations follow. They look around and see everybody around them is a Republican, and they decide they must be a Republican," Dowd said. When a man who likes to hunt, drive a four-wheel SUV, and barbeque on weekends moves to a new community, he is likely to pick a neighborhood where he sees SUVs in the driveways, barbeques in the backyards, and, in the fall, deer racks on the cars and trucks. As Dowd stated:

> Society is becoming much more homogeneous, and you com-
> pound that with the media choices that become confirmatory
> of that. They don't have to watch NBC, CBS, or ABC. They
> can go to find something that feeds their preexisting thoughts.
> They are sitting next to neighbors who are basically in agree-
> ment with them. And then they listen to or watch news that re-
> inforces that.

The growing trend toward self-segregation of Democrats and Republicans has, in turn, provided new opportunities for partisans in control of congressional redistricting to boost the number of seats held by their party. The classic Republican strategy has now become to create as many overwhelmingly Democratic districts (where a Democrat will win by 70 percent plus) as possible. From a Democratic vantage point, this scheme "wastes" votes by giving these few districts far more Democratic votes than a Democratic candidate would need to win. The strategy then calls for construct-ing as many districts as possible with modest Republican majorities to minimize "wasted" GOP voters, while creating the maximum number of Republican-majority districts.

This tactic was used with striking success in states such as Michigan and Pennsylvania (both Republican controlled in 2001–2002). In Pennsylvania, a state that in 2000 and 2004 voted for Al Gore and John F. Kerry over George W. Bush, the Republican-controlled redistricting process produced, after the 2002 midterm elections, a congressional delegation with twelve Re-publicans and seven Democrats. Michigan, which similarly sup-ported Gore and Kerry, emerged after the 2002 elections with a delegation of nine Republicans and six Democrats.

Creative Groundswell among Republican Consultants

Dowd's advocacy of polarizing the electorate produced a creative groundswell among Republican consultants. Among those working along the same lines as Dowd was Will Feltus, who first brought his ideas to the Republican consulting firm National Media and then marketed them to the Bush campaign and to the Republican National Committee. Also working in this vein was Alex Gage, who formed TargetPoint Consulting. Feltus and Gage turned Dowd and Rove's strategic theory into tactical reality.

For years, Feltus had been bothered by the Republican "GRP [gross rating point] gap." Surveys showed that 14 percent more Democrats watched television than Republicans. The result, from a political television time buyer's point of view, was that a substantial percentage of the money spent by Republicans on television was wasted on committed Democrats. During the 1988 campaign, Feltus had asked Nielson Media Research, which estimates audience size for broadcast and cable networks, how much it would cost to ask viewers if they were Republicans, Democrats, or independents and to get partisan ratings for every show and use the data to reduce the "television gap." The cost, however, was prohibitive—in excess of $1 million, Feltus said.

In 2001, however, Feltus met Bob Cohen, president and CEO of Scarborough Research. Scarborough had begun measuring newspaper readership and penetration in 1975. In the mid-1990s, Scarborough enlarged the scope of its work to become, in its own words, a "premier source for consumer insights. We measure the shopping patterns, lifestyles and media habits of consumers locally, regionally and nationally." The firm maintains local and national databases of consumer brand purchases, "retail shopping behaviors, lifestyle characteristics, in-depth consumer demographics, and media usage patterns."

Feltus recalled "flipping through the Scarborough questionnaire and there it was," about halfway through, right after a question about credit card use and right before a question on health club membership: "Do you consider yourself a Democrat, Republican, Independent, Independent but close to the Democrats, Independent but close to the Republicans, or none of these?" It was the basic political question. People filling out the questionnaire answered hundreds of other inquiries about consumer purchases, leisure pursuits, hobbies, recent movies, insurance coverage, drinking preferences, and so on. The data from the questionnaire, in combination with weekly television viewing diaries filled out by participants, are designed to be used by marketers and advertisers to make spending decisions and by newspapers, television stations, and other media outlets to make the case that they provide reliable access to targeted consumers.

For Feltus, the data became a political treasure trove, discovered just as the Bush White House and the Republican National Committee had begun searching for the most effective tools to zero in on key voter groups for the 2004 campaign. The Scarborough surveys showed, for example, the partisanship of car buyers, from decisively Republican Porsche owners (59 percent Republican, 26 percent Democrat), to bipartisan American car buyers (Chevy, Lincoln, Plymouth, Ford, Olds, etc.), to the increasingly Democratic Subaru (45 percent Democrat, 34 percent Republican) and Volvo owners (45 percent Democrat, 33 percent Republican).

More importantly, the Scarborough data provided guidelines for a much more effective use of television dollars. The huge expansion in the number of networks and channels available to cable viewers, in combination with the Scarborough findings, provided, for the first time, a means to get around the 14 percent GRP gap and save millions of campaign dollars. A campaign directed at Republican base voters could, according to Scarborough data, buy television time around *FOX News Sunday*, which is the most decisively partisan audience of any news show. For national buys, the campaign pointedly avoided the CBS *Morning Show*, CBS *Evening News*, and the CBS Sunday show *Face the Nation*. All these CBS news shows have decidedly Democratic audiences, although not approaching the Republican tilt at FOX.

Similarly, among entertainment shows, just as *JAG*, *NYPD Blue*, and *The Simpsons* have had strong Republican audiences, *West Wing* and *Girlfriends* have had decisively Democratic viewers. In picking which sports show to advertise on, it is important to know that the percentage of Republican viewers is higher for college football than for pro football. Scarborough can also rank by partisanship the audiences of all the major cable channels, using a system of subtracting the Democratic "index" from the Republican "index." The higher the positive number, the more decisively Republican the viewers are, whereas the higher the negative number, the more Democratic the viewers. Using this system, Speedvision, the Outdoor Channel, the History Channel, FOX News Channel, and the Golf Channel in 2004 ranked from plus 20 to plus 48 (the highest score being Speedvision, which specializes in NASCAR, motorcycle, and other vehicle competitions). Conversely, the strong minus (or pro-Democratic) numbers revealed Democratic-leaning audiences for BRAVO, Lifetime, Court TV, Nickelodeon, and TNT.

Even more important for a presidential contest focused on twenty battleground states, Scarborough provided partisan viewing patterns for individual metro-political markets, which often differed substantially from the larger national patterns. In Los Angeles, for example, Republicans are much more likely to watch CBS news than they are nationally, and a GOP ad buy at the beginning and end of *Face the Nation* or the *CBS Evening News* is cost-effective.

The wide range of choices and the increasing partisan differentiation in viewership have resulted in a basic change in the function of television news. Instead of providing ostensibly neutral information on which citizens can base opinions of leaders and events, the trend is toward television news-watching that increasingly serves to reinforce pre-existing dispositions and views. "It used to be that everybody sat down and watched ABC, CBS or NBC, and generally got the same news. Today, they get different versions of the news. They get the version of the news that seems to them to make them more comfortable," Dowd said.

These trends have contributed to a more than doubling of the percentage of voters who view the opposition party in sharply negative terms. Dowd described how, over the past half century, the way voters view their own party and the opposition party has changed radically. In the Eisenhower years (1953–1960), there was a thirty percentage point difference in a voter's positive assessment of his or her own party and his or her negative assessment of the opposition party. For example, a voter with an 85 percent favorable rating for his own party would give the other party a 55 percent favorable rating. During the Watergate years of the early and mid-1970s, that spread grew to forty points; under Ronald Reagan it rose to fifty; under Bill Clinton, to sixty; and under George W. Bush, to sixty-five points. In other words, voters in 2001–2005 gave an average 85 percent favorable rating to their own party and, to the opposition party, an average 20 percent favorable rating.

Anger Is a Much Stronger Motivation

At the same time that Feltus was putting together the Scarborough data to improve the efficiency of Republican television and radio time buys, Alex Gage and his partners, Brent Seaborn and Michael

Meyers, set about addressing two problems facing a Republican Party determined to mobilize and enlarge its base vote. Unlike Feltus, whose focus was on radio and TV advertising, Gage was determining cost-effective ways to reach individual voters, one by one, by phone, by direct mail, online, and through door-to-door canvassing. Gage and the entire Rove-Dowd-Mehlman team had been building a "ground war" strategy to counter the Democrats' traditional advantage in getting out the vote in the closing days of a campaign.

Gage was determined to enlarge the scope of past Republican targeting, which had limited get-out-the-vote (GOTV) activities to precincts that cast GOP majorities of 65 percent or more. These highly concentrated votes made up only 15 percent of the total Republican vote nationwide on election day. Gage wanted to find prospective voters for Bush wherever they were located—scattered in the black neighborhoods of Detroit and Cleveland, in the ranks of unionized autoworkers and teamsters, even in Ivy League faculty lounges where Republicans were few and far between. Finally, after seeking out these hard-to-find voters, Gage wanted to devise ways to tailor messages to the issue concerns of each person instead of using bland mail and recorded phone messages from popular figures making generic appeals.

If a voter was enraged about the legalization of same-sex marriage in Massachusetts, about sex education focusing on contraception in middle school, or about "activist judges" supporting "racial quotas" or free health care for illegal immigrants, Gage wanted that voter to get letters and phone calls promising that Bush would make every effort to put an end to the offense. If a voter's wrath was directed at politicians who raised taxes, that voter needed to be directly informed that Bush would lower federal taxes, not raise them. "We wanted to know what these voters' 'anger points' were," Gage said. "People don't vote because they're pleased with something President Bush did. Anger is a much stronger motivation."

Gage and his team worked off of detailed voter lists containing partisan registration and past turnout histories available from public sources and from information compiled by Acxiom, a major commercial processor of consumer data. The Republican strategists combed through Acxiom databases for information regarding demographics, home ownership, purchasing histories, and lifestyle activities for 111 million households and 176 million individuals nationwide. Gage oversaw exceptionally large surveys of 5,000 to 12,000 voters in each of the twenty presidential "battleground" states of 2004. Each survey respondent indicated his or her strongest anger points, on issues from gay rights to tax hikes, gun control, military strength, immigration, abortion, and affirmative action. Each survey respondent was then put into one or more of roughly thirty "clusters," including religious conservatives, antitax voters, pro-military voters, anti-lawyer voters, libertarians, and so forth.

For each of these clusters, it was possible to develop a detailed demographic portrait: their hobbies, buying habits, religious denomination and service attendance, income levels, cars, magazine subscriptions, marriage status, price of homes, boat ownership, NRA membership, children, preparations for retirement, and so on. It was then possible to extrapolate this information to the population of the entire state. "We wanted to be able to find out things like 'who are the 10,000 people in the city of Detroit whose top priority is to stop abortions,'" Gage said. With the "needle in a haystack" techniques Gage developed, it was possible to send pro-gun messages to NRA members within the United Automobile Workers Union.

The ability of the Republican Party to target their voters—not only in such large areas as exurbia and in sprawling suburbs but also within black and Hispanic churches, in unions, and in overwhelmingly Democratic college towns—stunned Democratic Party leaders. "They were smart. They came into our neighborhoods. They came into Democratic areas with very specific targeted messages to take Democratic voters away from us," said Democratic National Committee Chairman Terence McAuliffe in 2004. "They were much more sophisticated in their message delivery."

Polarization as a Republican Strategy: Christians to the Right, Media to the Left

Throughout most of the twentieth century, one of the Democratic Party's key advantages was that it could depend on four easily identified, sizeable, overlapping constituencies: trade unionists, African Americans, ethnic European Catholics, and members of big city political machines. The lines of communication to each group were direct, from the party to the leadership of labor, to the Catholic and African American churches, and to local big city politicians. Now, however, the Republican Party has its own equally accessible, large, and receptive core constituency: white evangelical Christians, as well as religious traditionalists of all faiths.

White evangelicals in 2004 made up somewhere between 34 and 40 percent of the Republican vote, the single biggest block within the GOP. These white evangelicals together with Mormons, conservative Roman Catholics, conservative-leaning Protestants, and evangelical Protestant Hispanics make up well over half, 61.2 percent, of GOP voters. Four political scientists specializing in the role of religion in elections, James L. Guth, Lyman A. Kellstedt, Corwin E. Smidt, and John C. Green, put it this way:

> The Republicans depend heavily on Evangelical Protestants, Latter-day Saints, and traditionalists from all major (and most minor) religious traditions, with the bulk of their remaining support coming from centrists in the three largest ones. The Democrats have clearly retained their historic identity as the party of most religious minorities, but depend far more heavily

> on secular citizens than ever before, with the bulk of their re-
> maining support coming from religious modernists and cen-
> trists. . . . [V]irtually every major issue of recent years has been
> shaped by religious politics: abortion, stem-cell research,
> same-sex marriage, judicial nominations, and the Iraq war, to
> be sure—but also tax policy, environmental politics and social
> welfare programs.

Traditionalist white evangelicals are much more supportive of Republican positions on a range of nonreligious issues than the population as a whole—a development that speaks to the efficacy of the Republican strategy of "bundling" or packaging key cultural/racial, national security, and economic issues together. In 2004, according to Pew data, twice as many traditionalist evangelicals believed the government should spend less (40 percent) than more (21 percent) in contrast to 26 percent less and 34 percent more among the general public. Similarly, a decisive majority (67 percent) of evangelicals described large tax cuts as "good," and only 25 percent described them as "bad," compared to a nearly evenly split general electorate, 48 percent good, 45 percent bad. While the general public strongly believes the United States has the right to initiate preemptive war—62 percent agree, 22 percent disagree—traditionalist evangelicals overwhelmingly affirm their support for such military action, 78 percent to 10 percent.

The same pattern holds for the war in Iraq. Among Republicans, white evangelical Christians were, in June 2005, far more supportive of the war than any other Republican group. Asked, for example, "All in all, considering the costs to the United States versus the benefits to the United States, do you think the war with Iraq was worth fighting, or not?" 88.5 percent of the Republican evangelicals said it was worth fighting, just over seventeen points higher than all other Republicans, 71.3 percent. Of the general public, 46 percent of all those surveyed said the benefits outweighed the costs. Asked about the number of U.S. casualties in the Iraq War, 63.7 percent of the evangelicals said the losses were "acceptable" compared with 47.7 percent of all other Republicans. For the entire sample, 29 percent described the casualties as acceptable.

Evangelical support for the GOP on nonreligious issues has, in turn, made it possible for the Republican Party to retain this base without the need to undertake extreme measures—without pushing to outlaw all abortion, for example—that might risk alienating moderate voters. The Republican Party has found many ways, substantive and symbolic, to appeal directly to and reward its most conservative "moral values" voters through programs, policies, rhetoric, and appointments that either stay under the radar of moderate conservatives and of the mainstream media or are sufficiently low-key that their full implications are more apparent to the Republican base than to its opponents. Thus the Bush administration—through a form of "narrowcasting"—is able to minimize the costs while maximizing the benefits of its polarization strategy.

For example, Bush's education secretary in 2005, Margaret Spellings, succeeded in having PBS remove from its children's programming an episode that featured a child raised in a lesbian household. Spellings wrote to PBS: "[M]any parents would not want their young children exposed to the life-styles portrayed in this episode." This confrontation with public television got enough media attention to gain the commendation of the faithful ("Education Chief Rips PBS for Gay Character"), but within such an insular milieu over such a trivial episode that it did not galvanize the cultural left.

In another arena, Bush not only signed the partial birth abortion ban but also the Unborn Victims of Violence Act of 2004, the 2001 ban on the use of federal dollars for research using new embryonic stem cell lines, and a 2004 bill that included a broad new federal "refusal clause" permitting any "health care entity" to refuse to perform, pay for, provide coverage of, or refer a patient for an abortion, regardless of federal, state, or local laws to the contrary. The strategy of chipping away at abortion rights appeals to evangelicals and to many traditional-values Catholics and others among religiously observant conservatives, intensifying their commitment to the GOP. This strategy thus serves the purposes of polarization without activating the kind of implacable opposition necessary to stop the conservative offensive. The 2005 John Roberts and Samuel Alito nominations to the Supreme Court can be seen in this light, drawing support from the right (both men are Roman Catholics) with neither man providing sufficient traction to the left to mobilize an effective counterforce.

The whittling away at abortion rights—new conditions and restrictions such as parental and spousal notification or consent, waiting periods, the banning of "partial birth" (third trimester) abortion, and "unborn victims" rights legislation, for example—infuriates the liberal opposition but does not, as a practical matter, rally dangerous levels of political opposition among the general public. Such opposition would be much more likely if the piecemeal approach were abandoned and if *Roe* were flatly overturned (unless nonsurgical abortion becomes widely available).

RELIGIOUS CONSERVATIVES: FAITH-BASED PATRONAGE

Religious activists within the right coalition have for years argued for a concerted effort to "defund the left" by eliminating federal grants to liberal organizations such as Planned Parenthood or the Urban League. During the Bush administration, this strategy has taken a step forward via a drive to use tax dollars to "fund the right."

With just one grant-making program—federal aid to abstinence education—the Bush administration has been able to channel well over 50 million federal dollars to organizations such as the following:

- Carenet Pregnancy Services of DuPage, Illinois, "an evangelistic organization that exists to help women experiencing unplanned or unwanted pregnancies choose life for their unborn babies," $295,442;

- The Door of Hope Pregnancy Care Center in Madisonville, Kentucky, "committed to the belief in the sanctity of human life, primarily as it relates to the protection of the unborn," $317,067;

- Pregnancy Support Center in Eugene, Oregon, endorsed by Oregon Right to Life, $368,560; and

- Bethany Crisis Pregnancy Services in Colorado Springs, Colorado, which warns women considering abortion that "your pregnancy ends with death. You may feel guilt and shame about your choice. You will remember taking a life," $631,873.

The Bush administration has used low-visibility appointments throughout the federal bureaucracy not only to reward supporters in the religious right but also to affirm the legitimacy of the views of Christian conservatives in the day-to-day process of federal decision making. These appointments include anti-abortion physician W. David Hager, the author of *As Jesus Cared for Women: Restoring Women Then and Now,* to chair the Food and Drug Administration's Reproductive Health Drugs Advisory Committee; Dr. Alma Golden, a leading advocate of abstinence as the only acceptable means of birth control, as deputy assistant health and human services secretary for population affairs; and Dr. Tom Coburn, an outspoken critic of condoms to prevent the spread of AIDS, as co-chair of the Presidential Advisory Council on HIV and AIDS until he won election to the Senate from Oklahoma in 2004.

The effectiveness of faith-based patronage has been demonstrated in a variety of ways. After Bush ordered creation of "Centers for Faith-Based and Community Initiatives" in ten federal departments including Education, Health and Human Services, Justice, and Housing and Urban Development on January 29, 2001, his proposal ran into unexpected opposition—from televangelist Pat Robertson, head of the Christian Broadcasting Network (CBN). On February 20, 2001, Robertson warned CBN viewers that "this thing could be a real Pandora's box. And what seems to be such a great initiative can rise up to bite the organizations as well as the federal government," channeling money to such groups as the Unification Church, the Hare Krishnas, and the Church of Scientology. Robertson's criticism was quickly silenced; on October 3, 2002, the Bush administration awarded a three-year, $1.5 million faith-based grant to Robertson's Operation Blessing International.

During the 2002 House and Senate elections, the administration dispatched officials to meet with black community and religious leaders in the districts and states where Republicans faced tough contests. In South Carolina, for example, where the late Senator Strom Thurmond's seat was open, the state Republican Party hosted a "seminar on Faith-Based and Community Initiatives" at which Jeremy White, White House director of outreach for the faith-based initiative, spoke. Ron Thomas, the South Carolina Republican political director, reported that about three hundred black ministers who were eager to learn how to obtain federal grants attended. Thomas called the event a "phenomenal success" that helped "put a human face on the party again."

Federal largess is not limited to domestic programs. On September 27, 2004, then-Secretary of State Colin Powell announced that the conservative Independent Women's Forum (IWF) was one of seven organizations sharing a $10 million grant "to train Iraqi women in the skills and practices of democratic public life." The IWF is a group that seeks to provoke and otherwise aggravate mainline feminists. Their promotional literature reads: "Are you sick of being told that you are a 'victim' of the men in your life? Are you bored with the media message that strong, competent women must be feminists?"

Similarly, in September 2005, the State Department awarded to Beverly LaHaye's Concerned Women for America (CWA)—a particular thorn in the side of traditional liberal women's groups ("CWA seeks to protect traditional values that support the Biblical design of the family")—a grant for $200,000 to train pro-life organizations in Mexico in methods of fighting prostitution and other forms of sex trafficking.

In addition to funding the social and Christian right, the administration has redirected some of the federal government's legal and regulatory powers to work on behalf of religious conservatives. The Civil Rights Division of the Department of Justice has, for example, shifted its emphasis away from defending the rights of racial and ethnic minorities and of working women. Republicans in charge of this division have instead created a new Religious Rights Unit and appointed Eric Treene, former litigation director for the Becket Fund for Religious Liberty, as special counsel for religious discrimination.

In a key case, the Civil Rights Division intervened to defend the right of the Salvation Army in New York to discriminate in its hiring practices. Former and current employees had sued the Salvation Army, contending that it violated nondiscrimination laws by calling on employees to embrace a new mission "to preach the gospel of Jesus Christ and to meet human needs in his name without discrimination." The Justice Department filed a brief in the case contending that the plaintiffs would violate "the federal statutory and constitutional rights of religious employers to define their character and maintain their religious integrity." On October 4, 2005, federal judge Sidney Stein ruled in favor of the Salvation Army, declaring that it would be "untenable for the Constitution to require a religion to water down its beliefs simply because it accepts government money." Jim Towey, head of the White House Office of Faith-Based and Community Initiatives, hailed the decision: "This is going to send a resounding signal out there in America because here you have an organization, the Salvation Army, that got 95 percent of its money from government to do its social service work. And the court held that they were allowed to hire on a religious basis, even though nearly the entire entity was funded by government."

This collection of actions and maneuvers by the Bush White House was designed to foster polarization, to mobilize the conservative base of the Republican Party, to motivate and repay its core voters, and to provoke the opposition—not to build bridges to the middle.

GAY RIGHTS: "OUR D-DAY, OR GETTYSBURG OR STALINGRAD"

America and the world are crying for courageous leadership. When President Bush stands in the face of Saddam Hussein, when he stands in the face of Osama bin Laden, when he stands in the face of the war on terrorism, when he stands in the face of the homosexual activist agenda and says "it's not right," let me tell you, people are drawn to that.

Ronnie Floyd, pastor
The Church at Pinnacle Hills
Rogers, Arkansas
and First Baptist Church
Springdale, Arkansas
November 5, 2004

More than any other Republican constituency, leaders and members of the Christian right have made a concerted effort to live within a universe as removed as possible from the liberal precincts in which Democrats thrive. White Pentecostal, fundamentalist, charismatic, and evangelical voters make up a third of the Republican electorate. More than any other GOP voting block, these Christians seek to separate themselves and their adherents from mainstream sources of information such as national newspapers, major universities and colleges, popular magazines, traditional television programming, and most of the entertainment industry. In many respects, the Christian right has created its own alternative world, with separate schools and universities, television networks, sources of news, entertainment, books, and other institutions and services.

From the perspective of these evangelical and fundamentalist Christians, "blue" or liberal media, educational, and other institutions are perceived in Manichean terms as instruments of a decadent culture, teaching godlessness, moral relativism, abortion, homosexuality, pornography, gambling, condom-based (rather than abstinence-oriented) sex education, divorce, father absence, debt, illegitimacy, and disrespect for the flag. These groups are also perceived as promoting a "feminism that encourages women to be as sexually active as their male counterparts" and "feminist egalitarianism with accompanying distortions or neglect of the glad harmony portrayed in Scripture between the loving, humble leadership of redeemed husbands and the intelligent, willing support of that leadership by redeemed wives." In recent years, these issues, interlocking with matters such as gay marriage and "the homosexual lifestyle," have become the top priority of social conservatives. They have recruited to the Republican cause mainstream voters who feel culturally besieged by what they view as a coarsening of the popular culture on a continuum from video games to visible tattoos, body piercing, rap music, and "transgressive" television—"daytime talk, the lowest form of Trash TV, ... the democratization of perversion," as well as shows such as *Desperate Housewives*, *Weeds*, *Six Feet Under*, *Queer As Folk*, *Queer Eye for the Straight Guy*, and so on.

The contrasting world outlook of evangelical Christians, conservative Catholics, and other religious traditionalists, on the one hand, and of secular Democrats, on the other, reflects polarized extremes. According to survey data gathered by Democratic pollster Mark Penn, a high percentage of both upper-income and low-income voters within the center-left coalition dismiss the idea that homosexuality is a sin, acknowledge looking at pornography, make no adverse judgments about a married person having an affair, regard sex before marriage as morally acceptable, and view religion as not a very important part of daily life. Compare these Democratic attitudes with those of Dr. Richard Land of the Southern Baptist

Convention, America's largest non-Catholic denomination with more than 16.3 million members and a key Republican constituency. Land, a Princeton graduate, sees liberalized sexual behavior as undermining the nation's essential strengths, and he opposes premarital sex—"abstinence before marriage is God's intended plan for healthy families"—as well as pornography. "[W]hen we're exposed to pornography," says Land, "our belief system begins to change. It takes as little as six, one-hour exposures to soft-core pornography to change your belief systems."

Land is one of the GOP's most outspoken opponents of "the radical homosexual agenda," referring to homosexual relations as "a deviance from God's norm":

> [T]he gay thought police have revealed themselves for what they really are—bullies who threaten and intimidate those who dare to speak out against them. We must ask who the real bigots are here. . . . As Christians, we will continue to support politicians who speak out against homosexuality and to oppose those who support special rights for homosexuals and those who seek to support societal approval of homosexual behavior.

The centrality Land ascribes to homosexuality in the cascading moral crisis that he believes is destroying America is striking—from pornography, to moral relativism, to the blurring of all distinction between human and animal life:

> Moral relativism eventually eviscerates moral character. When schools train students to "clarify" their own values, tell them they have the right to question parental or societal values, and that each person's values are as valid as any other person's values, then you have made all morals relative and each person becomes the final arbiter of what is "right" or "wrong" for them. When such thinking permeates society, . . . nothing is always right or wrong but entirely dependent upon the situation, circumstance, or personal opinion. . . . In such a society, . . . anything is possible. . . . For more than a decade now [a colleague] has been asking young people in various forums this question: "If your pet dog and a stranger were both drowning and you could only save one, which would you choose?" Consistently, one-third answer their dog, one-third answer the stranger, and one-third say it's too hard a question and they can't answer it.

To some extent, Land is waging an uphill battle. In a 1998 paper on American sexual behavior, Tom W. Smith, the director of the General Social Survey of the National Opinion Research Center (NORC) at the University of Chicago, found that 90 percent of the men born in the 1940s had sex before marriage, as had 63 percent of the women; of the women born since 1952, only 20 percent reported having been virgins when they married. Many men and women cherish the rights that fall under the post-1960s rubric of autonomy and personal freedom, strongly valuing their sexual independence and reproductive autonomy.

On the other hand, with homosexuals making up in the vicinity of 2 to 4 percent of the American population, by most reliable estimates, homosexuality is a more effective mobilizing tool for the conservative social movement than a major threat to the American family. Targeting homosexuality harvests much greater popular support than any proposed attempt to outlaw or reduce the incidence of divorce—which, in terms of its impact on "traditional families," is far more significant. The divorce rate in the Bible Belt, for example, is substantially higher than it is in the rest of the country. The Associated Press reported on November 11, 1999, that "no region of the United States has a higher divorce rate than the Bible Belt. Tennessee, Arkansas, Alabama and Oklahoma round out the Top Five in frequency of divorce. In a country where nearly half of all marriages break up, the divorce rates in these conservative states are roughly 50 percent above the national average."

Along the same lines, conservative Christian leaders focus on homosexuality rather than out-of-wedlock childbearing, even though the number of their parishioners who are unwed mothers is vastly greater than the number of gay congregants. The percentage of children born in 2000 to white unmarried mothers in states where evangelical and fundamentalist denominations are preponderant gives a sense of how much more difficult this issue might be as a political mobilization device than "the gay lifestyle." The percent of live births to unmarried white women in 2000 was as follows:

- Oklahoma City, Oklahoma, 29.1

- Albany, Georgia, 23

- Alexandria, Louisiana, 26

- Biloxi, Mississippi, 29.6

- Charleston, South Carolina, 21

- Chattanooga, Tennessee, 29.5

- Dallas, Texas, 24.3

- Colorado Springs, Colorado (home of Focus on the Family), 23.5

- Fayetteville, Arkansas, 26.4

- Fort Smith, Akansas, 30.2

- Lafayette, Mississippi, 28.5

- Lake Charles, Louisiana, 27.8

- Lakeland-Winter-Haven, Florida, 37.3

- Little Rock, Arkansas, 20

- Louisville, Kentucky, 28.8

In effect, the conservative crusade against homosexuals is a means of uniting the Christian evangelical troops and protesting the deregulation of sexual norms in general, without requiring much moral effort from the right-of-center heterosexual Christian electorate.

James Dobson, founder of Focus on the Family—a premier evangelical organization whose annual donations now reach into the nine figures—is one of the many influential conservative leaders to express his anxiety about the disintegrating American family. Dobson speaks primarily in terms of the battle against homosexuality—despite the fact that most families in his orbit, while deeply affected by the sexual revolution, have little or no involvement in the "gay lifestyle." In September 2003, Dobson issued a letter to his followers regarding the pressing need to pass the Federal Marriage Amendment (FMA), the constitutional amendment to outlaw same-sex marriage, a key recruiting tool for both the Christian right and for the Republican Party. The degree to which Dobson has invested his cause in this issue is demonstrated by the length and detail of his argument:

> It is with great concern that I share with you our considered belief that the institution of marriage is about to descend into a state of turmoil unlike any other in human history. The homosexual activist movement, which has achieved virtually every goal and objective it set out to accomplish more than 50 years ago, is poised to administer a devastating and potentially fatal blow to the traditional family. . . . The late 1960s and early 1970s, no-fault divorce laws, radical feminism and a sweeping sexual revolution combined here in the United States to rip open the fabric of the family. They left it shaken and wounded. . . . On June 26, 2003, the U.S. Supreme Court struck down the Texas law prohibiting sodomy in the *Lawrence v. Texas* decision. Writing for the majority, Justice Anthony Kennedy cavalierly stated that the law's ". . . continuance as precedent demeans the lives of homosexual persons." By ruling that sodomy is a constitutionally protected "right," the Court decided that considerations of morality and decency were irrelevant. . . . On July 28, the New York Board of Education announced the creation of a gay-oriented high school. . . . On August 5, the United Episcopal Church ordained its first gay bishop. . . . During the first week of August, the California State Legislature passed Assembly Bill 196 with the intent to "protect" transgendered people from employment and housing discrimination. Simply put, this bill would force Christian bookstores, and perhaps even the Boy Scouts, to hire or keep male employees who dress like women, or women who dress like men. The fine for violating this law is $150,000! The inmates are now fully in charge of the asylum. . . . It seems as if every episode of every sitcom on television now includes a gay character portrayed in a positive light. . . . It's gay, gay, gay, wherever you look. . . . To summarize, the legalization of homosexual marriage is for gay activists merely a stepping-stone on the road to eliminating all societal restrictions on marriage and sexuality. Perhaps it is evident now why I began this letter by predicting that unless we act quickly, the family as it has been known for 5,000 years will be gone. . . . The destruction of the traditional family will condemn millions of [children] to temporary relationships, involving multiple "moms" or "dads," six or eight "grandparents" and perhaps a dozen or more half-siblings who will come and go as those who care for them meander from one sexual

relationship to another. . . . Studies show that homosexual men, in particular, have a difficult time honoring even the most basic commitments of "marriage." A recent study conducted in the Netherlands—a "progressive" nation in which gay marriage has been legal for several years—found that the average homosexual relationship lasts only 1.5 years, and that gay men have an average of eight sexual partners per year outside of their "primary" relationship! Does that sound like a stable child-rearing environment to you? . . . This effort to save the family is our D-Day, or Gettysburg or Stalingrad. This is the big one.

CATHOLIC CONSERVATIVES

The leadership of the Catholic Church shares the Bush administration's opposition to abortion and to gay marriage but has generally voiced more tolerance for individual diversity than have evangelical leaders. Many conservative Catholics and other cultural traditionalists find themselves far less comfortable with "D-Day" rhetoric than Christian evangelicals do—even as their moral convictions put them squarely within the larger Republican camp.

Pope Benedict XVI, previously Joseph Cardinal Ratzinger, took what was widely considered to be a hard line in his 1986 Letter to the Bishops, declaring:

> [A]n overly benign interpretation was given to the homosexual condition itself, some going so far as to call it neutral, or even good. Although the particular inclination of the homosexual person is not a sin, it is a more or less strong tendency ordered toward an intrinsic moral evil; and thus the inclination itself must be seen as an objective disorder. Therefore special concern and pastoral attention should be directed toward those who have this condition, lest they be led to believe that the living out of this orientation in homosexual activity is a morally acceptable option. It is not.

In 1997, that view was echoed in a Vatican statement issued by Cardinal Dionigi Teltamanzi, archbishop of Genoa, in "Christian Anthropology and Homosexuality," which appeared in the March 12, 1997, issue of *L'Osservatore Romano*:

[A]dultery, for example, is no less sinful than homosexual relations. . . . Christians who are homosexual are called, as all of us
are, to a chaste life. . . . As everyone knows, this debate [over
homosexuality] is taking place in the context of highly politi-
cized demands that homosexual persons have completely equal
rights, including the right to marriage, adoption and political
asylum. More broadly, it is taking place in the context of the
so-called "gay" culture, which adopts a homosexual "life-style"
and is committed to getting this life-style accepted by society
(and civil law) as fully legitimate. In this cultural situation the
Church must exercise the greatest vigilance and take a coura-
geously prophetic stance (cf. Is 5:20): she is called, together
with every person of goodwill, to denounce the very grave personal and social risks connected with accepting such a culture.

These institutional views within the Catholic Church provided
the Bush campaigns of 2000 and 2004 with a direct avenue of access, without going to the lengths that the more fundamentalist
Protestant denominations sought. The Bush campaign—as opposed to the Christian right—took a more moderate tone on such
themes as gay marriage and abortion, using a subtler approach to
tap the anger points of mainstream voters and focusing on the
"softer" dimensions of these issues, such as the sanctity of marriage
and the "culture of life." This tactic paid off decisively among traditional Catholics.

In 2000 Bush substantially improved on Bob Dole's 1996 margin among Catholics while still losing among these traditionally
Democratic voters by a modest three percentage points, 47 percent
to 50 percent. In 2004 against Kerry (a Catholic), Bush carried 52
percent of the Catholic vote, according to exit poll data. Not only
did Bush's margin among Catholics improve strikingly from 2000 to
2004, but Catholic turnout grew by 11 percent.

Before the 2000 election, Bush had already begun developing a
"Catholic strategy," meeting in Austin with such conservatives as
pollster Steve Wagner, *Crisis* magazine publisher Deal Hudson, and
Princeton University political scientist Robert George. The theme
of "compassionate conservatism" was designed in part to appeal to
Catholics, who are stronger supporters of government intervention
on behalf of the poor than are evangelical Protestants.

Immediately after the 2000 election, Bush began to meet
regularly with Catholic bishops and adopted Catholic themes and

rhetoric in speeches. Under Rove's direction, his staff instituted a weekly conference call with an informal group of Catholic advisers. The Republican National Committee, in turn, set up a Catholic Task Force. In a March 22, 2001, speech honoring Pope John Paul II, to an audience that included Detroit Archbishop Adam Cardinal Maida and Cardinal Theodore McCarrick, Bush adopted the language of Catholic leaders:

> The culture of life is a welcoming culture, never excluding, never dividing, never despairing, and always affirming the goodness of life in all its seasons. In the culture of life we must make room for the stranger. We must comfort the sick. We must care for the aged. We must welcome the immigrant. We must teach our children to be gentle with one another. We must defend in love the innocent child waiting to be born.

Princeton's Robert George pointed out shortly after the speech that "in 1960, John Kennedy went from Washington down to Texas to assure Protestant preachers that he would not obey the pope. In 2001, George Bush came from Texas up to Washington to assure a group of Catholic bishops that he would."

In the months before the 2004 election, lawyers from religious advocacy organizations held briefings for conservative Catholic and Protestant clergy to outline exactly how far tax laws permitted them to go in taking moral stands on issues such as abortion and same-sex marriage and then linking those stands to specific political candidates or parties, implicitly suggesting that churchgoers vote for Bush. Although the media focused far more on evangelicals, many prominent Catholics aggressively pressed the moral case against Kerry. Archbishop Raymond Burke of St. Louis, backed by a number of others in the Catholic clergy, declared that Kerry should not be allowed to receive communion because of his position in favor of abortion and stem cell research. Bishop Michael J. Sheridan of Colorado Springs and Archbishop John J. Myers of Newark joined Burke in publicly asserting that, in the 2004 election, the obligation of Catholics to oppose abortion outweighed any other issue.

Archbishop Charles J. Chaput in Colorado told Catholics that a vote for Kerry was a sin. "If you vote this way, are you cooperating in evil?" he asked, rhetorically. "And if you know you are cooperating in evil, should you go to confession? The answer is yes." At another point, Chaput told a group of students, "The church says abortion is a foundational issue."

On April 8, 2005, on the occasion of the death of John Paul II, Bush became the first U.S. president to attend a funeral for a pope.

CHRISTIAN EVANGELICALS: A SEPARATE BEACHHEAD

In the view of evangelical Christian conservatives, the answer to the threat to their faith and families has been to set up a separate beach-head: a system of colleges and universities, home schooling, pub-lishing houses, televangelical and Christian radio broadcasts, church-based academies from K-3 to grade 12, news services, direct mail and email networks, political organizations, book stores, music, and popular literature. All these organizations are based on cultural products and curricula generated by the Christian right. Among the Christian television and radio networks in 2006 are TBN, Daystar, AFA Radio Network, Sky Angel Nationwide Satel-lite Television System, Trinity Broadcast Network, America Family Radio, Salem Radio, and Bott Radio Network.

According to the religious opinion research firm The Barna Group, nearly half of all adults—46 percent—listen to a Christian radio broadcast in a typical month, with that figure rising to 56 percent in the South, and 45 percent of adults watch a Christian television program during a typical month. While many African Americans belong to fundamentalist and evangelical denomina-tions—and may tune in to a range of Christian broadcasts—the "parallel universe" of the Republican Christian right is overwhelm-ingly white.

At the same time that parishes of the older, traditional religious denominations are frequently rusting and underfunded (the Catholic Church in America is in the grip of a financial crisis, with the propor-tion of non-Hispanic whites among church members falling—cur-rent membership is now one-third Latino), evangelical Christians have built huge and thriving mega-churches just off suburban high-ways in communities across the country—40 percent of them in the South and 32 percent in the West. Some of these enterprises are staggering in their size: Joel Osteen's Lakewood Church in Houston has 30,000 congregants and brought in $55 million in contributions in 2004. Rick Warren, a self-described fifth-generation Southern Baptist, is the pastor of the largest church in America, Saddleback Church in Orange County, California, with 80,000 names on its rolls.

These institutions have become seven-day-a-week service providers, using a business model and "corporate-style growth strategies, ... giving them a tremendous advantage in the battle for religious market share." They arrange for day care, singles groups, political debates, game nights, bridge clubs, affinity gatherings for everyone from motorcycle enthusiasts to weight-watchers, book groups, softball teams, AA sessions, church cafes, gathering places for teenagers, free financial advice, low-cost bulk food, music studios, divorce counseling, help for parents of autistic children, meals for the elderly, a "cars ministry" that repairs donated vehicles, and even a "fidelity group" for men with "sexual addictions." Some mega-church complexes have banks, pharmacies, and schools; others offer test preparation assistance, help in filling out tax forms, and assistance in buying houses.

According to *Business Week*, Rick Warren's 2002 book, *The Purpose-Driven Life*, has become the fastest-selling nonfiction book of all time, with more than 23 million copies sold, in part through a novel "pyro marketing" strategy. Tim LaHaye's *Left Behind* series of "end time" novels about those abandoned on Earth after Christ's second coming have sold more than 60 million copies since 1995.

The list of activities and services of Christian mega-churches is extensive, but from a political point of view, the signal development has been the creation of a profoundly influential community institution that meets a host of needs, personal and spiritual, that for millions of people are not available elsewhere. "'Mainline' is sideline now. They're not mainline anymore, they're sideline denominations. The mainline is evangelicalism," Rick Warren argues, with considerable justification.

Leaders and parishioners in the evangelical movement reflect and reinforce a common view of the world, a conviction that people must accept Jesus Christ as Lord and Savior to enter the gates of heaven, a deep aversion to the social and cultural left, and—by now—an ingrained loyalty to the Republican Party. While Osteen and Warren tailor their messages to capture vast numbers of the "unsaved" and do not bear down on issues of sin or wrongdoing, they preach a "prosperity gospel" congenial to free-enterprise Republican doctrine. Osteen's wife and co-pastor, Victoria, exhorts parishioners to donate generously to Lakewood in expectation of a return on their investment: "Let Him breathe the breath of life into your finances and He'll give it back to you bigger than you could ever give it to him."

Many of the fundamentalist denominations of the religious right combine a market-oriented approach with a values-laden message, preaching not only that giving increases the odds of being given to, but also that doing battle with liberal America in a drive to establish—to restore, in their view—a national consensus will support traditional values, the pre-feminist family, and pre-pill/pre-*Roe* sexual norms. This "virtuous" circle is demonstrated by one of the leading lights of the evangelical Christian movement, the Reverend Ronnie Floyd. On July 4, 2004, as video images of President Bush and John F. Kerry alternated on a screen behind him, Floyd delivered a sermon to his parishioners at the First Baptist Church in Arkansas:

> I believe this will be one of the most critical elections in U.S. history. Rarely have we seen two candidates so diametrically opposed in their convictions. One candidate believes that the United States is at war with terrorism. The other believes we're not at war at all, but in a lawsuit.
>
> One candidate believes in the sanctity of an unborn life, signing legislation banning partial birth abortion and declaring that human life is a sacred gift from our Creator. The other believes in abortion on demand, voting six times in the United States Senate against the ban and insisting there is no such thing as a partial birth.
>
> One candidate believes that marriage is a God-ordained institution between one man and one woman and has proposed a constitutional amendment protecting marriage. The other was one of only 14 U.S. senators to vote against the Defense of Marriage Act of 1996. One candidate publicly and unashamedly confesses faith in Christ and acknowledges that, "My faith helps me in the service to people."

THE STRONGEST, AND MOST SELF-SUFFICIENT, POPULATION WITHIN THE CONTEMPORARY REPUBLICAN COALITION

Floyd's weekly "message of hope, obedience to Christ and love" is, as of this writing, televised on WGN Superstation, FamilyNet Television, Sky Angel, Daystar, and the Church Channel on Direct TV. He is regularly interviewed on networks and programs geared to red America: *FOX News*, *WorldNetDaily*, *Janet Parshall's America*, *Washington Watch*, and American Family Radio. He has written ten books, all available in Christian bookstores—but virtually impossible to find in Harvard Square, Berkeley, or on the upper west side of Manhattan—including *The Gay Agenda*, *God's Gateway to Supernatural Power: A Resource, Testimony, and Practical Guide on Prayer and Fasting*, and *The Meaning of a Man*.

Floyd and the lives of those in his congregation are shaped by a large and growing network of church-based institutions that exercise influence in realms far beyond the church. Enrollment in the 105 member schools of the Council for Christian Colleges and Universities, whose mission is "to advance the cause of Christ-centered higher education and to help our institutions transform lives by faithfully relating scholarship and service to biblical truth," grew 70.6 percent from 1990 to 2004, from 134,592 to 229,649 students, five and a half times the rate for public campuses and two and a half times the rate of most private schools. The number of children being home schooled is growing rapidly, from an estimated 850,000 in 1999 to 2 million today, according to advocacy organizations. Such educational bodies, home-schoolers, and home-schooling networks are overwhelmingly white.

The Christian right is, in many respects, the strongest and most self-sufficient population within the contemporary Republican coalition. More than any other Republican constituency, religious conservatives are sustaining themselves within their own institutional structures. One of the most powerful examples of such institution-building and its integration into the Republican political structure is Patrick Henry College in Purcellville, Virginia, about fifty-five miles northwest of the nation's capital. A college primarily for the home-schooled, the vision of Patrick Henry College is "to aid in the transformation of American society by training Christian students to serve God and mankind with a passion for righteousness, justice and mercy, through careers of public service and cultural influence." Most students major in government with a strong emphasis during their last two years at the college on securing internships in the Washington political cosmos—in the White House, Congress, federal agencies, and conservative think-tanks—a teaching method the college calls "practical apprenticeship methodology."

An instructive example of the interface between Republican politics and the Christian evangelical community can be found in the life mission of Michael J. Farris, the founder of Patrick Henry. Farris embodies some of the principal strengths of the religious right as it seeks to drive a Republican realignment: the capacity for sustained devotion to a cause and the purposeful linking of that cause to political engagement. Farris founded the Home School Legal Defense Association in 1983, building it into a powerful force working on behalf of the home school movement and going on to found Patrick Henry College in 2000. More recently, Farris initiated a project called Generation Joshua to increase political activism among teenage home-schoolers in congressional districts across the country. This is all part of a vision that extends well into the future: "We will know that our home-schooling has been successful when we see real-life victories from our children. We believe that some day home-schooled young people will help reverse *Roe v. Wade*, stop same-sex marriage, and help reestablish a strong view of the freedoms established by our Founding Fathers."

USING RACE TO SPLIT THE ELECTORATE

From a strategic vantage point, religious conservatives do not need to be persuaded; they need only be motivated to turn out to vote in high numbers. The tactics of polarization are ideal for increasing turnout—often via targeted efforts to inflame conservative anger points—whereas strategies of consensus and moderation function only to diminish the number of conservative ballots cast on election day.

The 2004 election was the first in which the Republican Party put as many or more resources into a base-building strategy as into the persuasion of swing voters. This investment in turning out the base was rooted in recognition of the voting behavior of a polarized electorate. Since the late 1960s, conservative politicians have noted the growing divisions within the post–New Deal public and the advantages that might emerge from capitalizing on such divisions. Polarization became the accepted strategy among Republicans during President Nixon's first term in office. Nixon barely beat Hubert Humphrey in 1968, 31,783,783 to 31,271,839. In the future, Nixon and his backers recognized, the winner would be determined by the 9,901,118 votes cast in that election for independent candidate George C. Wallace, the segregationist Alabama governor.

The Nixon administration set out to convert the Wallace voters to the GOP. Indeed, direct-mail expert Richard Viguerie writes that he "came to an agreement with Wallace, and the hundreds of thousands of names of Wallace contributors he [Viguerie] amassed were later used to help conservative Republicans take over the South." In 1969, then-Vice President Spiro T. Agnew, with the full backing of the Nixon White House, declared, "I say it is time for a positive polarization. It is time to rip away the rhetoric and to divide on authentic lines." In 1971, Patrick Buchanan, then an aide to President Nixon, wrote a memo to urge the use of racial issues to split the electorate: "[T]his is a potential throw of the dice that could bring the media on our heads, and cut the Democratic Party and country in half; my view is that we would have far the larger half." Thirty years later, David Horowitz, a favorite of both Karl Rove and Tom DeLay, wrote:

> Politics is war conducted by other means. . . . In political warfare, you do not fight just to prevail in an argument, but to destroy the enemy's fighting ability. . . . In war, there are two sides: friends and enemies. Your task is to define yourself as the friend of as large a constituency as possible compatible with your principles, while defining your opponent as the enemy whenever you can.

THE LIBERAL MEDIA AS A WEDGE ISSUE

Early on in the drive to remake America, conservatives recognized that one of their key adversaries would be the media: the major mainstream newspapers—including the *New York Times*, the *Washington Post*, the news pages of the *Wall Street Journal*, the *Los Angeles Times*, and the *Boston Globe*—the weekly newsmagazines, and the big three network news shows. The threat posed by the media has been long understood by the leadership of the Republican Party.

On November, 13, 1969, Vice President Agnew fired what many on the right view as the first real salvo in what has become a sustained, and highly successful, drive to constrain the establishment media and to discredit its legitimacy. In a speech entitled "On the National Media," Agnew declared that a week earlier President Nixon had

> delivered the most important address of his Administration.... For thirty-two minutes, he reasoned with a nation that has suffered almost a third of a million casualties in the longest war in its history. When the President completed his address—an address that he spent weeks in preparing—his words and policies were subjected to instant analysis and querulous criticism. The audience of seventy-million Americans—gathered to hear the President of the United States—was inherited by a small band of network commentators and self-appointed analysts, the majority of whom expressed, in one way or another, their hostility to what he had to say."

Agnew then began his attack:

> The purpose of my remarks tonight is to focus your attention on this little group of men who not only enjoy a right of instant rebuttal to every Presidential address, but more importantly, wield a free hand in selecting, presenting, and interpreting the great issues of our nation. . . . A raised eyebrow, an inflection of the voice, a caustic remark dropped in the middle of a broadcast can raise doubts in a million minds about the veracity of a public official, or the wisdom of a government policy. One Federal Communications Commissioner considers the power of the networks to equal that of local, state, and federal governments combined. Certainly, it represents a concentration of power

over American public opinion unknown in history. What do Americans know of the men who wield this power? ... We do know that, to a man, these commentators and producers live and work in the geographical and intellectual confines of Washington, D.C. or New York City. ... The American people would rightly not tolerate this kind of concentration of power in government. Is it not fair and relevant to question its concentration in the hands of a tiny and closed fraternity of privileged men, elected by no one, and enjoying a monopoly sanctioned and licensed by government? The views of this fraternity do not represent the views of America.

Showering disparagement on the press—"nattering nabobs of negativism" and "an effete corps of impudent snobs"—Agnew's subsequent forced resignation from the vice presidency (he pled no contest to charges of tax fraud) masked for many the fact that he had tapped into a political goldmine. Watergate was a show of strength by the media, a demonstration that two reporters, Bob Woodward and Carl Bernstein, working for one paper, the *Washington Post*, could bring down a sitting Republican president, one who had just been re-elected by a landslide margin. The short-term lesson of Watergate appeared to be that a politician who takes on the "liberal" press does so at his own peril.

The national media, however, was vulnerable to attack. The liberalism of the media is not only or even primarily the liberalism of Roosevelt's New Deal—economically redistributive and pro-union. Instead, it is the newer social liberalism, firmly supportive of racial equality, of the women's and other liberation movements, of sexual autonomy, of abortion, and of reproductive and sexual privacy rights. The media's liberalism is that of a well-educated, professionally oriented elite, which makes the press susceptible to the same attacks that conservative populists have used against the Democratic Party. Combatants capitalize on fears of family breakdown, amorality, racial change, immigration, foreign enemies, "the homosexual agenda," an urban and inner-suburban "underclass," and the coarsening of the popular culture.

By the end of the 1970s, Republicans and conservatives fully recognized that they had in hand a powerful weapon—accusations of ideological and partisan bias—to weaken the influence and authority of the mainstream media. As attacks began to mount, conservatives found that their adversaries in the media were not quick to recognize their own ideological and partisan convictions and, thus, their own vulnerability to attack.

The liberal tilt of the traditional media has been documented repeatedly—particularly by ideologically conservative interests eager to capitalize on such findings. The first substantial effort was a survey of 240 journalists at the *New York Times*, the *Washington Post, Wall Street Journal, Time, Newsweek, U.S. News & World Report*, ABC, CBS, NBC, and PBS, published in 1981 by S. Robert Lichter, then at George Washington University, and Stanley Rothman, then at Smith College. That survey, backed by conservative foundation money, found that 81 percent of the journalists polled voted for the Democratic presidential nominee in the eight elections from 1964 to 1976. More than half, 54 percent, described themselves as "left of center," 90 percent favored abortion, 80 percent supported "strong affirmative action for Blacks," and 54 percent did not regard adultery as wrong.

A 1996 Freedom Forum survey of 139 Washington bureau chiefs and congressional correspondents found that 89 percent of those questioned had voted for Bill Clinton, 7 percent for George H. W. Bush, and 2 percent for Ross Perot. In 1997, the American Society of Newspaper Editors released a survey of 1,037 newsroom reporters and editors at sixty-one papers from all over the country. It found that 61 percent of the respondents were either Democrats or leaned to the Democratic Party, compared with 15 percent who were Republican or leaned to the GOP.

In 1996 the *Minneapolis Star Tribune* reported on another study examining the political leanings of the media:

> David Weaver and Cleveland Wilhoit, Indiana University journalism professors who surveyed journalists from all over the country in 1982 and 1992, found that during the 1980s, when the general population was becoming more conservative and more Republican, journalists became even more likely to call themselves left-leaning Democrats. Likewise, when the various surveys have asked journalists about their lifestyles or their positions on various issues that typically separate liberals from conservatives, journalists consistently have a greater tendency than the public at large to take the liberal position. Journalists, for example, are more likely to support abortion rights,

more likely to support gay rights and less likely to say that religion plays an important role in their lives.

While liberals during the 1970s and 1980s enjoyed dominance
in television and mass-circulation print, conservatives became more
adept at leveraging the advantages of an adversarial relationship
with the mainstream media, turning the "liberal media" into a bona
fide wedge issue of its own. As Republican and conservative successes in capturing the White House gave the right experience and
access to resources, entrepreneurial conservatives began to build
their own right-wing media network. William Buckley's *National
Review, Human Events*, and the neoconservative journals *The Public
Interest* and *Commentary* already had assumed a significant role in
conservative policy and strategy debates. In 1982, the South Korean
Christian evangelical Sun Moon began to publish the *Washington
Times*, providing a daily conservative voice in the capital.

In 1987 the Federal Communications Commission abolished
the Fairness Doctrine, arguing that the interest of citizens in "the
listening and viewing public" would be "fully served by the multi-
plicity of voices in the marketplace today." The Fairness Doctrine
had in some ways provided a safe haven for liberals, requiring stations to give free air time for responses to controversial opinions. Its
abolition provided an opening for incendiary and polarizing conservative talk radio programming. Among the first to take advantage of
this development was a former disk jockey known as Rusty Sharp,
then as Jeff Christie, and ultimately as Rush Limbaugh.

Limbaugh—with an estimated 20 million listeners a week—
has since been joined by a flood of right-wing radio hosts, among
them Sean Hannity, G. Gordon Liddy, Laura Ingraham, Michael
Savage, Bill O'Reilly, Michael Reagan, Hugh Hewitt, Dennis
Prager, Michael Medved, and Dr. Laura Schlessinger. Limbaugh
notes that "being a DJ teaches you the elements of broadcasting
that are crucial no matter what kind of a show you are doing—tim-
ing, brevity, quickness, get in and get out."

In recent years, conservatives have called and raised liberal journalists, in terms of their centrality to the debate, with a raft of online media productions—Web sites, podcasts, email and newslet-
ters, and blogs—as well as best-selling books by, among others,
Bernard Goldberg (*Bias*), Ann Coulter (*Treason, Slander*), Bill Gertz

(*Betrayal, Breakdown*), Dan Flynn (*Why the Left Hates America*), Sean Hannity (*Let Freedom Ring, Deliver Us from Evil*), Bill O'Reilly (*Who's Looking Out for You, The No Spin Zone, The O'Reilly Factor*), and Rush Limbaugh (*The Way Things Ought to Be, See I Told You So*).

These secular conservatives join Christian inspirational authors such as Timothy LaHaye in commanding not only the best-seller book lists but a vast online conservative empire as well, with an unprecedented ability to create a networked "reach" into the lives of American voters: rushlimbaugh.com, billoreilly.com, anncoulter .com (with photo gallery), a plethora of Christian sites (Reverend Rod Parsley's http://www.breakthrough.net/, Dr. Richard Land's http://sites.silaspartners.com/forfaithandfamily, James Dobson's http://www.family.org/, etc.), and an array of conservative blogs (Glenn Reynolds' *Instapundit*, *Michelle Malkin*, Ben Domenech's *RedState*, and so forth). The top 150 conservative blogs had just under 10 million page visits a week as of July 2005.

➤ ◄

Liberal activists have attempted to respond to Republican polarizing techniques by setting up their own talk radio empire but have failed to garner the audience that the right has. The late Democratic direct-mail specialist Roger Craver, founder of Craver, Mathews, Smith & Company, analyzed liberal vulnerability in this realm and found that, again, it touches on Alex Gage's concept of anger points:

> Those right-wingers have a hell of a lot of fun, and we have these wine and cheese parties to listen to this insufferable bullshit on the part of the liberals. . . . I think every liberal commentator wants to explain how we can work our way out of whatever problem's being discussed, whereas the right-winger will just say, "Well, the way we can work our way out of this problem is to kill the bastards." . . . It's a difference . . . between black and white . . . and gray. The conservatives have always been much more willing to view things through the lens of what I call a "morality play." I mean, they have basically been able to say, "This is good. This is evil. There is no in-between." Whereas the liberals will say, "Well, I see this is good, and this is bad, but you really ought to look at the background of these

underprivileged children" or whatever. It's just a whole different mindset.

Richard Viguerie sees the vulnerability of the contemporary left in its overreliance for media outreach on National Public Radio (NPR), writing that "when you rely on federal subsidies rather than the marketplace for your support, federal subsidies become a crutch. Maybe even more of a straitjacket. Rush can say anything he wants, but the NPR folks have to maintain some semblance of objectivity." On the other hand, the liberal blogosphere has taken off—with, by some estimates, 17 million weekly page views as of June 2006 for the eighty-eight most-trafficked progressive blogs: The Daily Kos (Markos Moulitsas), Eschaton (Duncan Black), Joshua Micah Marshall's Talking Points Memo, My DD (Jerome Armstrong, Chris Bowers, Matt Stoller), Crooks and Liars, and so on.

➤ ◁

On the op-ed pages, columnists David Brooks, George Will, Charles Krauthammer, Bob Novak, Michael Barone, and a host of others now present a daily array of well-honed conservative opinion pieces. Reporters at all the major media outlets—print and broadcast—are under strict scrutiny not to betray liberal leanings. Michael Massing in the *New York Review of Books* writes:

> [N]ewspapers find themselves less popular than ever before, at a time when the newspaper industry itself is losing readers while struggling to cuts costs and meet demands for ever larger profits. Today's journalists, meanwhile, when compared to their predecessors, often seem far less willing to resist political pressure from the White House. In the 1970s, for example, *The Washington Post* refused to buckle under intense White House pressure during Watergate, and *The New York Times* did not shrink from publishing the Pentagon Papers. Recently, in contrast, the *Times* had to apologize for uncritically publishing false government claims about Iraqi weapons of mass destruction, and *Time* magazine released the notes of its journalist Matthew Cooper to a government prosecutor without his consent. Conservative commentators and the administration have also been able to intimidate publications into shunning investigative reporting, as when, for example, *Newsweek* promised to

crack down on its use of anonymous sources after being criticized for its story about the mishandling of the Koran by the US military, and when CBS forced the resignation of four news employees after questions were raised about the *60 Minutes* broadcast on Bush's record in the National Guard. With the President's poll numbers down and infighting among conservatives more visible, the coverage of Washington has sharpened of late, but overall the climate remains hostile to good reporting.

Most important in the demonization of the mainstream press (and of the new progressive media) is the ability of conservatives and Republicans to turn the media into a wedge issue. Most members of the establishment media are college or university educated, work in the cities of "blue America," and live in the contemporary culture of upscale social liberalism—giving some heft to Agnew's charges of a "tiny fraternity . . . living in geographical and intellectual confines of Washington, D.C. or New York City." Many (but by no means all) members of this branch of the media exist in a universe distant from the anxieties, angers, fears, and moral convictions of those who are culturally conservative. Relative to the broader public, a substantial proportion of national reporters, editors, and producers view "red America," especially its evangelical religiosity, as alien. In March 2005, *New Republic* writer Michelle Cottle noted on CNN's *Reliable Source* that mainstream journalists "do behave as though the people who believe these things are on the fringe."

➤ ≺

In the polarized battle for political control, the mainstream media has, in the eyes of observers within the craft, begun to self-censor its coverage to screen out any tilt to the left. The threat posed to the conservative cause by the mainstream media has in many ways been conquered. The tarring of the establishment media as liberal has discredited its legitimacy across large swaths of the country, as substantial numbers of citizens have been persuaded of the charges Agnew first leveled twenty-seven years ago—that the national media networks "do not represent the views of America." The use of the "liberal media" as a wedge issue has scored a double victory for the GOP.

4
The Republican Party Weds
Corporate America

For the four nights of the 2004 Republican convention, well-dressed men and women, generally in their thirties or forties, all identifiable by bright badges and baseball hats in color codes, were scattered across the floor of Madison Square Garden. Yellow hats were for whips, who made sure that all the delegates voted according to party leadership instructions and that no one raised extraneous or unscheduled issues. Red hats identified members of the "official proceedings" task force, who guaranteed that all speakers stayed on message and that nothing altered the precisely timed-to-the-minute schedule.

Ohio delegate Juan Jose Perez, a Hispanic from a battleground state, had been carefully chosen to formally put Bush's name into nomination on opening night. When the moment came for Perez to rise and be recognized, there were two men, neither one known to the general public, at his side. For the four-day New York event, these two men, Mark Isakowitz and Bruce A. Gates, were volunteers for the Republican National Committee. Their role at that moment was to make sure that Perez' nomination speech came off without a hitch.

For most of the year, Isakowitz and Gates work in Washington. Isakowitz is a partner in the lobbying firm Fierce, Isakowitz and Blalock. In 2004, the firm collected $6 million in publicly reported fees from thirty-eight clients, including MCI, Miller Brewing, Intel Corp., the Federation of American Hospitals, the Business Roundtable, the American Gaming Association, and the American Forest & Paper Association. Gates, a partner at the lobbying firm Washington Council Ernst & Young, had sixty-six clients in 2004, including Eli Lilly, Edison Electric Institute, AT&T, General Electric, and Merrill Lynch. Gates' firm collected $12.6 million in lobbying fees in 2004.

Isakowitz and Gates were only the tip of the iceberg. Lobbyists ran the entire Republican convention. The convention's CEO, Bill Harris, lobbied on behalf of Quest Software Inc. and the U.S. Chamber of Commerce Institute for Legal Reform, the organization leading the business community's fight for tort reform. David A. Norcross, whose defense industry clients have included Raytheon Corp. and Boeing Co., chaired the arrangements committee. Bryce L. "Larry" Harlow, who was in charge of official proceedings, represented the National Association of Manufacturers, the American Petroleum Institute, Northrop Grumman Corp., and VISA. Anne Phelps, executive director of the Republican Platform Committee, works with Gates at Washington Council Ernst & Young, where her clients include R. J. Reynolds, the Securities Industry Association, Verizon, and Ford Motor Co. When then-Republican National Committee Chairman Ed Gillespie, himself a lobbyist, announced Phelps' appointment, he made no reference to her work in the private sector: "We are fortunate to have such talented people join us as the 2004 Platform Committee works to craft a proposal that reflects the president's goals and the beliefs of our party."

The dominant role of lobbyists at the GOP convention is only a single reflection of the consummation of the *merger* of the Republican Party, the conservative movement, and American business. More than ever before, business, from Main Street to Wall Street, has been fully integrated into the Republican Party structure, from campaigns to policy making, from voter mobilization to whipping the vote in the House and Senate. Traditional ethical borders and lines that separated interest groups from elected officials have been crossed so often that they are now totally obscured. Consultants who run the campaigns of House and Senate candidates regularly return to lobbying practices in the off-season between elections, pressing their clients' cases to the same men and women they helped put in office.

Defeated politicians who remain ambitious for public office are working as lobbyists between elections, only to re-enter the political fray in two or four years, paying little or no price for their advocacy for special-interest causes. Business advocates from the private sector are officially recognized as part of the Republican leadership structure in the House and increasingly in the Senate. In the past, disclosures that legislative or regulatory language had been written by a trade association or the law firm of a regulated company provoked accusations of wrongdoing; now, such disclosures occur regularly and do not even slow the movement of the legislation or regulation toward final adoption.

MERGER WITH THE CORPORATE ESTABLISHMENT HAS SET UP CONFLICT WITH THE GOP'S POPULIST CLAIMS

The alliance between corporate America and the Republican Party has worked to the advantage of both. American business and its leading trade associations have done better in recent years in winning approval of favored legislation in the nation's capital than at any time since the 1920s and, perhaps, better than at any time in the history of the United States. The Republican Party has, in turn, secured a reliable source of millions of dollars to finance campaigns and an army of private sector lobbyists to push legislation through Congress. It also has allies ready to create and finance independent political and advocacy committees to support key campaigns, to back judicial nominees, and to foster "grassroots," "grass tops," and "astroturf" support for legislative initiatives, mobilizing regular voters, opinion elites, and interest-group members, respectively.

The merger of business and the GOP has not, however, been without cost to the Republican Party. Republicans rose to power in the aftermath of the mid-1960s by taking up the populist cause of striving, once-Democratic white voters who felt oppressed by what they saw as an elite, "liberal" agenda of government support for racial and ethnic minorities, a war against religion, the glorification of sexual deviance, a popular culture fostering amorality, and unrestricted abortion perceived as enabling promiscuity. Many social conservatives voted Republican not because they were interested in or favorably disposed toward the needs of the business sector—for example, the top 2005 legislative priority of the oil refining industry, the methyl tertiary butyl ether (MTBE) waiver. Rather, these conservatives voted Republican because of a conviction that the Democratic Party was undermining the traditional culture of the United States, assaulting the two-parent family, sabotaging piety, endangering national security, transforming the nation's demographic composition, and subverting both male authority and male responsibility.

The Republican Party continues to support the perceived values and social goals of white working- and middle-class voters. Its merger with the corporate establishment, however, conflicts with the GOP's populist claim to serve "ordinary people" as the party seeks to accommodate its other primary constituency—and the source of its power and wealth—the world of the rich and of national and multinational commerce.

THE CONSOLIDATION OF BUSINESS ELITES

The George W. Bush administration united a broad and diverse American business community under the banner of the Republican Party. The tensions between the Main Street and Wall Street financial wings of the GOP, which characterized the 1952 Eisenhower-Taft fight for the nomination, the Goldwater-Rockefeller battle of 1964, the Reagan-Ford nomination battle in 1976, and the Reagan-George H. W. Bush contest of 1980, have been replaced by a powerful cross-sector business alliance consolidated in the years following the 2000 election.

With policies favorable to corporations—energy, defense, transportation, telecommunications, information technology, pharmaceutical, and agricultural—as well as to enterprises run by a new class of financiers, the George W. Bush White House has fused the wealthy southern and western renegade backers of the conservative movement, who came to dominate the Republican Party in the Goldwater and Reagan years, with a universe of entrepreneurs on Wall Street and in the wider technology-intensive financial services industries. This fusion built a new, turbocharged Republican money machine, replacing the old guard of the GOP previously dominated by Anglo-Saxon blood aristocracies.

The socially and racially conservative backers of the Goldwater and Reagan ascendancies brought into the inner circles of the Republican establishment independent oilmen, ranchers, and new-money magnates. The original backers of the Goldwater and Reagan movements within the GOP were anticommunist, viewing the Soviet Union and Maoist China as mortal enemies of capitalism, not as potential trading partners. The sources of political money for the post-Goldwater GOP venerated doctrines of free trade, even as they accepted the oil depletion allowance and hydroelectric, aerospace, agribusiness, and defense subsidies.

Among the important donors of the post-Goldwater GOP were southern businessmen who saw the Civil Rights Act of 1964 as an unconstitutional invasion of states' rights and as a threat to their freedom to engage in commerce on their own terms. Many in the Southwest and West had made fortunes in the extractive industries, dependent upon access to natural resources, and were infuriated by corporate financing of, and government support for, the environmental movement. Others were entrepreneurs who had broken into established markets by locating in anti-union, open-shop, lightly regulated states where labor was cheaper and more compliant than in the Midwest and Northeast, where the AFL-CIO held sway.

Two of the most important financial constituencies of post–Civil Rights Act conservatism were independent oilmen and ranchers. For the three-and-a-half decades between the Goldwater campaign and the 2000 election, one of the GOP's major sources of money, especially large, "soft money" donations from corporate and high-dollar individuals, came from business "outliers"—from new enterprises such as Amway, run by the intensely conservative DeVos and Van Andel families who gave over $6.2 million to GOP committees in those years, from oil conglomerates Chevron and Texaco, which merged to form ChevronTexaco (well over $3 million), and from companies such as El Paso Energy, Dow Chemical, Mesa Petroleum, and their top executives.

The George W. Bush administration has produced the consolidation of what can be described as a reconfigured financial services sector—the Wall Street wing populated by a new breed of financiers—with the independent oil money wing of the GOP. The crucial building blocks for this merger were the policies adopted during Bush's first term, especially tax legislation providing for cuts in capital gains and dividend tax rates. Before Bush 43[1] took office, however, operatives and senior personnel behind Bush's presidential bid created the innovative fundraising mechanisms that greatly facilitated the merger.

REPUBLICAN ELECTION CAMPAIGN FUNDRAISING

Breaking the Candidate Free from Spending Limits: Bush Rejects Public Financing Subsidies

The crucial step was taken by the Bush presidential campaign in late 1998, when his top strategists decided to reject public financing subsidies in the 2000 primary elections. This decision meant that the primary campaign would be entirely financed by private sources and that there would be no limits on the total amount that could be raised. The exclusive use of private sources of cash in the primaries and the determination by the Bush campaign to raise a record amount (ultimately $101.5 million in 2000 and nearly three times that, $271.8 million, in 2004) established an unprecedented framework for a mutually rewarding relationship between the Bush administration and its most prominent financial backers.

Four top Bush supporters—Texas oilman Donald Evans, a long-time Bush family friend and key strategist since 1978 in all of Bush's campaigns, who was to become secretary of commerce in 2001; Fred Meyer, former chairman of the Texas Republican Party; Jeanne Johnson Phillips, a political and charitable fundraiser; and James Francis, who had run the fundraising for Bush's 1994 and 1998 gubernatorial campaigns—together devised a mechanism designed to raise large amounts of money at a time when, under Federal Election Commission rules, individual contributions could not exceed $1000. To do this, the four proposed the creation of an honorific, the title "Pioneer," to those who could collect at least $100,000 in $1000

---

[1]George W. Bush is the forty-third president of the United States; his father, George H. W. Bush, was the forty-first president—thus their administrations are known respectively as Bush 43 and Bush 41.

donations. (This amount rose to $2000 in 2004.) Strict accounting rules were set to make sure that fundraisers received personal credit only for checks that carried specifically assigned, four-digit tracking numbers to assure recognition and to prevent any double or triple counting. Fundraisers received regular reports on donations for which they were credited, a system that allowed them to apply pressure to those who failed to fulfill promises.

"We purposely set the bar high [at $100,000]," Francis said. "These are very successful, very competitive people" and the requirement of raising at least $100,000 in contributions of $1,000 or less was designed "to tap into their competitive instincts." In 2004, the Bush campaign created two new categories: "Ranger" for those who raised at least $200,000 for the campaign, and "Super Ranger" for those who collected at least $300,000 for the Republican National Committee.

Unintended Consequences of Campaign Finance Reform

The two presidential campaigns of George W. Bush demonstrated the unintended consequences of campaign finance reform laws seeking to minimize the role of the wealthy by placing limits on the amount that any individual can give. In rejecting public financing for his two primary elections, Bush showed that it was not only possible but actually advantageous to raise cash from the private sector. The creation by the Bush campaign of a new elite in the world of campaign fundraising—Pioneers, Rangers, and Super Rangers—was a natural, if unintended and, by some, unanticipated, consequence of the 1974 post-Watergate reforms. Those reforms attempted to limit primary spending by setting limits on candidates who accepted public money, as did the ban in 2002 imposed by the McCain-Feingold campaign finance reform bill—a ban on unlimited donations of "soft money" to the political parties by individuals, corporations, and unions.

This unanticipated outcome of the campaign finance reforms of 1974 and 2002 transferred power from wealthy individuals and corporations able to write large soft money checks—many of them independent oilmen, entrepreneurs, venture capitalists, and investors—to a broader group of powerful men and women. Under these reform rules, the Pioneer and Ranger system sought to capitalize upon newly empowered CEOs and chairmen of large corporations, investment bankers, and other enterprisers who, rather than writing big checks themselves, could call upon large numbers of subordinates to contribute. The reformed campaign finance system also favored lobbyists with large client networks and numerous levels of personnel ripe for recruiting $1000 and, later, $2000 contributors. Similarly, developers and contractors who had extensive dealings with architectural and engineering firms and with networks of subcontractors, lenders, and others dependent on them for business proved adept at assembling large numbers of $1000 and $2000 checks.

Expansion of the Inner GOP Money Circle

Creation of the Pioneer-Ranger fundraising structure provided an ideal mechanism for full-scale recruitment of executives in the burgeoning financial services universe and of the nation's CEOs to the inner circles of Republican Party fundraising. These men (and a few women) had built-in fundraising constituencies, subordinates who would have difficulty rejecting their bosses' requests to support the Bush campaign. These investment bankers, brokers, and CEOs, in turn, had huge financial incentives for backing Bush: his administration had enacted tax cuts that, for people like themselves with incomes well in excess of $1 million annually, meant an average additional after-tax, take-home paycheck of at least $250,000 annually. In addition, for those in the stock brokerage and other securities businesses, a huge increase in commissions flowed in from clients' buying and selling in response to new tax policies.

This expansion of the inner GOP money circle helped consolidate the merger of a more politically unified corporate America with the modern Republican Party. As a result, at the start of the twenty-first century, the Republican Party has evolved from the conservative insurgency of Barry Goldwater and Ronald Reagan—once a movement that broke ranks with mainstream Eisenhower Republicans—into a party that has joined forces with the broader contemporary corporate establishment. In the process, the center of gravity in American politics moved to the right, and the once-dominant insurgent GOP wing allied its interests with those of the greater Republican universe.

The shift in the composition of interests supporting the Republican Party can be seen in the changing character of the sources of Bush's money between 2000 and 2004. In the 2000 Bush campaign, the Sunbelt claimed three of the five top metropolitan areas providing contributions. Washington DC came in first at $4.7 million, the Dallas metropolitan area was a close second at $4.5 million, Houston gave $4.2 million, New York, $3.1 million, and Los Angeles–Long Beach, $2.8 million.

In 2004, four years later, however, the tilt of Bush's money shifted back to the North to older preserves of influence and long-standing wealth. Dallas fell out of the top five altogether, and Houston fell to fourth. Metropolitan Washington remained first, but its total grew by 131 percent to $10.8 million. New York, home of Wall Street and a host of Fortune 500 headquarters, shot up to second place, growing at the fastest pace of all, 145 percent, to $7.6 million. Los Angeles rose from fifth to third place, growing by 118 percent to $6.1 million, and Chicago, another establishment corporate headquarters town, made fifth place at $5.9 million. Equally illuminating is the dominance by prominent Wall Street figures of Bush's list of top fundraisers in 2004—the Pioneers and Rangers who collected at least $100,000 each. None of the top money men in 2004 had been even minor players in 2000. No other group had benefited more, personally and professionally, from the tax cuts enacted during Bush's first term, and these investment bankers, hedge fund partners, and brokerage executives responded by doing everything in their power to keep their benefactor in office for four more years.

In 2000, only seven of Bush's Pioneers came from New York, and not one was the CEO or chairman of a major Wall Street or investment banking firm. In 2004, there were thirty Pioneers and Rangers from New York, and they were the cream of Wall Street. The nation's most prominent figures in finance—who just four years earlier had disdained political fundraising—not only made the list but also set national records:

- Philip J. Purcell, CEO in 2004 of Morgan Stanley, presided over employees who gave Bush $680,480, more than any other company in the nation.

- E. Stanley O'Neal, chairman, CEO, and president of Merrill Lynch & Co., whose employees gave $580,004, made his firm the second-ranking source of money for Bush.

- Joseph J. Grano, chairman and CEO of UBS Wealth Management, oversaw employees who gave Bush $468,075.

- Henry M. Paulson Jr., chairman and CEO of Goldman Sachs & Co., raised $388,600. (Paulson became Bush's secretary of the treasury in 2006.)

- John Mack, CEO of Credit Suisse First Boston Corp., raised $330,040.

- James E. Cayne, chairman and CEO of Bear Stearns & Co., gave $309,150.

An analysis of how much some of Bush's major fundraisers would receive from the administration's 2001 tax cut showed that in 2003 alone, Bush Rangers such as Merrill Lynch's O'Neal was eligible for $351,900; Henry McKinnell, the CEO of Pfizer, might save $244,214; William McGuire, CEO of UnitedHealth Group, $329,866; and Maurice Greenberg, then-CEO of American International Group, $276,000. These figures pale in comparison, however, next to the surge of income-generating transactions prompted by the tax changes enacted between 2001 and 2004. Lowered capital gains, corporate, individual, and dividend tax rates encouraged massive asset shifting on Wall Street as clients discovered that the variously lowered rates produced incentives to sell existing holdings and to move their money. "This tax cut will have a major impact on capital markets by creating more incentives for investors to save and invest," declared Steve Judge, senior vice president for government affairs at the Securities Industry Association. "As a result, more capital will become available, which will help companies to expand and hire new employees. This is a win-win for our economy, and the President and Congress are to be congratulated for their efforts on behalf of investors."

THE SHADOWY UNDERBELLY OF WASHINGTON HAS BECOME ITS PUBLIC FACE

The stage for the merger engineered by Bush was set by the Republican takeover of the House and Senate in 1994. As long as the two branches of Congress were in Democratic hands (1955–1995 for the House, 1955–1981 and 1987–1995 for the Senate), business interests were under an obligation to apportion their donations and support in order to retain access to lawmakers. When Democrats chaired such key committees as Appropriations, Armed Services, House Energy and Commerce, House Ways and Means, and Senate Finance, business had no choice but to be bipartisan.

The changing flow of money as power shifted was striking. In 1993–1994, the last session of Congress when Democrats were in control, defense industry PACs gave Democrats $2,937,459 and $2,138,388 to Republicans, a 57 percent to 43 percent split; as soon as the GOP took over in 1995–1996, the industry switched to a 72 percent to 28 percent margin favoring the Republicans, $4,051,907 to $1,564,640. The energy and natural resources industries went from a slight 53 to 47 tilt to the GOP, $6,604,225 to $5,637,728 prior to the GOP takeover, to an overwhelming 77 to 27 split favoring the GOP in 1995–1996, $10,207,407 to $3,065,220. The pattern was almost universal as business leapt on the opportunity to join forces with a party that explicitly supported its goals.

The shift of financial resources to House and Senate Republicans as the Democrats lost their half-century hold on the levers of power was the backdrop to what became known as the "K Street Project," a concerted and highly successful effort to convert basic political resources such as top-paying lobbying jobs, the money donated by business PACs, and the muscle of the Washington trade association and lobbying communities to the Republican cause. While presidential fundraising changed dramatically under Bush 43, at the congressional level what had been the shadowy underbelly of the money culture in Washington became its public face. The secretiveness and the element of shame that accompanied Washington special interest fundraising in the past have by now virtually disappeared.

House Republicans list their fundraising events with special interest sponsors on the National Republican Congressional Committee (NRCC) Web site. In early June 2005, for example, Frank Purcell, chief lobbyist for the American Association of Nurse Anesthetists, announced a $1,000-a-person "Healthcare Industry Dinner Honoring Congressman Duke Cunningham," Republican of California and a member of the Appropriations Subcommittee on Labor, Health and Human Services, Education, and Related Agencies, at the Capital Grille. For the same price that night at the Capital Grille, prominent Washington lobbyist Ann Eppard, whose specialty is port and highway spending bills, and the National Business Travel Association PAC held a dinner honoring Representative Frank LoBiondo, a New Jersey Republican who is a member of the House Transportation and Infrastructure Committee. A couple of nights later, the lobbying firm Blank Rome Government Relations, whose clients included Union Pacific Railroad, Holland America Lines, and the Alaska Railroad Corp., posted an invitation—$1000 for a person, $2500 for a PAC—"to a special birthday bash honoring Congressman Don Young," the Alaskan Republican who chairs the Transportation Committee. In June 2005 alone, 128 such events were listed on the NRCC Web site.

The changing culture of money in Washington throughout the years of the George W. Bush presidency has significant policy consequences. Tax cuts enacted during Bush's first term have been decisively tilted to the very rich. The joint Brookings Institution–Urban Institute Tax Policy Center has calculated that the net result of the 2001 and 2003 tax bills will be declines in after-tax income for the bottom 80 percent of taxpayers by 2010—annual losses ranging from $184 to $433. Conversely, those in the top 20 percent of the income distribution get an average tax cut of $1,128, and those in the top 1 percent get an average annual tax break of $22,335. This result broadens the inequality gap in the United States, already significantly wider here than in most other developed countries.

With virtually no outcry or opposition, Congress enacted, and Bush signed, 2005 bankruptcy legislation that places new burdens on debtors, including those forced into bankruptcy by medical catastrophe. The legislation restricts the ability of persons using the federal bankruptcy courts to wipe the slate of debt clean. In addition, in 2005 a hefty $14.5 billion energy bill was passed that primarily subsidizes the oil and gas industry and opens up public utilities to corporate acquisition.

Class Action, Tort, Liability, and Lawsuit Reform: Uniting the Interests of Business and of Social-Racial Conservatives

The financial and political importance of tort reform to American business should not be underestimated. The bottom-line cost of litigation and judgments, most of it paid for by corporations, was $246 billion in 2003 alone, the most recent year surveyed by Tillinghast-Towers Perrin, a well-known consulting firm. Tillinghast-Towers Perrin estimated that tort costs have risen two to three percentage points faster than the gross national product for the past fifty years and by a total of 35.4 percent just between 2000 and 2003. Any significant cutback in tort litigation—even slowing the rate of increase—is perceived as crucially important by American business.

Cutting liability awards, furthermore, weakens the ability of trial lawyers—among the most important sources of Democratic campaign contributions—to make donations to the Democratic Party and diminishes as well the ability of the plaintiffs' bar to fend off further corporate-backed changes in tort law. While it is difficult to separate campaign contributions made by trial lawyers from the money given by other legal practitioners, in 2004 lawyers of all kinds gave $182.6 million in political contributions, three-quarters, or $135.8 million, of which went to Democrats. If donations by Republican-leaning corporate lawyers are subtracted from those figures, trial lawyers constitute the overwhelming majority of donors, and their contributions went to Democrats by a ratio of 85 to 15, at least. As a result, any legislation cutting the income of trial lawyers is very likely to reduce the available pool of discretionary money that they can donate to Democratic candidates.

Political scientist Thomas Burke, in *Lawyers, Lawsuits, and Legal Rights*, writes,

> Changes in procedural rules [over the past decades] made it easier to bring "mass torts" and class action lawsuits for injuries either proven or alleged to be caused by asbestos, Agent Orange, breast implants, diet pills, genetically modified foods,

HMOs, even the Holocaust—as well as such lesser evils as defects in the Pentium computer chip. Enterprising plaintiff lawyers developed new theories of damages, and awards for "pain and suffering," loss of a family member, and punitive damages ballooned. As a result both the opportunities for and potential rewards of tort litigation have greatly increased.

Tort and liability litigation provides a form of market regulation in this country that has a tradition of generally restricting direct government regulation. From the perspective of consumers and voters, class action suits, tort litigation, and liability action provide substantial protection—and sometimes the only protection—against defective products, medical malpractice, corporate negligence, environmental hazards, personal injury, fraud, and so forth.

In the view of those who support the plaintiffs' bar, legal action is the best way to ensure that just compensation is paid by large corporations and other defendants with deep pockets to those suffering damages caused by unsafe goods, pollution, medical errors, corporate negligence, and so on. According to this line of argument—one generally advanced by Democrats and liberals—businesses run cost-benefit calculations when weighing consumer well-being against the expense of increasing product safety; thus, imposing substantial costs on producers for injuring people or for damaging property is the most effective way of correcting those wrongs and compensating victims. Conversely, supporters of lawsuit reform—generally Republicans and conservatives—argue that the use of tort remedies provides a highly random and inequitable system of compensation, with some victims getting large settlements and others getting nothing at all. At the same time, they argue that the system imposes crippling costs on the American economy and encourages a risk-adverse corporate culture, antithetical to innovation and experimentation.

The conservative movement and the Republican Party have more at stake in class action and liability reform than just business profits, however. The conservative demand for class action and liability reform represents not only a business imperative; it also unites the objectives of corporate interests with those of social, racial, and cultural conservatives. This unity of interest in curbing "lawsuit abuse" stems from the fact that class action suits, rooted in antidiscrimination and civil rights laws passed over the course of the past fifty years, have become an avenue by which litigators have been able to force social and racial change.

Thomas Burke details the history of the targeted use of class action and liability law over the past five decades to provide expanded civil and citizenship rights:

> Out of *Brown v. Board of Education*, the Supreme Court's 1954 ruling that segregation in public schools is unconstitutional, grew the notion that law could be used to transform society and achieve social justice. One of the crowning achievements of the civil rights movement, the Civil Rights Act of 1964, gave minorities the right to sue discriminating employers. That model—of giving victims of discrimination the right to bring lawsuits—has since been expanded to cover women, the aged, gays and lesbians, religious minorities, and people with disabilities and has inspired a panoply of civil rights laws at the national, state, and local levels. Alongside these statutory antidiscrimination rights, the Supreme Court expanded the bases for claims under the Constitution's Equal Protection Clause to include discrimination on the basis of sex and other attributes. Both constitutional and statutory antidiscrimination law has grown to govern more and more domains, from education and employment to law enforcement and public accommodations. With the Supreme Court's 1964 *Baker v. Carr* decision, holding that unequally sized voting districts could be challenged under the Constitution, and with Congress's passage of the 1965 Voting Rights Act, many aspects of the U.S. electoral system have also become subject to litigation.
>
> As the range of civil rights laws has grown, so have the damages available to plaintiffs. While the Civil Rights Act of 1964 allowed successful plaintiffs to claim only back pay, reinstatement in their jobs, and attorney's fees, courts and legislatures have in many instances also granted punitive and pain-and-suffering damages, enlarging the potential rewards of litigation. The 1991 Civil Rights Act, for example, gave women, minorities, and disabled people the right to collect up to $300,000 in punitive and pain-and-suffering awards. Thus the potential rewards of civil rights litigation have continued to grow.

Walter K. Olson, senior fellow at the conservative Manhattan Institute, also lays out the reasons that the Republican Party and its allies have invested so much of their political capital in the broad arena of lawsuit reform:

During the Sixties and Seventies, new conceptions of the function of law rapidly gained ground: law was seen as a powerful tool to remake society. . . . One early result was a great blossoming of institutional-reform litigation identifying inequalities, unfairnesses or harsh outcomes in the operation of public (and some private) institutions and demanding such remedies as cross-district racial busing in school systems, court takeovers of prison and mental health systems for the sake of protecting inmates' rights, expanded due process rights for welfare recipients, and much more. Hundreds of ambitious suits met with success, frequently resulting in the negotiation of consent decrees in which the government or other parties being sued agreed to revamp old policies and sometimes seek permission from the plaintiff's groups before adopting new ones. . . . [T]he movement continues to rack up many successes, notably with the campaign to persuade courts to order "Robin Hood" school finance reform, . . . [which forces] the allocation of higher sums to underperforming schools or districts.

Olson goes on to cite the success of class action suits in forcing punitive awards and legal action favoring plaintiffs in affirmative action, sex discrimination, and sexual harassment lawsuits. This "lawsuit culture" can and does expand to cover matters ranging from "handicap-accommodation law to age discrimination law to family leave to new common-law doctrines making employers liable for 'wrongful termination,' 'workplace defamation,' and much more."

Business and trade associations have fused their interests with those of social conservatives in the arena of liability reform. In recent years, corporations and trade associations have invested between $95 million and $110 million annually in publicly reported lobbying payments supporting tort reform, according to a summary by PoliticalMoneyLine of data contained in publicly filed lobbying reports. President Bush and the Republican Party have, in turn, found that tort reform is a goldmine for raising money, and Bush has unrelentingly promoted legislation along these lines since he first ran for Texas governor in 1994.

Among the groups pushing for a restructuring of lawsuit rules in 2005 were the following:

- The Asbestos Study Group, an alliance of Fortune 500 companies that are defendants in asbestos suits, which paid annual lobbying fees of more than $10 million over the past two years.

- The American Medical Association—determined to protect doctors in malpractice cases—which has an annual lobbying budget of more than $17 million.

- The American Insurance Institute, which spends about $5 million annually, a significant share of which goes to efforts to restrict lawsuits.

- The Institute for Legal Reform of the U.S. Chamber of Commerce, which spent $19.8 million in 2005.

In addition, a significant share of the American Hospital Association's $19.8 million 2005 lobbying budget, of General Electric's $17.8 million, of Altria's $13.5 million, and of the Pharmaceutical Research and Manufacturers of America's $13.5 million went to the issue of lawsuit reform.

Republican officials and business groups direct public attention to "excessive litigiousness" that, they argue, limits access to or drives up costs of medical care and closes down parks, playgrounds, and other public amenities. The debate led by conservative policy advocates in such books as *The Death of Common Sense: How Law Is Suffocating America* by Philip Howard systematically diverts attention away from the social justice issues advanced by class action litigation. The role of class action settlements in mandating the advancement of women, minorities, and other once-marginalized groups is rarely if ever made the subject of public comment by politicians running national campaigns, even as they strenuously advocate lawsuit reform.

Bush on the campaign trail, for example, while making liability reform a central campaign issue, casts the matter in terms of driving down medical costs:

> And you know what else we need to do in order to make sure health care is available and affordable? Medical liability reform. These lawsuits are making—[applause]. I'm telling you, the frivolous lawsuits are running up the cost of health care and they're driving doctors out of business and they're hurting our hospitals. [Applause] And I don't think you can be—I don't

think you can be pro-patient and pro-doctor and pro-trial lawyer at the same time. [Applause] I think you have to choose. My opponent [Kerry] has made his choice and he put him [trial lawyer John Edwards] on the ticket. [Laughter] I made my choice. We're standing with the patients and the doctors and the small business owners.

Rhetoric invoking "frivolous lawsuits" and "lawsuit abuse" has, however, been added to language targeting "activist judges" and "liberal courts" as an effective sub-rosa signal to social conservatives—particularly to those concerned with cultural and racial issues—that legislation putting an end to "lawsuit abuse" potentially contains broad social implications, implications welcome to many voters on the right.

Democratic politicians see the matter differently. "*Brown v. Board of Education* might have been [considered] frivolous," said Representative Sheila Jackson Lee, an African American Democratic congresswoman from Texas in opposition to limiting so-called frivolous lawsuits. "I don't want a law that says you can't go into the courthouse."

In point of fact, there has been an explosion of class action lawsuits in recent years seeking to further redistribute rights and resources, including the following settlements:

- race discrimination against Texaco ($176 million);

- race discrimination against Coca-Cola ($192 million);

- sex discrimination against the U.S. Information Agency and Voice of America ($508 million);

- sex discrimination against Home Depot ($104 million);

- race discrimination against Shoney's ($105 million);

- sex discrimination against Publix Markets ($81 million);

- race discrimination against Abercrombie and Fitch ($40 million);

- race discrimination against Norfolk Southern Corp. ($28 million); and

- sex discrimination against State Farm Insurance Co. ($157 million).

Mitsubishi settled two sexual harassment cases for $45 million. A jury awarded $80.7 million to a UPS female supervisor who alleged a male supervisor poked her breast during an argument. A recently filed sex discrimination suit against Wal-Mart threatens to set a new record.

Last year, 23,152 suits alleging race, sex, disability, or age discrimination were filed in federal courts, more than double the 1992 total of 10,771. In October 2005, thirteen current and former employees of the Commerce Department filed a $500 million class action lawsuit alleging race discrimination in hiring and advancement practices. On March 31, 2005, four female financial consultants filed a national class action lawsuit charging sex discrimination at Smith Barney, the retail brokerage arm of Citigroup, the nation's largest financial institution.

In August 2004, the law firms Lieff Cabraser Heimann Bernstein and Davis Cowell Bowe filed an employment discrimination class action lawsuit against Costco Wholesale Corporation, charging that Costco operates a "glass ceiling" at the store-management level that stops women from getting promoted to assistant manager and general manager positions. In January 2006, the Borgata Hotel Casino Spa was slapped with a $70 million suit claiming that "the gaming hall discriminated against female employees in its zeal to keep its skimpily attired cocktail servers slim and sexy. The litigation stems from the casino's controversial policy, enacted last year, that prohibits the 'Borgata Babes' cocktail servers from gaining more than 7% of their body weight. Two former Borgata Babes, Renee Gaud and Trisha Hart, allege in the state Superior Court suit that the casino created a hostile workplace tainted by discrimination and sexual stereotypes."

➢ ⊰

In the broadest sense, laws facilitating tort and class action suits gather support from the have-nots and opposition from the haves because successful lawsuits are inherently redistributive. They transfer rights, resources, and benefits from dominant players in society, who are most often the defendants in such cases, to the ranks of the relatively disadvantaged, the plaintiffs who usually have fewer or no assets. The relative nature of this dominance relationship is true also in business litigation; for example, the biggest lawsuits targeting Microsoft have been brought by companies that were "plowed under by the Microsoft juggernaut." Trent Lott, the powerful Republican senator from Mississippi, recently had cause to feel himself thrust into the class of have-nots when his beachfront Pascagoula home was razed by Hurricane Katrina. Lott bolted his party's orthodoxy on "lawsuit abuse" and sued his insurance company, State Farm, when the firm denied his claim that his house was destroyed by wind (covered), not floodwater (uncovered). It was, ironically, Lott who lost his leadership position as a result of displaying his hostility to decades of civil rights law, much of it advanced through class action litigation, when he observed at Senator Strom Thurmond's one hundredth birthday that, if Thurmond had won in his 1948 Dixiecrat segregationist bid for the White House, the United States would have been better off. "I want to say this about my state," Lott declared. "When Strom Thurmond ran for president, we voted for him. We're proud of it. And if the rest of the country had followed our lead, we wouldn't have had all these problems over all these years, either."

One key goal of recent federal tort reform legislation signed by G. W. Bush has been to move important classes of liability litigation from the state to the federal court system, where business interests and Republican strategists see a far more restrictive environment for plaintiffs and a reduced likelihood of lawsuits being approved. This political goal contradicts the historic conservative advocacy of states' rights and the fear of big or centralized government, which, according to Republicans, a federal presence inevitably promotes.

For business interests, liability reform is all about money. That the issue in addition has recruited racial and cultural conservatives, opposed to the use of the courts to advance a liberal rights agenda by means of lawsuits, is profoundly advantageous. It allows corporate powers within the GOP coalition ever greater leeway in Washington while being solidly backed by loyal social-issue voting constituencies. The Republican battle for "tort reform" thus captures almost every aspect of the fundamental Republican partisan electoral strategy, simultaneously uniting, in a perceived common cause, the two major wings of the GOP—social and racial conservatives on the one hand and corporate America on the other.

The Bush Administration Delivers

Since George W. Bush took office in 2001, seven measures falling under the rubric of legal reform—most involving changes in tort law benefiting corporate defendants—have been enacted as of this writing; two other bills sought by corporate America have been passed by the House and await action by the Senate. The biggest victory for the Chamber of Commerce, the National Association of Manufacturers, and their allies was passage of the Class Action Fairness Act of 2005, which moved jurisdiction over large, interstate class action cases from state courts to federal courts. Rules and precedents in federal courts are traditionally more favorable to defendants than in state courts, and the shift is expected to significantly reduce the number of cases that trial lawyers are allowed to bring. When he signed the act, Bush gave the public his description of the abuse the legislation is designed to curb—"a woman who purchased a faulty television got a $50 rebate on a new TV from the same company while the lawyer who brought the suit got $22 million."

In addition, separate bills passed by Congress have provided new protections against lawsuits to specific groups: most notably to gun manufacturers; to companies providing terrorism risk insurance; to car and truck leasing companies in cases involving accidents caused by renters; to the manufacturers of vaccines used to fight pandemics, anthrax, or other pathogens; and to the producers of antiterrorist technologies purchased by the Department of Homeland Security. The two remaining bills that have passed the House and await action by the Senate are the Personal Responsibility in Food Consumption Act, or the "Cheeseburger Bill," which would exempt McDonald's and other fast-food operations from charges of contributing to obesity, and the Lawsuit Abuse Reduction Act, which would impose mandatory fines on plaintiffs' lawyers bringing "frivolous" suits and would prohibit "venue shopping." In addition, two measures awaiting action as of this writing by both branches of Congress are among the highest priorities of the lobbying community. The first would limit suits against doctors and health care providers; the second would create a special fund for asbestos liability cases to permit corporations now in bankruptcy or threatened by it to return to normal operations.

Tort reform will remain at the top of the conservative agenda. As he explores a bid for the 2008 GOP presidential nomination, Senate Majority Leader Bill Frist (R-Tennessee) stresses the issue on the stump. At a February 3, 2006, Lincoln-Reagan Day Dinner in Hampstead, New Hampshire, Frist told the gathering:

> For years, frivolous lawsuits have clogged our courts, burdened our economy, and diminished your access to health care. So Republicans said, "We're gonna do something about it. We're gonna fix this broken system."
>
> Folks on the sidelines said, "It'll never happen. The trial lawyer lobby is simply too strong."
>
> They were wrong. We pushed, and we pushed and we pushed. And where Congress after Congress failed, this current Congress—step by step—succeeded in passing:
>
> First, class action reform. Then bankruptcy reform. Then gun liability reform. And then avian flu and bioterror liability reform. And now today, after nearly a decade of partisan obstruction, lawsuit abuse reform is a reality.
>
> What does that mean for you? It means a legal system that's fair . . . and an America that's poised to compete against China and India in this 21st century global economy.
>
> And mark my words, . . . we're not finished.
>
> When trauma centers in America are closing, when skyrocketing premiums are driving my colleagues in medicine out of business, . . . when moms in New Hampshire can't find doctors to deliver their babies, it's time to reel in those predatory trial lawyers and pass meaningful medical malpractice reform! (And we will do it!)

BREAKDOWN OF THE BOUNDARIES BETWEEN LOBBYISTS AND POLITICIANS

By constantly wearing down the boundaries between money and politics, the Republican Party has, at least for the moment, succeeded in transforming the norms of interaction in Washington between conservative interests and politicians. Newspapers today generally treat as unexceptional elements of the Washington landscape that, a generation ago, were considered scandalous examples of corruption.

On February 3, 1987, for example, the *Washington Post* disclosed that then-Senate Finance Committee Chairman Lloyd Bentsen, Democrat of Texas, had created a $10,000-a-head breakfast club called the "Chairman's Council." Lobbyists who put up $10,000 were invited to attend monthly breakfasts with Bentsen. "I will be relying on members of the Chairman's Council for advice, assistance and early financial support crucial to a successful campaign," Bentsen wrote in a letter to two hundred lobbyists. Three days after the news story appeared, a shaken Bentsen announced that he was folding the breakfast club. "I'm not known to make many mistakes, but when I do, it's a doozy. And in forming the breakfast club, I really blew it. . . . The last thing I want is anything that would reflect on my integrity. The club will be disbanded today. The contributions to the campaign will be returned to the contributors."

Fewer than fifteen years later, the $10,000 donations that had so deeply embarrassed Bentsen would be viewed as chickenfeed in a transformed Washington money culture where corporations routinely donate huge sums and, in return for their investments, reap huge rewards. Between 2000 and 2002, just one PAC, House Majority Whip Tom DeLay's Americans for a Republican Majority Non-Federal PAC (ARMPAC), got $195,000 from SBC Communications Inc., $110,000 from the Altria Group Inc. (Philip Morris, Kraft Foods), $100,000 from Reliant Energy Resources Inc., and $75,000 from the Union Pacific Corp. Many of these same companies gave heavily to House Majority Whip Roy Blunt's "Rely on Your Beliefs Fund": SBC, $135,540; Altria, $109,452; Union Pacific, $50,000; and Reliant, $50,000. Democrats belatedly attempted to join the same bandwagon of high-dollar donors. Former Senate Minority Leader Tom Dashcle, Democrat of South Dakota, limited top donors to $10,000 through the 2000 election, but, facing the prospect of a tough challenge in 2004, he lifted the limits, taking contributions ranging from $25,000 to a top limit of $60,000, with the largest gifts coming from trial lawyer firms.

Until recently, most politicians assumed that, if they attempted to cash in on their elective careers by taking jobs as lobbyists, they were in effect foregoing all future prospects of running for office. The act of becoming the representative of private special interests effectively precluded representation of the public interest, in this assessment of the electorate's view of lobbying. Recently, however,

Republicans have been demonstrating that this political truism is false. In 2000, Representative James Talent, Republican of Missouri, ran unsuccessfully for governor of his state, and two years later, Representative John Thune, Republican of South Dakota, ran unsuccessfully against Democratic Senator Tim Johnson. During the two years that each of these men was out of office, both became registered lobbyists. Talent's clients included the National Federation of Independent Business, the premier small business lobby, as well as UniGroup Corporation and the National Grain and Feed Association. Thune's client list included the National Milk Producers Federation, the Motor and Equipment Manufacturers Association, and Laserscope Inc. When Talent in 2002 and Thune in 2004 ran for the Senate, their lobbying interludes were raised as issues by their opponents, but these accusations did not prevent them from winning office.

Perhaps the quintessential case study in the breakdown of boundaries between the world of lobbyists and the world of politics was the 2003 election of Haley Barbour as governor of Mississippi, once a populist state with a deeply entrenched suspicion of Washington special interests. In the seven years before his election, Barbour, who had been chairman of the Republican National Committee from 1993 to 1996, built the most successful Republican lobbying firm in the history of the nation's capital, specializing in the representation of clients with interests that often collide with the interests of the general public: tobacco (Brown & Williamson Tobacco, $120,000 yearly, Lorillard Tobacco, $440,000), drug companies (Bristol Myers Squibb, $200,000, GlaxoSmithKline, $120,000), long-term health care and the health maintenance organization industry (Kindred Healthcare, $320,000, Medcath Corporation, $320,000, UnitedHealth Group, $320,000, Alliance for Quality Nursing Home Care, $520,000), and major electric utilities (Electric Reliability Coordinating Council, $440,000, The Southern Company, $200,000). This work did not stop Barbour from winning the Mississippi governorship with 53 percent of the vote.

Presidential campaigns not only turn to prominent lobbyists to run conventions but also to serve as semi-official campaign spokesmen. They appear regularly on cable television and in newspaper stories, rarely if ever identified as lobbyists, and they run campaign operations in different key states where they began their careers as political operatives. All these practices take place in both the Republican and Democratic parties, but they have overwhelming originated in the GOP and are far more prevalent there.

Little of the Embarrassment and None of the Shame

What makes this system work is that many, if not most, Republican leaders, lobbyists, and political operatives see their advocacy of the interests of American business as an entirely legitimate public mission. Both in Congress and in the Bush administration, this Republican mission is carried out explicitly and publicly. Unlike the Democrats, for whom both unions and corporations are "special interests," contemporary Republicans experience little of the embarrassment and none of the shame characteristic of their Democratic counterparts when legislation or regulation is shown by the media to be overwhelmingly tilted in favor of corporate interests, of the affluent, or of corporate goals generally.

Democratic political operatives will go out of their way to avoid registration as lobbyists, becoming, instead, "strategic advisors" or public relations consultants. For example, Howard Wolfson, strategic adviser to Hillary Clinton and former executive director of the Democratic Congressional Campaign Committee, Jim Jordan, manager of John F. Kerry's presidential campaign and former executive director of the Democratic Senatorial Campaign Committee, Mike McCurry, President Clinton's chief spokesman, and Joe Lockhart, who followed McCurry as Clinton's spokesman, are involved in influence peddling, but each has—whenever possible—chosen ways to do so without falling under the jurisdiction of the Lobby Registration Act.

Republican campaign operatives-turned-lobbyists show no such reticence. If anything, the Republicans have found that disclosing the high fees they get only serves to increase their clientele. The ability to act without shame is a powerful political weapon, allowing politicians to remain indifferent to accusations of opportunism, self-interest, or greed. Republican straightforwardness—which Democrats call corrupt or brazen—has been accompanied by the general curtailment on the part of the media of its role as watchdog when political self-dealing and influence peddling reach levels that might have been treated as scandalous in the recent past. Stories describing the role of lobbyists in writing legislation, reports demonstrating the regressive nature of tax bills, or stories exposing the weakening of environmental protections are now most often relegated to the inside pages of newspapers, if assigned or covered at all, and left untouched by television.

New electronic media—left and right blogs—have at present no systematic way of covering the full range of Washington politics, although they are effective in documenting the failings of the mainstream media. The specialty press (*Consumer Electronics Daily, Petroleum Economist, Contractor, Aviation Week,* etc.) targets professional audiences and is invisible to the general public. Publications such as *The Chronicle of Higher Education* have revealed in detail the interrelationship between public officials and the finances of the companies and institutions they oversee, including coverage of former Education and the Workforce Committee Chairman John Boehner (R-Ohio) and his favorable treatment of student lending giant Sallie Mae, but such stories are rarely picked up by the mainstream media.

With some notable exceptions—the 2005 and 2006 coverage of former House Majority Leader Tom DeLay and his ties to lobbyist Jack Abramoff—the media has been remarkably hesitant to aggressively examine the policies enacted or the procedural practices adopted during the era of Republican control of the Congress and the White House. Starting with the election of 1980, the daily establishment media have struggled with the fear of being labeled "liberal," which has led to reluctance to send reporters out to cover the extraordinarily lucrative relationship between Republicans and business.

Without effective challenge, the Republican-corporate merger has brought forward a jointly produced legislative and regulatory agenda backed by major business interests as well as by the White House, by the leadership on Capitol Hill, and by the formal institutionalization of business lobbyists as key shapers and promoters of legislation. This agenda, furthermore, is often vigorously backed by the religious right and the universe of social-conservative interest groups. The Republican whip operation in the House has turned a network of 1,200 lobbyists into a recognized arm of the Republican leadership, abandoning all pretense of a separation between elected officials and those seeking to influence their decisions. Acting simultaneously in behalf of their own clients and the Republican leadership, these lobbyists are empowered not only to pressure House members and senators in support of key legislation but also to negotiate deals for amendments and language changes in legislation designed to simultaneously benefit clients and to pick up votes.

On Thursday, April 16, 2005, for example, some 250 Republican lobbyists gathered in a basement room on the House side of the Capitol building to celebrate past achievements and to get briefed on the status of pending legislation by House and Senate leaders. The lobbyists had already helped win approval in early 2005 of the bankruptcy bill significantly limiting the rights of those in debt and of class action legislation limiting the ability of plaintiffs to sue corporations for damages. There was still much on the common agenda of business and the Republican leadership, including more tax cuts, structural changes in federal pension law, and enactment of the Central American Free Trade Agreement (CAFTA).

Looking out to a room packed full of lobbyists, House Majority Whip Roy Blunt (R-Missouri) said, "Gathered in this room is where policy meets politics, where the rubber meets the road. Thank you to all of you for all that you've done to help us. We couldn't have gotten this far without your assistance." Under Blunt's guidance, the Republican whip's office has built a small army of business and trade association lobbyists. These lobbyists are "willing to work with leadership, in a broad generic way," said Gregg Hartley, who ran the "business liaison" operation for Blunt until becoming a K Street lobbyist himself. "We have a commitment from them to whip the vote on the outside."

At the top of the Republican leadership at the time, there was a de facto "executive committee," a hardcore base of about twenty-five lobbyists that included Hartley, Ed Gillespie, former Republican Party chair, Mark Isakowitz, formerly with the National Federation of Independent Business, Drew Maloney, DeLay's former assistant chief of staff, Lyle Beckwith, senior vice president of the National Association of Convenience Stores, Bruce Gates of Washington Council Ernst & Young, Henry Gandy of the Duberstein Group, and Dirk Van Dongen of the National Association of Wholesaler Distributors. The composition of the informal executive committee changed to include Gates, Gandy, and Van Dongen in early 2006 when John Boehner (R-Ohio) replaced DeLay as majority leader.

The power and leverage of the K Street lobbying arm of the Republican whip's office proved most effective in 2004 when the House faced a seemingly insurmountable election-year hurdle: the World Trade Organization had ruled that an export subsidy providing corporations with $50 billion in tax breaks over ten years was in violation of international trade agreements. Unless the United States repealed the tax provision, foreign trading partners would be authorized to impose restrictive tariffs on U.S. goods. Representative Mike Rogers (R-Michigan), Blunt's deputy whip with responsibility for dealing with allies in the lobbying community, saw proposed legislation eliminating the subsidy as facing daunting prospects.

Rank-and-file Republicans, especially those from Midwestern industrial states with large manufacturers in their districts, saw millions in annual losses for major companies such as Boeing, Caterpillar, United Technologies, Honeywell, and Emerson. "When we started, the whip count on that bill looked as bad as I have ever seen," Rogers said. An attempt to make up for the elimination of the illegal $50 billion tax provision with a $50 billion tax break that did not violate trade agreements would only serve to create a new set of winners and losers, and losers are almost invariably stronger in opposing legislation than prospective winners are in backing it.

The solution to breaking the logjam turned out to be straightforward and simple: the corporate lobbying community was unleashed to find out what it would take to piece together a minimum of 218 votes, a House majority, and lobbyists were empowered to cut deals for those votes. Simple repeal of the export subsidy grew into a 633-page bill, and a small-type, line-item list of the revenue changes required twelve pages. The result was that every influential lobbying interest got something, and Republican opposition to the measure collapsed. American companies with overseas operations were granted a virtual tax holiday on repatriated income, with the rate falling from 35 to 5.25 percent. Railroads won the elimination of a 4.3 cent-per-gallon tax on diesel fuel, and the tax on manufacturing income was reduced by three percentage points. NASCAR track owners could write off $101 million worth of improvements over ten years. The tariff paid by Home Depot on ceiling fans imported from China was temporarily suspended. General Electric, the single biggest corporate beneficiary of the measure, paid its lobbyist, Ken Kies, former chief of staff of the Joint Committee on Taxation, a $1 million bonus, boosting the fee to Kies' firm from $260,000 for the first six months of 2004 to $1.28 million for the second half of 2004.

As new tax breaks were added to the bill, the vote count "just got better and better," said Rogers, who worked closely with Blunt on the mobilization of lobbyists. "It was incredible." On the final vote, Republicans favored the bill 203 to 23, whereas Democrats opposed it 154 to 48.

The "K Street Project" has been the moving force behind the alliance between the corporate and trade association lobbying community and the Republican House leadership. The project effectively began the moment the GOP took over Congress in the "Gingrich revolution" at the start of 1995, when business interests no longer had to contend with Democratic control of the House and Senate. DeLay, working with Grover Norquist, president of the antitax Americans for Tax Reform and a lobbyist in his own right, determined that a formal structure was needed to ascertain which of the lobbies and trade associations that line Washington's K Street gave most of their contributions to Republicans and hired Republicans as top staffers, and which needed to be told that they were giving too much to Democrats and that Democratic staffers needed to be replaced with Republicans.

DeLay, then majority whip, promoted his role as enforcer, delighting as lobbyists and reporters traded stories of how he met with K Streeters while standing by his desk with a book that detailed how their political action committees had distributed contributions between Democrats and Republicans. "Unfortunately in this town over 40 years, people that should be conservative, should be pro-business, should be pro-free enterprise, have prostituted themselves in this town," DeLay said in 1996, well before the 2005 Jack Abramoff scandal made him more cautious in describing his activities.

> You've got business organizations, for instance, that give 60, 70 percent of their money to liberal Democrats that stab them in the back, and that just doesn't make sense to me. . . . I do have

a book that lays out on my desk that has a report on who gives money to whom. I never use it. I never open it. But people that come to see me I'm sure see that book laying out there and they know that I know what they've done to further the revolution or not. It's just a nice little hint.

DeLay was candid about what he planned to do with the information. In 1995, before he faced his first barrage of complaints to the House Ethics Committee, DeLay told the *Washington Post*: "There are just a lot of people down on K Street who gained their prominence by being Democrat and supporting the Democrat cause, and they can't regain their prominence unless they get us out of here." DeLay made it clear that he would not tolerate the status quo: "We're just following the old adage of punish your enemies and reward your friends. We don't like to deal with people who are trying to kill the revolution. We know who they are. The word is out." Representative Bill Paxon, formerly a Republican member from New York and then chairman of the National Republican Congressional Committee, told lobbyists who had given to Democrats: "Why do you support the enemy? Why do you give money to people who are out there consciously every day trying to undermine what's good for you?"

DeLay would not have become Republican whip if it had not been for his K Street lobbying allies. When Republicans took over the House in 1995, Gingrich's personal choice for whip was Pennsylvania Republican Bob Walker. Gingrich viewed DeLay as a potential threat—correctly as it turned out—and he saw that the addition of DeLay would create an all-southern GOP leadership, with one Georgian and two Texans. DeLay appeared to be a certain loser, except for two developments that had gone largely unnoticed by Gingrich and Walker: during 1994, as the possibility of a GOP takeover became more likely, DeLay had called on his K Street allies to funnel cash to Republican candidates making sure that DeLay got credit, and, after the election, he had asked them to work the Republican members in behalf of DeLay, just as they would in behalf of key legislation. In analyzing his own victory, DeLay said:

> You cannot be effective in this job unless you have an outside group that supports what you're doing inside. So in anything, in any project that I've ever worked on, I've always had a steering

group of outside people that I can trust, that can get things done, and they've proven they can get things done. And that's what I did in the whip race. . . . My closest allies that have worked on things they weren't even paid for during my 10 years here, but at the same time, were very interested in me and making sure that I won, that we were philosophically in tune, and they wanted to see that I carried on.

Key members of the DeLay K Street team at that time were Bruce Gates of the National-American Wholesale Grocers Association, David Rehr of the National Beer Wholesalers Association, Dan Mattoon of BellSouth Corporation, Robert Rusbuldt of the Independent Insurance Agents of America, and Elaine Graham of the National Restaurant Association. "We'd rustle up checks for the guy and make sure Tom got the credit," said the beer wholesalers' Rehr. "So when new members voted for majority whip, they'd say, 'I wouldn't be here if it wasn't for Tom DeLay.'" The result was that DeLay beat Walker 119 to 80, with the crucial help of Republican freshmen elected with DeLay-raised cash: 52 of the 73 GOP freshmen backed DeLay.

DeLay—who at this writing stands indicted by a Texas grand jury for conspiring to illegally funnel corporate money into state legislative contests and is under investigation in connection with the lobbying activities of Jack Abramoff—established a precedent for winning and exercising power by building a rock-solid alliance with business and with the lobbying community. The man who in February 2006 replaced Delay as his colleagues sought distance from mounting lobbying scandals, Education and the Workforce Committee Chairman John Boehner, is as close to K Street as anyone in the House. Blunt, DeLay's protégé, has followed DeLay's footsteps both in his fundraising practices and, as majority whip, taking over responsibility for developing a formal structure for the relationship between lobbyists and the House leadership. As DeLay's troubles worsened in the fall of 2005 and the jockeying between Blunt and Boehner to replace him intensified, Boehner's supporters pointedly leaked a story to The Hill, a publication that focuses on Congress, listing the influential members of Boehner's lobbyist inner circle. The story, designed to counter Blunt's growing strength among lobbyists, had an ideal headline from Boehner's point of view, "Boehner can rely on K Street Cabinet." While in the not too distant past linkage with lobbyists would have been a liability for an aspiring leader, it is currently an asset.

Now that Republicans have pushed the ethics envelope further than it has ever been pushed, Democrats are following suit, cementing the politician-lobbyist alliance as an accepted Washington practice. House Democratic Whip Steny Hoyer (D-Maryland) has initiated his own "K Street Project." Stacey Farnen, a Hoyer spokeswoman, declared, "We're not ceding ground to Republicans in the business community. This is a long-term effort to build relationships and work with business where we can." Senate Minority Leader Harry Reid (D-Nevada) meets every two weeks with "Democratic-leaning" business lobbyists, who noted that Reid supported business-backed bankruptcy legislation and did not block class action lawsuit legislation. Most Democratic constituency groups, including plaintiffs' lawyers, organized labor, and consumer groups, opposed both bills.

Rewards of the Merger: Each Gaining Advantage from the Presence of the Other

The rewards for those on both sides of the merger between business and the Republican Party have been plentiful. For those on the political side of the ledger, Republican candidates are winning. There is a guaranteed source of revenue for campaigns and the party organizations, and Washington lobbying is a lucrative and expanding industry with more than $2 billion in annual reported revenues, offering opportunity and jobs to political operatives, congressional staffers, and out-of-office elected officials. On the business side of the ledger, corporate tax burdens have fallen, regulations have been weakened, trial lawyers have been reigned in, bankruptcy laws have been tightened to the advantage of creditors, and the share of income and wealth going to those at the top of the income distribution has grown dramatically. In effect, the GOP has become the party drawing unified support from corporate America just when the balance of private sector power has become decisively tilted in favor of business and against its challengers in organized labor, the environmental movement, and liberalism generally.

After years of winning elections on the basis of a conservative populism that capitalized on hostility to elites—both liberal and corporate—the Republican Party of George Bush, Tom DeLay, Dennis Hastert, and Bill Frist has developed techniques to keep both E. Stanley O'Neill, president and CEO of Merrill Lynch, and James Dobson, the fire-breathing head of Focus on the Family, not only in the same political family but each gaining advantage from the presence of the other. The result has been the creation of a Republican fundraising and patronage machine, with the party organizations, the elected officials and their staffs, the lobbying–trade association community, the religious right, and the broader sociocultural conservative community all working synergistically together. The system provides a career path that ends in riches for the loyal and successful, in a source of political money, in organized leverage over members of the House and Senate, and in favorable legislation and beneficial executive branch decisions for the lobbying community.

GOING FOR THE JUGULAR

Nowhere is a major difference between liberals and conservatives more apparent than in their differing use of tax-exempt, nonparty, independent expenditure organizations, known as 527s and 501(c)(4)s, depending on which section of the tax code they are organized under. From 1980, when Terry Dolan's National Conservative Political Action Committee (NCPAC) helped to defeat six Democratic senators, to the 2004 campaign when Swift Boat Veterans for Truth (a 527 organization) ran crucial television ads, the Republican "independent" or third-party groups have gone for the kill, determined to extinguish their Democratic rivals. Democratic independent groups, in contrast to their Republican counterparts, concentrated much more on filling a role traditionally performed by the state and national parties—getting out the vote—and to a limited, and generally unsuccessful, extent on running anti-Bush ads, none of which proved to have the lasting value of the Republican-allied ads in shaping the campaign.

The Republican 527 groups set out with the explicit goal of making Kerry unacceptable to the voters, and they were prepared to do whatever it took. Chris LaCivita, senior adviser to the GOP-backed 527 organization Swift Boat Veterans for Truth, speaking in

December 2004 to a post-election conference of campaign managers at the Institute of Politics at Harvard, described the role of his tax-exempt nonprofit group and the eleven swift boat ads it generated in the Bush-Kerry race:

> The Swift Boat wasn't a specific ad, because we did eleven, but I think it was the entire campaign effort. Basically, the bottom line was this. In June about ten of those guys [veterans opposed to Kerry] came to me and said, hey we held a press conference in May and no one bothered to give us any attention. . . . How do we get attention? I said, the only way you can essentially get attention is if you raise enough money and put it on TV. . . . That first ad was a buy of a half million dollars. The intention was not to generate repetition through gross rating points. . . . Where they [Democratic strategists] underestimated was that it was nothing but an earned [free] media play, plain and simple. The pure intention of that first ad was to generate earned media about the message we were conveying. And yes, it was in your face. There was no other way to communicate it. . . . [T]he fact of the matter is that—granted I need to say this for the record because my lawyer's here—our intention was never to influence the outcome of the election. [Laughter] We are an issue advocacy group and the purpose of our organization is to educate the public about issues. Never once in our ads, or in the $3 million worth of mail that we did, did we ever say "defeat John Kerry" or "vote for George Bush."

According to the American Enterprise Institute, "In the end, the Swift Boat vets raised more than $26 million and took their message directly to the public with a grassroots advertising and personal testimony campaign. Their first ads appeared in early August when Kerry was leading the Presidential race. They were widely credited with reversing that lead, which Kerry never won back."

The attacks on Kerry by the Swift Boat Veterans were supported on a number of fronts and coordinated with a series of other events. The top lawyer in President Bush's reelection campaign, Benjamin L. Ginsberg, acknowledged on August 24, 2004, that he had been advising the Swift Boat Veterans seeking to discredit Kerry's military record. Ginsberg, the chief outside counsel to the Bush campaign, said in an interview: "I've done some work for them [Swift Boat Veterans]. . . . The law lets lawyers do that . . . and does not include lawyers among the coordinated political activities" that are prohibited by federal election law. Nonetheless, Ginsberg stepped down from the Bush campaign the day after his involvement with the Swift Boat Veterans appeared in the newspaper.

Former senator and presidential nominee Bob Dole, a Bush campaign surrogate, appeared on August 22, 2004, on CNN's *Late Edition*, shortly before the beginning of the Democratic convention. Dole joined in the attack on Kerry for his role as a leader of the Vietnam Veterans against the War and for giving testimony, in that capacity, in 1971 before the Senate Foreign Relations Committee, casting aspersions on Kerry's heroism in winning a silver star, a bronze star, and three purple hearts:

> I mean, one day he's saying that we were shooting civilians, cutting off their ears, cutting off their heads, throwing away his medals or his ribbons. The next day he's standing there, "I want to be president because I'm a Vietnam veteran," . . . making these allegations of atrocities, if you will, war crimes committed by U.S. troops. . . . Maybe he should apologize to all the other 2.5 million veterans who served. He wasn't the only one in Vietnam. And here's, you know, a good guy, good friend. I respect his record. But three Purple Hearts and never bled that I know of. I mean, they're all superficial wounds. Three Purple Hearts and you're out [exempt from combat duty].

Five days before Dole's August 2004 TV appearance, the conservative nonprofit group Judicial Watch filed a highly publicized complaint with the inspectors general of the Department of Defense and the Department of the Navy calling for an investigation into Kerry's war medals.[2] The formal complaint read:

> The recent publication of the book, *Unfit for Command* by John E. O'Neill and Jerome R. Corsi, PhD, . . . raise[s] extremely grave questions concerning the legitimacy and propriety of the

---

[2] The Associated Press reported on September 18, 2004, that "the Navy's chief investigator concluded Friday that procedures were followed properly in the approval of Sen. John Kerry's Silver Star, Bronze Star and Purple Heart medals, according to an internal Navy memo" (Robert Burns, "Navy Says Kerry's Service Awards Were Properly Approved," The Associated Press, September 18, 2004, available online at http://pqasb.pqarchiver.com/ap/699846201.html?did=699846201&FMT=ABS&FMTS=FT&date=Sep+18%2C+2004&author=ROBERT+BURNS&pub=Associated+Press&desc=Navy+says+Kerry%27s+service+awards+were+properly+approved [accessed May 2006]).

awards Senator Kerry received for heroism and wounds received from enemy fire in combat. . . . Questions of fraud, false official statements and abuse by Senator Kerry must be answered. . . . A second matter concerns . . . dishonorable and possibly unlawful actions by Senator Kerry during the early 1970s, . . . so grievously damaging to the dignity, honor and traditions of the U.S. Navy and the American republic that the Secretary of the Navy may be compelled to revoke Senator Kerry's awards.

Regnery—the premier American conservative publisher—in August 2004 released *Unfit for Command: Swift Boat Veterans Speak Out against John Kerry* by former Swift Boat Captain John O'Neill. O'Neill had been a political enemy of Kerry's since 1971 when, representing Vietnam Veterans for a Just Peace, he had debated anti-war veteran Kerry on ABC's *The Dick Cavett Show*. According to Michael Dobbs of the *Washington Post* writing on August 28, 2004,

> Archival records show that O'Neill, who has been making the rounds of the TV talk shows this month to promote his best-selling anti-Kerry book, *Unfit for Command*, was encouraged to go on television in 1971 by President Richard M. Nixon and his aide Charles W. Colson. Nixon regarded Kerry as the antiwar movement's most effective and articulate spokesman, and the president was desperate to undercut the activist's popular appeal.

Ken Mehlman summarized the 2004 Republican election strategy this way: "We had to . . . remind people why we went to war, remind people about the War on Terror, and remind people about Senator Kerry's, shall we put it, complicated record on discussing these questions."

➤ ◄

The additional discrediting of Democratic presidential candidate General Wesley Clark reflects the resources that conservatives and the Republican Party were willing to invest to crush the Democratic opposition. Clark had outstanding military credentials— thirty-four years in the army, the Defense Distinguished Service Medal, Silver Star, Legion of Merit, Bronze Star, Purple Heart,

Meritorious Service Medal, the Army Commendation Medal, and the Presidential Medal of Freedom. He also had international experience that was unusually strong for an American presidential candidate. Clark had served as supreme allied commander–Europe, NATO, 1997–2000; commander-in-chief–U.S. European Command, U.S. Army, 1997–2000; commander-in-chief–U.S. Southern Command, U.S. Army, Panama, 1996–1997. Finally, Clark had been first in his class at West Point and a Rhodes Scholar.

Those credentials had promised to insulate Clark's candidacy from charges of Democratic weakness on national security, and his military record stood in direct contrast to Bush's own controversial service in the Air National Guard during the Vietnam war. Clark, however, faced an exceptionally hostile reception from the conservative military establishment from the moment that he presented himself as a Democratic candidate in the 2004 race.

At a forum in September 2003, retired General Hugh Shelton was asked if he would support Wesley Clark for president. Shelton, the former chairman of the Joint Chiefs of Staff, providing no further detail, said: "I've known Wes for a long time. I will tell you the reason he came out of Europe early had to do with integrity and character issues, things that are very near and dear to my heart. . . . I'll just say Wes won't get my vote."

On November 6, 2003, retired General Norman Schwarzkopf, George H. W. Bush's commander-in-chief of U.S. forces during Operation Desert Shield/Storm (1990–1992), said on CNBC, also without providing detail or evidence, "I think the greatest condemnation against [Clark] . . . came from the chairman of the Joint Chiefs of Staff when he was a NATO commander. I mean, he was fired as a NATO commander, and when Hugh Shelton said he was fired because of matters of character and integrity, that is a very, very damning statement, which says, 'If that's the case, he's not the right man for president,' as far as I'm concerned."

Clark's appointment as supreme allied commander–Europe (SACEUR) was terminated in May 2000, several months early, by Secretary of Defense William Cohen. Cohen was at that time the only Republican serving in Clinton's second-term cabinet. Clark's NATO job went to General Joseph Ralston, who went on to become vice-chairman of Cohen's lucrative Washington defense lobbying firm, the Cohen Group.

Coordination Prohibited by Federal Election Law

Tax-exempt, independent expenditure groups are prohibited by federal election law from coordinating with the presidential campaigns themselves. Nonetheless, a high degree of mutually reinforcing activity appeared in the advertising strategies of the conservative 527 groups and the Bush-Cheney campaign. In October 2004, less than a month before the election, the Bush-Cheney campaign itself ran a television commercial known as "Wolves":

> ANNOUNCER: In an increasingly dangerous world, . . . even after the first terrorist attack on America, . . . John Kerry and the liberals in Congress voted to slash America's intelligence operations—by 6 billion dollars—cuts so deep they would have weakened America's defenses. And weakness attracts those who are waiting to do America harm.
>
> *[On screen: Several wolves eye the camera, as if preparing to attack.]*
>
> BUSH: I'm George W. Bush and I approve this message.

➤ ◄

Progress for America (PFA), a conservative 527 organization and thus prohibited from consulting with the Bush-Cheney campaign, moved in the summer of 2004 to make the war on terror central to the election. In a series of nine commercials that began on July 4, the group paid for ads titled "What If" and "Why Do We Fight," culminating in the widely viewed "Ashley's Story" commercial.

"Ashley" had first been shown to donors early in the summer. According to Brian McCabe, the executive director of PFA, "We knew we had a goldmine. The emotional response from donors was amazing. We had 50 percent of the people cry the first time they saw the ad." The Ashley ad was held until the closing two weeks of the campaign for maximum election day impact. "We sharpened the focus on the issue of the War on Terror. From when we ran the first ad in June all the way through for us it was the War on Terror. We wanted to compare different people's policies and issues and beliefs on the War on Terror. Ashley's story fit right into that," McCabe said.

PFA raised and invested a total of $35 million in the Ashley commercial, $16.7 million for actual television time and the rest for a "surround" campaign, including the widespread purchase of Internet banner ads, 20 million emailed copies of the Ashley ad itself, production, and other promotional costs. In three separate post-election surveys of voters, the Swift Boat, Wolves, and Ashley commercials topped all competitors as the most effective.

"Ashley's Story" Script

LYNN FAULKNER: My wife, Wendy, was murdered by terrorists on September 11.

[On screen: Lynn Faulkner, Mason, Ohio]

ANNOUNCER [v/o]: The Faulkners' daughter Ashley closed up emotionally. But when President George W. Bush came to Lebanon, Ohio, she went to see him as she had with her mother four years before.

[On screen: Lebanon, Ohio]

LINDA PRINCE: He walked toward me and I said, "Mr. President, this young lady lost her mother in the World Trade Center."

[On screen: Linda Prince, family friend]

ASHLEY FAULKNER: And he turned around and he came back and he said, "I know that's hard. Are you all right?"

[On screen: Ashley Faulkner, Mason, Ohio]

LINDA PRINCE: Our president took Ashley in his arms and just embraced her. And it was at that moment that we saw Ashley's eyes fill up with tears.

ASHLEY FAULKNER: He's the most powerful man in the world and all he wants to do is make sure I'm safe, that I'm OK.

LYNN FAULKNER: What I saw was what I want to see in the heart and in the soul of the man who sits in the highest elected office in our country.

ANNOUNCER [v/o]: Progress for America Voter Fund is responsible for the content of this message.

A Powerful Tool to Motivate Major Republican Donors

The major Democratic 527 organization, America Coming To-gether (ACT), was designed to fill in for weak Democratic Party apparatus in many key battleground states. ACT did so by creating what was intended to become a permanent, ongoing structure in these states. It was to remain available both in future national elections and for voter mobilization to influence state legislatures, city councils, and congressional delegations. Instead, the major donors to ACT, George Soros and Peter Lewis, both committed social liberals who had—with much public attention—donated millions of dollars to support the decriminalization of marijuana, ceased contributing after the 2004 defeat of Kerry, and ACT folded. From the Republican vantage point, Soros and Lewis represented a major threat, but their huge contributions to Democratic groups (Soros $27 million, Lewis $24 million) paradoxically served as a powerful tool to motivate Republican donors.

The Soros money encouraged deep-pocketed Republicans, including Texas developer Bob J. Perry, who gave $8.1 million to conservative 527s; Texas corporate-takeover specialist T. Boone Pickens, who gave $5.2 million; San Diego developer and Chargers football team owner Alex Spanos, $5 million; subprime lender Ameriquest's Roland and Dawn Arnall, $5 million; radio network owner Jerry Perenchio, $4.1 million; Wal-Mart heir Alice Walton, $2.6 million; and Amway executives Richard DeVos Sr. and Jay van Andel, $2 million each. The Arnalls are calculated to have donated or raised more than $12 million for the GOP from 2000 through 2004.

DEMOCRATS: MONEY PUSHES THE PARTY LEFT

The financing of the 2004 presidential election strengthened the power of the already dominant culturally liberal elite within the Democratic Party, pushing the Democrats farther to the left on key social issues and in essence handing the Republican Party yet another incremental advantage. In effect, the McCain-Feingold campaign finance reform legislation served to profoundly accelerate partisan polarization in the 2004 campaign cycle, a development beneficial to the GOP that year. This polarization was accentuated by the socially progressive/liberal sources of financing for Democratic presidential candidates. Here is what happened:

During the 2003–2004 primaries, both major party nominees raised record amounts, more than doubling the $101.5 million record set just four years earlier by George W. Bush. For the 2004 race, Bush raised $260,565,424, and John F. Kerry was close behind with $248,021,185. Kerry not only came within striking distance of Bush, but he also tapped into the small donor universe to a degree that had never been even approximated on the Democratic side of the aisle.

For decades, starting in the 1960s with the help of conservative fundraiser Richard Viguerie, among others, the GOP had built a steadily growing base of direct mail contributors, many of them social-racial or economic conservatives—often both. Until 2004, the Democratic Party and its candidates had largely neglected development of a parallel direct mail base. With little continuity in the leadership and staff of the major Democratic committees—national, senatorial, and congressional—Democrats depended much more than Republicans on the quadrennial cultivation of culturally liberal major donors to prop up their finances.

In the 2004 primary contest, a sequence of events turned the election in a financially transformative direction for the Democrats. First, Howard Dean demonstrated that strong opposition to the Bush administration, a position against the Iraq war, advocacy for gay rights, and support for "participatory democracy" could produce a groundswell of financial backing from men and women who had never before given to a candidate but whose intense hostility to Bush and desire to push American politics in a progressive direction were prime motivators. The Internet provided the means to access these progressive, wired Bush-haters. In contrast to direct mail that worked to the political advantage of Republicans, the Internet had become, in the years before the 2004 election, an increasingly powerful tool for liberals and the left. Early evidence of its influence emerged during House and Senate proceedings to impeach President Clinton, when software millionaires Wes Boyd and Joan Blades created MoveOn to oppose impeachment and to encourage voters to "move on" to other issues. Boyd and Blades soon discovered that they had created a liberal grassroots cyber-movement that could be mobilized for multiple goals, including massive email and letter-writing campaigns, new forms of political interactivity, and Internet fundraising.

Dean's campaign manager, Joseph Trippi—a longtime Democratic operative who hitched the Dean campaign to MoveOn and to the online social networking portal MeetUp—had a background in technology as well. A former aerospace engineering major from San Jose State, Trippi had worked at two information technology firms between campaigns—Progeny ("managing customized Linux platforms") and Wave Systems ("offering a comprehensive trusted computing ecosystem"). Both firms were unusual in their reliance on Internet feedback from customers and investors. According to Trippi, Wave was "attracting hundreds of posts per day from so-called 'Wavoids'—at all hours of the night. What kept them coming back was the fact that Wave executives were actually reading what the investors wrote. . . . The people involved in this community were doctors, neurosurgeons, psychiatrists, professors." These people were just the kinds of highly educated and engaged Web users Dean would set out to recruit.

Trippi saw the potential for the Dean campaign in this kind of "democratized user participation." As Trippi puts it, "I always wondered how could you take that same collaboration that occurs in Linux and open source and apply it here. What would happen if there were a way to do that and engage everybody in a presidential campaign?" Trippi drafted young, tech-oriented operatives—most importantly, by his account, Matt Gross—to set up a Dean Web site and blog, eventually with a feedback comments section and—critically important—credit card donation capabilities.

As of January 1, 2004, Dean had netted a total of $41.02 million, with about $27 million raised through the Internet. As one online observer put it, "The Internet is the killer application for generating grassroots political interest." By early 2004, Trippi and his team had established the Web as the single most important political fundraising advance since Richard Viguerie began the direct mail revolution forty years earlier.

Kerry Back in the Money Game

Dean and MoveOn mobilized massive Democratic constituencies so that, when John Kerry effectively locked up the nomination in early March of 2004, he became the beneficiary of thousands upon thousands of liberal Democrats and Bush critics who were waiting for the selection of a Democratic candidate they could support. Less than a month after locking up the Democratic nomination in March 2004, Kerry—with twenty-one-year-old antiwar activist Eli Pariser, former union organizer and software programmer Zack Exley, and thirty-two-year-old former Silicon Valley entrepreneur Josh Ross providing high-tech skills—was back in the money game, despite having had to mortgage his Beacon Hill townhouse just a few months earlier to stay afloat during the primaries.

"The best fundraiser for John Kerry's presidential campaign is George W. Bush," said Miami business lawyer John Cosgrove, who collected roughly $150,000 for Kerry and more than that for the Democratic National Committee. "The world changed for us on January 19," the day Kerry won the Iowa caucuses and became the most likely candidate to take on Bush, Kerry fundraising chair Louis Sussman said. "There had been somebody I had been trying and trying to reach, but he never returned my calls. After Iowa, he called and wanted to know if I had changed my cell phone, that he had been trying to call me."

Double the Number of Small Donations, 2000 to 2004, from Culturally Progressive Democrats

The contrast to the election four years earlier was striking. In 2000, Al Gore received $6,833,27 in small donations under $200, or 20 percent of the total $34,477,100 that he raised from individuals. In 2004, Kerry raised 11.5 times as much in small gifts as Gore had done, $78,824,097, which made up 37 percent of Kerry's total. Bush, in turn, raised virtually the same amount of money as Kerry in small, under $200 gifts, or 31 percent of his 2004 total, a significant increase from the 20 percent in small donations to Bush in 2000.

These new Kerry-Democratic donors—many inherited from the Dean camp—were often secular progressives, white, wealthier, better educated, and less ethnically diverse than other Democrats, and adamantly against the war in Iraq. A disproportionate number were well-educated baby boomer college graduates between the ages of forty-five and sixty-four. Many were driven by anger at President Bush and by anger at what they saw as the punitive moralism of the Christian right. "I'm very disturbed by Bush, the theocratic nature of his presidency, the subliminal nature of his speech that makes references to the Bible," said Thomas Anderson, forty-six, of Baton Rouge. Anderson, owner of a security firm, had never given more than $20 to a political candidate before 2004. By mid-August 2004, Anderson had given $300 in three $100 Internet donations to Kerry, and he expected to give as much as $1,000. "This was a big decision of ours; this means we are not going to go out to dinner a few times," Anderson said. A supporter of gay marriage, Anderson objected strenuously to what he saw as the Christian right's attempt to impose moral conformity on society: "No one has the right to tell anyone how to live, as long as they are not hurting anybody."

Patrick Rankin, an antiques dealer in Pilot Point, Texas, gave Kerry $1,000 and said he was particularly disturbed over "this unprecedented move to invade Iraq." Rankin voiced particular concern that when Bush makes decisions it's "just him and the Lord."

Another major source of Democratic cash was the angry gay and lesbian community, again driven by Bush and his election-year advocacy of a constitutional amendment banning gay marriage. Robert Farmer, Kerry's chief fundraiser and both Clinton's and Dukakis' before that, is gay, and he was joined in the drive for Kerry by many leaders of local and national gay movements, including Tom Daley, a consultant to Hotels.com, Washington DC investor Claire Lucas, and Jeff Anderson, finance co-chair of the Alice B. Toklas Lesbian, Gay, Bisexual, Transgender Democratic Club, and his partner, Jeff Soukup.

The strongest economic interest group to back Kerry was the trial lawyers' or plaintiffs' bar. This support cannot be construed, however, as backing from the business community; trial lawyers thrive on suing major American corporations and carefully select as defendants businesses with vast reserves to pay off large judgments. Opposition to trial lawyers has unified most of the business community in support of Bush-backed legislation to severely restrict the ability of the plaintiffs' bar to file suit. Indeed, one of the first priorities of the Bush administration was tort reform.

Kerry received substantial contributions from men and women who work for major corporations such as Time Warner and Microsoft and for the large Wall Street investment backing firms. These donors were not making contributions to advance the interests of their employers through tax breaks or favorable trade legislation, however, as were their Republican counterparts. In fact, Kerry threatened to rescind many of the Bush tax cuts that helped their employers. These donors were giving in the main because they were social liberals.

"Democrats have a different demographic," Green said. "They tend to be drawn much more from professionals, a lot of lawyers who do not work for corporations, especially trial lawyers, lots of engineers, computer folks, college professors, journalists, academics, artists and entertainers." These findings are strongly supported by the occupation data listed by presidential donors. Five times as many corporate CEOs, presidents, and chairmen gave to Bush as to Kerry: 17,770 to 3,393. Conversely, the number of professors who gave to Kerry is eleven times the number of those who gave to Bush, 3,508 to 322. Actors split 212 for Kerry, 12 for Bush; authors, 110 to 3; librarians, 223 to 1; journalists, 93 to 1; social workers, 415 to 32. At the top of the fundraising pyramid—the fundraisers who individually collected $100,000 or more—top executives in major industries such as energy, agribusiness, construction, and transportation were plentiful in the Bush campaign but nonexistent in the Kerry campaign.

Kerry's fundraisers were members of the Democratic liberal social elite:

- Susie Tompkins Buell, co-founder of Esprit Clothing, backer of groups supporting abortion rights such as Emily's List, America Coming Together (ACT), and other causes on the left;

- Peter Buttenweiser, benefactor of the Brady Center to Prevent Gun Violence;

- Anne Cox Chambers, supporter of liberal international organizations such as the Institut Pasteur and the Council of American Ambassadors;

- Lana Moresky, former president of the Ohio National Organization of Women;

- Nancy Zirkin, deputy director of the Leadership Conference on Civil Rights; and

- Kim Cranston, director of the Institute for Organizational Evolution, program manager of TransparentCommerce.org, member of the Social Venture Network Advisory Board, former director of Corporate Social Responsibility, and co-founder and former president of the Center for Participation in Democracy.

The first clear signal of the consequences of the growing power of the cultural left in the Democratic Party after the 2004 Kerry defeat was the selection of Howard Dean to become chairman of the Democratic National Committee. Filling a post that has traditionally gone to a backroom negotiator skilled at keeping factional disputes to a minimum and at winning the hearts and wallets of wealthy donors, Dean is the first explicitly ideological chairman of the DNC. Dean's claim to fame is that he was the presidential candidate of 2004 able to recruit a new universe of liberal small donors online, attracting support primarily through his outspoken opposition to the Iraq War, his claim to represent "the Democratic wing of the Democratic Party," and his sponsorship of gay civil union legislation as governor of Vermont.

Dean's campaign mobilized half a million donors and political volunteers, and those supporters helped put him, in 2005, in charge of the Democratic Party. The demographic and ideological characteristics of Dean's supporters, as analyzed by the Pew Research Center, reflect, at least in part, the future direction of the party. They are, first and foremost, socially and morally liberal, as are many of Kerry's strongest supporters. Eighty-two percent of Dean activists describe themselves as liberal, twice as many as the 41 percent of Democratic convention delegates and three times as many as Democratic voters. While half of Democratic voters and a majority of the electorate as a whole oppose gay marriage, 91 percent of Dean backers support gay marriage. They are much richer than the majority of Democratic voters, with 29 percent having family incomes over $100,000 compared with just 10 percent of those who cast Democratic ballots. This constituency will not define the Democratic Party, but it will, at least through the 2008 election, significantly shape the character and agenda of the party.

FUNDRAISING CONSTITUENCIES OF THE TWO PARTIES

Looking toward the elections of 2008 and beyond, there are striking differences in the fundraising constituencies of the two parties. The business-corporate commitment to the GOP is likely to remain durable as long as the Republican Party candidate is competitive. There is little doubt now that on regulatory, tax, and other key federal policies, the Republican Party is firmly aligned with business leaders; there is little reason to anticipate a collapse of backing from corporate America. As long as business is perceived as the prime source of national well-being and as the generator of jobs and wealth, the liabilities of this alliance are outweighed by the benefits.

The Democratic Party, in contrast, faces two substantial problems given the marked social liberalism of its newfound Internet donor base. The first is whether this donor base will continue to be active if the Republican Party does not nominate someone in the style of George W. Bush who provokes liberals' anger and fear. Will this base be active in 2008 if, for example, the GOP nominates Senator John McCain or a comparable candidate? When McCain ran in 2000, his strength was in his appeal to independent and Democratic voters—so-called crossover voters. The primaries he won were in states that were not restricted to registered Republicans and that allowed Democrats and independents to vote in Republican primaries. McCain and Republicans in his social-libertarian mold who also credibly support civil rights have neither the agenda nor the style to provoke the left.

The second problem is that the emerging Democratic Internet donor base may demand that an eventual nominee take stands on issues that will make him or her unelectable in the November general election. Although the issue framework of 2008 has yet to be determined, the financial pressure on Democratic candidates to endorse same-sex marriage, to take a less forceful tack in the war on terror, to push farther left on issues of secularization, crime, illegal immigrants, and other controversial matters is considerable. Such stands could generate pushback from large numbers of even strongly Democratic voters and prove difficult to defend on the stump.

➤ ◄

The complexity of the role of money in elections pales in comparison with the subtle but powerful ways race and sex, especially the sexual and women's rights revolutions, have altered the nation's politics and parties over the past forty years. The next chapter explores further the crucial role of these issues in building the contemporary Republican Party.

5 The Two Revolutions

Political polarization, the rise of the conservative movement, and the success of the Republican Party are best understood in the context of larger movements within American society. Over the past three and a half decades, America has passed through two major revolutions. The *first* is social and cultural, driven by a commitment to equality and the extension of rights to previously marginalized groups, including the 51 percent of the population made up of women. The *second* is technological, scientific, and economic, opening up a new era of hypercompetition.

These revolutions have created two roughly equal partisan coalitions, one on the left, the other on the right. Neither coalition is based solely on socioeconomic class, and each has the potential to produce an election-day majority. The Republican Party, spearheading the center-right coalition, has been determined to prevent the emergence of a liberal majority, and the effort has been hugely successful. To assemble a winning political majority, the GOP, with strategic and tactical acumen, has tapped into and capitalized on the sense of dislocation and conflict generated by rapid cultural modernization among many middle- and working-class voters.

OVERVIEW OF THE TWO REVOLUTIONS

The Civil Rights, Women's Rights, and Sexual Revolution

The sociocultural revolution, encompassing the civil rights, immigration rights, women's rights, and sexual revolutions, was set off by a burgeoning, post–World War II human rights movement (including decolonization and liberation movements around the world). American society experienced a race-based freedom movement; the deregulation of sexual mores—pioneered by male vanguardists such as Henry Miller, Jack Kerouac, Allen Ginsberg, and Hugh Hefner; claims for women's rights—with avatars such as Simone de Beauvoir, Anaïs Nin, Erica Jong, and Nancy Friday; and the invention of new contraceptive technologies, most notably, in the early 1960s, the oral contraceptive pill.

The contraceptive revolution—as well as innovations in antibiotics, surgical abortion, fertility techniques allowing women to postpone childbearing, the industrialization of infant nutrition (bottles, formula, baby food), and the professionalization of childcare—eliminated many of the principal factors determining the historic imbalance of power between the sexes and the traditional shape of the social world. Biomedical invention played a critical role in emancipating women from their subordinate status. Scientific breakthrough dovetailed with new government policies prohibiting race- and sex-based discrimination; together these developments made possible the massive entry of women into the workforce—including, increasingly, the mothers of small children—empowered for the first time to reliably control pregnancy and family size.

Further consequences of these new, interrelated developments were visible in Vatican II (1965), which spurred a new level of tolerance (and reaction) toward modernized sex and sex roles within the Catholic Church. Other developments included the spread of no-fault divorce, first enacted into law (by an all-male legislature) in California in 1969, the beginning of the end of marriage as a life-long commitment, and the extension of the right of sexual privacy to married couples (*Griswold v. Connecticut*, 1965), then to unmarried couples, and last to gays and lesbians (*Lawrence et al. v. Texas*, 2003). Thus the sexual revolution became a mass movement for both men and women, accompanied by an outpouring of cultural production supporting a ripening ethos of individualism and self-actualization. At the same time, it stimulated the emergence of new political polarizations—proponents of these changes on one side and a backlash against them on the other—resulting in the emerging "culture wars."

These wars have not been confined to American soil; they underpin much of the antagonism between fundamentalism and modernism that characterizes both domestic and international affairs. According to research by University of Michigan political scientist Ronald Inglehart and Pippa Norris of Harvard University, "The most basic cultural fault line between the West and Islam does not concern democracy—it involves issues of gender equality and sexual liberalization."

The Technological, Scientific, and Economic Revolution

The second great transformation of the past fifty years was the technological-scientific-economic revolution, which contributed not only to the women's rights and sexual freedom movements but also to an ongoing business revolution. This change resulted in the globalization of commerce, economic deregulation, the spread of quantitative methods, the emergence of a digital sector, the development of new forms of financial engineering—including new forms of mortgage finance—multinational corporations, new developments in weaponry, and an increasingly powerful and contentious role for America in the world.

While generating economic growth and higher standards of living, including the highest levels of home ownership ever recorded, this transformation eroded safe harbors such as unions, protected industries, hereditary oligopolies, secure lifetime employment, and traditional community structures—as well as, over time, international support for America's global dominion. Scientific and technological advances have forced an explosion of entrepreneurial innovation, breakthroughs in information and communications technology, the electronic control of capital, and groundbreaking progress in medicine, biotechnology, and genetics. They have also generated unparalleled levels of wealth and debt (national and household), sharply intensified competition and inequality, increased the potential lethality of war, magnified the dangers of conflict, reduced child mortality, increased longevity, swelled the population, threatened the environment (even while offering potential solutions), and raised the stakes for both winners and losers.

The Two Revolutions: Opportunity and Backlash

In many respects, the social/cultural and the technological/economic revolutions have been mutually reinforcing. Without new reproductive technologies, there would have been no women's rights or sexual revolution. Without the mechanization of agriculture, there would have been no civil rights revolution. In other respects, the two revolutions are in conflict, generating tension between America's historic dedication to equality, on the one hand, and the entrenched commitment to achievement, competition, meritocracy, scientific innovation, wealth generation, risk-taking, and change, on the other—a commitment viewed by many as essential to the maintenance of America's position in the world.

To a remarkable degree, the technological/scientific/economic revolution, while opening doors for African Americans, for previously marginalized ethnic groups, and for women, also further empowered those on the top rungs of the socioeconomic ladder, making the rich richer and broadening the inequality gap. The sociocultural revolution, which had the explicit goal of giving power to women, has also worked to free men from many of the restraints and obligations in the realm of family relations to which they had been subject in the past.

Just as hypercompetition eliminated the economic shelters found within protected markets and paternalistic organizations, producing upward mobility for many but also widespread anxiety and concentrations of joblessness and poverty among the disadvantaged, the social and cultural revolutions have eaten away at the once-safe enclaves of the family, marriage, religion, the neighborhood, and tribal ties. The expansion of modern contraception in the sixties, coupled with the guarantee by the state (through the civil rights legislation of that era) of full citizenship rights for minorities and women, recast what had been widely accepted as the "natural" order. In the aftermath, men and women, blacks and whites, native-born Americans and immigrants from less-developed countries directly competed for resources—jobs, status, territory, political power, authority, and agency. Although many formerly subordinated racial and ethnic minorities and women improved their positions significantly, the advantage accruing to the most powerful and dominant members of society remained substantial and even grew.

As the structure of custom, law, and morality that maintained the old order broke down, one of the most striking developments was the atrophy of marriage as a permanent institution. Along with the partial de-institutionalization of marriage and the growing acceptance of nonmarital sex, an earlier ethos of male and female honor was transformed. Within a very short period of time, chastity was no longer a mark of virtue in a woman, nor was serial seduction and betrayal any longer widely viewed as a mark of dishonor in a man.

In the course of the social upheavals of the sexual revolution, the ideals of sexual virtue and of self-sacrificing motherhood were demoted, as was the heroism of the soldier and the Olympian figure of the father who "knows best." Traditional gender roles were deposed by the historically novel principle of the equality of the sexes. In that context, transient consensual sexual relations for men and women became normative, as did single motherhood and a shift from an ethic of life-long family obligation to one of serial monogamy—or of even shorter-term liaisons.

➤ ◄

Medical science and public health measures (sanitation of water and waste, quarantine, inoculation, and antibiotic therapies) also fueled social trends by ensuring higher rates of survival for American children than in the past:

> Around the time of World War I, 1 in 10 babies born in the United States died before age 1. The infant mortality rate for minority infants approached 1 in 5. These rates are similar to those found today in some of the poorest countries of the world, such as Sierra Leone and Ethiopia. Today infant and child deaths are much less common. There are 7 infant deaths for every 1,000 babies born in the United States. In 2000, the death rate for children ages 1 to 4 was 0.3 per 1,000 population.

As parents had fewer children and could reliably expect them to survive to adulthood, they made a greater investment in each child, giving rise to a heightened sense of individualism and entitlement among those raised in this way. A vast constituency of Americans (and others in affluent countries) was thus created, people committed to political regimes in which individual rights—social, sexual, and material—have become democratized and sacrosanct.

Technological and scientific advances ensured that the survival of individual children was less dependent on having a biological father present. Working mothers, maternal kin, government, and charitable services became sufficient to sustain the lives of children. The advent of contraception controlled by women relieved men of the sense of responsibility for out-of-wedlock pregnancy, and shotgun marriages became scarce. Men came to believe that women who did not adopt contraceptive measures or who were "careless" had taken the obligations of child-raising upon themselves. By 2000, the nonmarital birthrate had skyrocketed to one out of three newborns in the United States, with the rate rising to almost seven out of ten among African Americans. Freedom from the need to maintain the marital or procreative bond has facilitated the introduction of market competition into mating relationships, with the prospect of finding a better future partner often encouraging both men and women to withhold unshakable, life-long commitment.

To social conservatives, these developments have signaled an irretrievable and tragic loss. Their reaction has fueled, on the right, a powerful traditionalist movement and a groundswell of support for the Republican Party. To modernists, these developments constitute, at worst, the unfortunate costs of progress, and, at best—and this is very much the view on the political left as well as of Democratic Party loyalists—they constitute a triumph over unconscionable obstacles to the liberation and self-realization of much of the human race.

Changes in the Economy

For American workers, especially the less upwardly mobile whites who had once been aligned with the Democratic Party, the late 1960s and early 1970s produced not only changes in traditional hierarchies—in the role of women, in the family, and in relations between blacks, whites, and Hispanics—but also wrenching changes in the economy forced by a "third industrial revolution"—a combination of global competition, the rapid erosion of domestic manufacturing, and the ascendance of information technologies and new financial instruments and institutions. Traditionally well-paying manufacturing jobs disappeared by the millions, followed by a winnowing of the ranks of white-collar workers. Unions lost their partnership status with American corporations, and the new information and computer-centered workplace demanded skills—both cognitive and behavioral—not easily available to many American workers, particularly those with minimal education, even while economic transformation generated new jobs.

Outsourcing and immigration transformed the global marketplace. First, U.S. firms developed the technological capacity to send jobs offshore, including manufacturing and knowledge processing—software design, engineering, legal work, scientific research, financial analysis, data-input operations, tech support, and virtually all services and functions provided more cheaply at a distance. Second, revised immigration laws provided a new source of low-wage labor within the country. After a Democratic Congress passed and a Democratic president signed the Immigration and Nationality Act amendments of 1965 liberalizing immigration from previously underrepresented regions and countries, including Latin America, Asia, and Africa, the number of legal immigrants grew from 2.5 million during the decade of the 1950s to 3.3 million in the 1960s, 4.5 million in the 1970s, 7.3 million in the 1980s, and 9.1 million in the 1990s. The figure continues to rise.

Bear Stearns, in a 2005 economic forecasting study, reported that the number of illegal immigrants living in the United States "may be as high as 20 million people, more than double the nine million people estimated by the Census Bureau." According to the Pew Hispanic Center, the U.S. foreign-born population, regardless of legal status, was even higher—35.7 million in 2005.

At the same time, over the past four decades imports of foreign goods surged into the United States from countries around the world ranging from China to Japan, Romania, and Madagascar— autos, steel, electronics, pharmaceuticals, clothing, entertainment, and a host of other products—with quality often matching or surpassing that of domestically produced goods at a fraction of the price. While the legal minimum hourly wage of a worker in China was reportedly forty-one cents an hour in 2005, the average hourly wage of a U.S. worker, according to the *2006 Economic Report of the President*, actually fell slightly in constant 1982 dollars, dropping from $8.21 in 1967 to $8.17 in 2005.

As an indication of the weakened bargaining position of American workers vis á vis their competitors in low-wage countries, the first post–World War II U.S. trade deficit occurred in 1971, a modest $2.26 billion. By 2005, the U.S. trade deficit had exploded to $665.39 billion.

Traditional Democratic policies that depend on government intervention and regulation were of little use in fending off competition from abroad; similarly, the party of the "working man" was unable to counteract the downward pressure on wages from outsourcing and from immigration—both legal and illegal. In 1969, well-paying, unionized manufacturing jobs accounted for 26.3 percent of all employment; by 2005, they amounted to only 10.9 percent of the national workforce. Over the same period, the average wage fell by more than $40 a week, from $316.93 to $275.93 calculated in constant 1982 dollars. Growing numbers of white workers, especially white men, began to believe that the Democratic Party had abandoned them at a critical juncture of economic crisis and moral challenge. These white male voters believed that, when the going got tough and resources were few, the Democratic Party had taken the side of African Americans, feminists, and migrants from developing nations.

➤ ◄

For the past four and a half decades of Republican ascendancy, American politics has been driven by these two revolutions, revolutions that to date have created more political opportunities for the conservative movement and for the Republican Party than for their opponents on the left.

THE SOCIOCULTURAL REVOLUTION: RACE, SEX, AND WOMEN'S RIGHTS

I would say the majority of our social problems today, maybe all of them when you stop and think about it, but at least the majority, revolve around sex. Like homosexuality is a sex problem, choosing your sex partner. Abortion is a sex problem. If you didn't have sex, you wouldn't have the need for abortion. Pornography, sex problem. Just everything you deal with that are major social problems today, almost everything comes back to sex, revolves around sex. And see, AIDS ties in again. Very seldom do you get AIDS without sexual activity; it's usually promiscuous sex activity that brings about AIDS, not monogamous. Why did we need welfare reform? Because we have too many people on welfare, and people on welfare tend to get pregnant and have more kids.

> *Reverend Duane Motley*
> *Executive Director*
> *New Yorkers for Constitutional Freedoms*

Turning Point: The Election of 1964

For the Republican Party, the election of 1964 was the first step in what became a larger strategy to deal with the racial, sexual, and cultural revolutions. The GOP nominated as its presidential candidate Barry Goldwater, an opponent of the landmark Civil Rights Act of that year. Goldwater lost in a landslide, but he broke the Democratic hold on the South, carrying the states of the old Confederacy most adamantly opposed to integration: Alabama, Georgia, Louisiana, Mississippi, and South Carolina. The Goldwater campaign set the stage for the strikingly successful southern strategy carried forward by Richard Nixon and Ronald Reagan.

The combination of the Goldwater campaign and the enactment under a Democratic president, Lyndon Johnson, of the 1964 civil rights legislation and the Voting Rights Act of 1965 established, for the first time, racial identities for the two political parties. The Democrats became the party of racial liberalism, and the Republicans, the party of racial conservatism.

The Republican Party, Goldwater declared in his speech accepting the nomination,

> has but a single resolve, and that is freedom. Freedom made orderly for this nation by our constitutional government. Freedom under a government limited by laws of nature and of nature's God. Freedom balanced so that liberty lacking order will not become the slavery of the prison cell; balanced so that liberty lacking order will not become the license of the mob and of the jungle.

Over time, the GOP would become home to those seeking to preserve a negative freedom—the freedom to defend institutions, values, and traditions challenged by blacks, ethnic minorities, feminists, and sexual privacy advocates, including homosexuals.

The role of racial issues in producing Republican victories is clearly reflected in the post-1964 realignment of the deep South, where the black-belt states are divided between a white Republican Party and a majority-black Democratic Party. Among African Americans, the 1964 election was the turning point. Nationally, in the elections from 1948 through 1960, an average of 70 percent of black votes were cast for Democratic candidates. From 1964 through 2004, the percentage of the black vote going to Democratic candidates shot up to 93.5 percent. The number of whites voting Republican rose from 55 percent before 1964 to 58 percent after 1964.

The much smaller percentage shift toward the GOP among white voters may seem far less significant than the Democratic shift among black voters, *but because the overall size of the white vote is so much larger, the actual shift in the number of votes switching parties is very similar*. Take two very close elections, 1960 and 2004. The number of white Republican votes cast rose from 32 million for Nixon to 49.1 million for George W. Bush, a gain of 17.1 million votes for the GOP. Conversely, the white vote for John F. Kerry increased by just 7.2 million over the white vote for John F. Kennedy. Among black voters, the gain for Kerry over Kennedy was 13 million, whereas the total number of blacks voting for Bush was just over 150,000 more than for Nixon. Thus the shift has tended, over the past forty years, to produce a net benefit for the GOP.

Divergence of the Two Parties on Women's and Civil Rights

Just as the civil rights movement in the South was reaching its zenith in the early sixties, with public attention riveted on demonstrations, marches, and police beatings of nonviolent protestors, the sexual and women's rights revolutions were beginning to gain momentum. In the words of Stanford chemist Carl Djerassi, the oral contraceptive pill, of which he was an inventor, had "the biggest social implications of anything in science that you could do other than drop another atomic bomb." By 1962, 1.2 million women were using the pill, growing to 2.3 million in 1963 and, by 1973, more than 10 million.

In 1963, Betty Friedan published *The Feminine Mystique*, "the book that pulled the trigger on history." Friedan described a

> problem that has no name. . . . It is the key to these other new and old problems which have been torturing women and their husbands and their children, and puzzling their doctors and educators for years. It may well be the key to our future as a nation and a culture. We can no longer ignore that voice within women that says: "I want something more than my husband and my children and my home."

The impact of the civil rights movement on politics was more immediately dramatic, as laws protecting African Americans were passed, the Great Society launched, and urban riots erupted. A conservative backlash and political polarization emerged almost immediately. In one election, 1964, the two parties diverged, and the issues of school and housing integration in the North and South, affirmative action, and the racially charged problems of urban crime, welfare dependency, and family dissolution—as well as the swelling of a large new black middle class—all quickly became central to the national debate.

For the women's rights and sexual revolutions, the political process was slower and more subtle. One of the early demonstrations of the emerging divergence of the two parties on the issues of women's rights can be found in the changing partisan pattern of votes in Congress for and against the proposed Equal Rights Amendment (ERA) to the Constitution, first in the early 1970s and then in the late 1970s. In votes cast in 1971 and 1972, hardly any difference was evident between Democrats and Republicans on the amendment, which read: "Equality of rights under the law shall not be denied or abridged by the United States or by any state on account of sex."

	1971 Final House ERA Vote		1972 Final Senate ERA Vote	
	Yes	No	Yes	No
Republican	137	12	37	6
Democrat	217	12	47	2

The next few years, however, were stamped by the politics of sex and the changing role of women. The most important and transforming event was the 1973 *Roe v. Wade* decision establishing a woman's right to an abortion, providing women with the freedom to act as they chose without fear of unplanned children.

Roe was only one front in the struggle for new rights. During the 1970s, girls were admitted to Little League baseball, women gained entry into naval flight training and into the military academies as well as into all-male Ivy League bastions, the American Psychiatric Association struck homosexuality from its list of mental disorders, Billie Jean King defeated Bobby Riggs in the tennis Battle of the Sexes, Judy K. Hartwell, twenty-nine, of Belleville, Michigan, successfully used self-defense to justify killing her husband, and Tucson, Iowa City, and Aspen adopted the first local laws barring discrimination against homosexuals.

As these issues came to the forefront, the political climate saw the institutionalization of partisan polarization. In one of the earliest backlash responses to the women's rights movement, Phyllis Schlafly founded the anti-ERA Eagle Forum in 1975. Further evidence of increasing polarization on women's rights issues found expression in the 1978 votes on the ERA:

	1978 Final House ERA Vote		1978 Final Senate ERA Vote	
	Yes	No	Yes	No
Republican	41	103	16	21
Democrat	186	85	44	15

In a matter of just seven years in the House and six in the Senate, decisive Republican majorities in favor of granting women equality under the Constitution shifted to majorities opposed. In 1971–1972, 90.6 percent of House and Senate Republicans voted for the ERA. In 1978, 68.5 percent voted against it. Solid majorities of Democrats continued to support the ERA, although the margin in favor dropped. In the House, which more quickly reflects social and cultural trends given elections every two years, the 1978 GOP majority in opposition was overwhelming, better than 2 to 1 opposed.

The GOP Downplays Its Cultural Agenda

The shift in the GOP was the first strong evidence that the sexual revolution and the parallel women's rights movement were changing

166 < BUILDING RED AMERICA

the nature of political competition in America. Women's rights and the sexual revolution became "the driving engine of partisan polarization," wrote political scientist and feminist Jo Freeman in her 1999 book, *We Get What We Vote For.* "While race was the lead mare of the progressive team, sex was the wicked witch that spurred the opposition. Abortion in particular was a realigning issue because it merged concerns about changing sex roles and the consequences of sex acts and gave them a political basis." The antiwar and student movements—which also challenged historic gender roles (including the duty of men to be soldiers)—added fuel to the fire.

From Nixon's courting of the Wallace vote in 1972, to the cultivation of Reagan Democrats in the 1980s, to the Angry White Men of 1994, the Republican Party has successfully capitalized on anger and resentment over progressive-liberal social movements. Democrats, in turn, have gambled on becoming the party of cultural insurrection, committed to the civil rights, antiwar, and women's movements and supportive of the newly claimed rights of sexual freedom, including abortion, gay and lesbian rights, rights to non-traditional family structures, and the right to personal privacy.

As the social and cultural revolutions became less and less controversial and the changes they wrought became increasingly accepted, the Republican Party sought to maintain its centrist credentials and to "narrowcast" the reactionary or traditionalist aspects of its cultural agenda. The GOP—and much of the larger conservative movement—now prohibits expressions of overt racism, tolerates (some) homosexuals in its ranks, and supports—indeed highlights—the election and appointment of women and minorities to positions of power and authority, as can be seen by the women the conservative movement showcases, from Karen Hughes to Condoleeza Rice, Laura Ingraham, and Ann Coulter.

Tanya Melich, a Republican delegate to the 1992 GOP presidential nominating convention, notes the Republican strategy of downplaying any radical dimension to the party's sociocultural positions:

> When [anti-abortion leader] Randall Terry called for "restructuring the [U.S.] as a Christian republic with laws drawn from the Bible," few politicians responded. When Ralph Reed repackaged these ideas and made them more palatable by saying "this was not a Christian agenda, but a pro-family agenda," the Republican leaders took notice. The Christian Coalition

borrowed a page from Reagan's book on how to bring about revolutionary change. Put your ideas in a simple "family values" framework, talk gently and with feeling about how you want only the best for America, recall the happy simple past, and don't threaten. . . . As Reed said, address "what we believe is the most pressing issue in American politics today, and that is the fraying of the social fabric, the coarsening of the culture, the breakdown of the family."

Whenever the Democratic Party or socially progressive public officials manifest highly visible or novel forms of cultural liberalism, however, the Republican Party and the conservative movement are quick to capitalize on backlash. This was the case regarding conservative response to the 2004 decision of the Massachusetts Supreme Judicial Court to allow same-sex marriages. Richard Land, the head of the public policy arm of the 16 million-member Southern Baptist convention, pointed out after the Massachusetts decision that, whereas it had taken six years after *Roe v. Wade* for abortion opponents, including evangelicals and Catholics, to join together as the Moral Majority, the battle over same-sex marriage was engaged at lightning speed because "the wiring was already up and ready to go. The institutional connections, the personal relationships—it was all built over the last 30 years by the pro-life movement."

Similarly, Michael Cromartie, director of the Evangelical Studies Project at the Ethics and Public Policy Center, said of the Massachusetts ruling, "For anybody who thought the culture wars were over, this will reignite them and ensure that they will be here for years and years to come. In that sense, it's very much like the abortion issue. New careers on both sides will grow out of this, the polarization will continue and grow, and the room for compromise will diminish."

On Issues Important to Women's Rights Groups, the Democratic Party Is Overwhelmingly More Supportive Than the Republican Party

At a time of growing instability domestically, with continuing job losses and intense workplace competition, and internationally, with the threat of violence and terrorism, the Republican Party has been viewed for the better part of the past forty years as the party of military credibility, economic know-how, cultural constancy, and tradition. The Democrats have more often been seen as asserting the priority of personal freedom and autonomy over stable institutional structures, over religiously based guidelines, over hard-and-fast moral rules, and over the imperatives of national security.

The culture wars and racial conflicts have thus altered the character of the two parties. Not only has black loyalty to the Democratic Party strengthened as white support has waned, but *on every issue of importance to liberal women's rights groups, the Democratic Party is overwhelmingly more supportive than the Republican Party*. Abortion rights, affirmative action, access to the "morning-after pill," sexual harassment, gay rights, hate crime legislation, Title IX mandates for gender parity in college sports, criminalizing violence against women, government-funded day care—all of these receive substantially stronger backing from Democrats than from Republicans at every level, from regular voters to political elites.

Although the Democratic and Republican parties have split on racial issues—a pattern reflected in congressional voting on busing, affirmative action, civil rights remedies, and the enforcement and extension of the Voting Rights Act—their split on the central issues of the women's rights and the sexual liberation movements is also evident—abortion, access to advanced contraceptive technologies (Plan B), and even sex education in the schools. The Republican Party platform has explicitly opposed abortion since 1980—arguably as much out of a desire to roll back the sexual revolution as to affirm the rights of the unborn. In this context, parental notification and consent laws, as well as spousal notification laws, are also designed to create disincentives to recreational sex as well as to promote the rights of the unborn.

The changing character of the political parties is, then, a striking outcome of the major social upheaval of the past half century: the unprecedented transformation of the role of women—at work, in the home, in their sex lives, and in their control over their own reproductive destiny. The two sides in the women's rights and sexual revolutions have found a home—in terms of the fight for legal reform—in each of the two political parties, just as the two sides in the civil rights revolution—pro and con—have found a partisan home based on the same schism.

Transformation of the Moral Order
Reconfigures the Two Parties

A once-prevailing moral order designed to ensure stable family structures no longer holds sway. In part, this transformation has been made possible by technological advances, as sex and procreation are no longer irrevocably linked and as the survival of children is no longer as dependent on their fathers. The change for both sexes has been dramatic. Among men who reached adulthood between 1951 and 1960, 41.5 percent reported having had sex by the age of eighteen. Thirty years later for those reaching adulthood between 1981 and 1992, the percentage rose to 60.3 percent, a 45 percent increase. Among women, the changes were even more dramatic: the percentage that reported they had sex by the age of eighteen grew from 18.5 percent to 52.8 percent for the same time period. The rate of early sexual experiences for women thus grew by 185 percent; in other words, the percentage of women who lost their virginity by the age of eighteen grew four times faster than the rate for men over the past half century.

The women's rights movement transformed not only women's sexual behavior but also family and workplace organization and structure. By gaining personal control over reproduction, women were able to take unprecedented control of their lives. The pill destroyed the argument that educating or hiring a woman for a professional career would result in a wasted investment as soon as she got pregnant—a prevalent view in the past.

In place of traditional morality configured around norms of self-denial and delayed gratification, a new ethic gained strength among progressives and liberals. This morality placed the strongest emphasis on the self—on self-fulfillment, self-potentiation, self-nurturance, and self-actualization. The new morality produced the "cult of the therapeutic," a morality with little or no emphasis on "discipline," sin, renunciation, or contrition. At the same time, this new morality tapped into the American tradition of individualism and personal freedom, of putting past failings behind you and "moving on," captured in the Democrat's MoveOn.org response to the Monica Lewinsky/impeachment scandal—"Let's move on." (Indeed, one of the most influential promulgators of the sexual revolution, Dr. Irene Kassorla, author of *Nice Girls Do—And You Can Too*, would become Monica Lewinsky's therapist during her affair with President Clinton.) The "moving on" concept was already evident in the Fleetwood Mac song that Clinton chose for his 1992 campaign, "Don't Stop Thinking about Tomorrow":

> If you wake and you don't want to smile
> Just you wait, wait a little while
> Open your eyes and look at the day
> You might see things in a different way
> Don't stop thinking about tomorrow. . . .
> Why not think about times to come,
> And not about the things that you've done. . . .
> I know you don't believe that it's true,
> I never meant any harm to you. . . .
> Don't you look back,
> Don't you look back.

This is not to suggest that Republican officials behave more chastely than Democrats. Newt Gingrich, Bob Livingston, Bob Barr, Henry Hyde, and Dan Burton—all ardent pro-life GOP members of the House who led the charge against Clinton, actively pressing for his impeachment—were identified in the news media at that time as having had extramarital affairs. Similarly, Bob Dole's former mistress declared herself to the *Washington Post* during the 1996 election, keeping the Dole campaign in a state of disabling suspense during the spring and summer months prior to the revelation.

The Demise of Separate Spheres: New Competition between Men and Women

The transformed role of women along with the changes in status of racial and ethnic minorities are the two most powerful factors shaping what have become known as the culture wars. In the aftermath of the sexual and women's rights revolution, the "ideal" model of the relationship between men and women in the United States underwent a dramatic change. In the pre-pill era, men and women spent much of their time in largely separate spheres. Gender archetypes dictated that men join the paid labor force, insofar as work was available, to provide financial support, food, housing, and other necessities of life for their families, whereas a majority of mothers (there were always exceptions) worked in the household, watched over the children, prepared food, performed tasks (often arduous, as in farmwork) compatible with these duties, and—where material conditions permitted—labored to create "a haven in a heartless world." Those many women who did work outside the home rarely competed with men, generally holding subordinate jobs in factories and commerce or working as teachers, nurses, librarians, domestics, and in other occupations (sometimes agricultural) designated as "women's work."

In 1900, southern white women living on farms averaged six children, black women had five children, and foreign-born white women had 4.54 children. German immigrant women had 7.22 children, Irish immigrant women had 7.34 children, and native-born white American women had 3.56 children. According to historian Judith Walzer Leavitt, "Pregnancy, birth, and postpartum recovery occupied a significant portion of most women's adult lives, and motherhood a major portion of their identity." Widowed or abandoned women, unmarried mothers, and "spinsters" in general lived toward the periphery of the larger social order.

In the post-pill era, this gendered structure was shattered for large segments of the population—at every rung on the socioeconomic ladder. Figures from the National Center on Health Statistics demonstrate that, by the mid-1970s, the total U.S. fertility rate fell to about 1.8 births per woman. During the 1990s, fertility rates fluctuated between 2.0 and 2.1 births per woman, generally a rate still below the level required for the natural replacement of the population (about 2.1 births per woman). By 2004, the average number of children that American women aged forty to forty-four had given birth to was 1.9.

In this new order, the spheres of men and women—no longer as sharply delineated by reproductive roles—overlapped, leading to new levels of both conflict and cooperation. Women by the 1970s began to compete directly with men both at work and at all levels of schooling. One of the most consequential results of the sociocultural upheavals of recent years can be found in employment trends. From 1955 to 2004, the labor force participation rate for men has fallen from 82.3 percent to 73.3 percent. During the same forty-nine years, the participation rate for women rose from 34.5 percent to 59.2 percent. The labor force participation of married women with children under six was 62.2 percent in 2003, and for married women with children six to seventeen it was 77.5 percent, higher than the participation rate of all men.

Since the beginning of the sexual and women's rights revolutions, the divorce rate has nearly tripled, further compounding the adversarial component in the relationship between men and women. Almost half of all marriages now end in divorce (and have done so since the 1970s), frequently involving bitter fights over income, assets, and children. These disputes often continue through years with arguments over child support, alimony, visitation, and other issues, compounded by disputes over stepchildren, blended families, and increased rates of divorce for second and third marriages. For anyone entering a marriage, and for those experiencing the difficulties of married life, the possibility of divorce is now a far more realistic prospect than it was in any other historic era.

The Drive to Lessen Traditional Built-in Advantages for Whites and for Men

One political goal of women entering the contemporary workplace and the unstable universe of modern family life is to change workplace and marketplace rules—including family law—to lessen traditional built-in advantages for men. The civil rights movement for African Americans—over a hundred years in the making—set a pattern for the adjudication of conflict over women's rights. The courts, the Congress, and the regulatory apparatus redistributed power between men and women as they had between blacks and whites. What quickly became a substantial body of law and regulation enabled women to challenge the constitutionality of laws giving men preference over women, to bring suit on grounds of sexual harassment, to redefine unwanted marital sex as rape, to require both the public and private sectors to seek out women as employees, to sue employers imposing tests or physical requirements that exclude a disproportionate number of women, and to collect punitive damages in civil rights suits.

Although women's rights were becoming institutionalized across the developed world, crucial to the process in the United States was the addition of the word "sex" to Title VII of the 1964 Civil Rights Act: "It shall be an unlawful employment practice for an employer . . . to fail or refuse to hire or to discharge any individual, or otherwise to discriminate against any individual with respect to his compensation, terms, conditions, or privileges of employment, because of such individual's race, color, religion, sex, or national origin." The amendment was added by the Democratic Virginia Congressman Howard W. Smith in a failed attempt to kill the bill by adding controversial and burdensome provisions.

The Equal Employment Opportunity Commission (EEOC) issued rulings in 1968 that airline stewardesses could not be forced to quit when they got married, became pregnant, wore glasses, gained weight, or entered their middle thirties, and that separate want-ads for men and women were unlawful. Nothing caught the attention of corporate America more decisively than the EEOC's 1973 success in its first major sex discrimination case, forcing AT&T to pay an unprecedented $31 million in damages and to end sex discrimination in hiring and promotion. The AT&T case was the first of many multimillion dollar awards in similar cases.

The EEOC regulatory apparatus was reinforced by the Office of Federal Contract Compliance Programs and by the creation in each cabinet department of separate divisions assigned to ensure compliance with civil rights laws. By 1984, 13,675 federal workers were employed in departments, agencies, and regulatory bodies to enforce anti-discrimination laws affecting racial minorities and women, 3,202 of them devoted to making sure the private sector complied with the law.

The Supreme Court, in turn, began handing down a series of decisions profoundly changing the American social order, including rulings invalidating state laws treating children of unmarried mothers differently from those of married mothers (*Levy v. Louisiana*, 1968) and laws denying benefits to male spouses of females serving in the military (*Frontiero v. Richardson*, 1973). It also held that corporate hiring and promotion policies and tests that were on their face neutral violated Title VII if such policies had a "disparate impact" on blacks or women (*Griggs v. Duke Power Co.*, 1971).

Much of the legal fight for women's rights involved the question of "bona fide occupational qualification" (or BFOQ). According to Sonia Pressman Fuentes, staff attorney with the EEOC from the middle sixties onwards,

> It [BFOQ] was really the first big issue. The question was: Did you really have to hire a woman for every job that a man could do? People said, "Oh, women can't lift," they couldn't be a fireperson, and they couldn't be a police person. You couldn't become a construction worker. People did not consider women in those days for those jobs. I drafted the EEOC's first Annual Digest of Legal Interpretations, and we finally ended up saying the only jobs for which sex could be a BFOQ were sperm donor and wet nurse. . . . Beyond those jobs (which, to my knowledge, never came up in actual cases), sex was not a BFOQ. . . . One of the early issues involved state protective legislation. That issue arose out of activities in the labor movement in the past. Years ago, women's groups and labor unions supported protective legislation for women—legislation that limited women to working a certain number of hours a day, limited the amount of weight they could lift, and otherwise restricted women's working conditions. . . . These laws served only to keep women from being hired into, or promoted into, decent jobs and earning decent money. And some of these laws were ludicrous. In Utah, for example, legislation prohibited women from holding jobs which required lifting more than fifteen pounds! State protective laws were a terrible barrier to women. Women couldn't be supervisors because a supervisor might have to work longer hours or work in the evening.

"You're moving from the historical concept of discrimination, which was to exclude women for the sake of excluding women, to telling employers that they have to adopt what may be, in their views, reasonably thought to be less efficient or less perfect mechanisms in order to increase the representation of women," said Geoffrey Stone, provost of the University of Chicago and a former clerk to Justice William Brennan.

Court and federal regulatory victories were reinforced by the enactment of new federal laws. Women won passage of the 1978 Pregnancy Disability Act (PDA), explicitly prohibiting discrimination against pregnant workers in hiring, promotion, seniority rights, and job security and requiring company-provided health and disability policies to include coverage for pregnancy and childbirth. When court rulings were adverse to the interests of women and blacks, women led the charge to persuade Congress to overrule the court. In 1988, Congress overturned *Grove City College v. Bell* and restored the power of the federal government to end subsidies to educational institutions with records of sex discrimination. In 1991, Congress passed legislation overturning a series of Supreme Court decisions that had restricted enforcement of affirmative action policies. The Civil Rights Act of 1991 expanded plaintiffs' rights in sex-related employment discrimination suits and, crucially, allowed compensatory and punitive damages over and above back pay.

Push-back from Leaders of the Republican Party

The legal push toward gender and racial liberalism produced a major push-back from leaders of the Republican Party. Ronald Reagan picked William Bradford Reynolds, an outspoken critic of gender- and race-based affirmative action, as his assistant attorney general for civil rights. "I regard government tolerance of favoring or disfavoring individuals because of their skin color, sex, religious affiliation or ethnicity, to be fundamentally at odds with this country's civil rights policies," Reynolds wrote. Reynolds was joined by Clarence M. Pendleton Jr., the Reagan-appointed chairman of the U.S. Civil Rights Commission, and Clarence Thomas, executive director of the EEOC, both of whom held similar views.

In terms of Republican push-back on race, Reagan in 1981 unsuccessfully attempted to weaken provisions of the Voting Rights Act that required local jurisdictions with histories of discriminatory policies to get Justice Department "pre-clearance" of any change in voting laws, after calling the requirement "humiliating to the South" in his election campaign. In 1982, Reagan rescinded an IRS ruling that barred tax-exempt status to Bob Jones University and other private schools that discriminate, contending that the ruling had "no basis in law." In 1983, however, the Supreme Court rejected Reagan's position in an 8 to 1 decision affirming the authority of the IRS to penalize discriminatory private schools. Five years later, when the Democratic Congress overturned the Supreme Court's *Grove City College* decision, Reagan vetoed the legislation, agreeing, in effect, that federal aid and subsidized loans could be granted to students attending colleges that refuse to sign a non-sex discrimination pledge required by the Department of Education. The veto was overturned.

President George W. Bush has followed Reagan's lead. He has appointed two Health and Human Services secretaries, Tommy Thompson and Michael Leavitt, who are outspoken opponents of abortion, along with many others holding similar views to regulatory positions throughout the federal government. Bush has tried, unsuccessfully, to end a requirement that federal employee insurance plans include coverage of five types of contraception, the pill, the intrauterine device (IUD), Norplant, Depo-Provera, and the diaphragm.

Bush appointed Samuel Alito, who has written about his opposition to *Roe v. Wade*, to the Supreme Court, along with at least eighteen other appointees with records of opposing abortion, to the federal appeals courts. By signing both S.3, the Partial Birth Abortion Ban Act (2003), and the Unborn Victims of Violence Act of 2004, Bush made an unambiguous attempt to undermine the determination arrived at in *Roe v. Wade* that a fetus is not a legal "person" for the purposes of constitutional protection.

In December 2004, Bush similarly indicated the views of his party by signing legislation allowing physicians or other health care professionals, hospitals, HMOs, and insurance plans to defy state laws mandating access to abortion services, known as the "refusal" clause. In 2005, Bush's Department of Education issued a "clarification" of rules used to determine whether a school, under Title IX, requires equal access to sports for men and women; the clarification allows colleges to use much less stringent survey methods—email and web-based—to determine if there is a lack of women's interest in any given sport.

More Dimensions of Polarization

These legal, regulatory, and administrative battles have intensified the divergence of the Republican and Democratic parties on issues directly linked to civil rights, women's rights, and the sexual revolution. Polarization now extends to virtually all of those issues on which there is significant statistical difference between the views of men and women, creating an issue-based gender gap. Such issues run the gamut from military spending to the domestic safety net, tax cuts, and gun control. In each case, Democratic partisans side with the majority of women on these issues, and Republican partisans side with the majority of men.

Take military spending for example: from 1980 to 2004, according to National Election Studies (NES) data, support for increased military spending has been eleven percentage points higher on average among men than among women, reaching a fifteen-point difference in 2000 and 2004 based on answers to this survey question: "Some people believe that we should spend much less money for defense. Others feel that defense spending should be greatly increased. Where would you place yourself on this scale?" In vote after vote on military spending and on new weapons systems, Republicans in the House and Senate are consistently more supportive of the Pentagon than are Democrats. In 2004, the Peace Action Education Fund, which grew out of a merger of two peace groups, SANE and the Nuclear Freeze Movement, evaluated members of the House and Senate based primarily on their votes on military appropriation and authorization bills. Every one of the twenty-two senators and all but one (Bernie Sanders, Independent of Vermont) of the ninety representatives receiving 100 percent ratings from the Peace Fund by voting against the spending measures were Democrats. Conversely, fifty of the fifty-two senators receiving zero ratings were Republicans.

Similarly, a major survey by the National Opinion Research Center (NORC) in 1999 found a decisive gender gap on the issue of gun control:

> Men and women have fundamentally different viewpoints on firearms and their regulation. . . . Across all 36 topics women are more concerned about guns and more in favor of their regulation, and 34 of the differences are statistically significant. The differences are often quite pronounced. In 15 cases they range from 10 to 20 percentage points and in 10 instances, over 20 percentage points.

The National Rifle Association, the leading opponent of gun control bills, rated members of Congress in 2004. Of the 204 senators and representatives with 90 to 100 percent "correct" votes, 177 were Republicans and 27 were Democrats, a ratio of 7.5 to 1. Among the 137 members who got zero ratings, 135 were Democrats and 2 were Republicans, a ratio of 68.5 to 1.

The pattern of Republican and Democratic congressional voting on domestic social spending and foreign military intervention follows the same pattern: as for congressional votes, the Republican position on tax cuts tracks with views more often expressed by men, and the Democratic position follows views more commonly expressed by women.

As members of Congress have become polarized not only on issues of culture but also on taxes, military intervention, the environment, class action suits, union rights, civil liberties, and so forth, these issues have become "co-branded," to use Matt Dowd's terminology,[1] in the perception of voters. A Republican politician who promotes tax cuts is likely to support a conservative social agenda on race, sex, minority rights, and religion and to oppose social spending, to support gun rights, to advocate a foreign policy strong on offense, and to back executive authority rather than civil liberties.

After 9/11: Republicans Capitalize on Their Advantage on the Use of Force

The profound differences between members of both parties in their attitudes toward the military and the use of force have become a major weapon in the Republican arsenal. Throughout the Cold War and more recently during the post-9/11 war on terrorism, the GOP and its leaders have leveraged this difference.

In the 1980 campaign, when fifty-two American hostages were being held in the U.S. embassy in Teheran and when the U.S. helicopter rescue mission failed, Ronald Reagan challenged Jimmy Carter's ability to lead, declaring:

> Who does not feel a growing sense of unease as our allies, facing repeated instances of an amateurish and confused administration, reluctantly conclude that America is unwilling or unable to fulfill its obligations as the leader of the free world? Who does not feel rising alarm when the question in any dis-

---

[1]See chapter 2 for Matt Dowd on the Republican "brand."

cussion of foreign policy is no longer, "Should we do something?" but "Do we have the capacity to do anything?" The administration which has brought us to this state is seeking your endorsement for four more years of weakness, indecision, mediocrity and incompetence. No American should vote until he or she has asked, is the United States stronger and more respected now than it was three-and-a-half years ago? Is the world today a safer place in which to live?

The same theme—of Republican superiority in the realm of national security—has been used by Republicans for over a quarter of a century. Four months after 9/11, Karl Rove was able to confidently tell members of the Republican National Committee that the electorate had more confidence in the GOP than in the Democratic Party to handle the threat of terrorism: "We can go to the country on this issue, because they trust the Republican Party to do a better job of protecting and strengthening America's military might and thereby protecting America." On June 22, 2005, Rove expanded on this theme, telling members of the New York Conservative Party that liberals, that is, Democrats, pose a danger to the nation: "Perhaps the most important difference between conservatives and liberals can be found in the area of national security. Conservatives saw the savagery of 9/11 and the attacks and prepared for war; liberals saw the savagery of the 9/11 attacks and wanted to prepare indictments and offer therapy and understanding for our attackers."

This rhetoric was reinforced in December 2005 when the Republican National Committee aired on television the following commercial:

ANNOUNCER: Democrats have a plan for Iraq: Retreat and Defeat.

HOWARD DEAN: The idea that we're going to win this war is an idea that unfortunately is just plain wrong.

BARBARA BOXER: So there's no specific timeframe but I would say the withdrawal ought to start now, right after the elections December 15th.

JOHN KERRY: There is no reason . . . that young American soldiers need to be going into the homes of Iraqis in the dead of night terrorizing kids and children, you know, women.

[On screen: "Our country is at war. Our soldiers are watching and our enemies are too. Message to Democrats: Retreat and Defeat is not an option."]

Different Classes of Men and Women Join Together on Either Side of the Partisan Divide

The issues that separate the parties do not pit men against women. Instead, the Republican Party's agenda joins certain classes of men and women, just as the Democratic Party unites a different set of women and men. The Republican side includes those committed to a traditional moral order, often religiously observant, those opposed to the various aspects of the women's, black, and gay rights movements, and those who are the dominant beneficiaries of the free market, including corporate executives and their spouses, the affluent, and those convinced they will achieve such status. The Democratic Party unifies members of both sexes who stand to gain from the insurgent sociocultural movements, who sympathize with and support the marginalized, and who for various reasons have difficulty competing in the twenty-first-century workplace.

In many ways, some of the statistical differences in the voting behavior of men and women reflect rational self-interest. For example, women make up the overwhelming majority of the victims of sexual assault, 84 percent of the victims of violent spousal abuse, and 86 percent of the victims of violence by a friend or lover, almost always a man, according to the Bureau of Justice Statistics. In this context, it is more than reasonable for women to seek protection from these risks through the provisions of the Violence against Women Act.

Similarly, the strong support of single and working women for government safety net programs is a reasoned choice. A woman venturing into the workplace with the ambition to climb the corporate or professional ladder is, in contrast to her similarly ambitious male counterpart, much more likely to be single and therefore more potentially reliant on resources outside of marriage, such as government benefits and protections, in the event of job loss, illness, forced retirement, or other circumstances outside of her control.

In findings that have been replicated in a number of studies, the University of Michigan Retirement Research Center has found that men who are successful in the labor market are much more likely to get married than those who are not and that, for white men, raised earnings and longer work days increase the likelihood of marriage. Exactly the opposite is true for white women: the higher the wages and the longer the hours put in at work, the lower the likelihood of marriage. Black men who work more hours every week are more likely to be married. Black women who work longer hours and have higher earnings are no different in their marriage patterns from black women who have lower earnings.

The logic of stronger support for the government safety net among women is obvious when looking at the demographics of the senior population. Among the elderly, who are most dependent on government support for survival—Medicare, Medicaid, and Social Security, among other services—the number of women far exceeds the number of men: 58 percent of those sixty-five and over and 69 percent of those eighty-five and over are female. Nearly three-quarters of men sixty-five and over are married and living with their spouse, compared to just 50 percent of women.

The same logic of self-interest is true in the case of gender-based affirmative action. Ambitious goals will drive men to invest huge numbers of hours in work and to impose sacrifices on their families and home lives in order to win raises and promotions. Women are not inclined in as large numbers to surrender their children's and family lives, and faced with this competition from men, they clearly benefit from affirmative action policies. In 2004, according to a U.S. Census/Department of Labor survey of full and part-time workers, men put in an average of 4.5 hours more a week than women. Over a year, that amounts to 216 hours, a difference of more than a month annually.

Conversely, many more white men than women are likely to prefer that outcomes of competition with women and minorities be decided by unbuffered contests, not by gender or race-based preferences ("quotas"). Such men logically oppose both affirmative action and the laws and regulations, aimed largely at curtailing male behavior, that prohibit the creation of a "hostile workplace environment for women."

Regulating the Behavior of Men

Since the 1960s, under the prodding of the women's rights movement, a large body of law has been built up to regulate and constrain the behavior of men in their relations with women. These regulations are based on the implicit assumption that men are far more likely than women to be physically aggressive, opportunistic, and violent; that men may respond in dangerous ways when jealous or threatened; that some men are sexually predatory; and that many men do indeed fall easily into a pattern of seeing women as "sexual objects."

Sexual harassment law is based on the experience of many women who, without legal protection, find they are often subject to "repeated or unwanted verbal or physical sexual advance, sexually explicit derogatory statements, sexually discriminatory remarks offensive or objectionable to them or which cause them discomfort or humiliation or interfere with their education or job performance." Sexual harassment, according to guidelines developed by NOW and the Working Women's Institute, may include one or more of the following:

- verbal harassment or abuse of a sexual nature

- unnecessary touching, patting, pinching, or brushing against a person's body

- subtle pressure for sexual activities

- leering (excessive staring) at a person's body

- displaying sexually explicit or suggestive pictures or cartoons

- nonverbal gesture of sexual nature

- sexually explicit cards, notes, or other written correspondence

- demanding sexual favors accompanied by implied or overt threats concerning one's academic or job performance, evaluation, promotion, and so on

- physical and/or sexual assault

- denying a qualified employee an opportunity or benefit that was granted another employee because he/she submitted to the employer's sexual advances or favors

To equalize the sexual balance of power in the workplace—and in interpreting Title VII of the 1964 Civil Rights Act—the Supreme Court in 1986 granted women a potent weapon with which to fight sexual harassment. In the landmark case *Meritor Savings Bank v. Vinson*, the Court found that sexual harassment was a form of sex discrimination under Title VII and prohibited by law. The decision, and others that followed, put corporations on the defensive, and men on the alert.

The Democratic Party has been the natural home for the drive to provide government-enforced legal protection to working women. But women make up 53 percent of the electorate, hence no Republican officeholder in recent memory has come out against sexual harassment laws, no matter what their private thoughts. Conservatives in the private sector are not so constrained. Rush Limbaugh boasted that a sign on his office door reads, "Sexual harassment at this work station will not be reported. However, . . . it will be graded!!!"

A truly conservative Republican position on sexual harassment might look something like this:

> The only thing women or men can properly demand of the law is that it protect persons and property from aggression. Not that it regulate attitudes, words, or offensive behavior that is non-aggressive. Private workplaces are just that . . . private property. The environment should be controlled through policies instituted by the owner and agreed to by the employees, as evidenced by their continuing presence as employees. At this juncture in society, most companies would almost certainly institute some . . . safeguards, . . . if only to ensure that they do not lose competent female employees or incur bad publicity that would alienate customers. But if a company's owners tolerate sexist remarks, etc., in the workplace, then the law has no more right to enter those premises to control attitudes than it has a right to enter your parlor for the same purpose.

The commitment of liberals, progressives, and the Democratic coalition to regulate male behavior does not stop at sexual harassment. Under the Democratic White House in 1994, new priority was given to collecting child support from "Deadbeat Dads." While mothers can be the target of such enforcement and regulation, it is far more often fathers who disappear than mothers:

> National statistics from 1979 showed that, while the majority of divorced fathers (55%) have visitation privileges, only a minority (approximately one-third) of children who live apart from their fathers saw them at least once a month in the previous year; 15% saw their fathers less than once a month, 16% had some contact in the past one to five years, *and 36% had not seen their fathers at all in the past five years or did not know where their fathers were living.* [emphasis added]

These figures do not take into account unmarried fathers, who abandon their offspring at far higher rates. The Clinton administration, as part of the Welfare Reform Act of 1996, instituted stringent methods to ensure maximum collection of delinquent child support payments from absent fathers, using IRS information "to locate noncustodial parents and to verify income and employment, . . . [to] locate additional nonwage income and assets of noncustodial parents who are employees as well as income and asset sources of self-employed and nonwage earning obligors." Child Support Enforcement (CSE) provisions in the 1996 law required

> states to implement procedures requiring that the SSN of any applicant for a professional, driver's, occupational, recreational, or marriage license be recorded on the application. . . . [They require] that the SSN of any individual subject to a divorce decree, support order, or paternity determination or acknowledgment be placed in the records relating to the matter, . . . [and that] automated registries of child support orders containing records of each case in which CSE services are being provided and each support order [be] established or modified on or after October 1, 1998. Local registries could be linked to form the State registry. The State registry is to include a record of the support owed under the order, arrearages, interest or late penalty charges, amounts collected, amounts distributed, child's

date of birth, and any liens imposed. The registry also will include standardized information on both parents, such as name, SSN, date of birth, and case identification number.

In one of the most important child support reforms in recent years, the 1996 law required states, by October 1, 1997, to establish an automated directory of new hires containing information from employers. . . . The new law also requires the establishment of a Federal case registry of child support orders and a national directory of new hires. . . . In fiscal year 1998, there were more than 1 million matches in which employment and address information was returned to states to assist in the location of noncustodial parents who owed child support. In fiscal year 1999, with the addition of the case registry to the matching system, there were 2.8 million matches.

Much of the Clinton-era 1994 Omnibus Crime Bill was aimed at male violence against women. Provisions of the bill made stalking and domestic abuse federal crimes and barred evidence of a victim's past sexual behavior in federal civil and criminal cases involving sex crimes. They allowed rape victims to demand HIV testing of alleged assailants, made "crimes of violence motivated by gender" a civil rights violation, made protective court orders issued in one state valid and enforceable in all states, and set up a domestic abuse 800 number hotline. The bill also established a $1.6 billion grant program for local government programs to fight violence against women, with financial incentives for local communities to adopt mandatory arrest policies in domestic abuse complaints and requirements that grant recipients pay the costs of medical exams of rape victims and the court fees of domestic abuse victims who file criminal charges. Under the law, victims of gender-related crimes could initiate civil actions to take assets and income from their abusers under relatively liberal rules of proof—"a preponderance of evidence" rule—with no requirement that the abuser be convicted of a crime. The legislation also included the "Megan's Law" section requiring community notification when a convicted sex offender moves into a neighborhood. More than 95 percent of sex offenders are male.

The law was valuable to women in the same way that Supreme Court rulings such as *Griggs v. Duke Power Co* (1972) empowered women. In *Griggs*, the disparate impact upon minorities of seemingly routine employer practices established grounds to suspect, and possibly prove, discriminatory employment policies. A classic example as applied to women was the use of strength tests in hiring firefighters. Proponents of the test argued that the ability to physically carry an injured person was a legitimate job requirement; critics countered that setting a high strength bar prevented most women from a chance to compete for the job. In many cases, employers have adopted race- and gender-based affirmative action policies calling for hiring in proportion to the racial and gender makeup of the available labor pool (see Bona Fide Occupational Qualification, above).

This body of laws, court rulings, and regulations enacted under Democratic leadership since the mid-1960s has altered the rules of the workplace and of the home to reflect the changing rights of women, and has been crucial to the workforce participation of women. At the same time, during a time of polarization, such regulation has, in an unintended outcome, created adherents of the contemporary conservative movement and the Republican Party.

The Exodus of White Males from the Democratic Party

The gender gap first emerged in force in the 1980 election. Contrary to the claims of some women's groups that the gap resulted from a rejection of Ronald Reagan's social and economic policies, it in fact emerged as a result of white men's abandonment of the Democratic Party. From 1948 to 1976, men cast a higher percentage of Democratic presidential ballots than women, or exactly the same percentage, in every election except the 1972 contest between Richard Nixon and George McGovern. In 1980, and in every election after that, the pattern was reversed, with men consistently casting more Republican presidential ballots than women. Data on partisan allegiance show that support for the Democratic Party among men began to drop from the high 50s and low 60s down to the 50 percent range between 1972 and 1982, and then dropped further into the high-to-middle 40s from 1984 to 2004. Women's loyalty to the Democratic Party, in contrast, has remained relatively unchanged for more than fifty years, hovering in the low to middle 50s in most years, including in 2004 when it was 53 percent Democratic, whereas men were 45 percent Democratic that year. Similarly, Republican allegiance, as opposed to actual voting, among men held in the low 30s between 1952 and 1982, and then rose to the low to mid-40s thereafter; women's Republican allegiance, in contrast, has remained in the mid-30s throughout these decades.

The shift to the Republican Party among men has been crucial to the GOP's record of winning five of the past seven presidential elections. If men had shifted allegiance and voting patterns only as much as women did in recent decades, George W. Bush would have lost in both 2000 and 2004, and his father, George H. W. Bush would have won by a tiny margin instead of by 7.8 percentage points in 1988.

Among male and female whites with high school degrees or less—a measure used by some pollsters as a proxy for determining working-class status—Al Gore lost to Bush by seventeen points, and Kerry lost by twenty-three points. Both Democrats did much better among college-educated whites, losing them by only nine and ten points in 2000 and 2004. In the 2000 and the 2004 elections, Bush's margin among white men with only high school degrees was substantially higher, twenty-nine points in 2000 and thirty points in 2004, than among comparable white women, seven points in 2000 and eighteen points in 2004. These working-class whites, male and female, not only trusted Bush more than Kerry to handle the threat of terrorism, 66 percent to 35 percent, but they also thought Bush was better able to handle the economy, 55 percent to 39 percent.

Sexual Mores Drive Partisanship: Penn Polling Data (Blue Movie)

By 1996, pollsters were finding that a wide range of issues directly related to the sexual revolution had become integral to partisan divisions. Dick Morris and Mark Penn, two of Bill Clinton's chief advisers, discovered a polling technique that proved to be one of the best ways to predict the likelihood of a vote for Clinton or for Bob Dole. Respondents were asked five questions. Four of the questions tested attitudes about the sexual revolution and its aftermath:

Do you believe homosexuality is morally wrong?

Do you ever personally look at pornography?

Would you look down on someone who had an affair while they were married?

Do you believe sex before marriage is morally wrong?
The closely related fifth question was:

Is religion very important in your life?

None of the questions dealt with traditional divisions of rich versus poor or of haves versus have-nots. The first four questions revolved not around sex per se but rather sexual behavior outside of monogamous marriage. The fifth question touched upon adherence to the institutions charged with upholding traditional ethical codes regulating sexual behavior.

A liberal, in this context, is someone who dismisses the idea that homosexuality is morally wrong, admits to looking at pornography, does not look down on a married person having an affair, views sex before marriage as morally acceptable, and does not treat religion as an important part of life. The Morris-Penn data showed that if the respondent—male or female—took the "liberal" stand on three of these questions, he or she was likely to be a Clinton voter by a two-to-one margin and by higher margins for those taking liberal stands on four or all five of the questions. The same was true in the opposite direction for those taking "conservative" stands on three or more of the questions. These questions were better vote predictors than all others, according to Morris and Penn, except for the race of the voter or the voter's partisan self-identification as a Democrat or Republican.

Women's Issues: A Democratic Vulnerability and Fodder for the Conservative Campaign for Permanent Power

The degree to which women's rights and questions concerning the sexual revolution have become enmeshed in the nation's politics was made glaringly apparent during the Clinton presidency. Bill and Hillary Clinton epitomized, in the eyes of many, the post-sexual and women's rights culture. Their marriage, their notion of a "co-presidency," their acknowledgment of Clinton's past affairs, their support of abortion and gay rights, her re-claiming of her maiden name, her tolerance of his ongoing infidelity in apparent return for his grant to her of substantial political authority and power, his rhetorical insistence on "responsibility" and "playing by the rules" and his personal inattention to just that—all of this represented a direct assault on the more traditional values that underpinned the Republican coalition. Clinton survived disclosure of his activities in large part because his wife did not leave him (as many women's rights advocates advised her to do) and because so many of his Republican accusers were revealed to have similar sexual track records.

The Republican Party recognized that Clinton's behavior highlighted the most vulnerable link in social liberalism—the moral vacuum liberating to some but frightening to others. Indeed, Clinton himself had long realized the extraordinary salience that fear among "ordinary" voters of this particular moral vacuum had for the left coalition. As early as the 1992 Democratic convention Clinton had set about to change the face (but perhaps not the soul) of the progressive movement. Clinton's acceptance speech at the 1992 Democratic convention set the bar high:

> I do want to say something to the fathers in this country who have chosen to abandon their children by neglecting their child support: Take responsibility for your children or we will force you to do so. . . . We offer our people a new choice based on old values. We offer opportunity. We demand responsibility. . . . One of the reasons we have so many children in so much trouble in so many places in this nation is because they have seen so little opportunity, so little responsibility. . . . You must be responsible. . . . That's what this New Covenant's all about. . . . Responsibility starts at the top. That's what the New Covenant is all about. . . . Opportunity, responsibility, community, . . . every one of us has a personal moral responsibility.

➤ ◄

Much of the public debate between 1992 and 2000 was dominated by matters at least tangentially related to the sexual revolution and to the volatile mix of issues that Bill and Hillary Clinton made salient. If Republicans were ready and willing to trap the philandering, risk-courting president who fueled anxiety on the part of centrists and conservatives alike about this moral vacuum, the president appeared more than willing to walk into the trap.

The trap was certainly laid: the Clinton years were marked by an unprecedented and sustained assault by Republican and conservative activists not only on Clinton himself but on the culture and values he espoused and exemplified. As early as the 1992 campaign, Republicans sensed their target, capitalizing on the allegations of Gennifer Flowers and other "bimbo eruptions," escalating to new heights "the politics of personal destruction."

These Republican strategies were designed to bring down not only a man, Clinton, but also the values and ideology he represented. The costs of this strategy to the GOP included the public reaction to the impeachment of President Clinton and its accompanying invasion of his private life. Public opinion ultimately recoiled from the prurient detail in *The Starr Report*, from the indignity of DNA analysis of the president's semen on Monica Lewinsky's "blue dress," from the urological inspection of the president required in the Paula Jones proceedings, from the surreptitious taping by Republican loyalists Linda Tripp and Lucianne Cummings Goldberg of Monica Lewinsky's alternately tearful and triumphant confessions, and from the attempt to cull fame and wealth by many of the women with whom Clinton had sexual relations.

In the long run, however, the Republican strategy—and the coordinated machinations of the conservative movement—paid off. Indeed, the "vast right wing conspiracy"—whose job Clinton made easy—weakened the 2000 Gore campaign so much that Bush was able to eke out an electoral college victory while losing the popular vote.

> ◁

Questions rooted in new women's rights and roles, sexual freedom, personal responsibility, and the social control of male behavior dominated not only the impeachment process but also the entire Clinton presidency. The unprecedented role adopted by First Lady Hillary Rodham Clinton, her responsibilities in the health care debate, and her victim status as the wronged wife ("I'm not sitting here as some little woman standing by my man like Tammy Wynette," Mrs. Clinton said during her *60 Minutes* televised campaign interview) are not the only examples. Important, as well, were the sustained debate over the "don't ask, don't tell" policy toward homosexuals in the military, the lifting of the "gag order" that had barred abortion counseling at federally funded clinics, and the elimination of restrictions on the use of fetal tissue for government-financed research (on Clinton's second day in office); not to mention the witness to sexual liaisons borne by Gennifer Flowers, Dolly Kyle Browning, Elizabeth Ward Gracen, and Marilyn Jo Jenkins, the accusation against the president of sexual harassment by Paula Jones, and the accusations against the president of rape by Juanita Broaddrick and of sexual harassment by Kathleen Willey. All these reflected the importance of the after-effects of the sexual and women's rights revolutions in the Clinton presidency.

At the same time, a hallmark of the Clinton years was the ruthless drive of, first, the conservative movement and, then, the Republican Party to turn the president's private life into a public issue. Richard Mellon Scaife, a major benefactor of the right, financed the "Arkansas Project," an effort by the conservative *American Spectator* to delve into every aspect of Bill and Hillary Clinton's private lives in Arkansas. Paula Jones first disclosed her accusations of sexual harassment against Clinton at a press conference during the 1994 annual Conservative Political Action Conference. The Independent Counsel (IC) investigation of Clinton, initially in connection with Whitewater (an Arkansas real estate development) and then expanded to include allegations regarding Monica Lewinsky, was conducted by conservative lawyer Kenneth Starr (solicitor general under George H. W. Bush). Starr was appointed to the IC by a three-judge panel headed by David Sentelle, a protégé of ultraconservative North Carolina Republican Senator Jesse Helms.

The 1996 election made clear to Republicans that the party was engaged in a life-or-death struggle with the liberal coalition and that, for the conservative coalition to remain ascendant, a sustained assault on the opposition was required. The "Clinton majority" that gave the president a second term was heavily minority, disproportionately weighted toward single voters, supportive of feminist goals, of sexual privacy, and of abortion rights, hostile to the religious right, and ideologically progressive on economic issues. The Republican congressional majority coalition was richer, whiter, majority male, Protestant (especially evangelical), more ideologically conservative, supportive of gun rights, more inclined to oppose abortion, much more religious, far less culturally tolerant, more inclined toward "discipline" than "therapy," hostile to doctrinal feminism, and far more concerned with lowering the deficit and taxes than were voters who backed Clinton.

The gulf between the "red" Republican and "blue" Democratic majorities came to be reflected in the increasing polarization of national opinion for and against Hillary Rodham Clinton, who had become, by 1996, an even more divisive figure than her husband. Among Bill Clinton voters, Hillary Clinton was viewed favorably by a margin of 81 to 15. Among voters for Republican candidates, she was viewed unfavorably by a margin of 79 to 21.

As the Republican Party and the conservative movement struggled toward their goal of a center-right realignment of the American electorate, the detailing of Clinton's sex life became a cottage industry on the right. *The Starr Report*, released to the public on September 9, 1998, included graphic details of seven "sexual encounters" between Lewinsky and Clinton. The lurid detail into which Starr went ran to 336 pages. At the same time, no credible evidence has ever emerged to suggest that any of Starr's report on Clinton's sex life was exaggerated or untrue.

When the Senate voted on February 12, 1999, to reject the articles of impeachment passed by the House, the widespread assessment on both the left and the right was that the attack on Clinton had backfired on the conservative movement, reaffirming and bolstering the liberal sociocultural values Clinton stood for. In an open letter to fellow conservatives, Free Congress Foundation President Paul Weyrich wrote: "The culture we are living in becomes an ever-wider sewer. . . . If there really were a moral majority out there, Bill Clinton would have been driven out of office months ago. . . . I no longer believe that there is a moral majority. I do not believe that a majority of Americans actually shares our values."

Weyrich's assessment of the national culture was soon proven to be far too pessimistic. As the 2000 election approached, every predictive model suggested that Al Gore should win decisively, with the economy strong, the deficit gone, and his mentor, Bill Clinton, continuing to be popular with the electorate. These economic and political science models predicted Gore would receive from 53 to 60 percent of the vote. "It's not even going to be close," declared the University of Iowa's Michael Lewis-Beck, who had predicted Clinton's share of the two-party vote to one-tenth of a percentage point four months before the 1995 election and who, in May 2000, declared that Gore would win with 56.2 percent of the two-party vote.

Instead, Gore received just 50.065 percent of the two-party vote, and Bush got 49.935 percent. This 0.13 percent difference was small enough to give Bush a win in the electoral college, and there is strong evidence in the exit poll data that Bush was able to close the margin in large part because of the polarization, slightly favoring the GOP, created by Bill Clinton and his conservative critics over the previous eight years. In exit polls, voters gave higher marks to Gore than to Bush on ability to manage government (61 to 34), the issue of prescription drug benefits (60 to 38), health care generally (64 to 33), handling the economy (59 to 37), education (52 to 44), and Social Security (58 to 39). By a decisive 75 to 19 percentage points, voters said that Gore better "understands issues" than Bush, by 63 to 31 said Gore "cares about people" more than Bush, and by 82 to 17 said Gore had more experience than Bush.

Despite all those seemingly decisive advantages on key issues and concerns of voters, Gore could not pull solidly ahead of Bush. Bush's advantages are connected, directly or indirectly, to the character issues and to the sociocultural values raised during the Clinton administration. Among those seeking moral leadership in the presidency, Bush beat Gore 69 to 28; among those for whom the Clinton scandals were very important in casting their votes, Bush won 80 to 18; among voters placing a high priority on the honesty and trustworthiness of the candidates, Bush won 80 to 15; and voters who thought the moral condition of the country was heading downward backed Bush 62 to 33.

The high-risk strategy by the conservative movement and the Republican Party of forcing wedge issues, of leveraging every marginal advantage, and of bearing down hard on morality and sex, in fact, paid off with a presidential victory. Not only did the Republican strategy give Bush a slight but decisive advantage in the 2000 campaign, but it also established a framework for the aggressive use of the issue of gay marriage in 2004 and the overall approach of the Bush campaign to abandon swing voter strategies. The new orientation would stress base-building polarization, laying the groundwork for successful attacks on Kerry's honor and manliness, on his heroism and trustworthiness, in the 2004 campaign.

6
The Business Revolution:
An Enormous Expansion in
the Role of Market Forces

Steve Carr went to work for Hertz at the age of twenty, changing oil and tires. A hard-working evangelical Christian, a graduate of an automotive repair training program, Carr impressed his supervisors and by the age of twenty-nine was promoted to manager of the maintenance shop at the Reno, Nevada, airport location. One of his best workers was Ben Martinez. Martinez suffered from bouts of severe arthritis, but he was always willing to put in extra time. Driving one of the rental cars from Reno to Sacramento, Martinez stopped for a coffee break. In the restaurant, the arthritis in his left shoulder began to act up.

After eating, Martinez got back into the automobile, "put it into reverse, and realized that the emergency brake was still on," Carr recounted. The arthritis in Martinez' left arm and shoulder made it impossible for him to reach down and release the handle to the left of the steering column. "So then he opened the driver's [side] door. And he put his leg outside to get to it [the brake release] with his right arm. And it's still in reverse, he forgot to put it back in 'Park.' He pulled on the emergency brake with his right arm, the automobile began moving backwards down the incline, and then the left tire grabbed a hold of his leg and pulled him out of the car. The car ran over him, his crotch, up his stomach, and dropped off right before his shoulder."

Months later, after recuperating, Martinez returned to work. Carr, acting under company policy, fired him. "You had to let him go, because he violated the safety thing. . . . The toughest part is letting people go. That was tough, I prayed about it," Carr said. "Still, there are a lot of guys that would take my job if I said no. They cut managers too. You've got to go with the punches when a corporation lays stuff down."

C arr and Martinez were caught in the riptide of the business revolution—a revolution ultimately favorable to the Republican
Party and to the conservative movement. The business revolution,
fueled by advances in science and technology, first became visible to
the general public during the economic crisis of the 1970s: the
OPEC embargo, rising energy costs, a severe economic recession,
the rise of global competitors, stagflation, deregulation, and deindustrialization—all led to a transformation that came to dominate
virtually every sector of the economy.

The revolution resulted in an enormous expansion in the role of
market forces—"the manic logic of capitalism"—improving efficiency, generating increased productivity, creating spectacular
wealth, and raising standards of living throughout America, even
while sowing destruction and widening the gap between the rich
and the poor. Conservative economic theorists gained new prominence, arguing that centrally planned economies failed as they attempted "to concentrate knowledge, authority, and decision-
making power at the center rather than pushing the power to act,
the freedom to do so, and the incentive to act productively out to
the periphery where the people-on-the-spot have the local knowledge to act effectively."

Friedrich von Hayek, perhaps the premier defender of free
market capitalism, won the Nobel Prize in 1974, and Milton Friedman won the prize in 1976. Von Hayek's *The Road to Serfdom* gained
new currency (thirty-two printings by 2004), and Friedman took
advantage of the opportunity to publicize key ideas about market
economies in a widely viewed televised series on PBS. Videotapes
and transcripts of the lectures were circulated, and his book, *Free to
Choose*, reached a far larger audience than had ever before been exposed to such concepts. Von Hayek's observation that "it is merely a
question of time until the views . . . held by the intellectuals become
the governing force of politics" contributed to the new determination to see a conservative intelligentsia installed to combat the liberal tenor of academia and of public policy discourse that had, since
the 1930s, become dominant.

Liberal economics writer Robert Kuttner noted that, over the
course of the 1970s and 1980s, free market champions came to dominate academic economics departments and that "tens of millions of
dollars [were] pumped into right-wing foundations to bolster

unregulated, free-market capitalism. And, apart from isolated individuals, there [was] no response from the left of center." Kuttner added that support also came from "[t]he high-tech industry as a whole [which tended] to be very libertarian. Technology is changing so fast, utopians say, that government should just get out of the way. They claim that, thanks to information technology, markets can really work more like they do in the textbooks, that any producer in the world can find any consumer in the world."

Financial journalist Joseph Nocera noted the extraordinary successes of free market capitalism: "Over the past two decades, we've been participating in nothing less than a money revolution," wrote Nocera in 1994.

> "Money revolution" is not a term I use lightly. When one recalls what the financial life of the middle class was like 20 years ago—when thrift was the highest value, when the daily movement of the Dow Jones average had almost no relevance to our lives, when few of us knew what a mutual fund was, much less the distinction between, say, a growth fund and a balanced fund—it's hard not to conclude that the change has, indeed, been revolutionary.

Nocera argued that the change came about because of a series of major financial innovations: the credit card, which democratized debt; the mutual fund and the discount brokerage house, which democratized investment; and computer technology, which "made the money revolution possible. Computers are the hidden spine of every modern financial device." These developments eventually tore down the legal barriers that once separated banks and brokerage houses from savings accounts and money-market funds. Once these barriers fell, the middle class walked through the breach and settled in for the long haul.

The democratization of credit and investment opened up avenues of wealth accumulation to the middle class, creating more conservative voters willing to cast their ballots for Republican candidates, as Grover Norquist's "investor class" expanded. Word of American prosperity and opportunity traveled, attracting greater numbers of immigrants from every corner of the Earth, men and women willing to undergo extraordinary hardship and danger to gain entry, legally or illegally.

➤ ◄

The American middle class over the past half century has grown vastly—well-nourished, well-housed, and well-clothed by historic standards—with an unprecedented array of work opportunities, family configurations, consumer goods, leisure activities, and dreams fulfilled. In this regard, the Democratic coalition is the victim of its own success.

At the same time, America can be a place of misery, as a walk through any ghetto, bar, emergency room, mental health clinic, unemployment office, social service agency, bus station, twelve-step program, family court, homeless shelter, halfway house, prison, domestic violence center, or breadline can attest. One indicator of the anxiety and despair induced by hypercompetition and insecurity can be seen in the pattern of stress-related medication consumption: antidepressants are now the top-selling category of prescription drugs in the United States with $12.5 billion in retail sales in 2001, up 20.2 percent from the previous year. Antidepressants also were responsible for the largest share (9.4 percent) of the one-year increase in 2001 drug spending. Risk and the absence of security have become central features of American life, for workers, managers, speculators, and owners.[1] There are few safe havens.

AN ENTREPRENEURIAL AND RISK-TOLERANT CORPORATE INSURGENCY

By 1973, the stage was set for the ascendancy of a new elite within the business universe. This new elite challenged vested interests across every domain: formerly protected industries including airlines, railroads, and communications, the monopoly of old-line

---

[1] Superior risk management skills are prized by Republicans and by corporate leaders, figuring significantly in Bush's May 30, 2006, appointment of Henry M. Paulson Jr., CEO of Goldman Sachs Group, as treasury secretary: "Think of Paulson as 'Mr. Risk,'" wrote *Business Week*. "He is one of the architects of a more daring Wall Street, where securities firms are taking greater and greater chances in their pursuit of profits. . . . Clearly, Paulson isn't scared by debt and risk-taking" (Michael Mandel, "Mr. Risk Goes to Washington," *Business Week*, June 12, 2006, pp. 46–48).

banking interests, the once-powerful industrial manufacturing sector, and the hereditary Protestant establishment. By the mid-1970s, a new, more entrepreneurial corporate insurgency began to emerge, challenging the old order and fueled by waves of rapidly accelerating scientific and technological change and the abrupt emergence of escalating competitive pressures. Computerization and information processing, increasingly sophisticated marketing techniques, accumulating technological breakthroughs, exponential advances in telecommunications, the development of the Internet, and the inexorable pressures of international trade augmented and extended the money revolution, ushering in a period of pervasive global hyper-competition unprecedented in terms of velocity and scale.

"Everybody was asleep at the wheel and didn't see that there was . . . a third industrial revolution," said Thomas K. McCraw of Harvard Business School. Management consultant Peter Drucker described the situation by the 1990s thus:

> [I]n the 1950s, industrial workers had become the largest single group in every developed country, and unionized industrial workers in mass-production industry (which was then dominant everywhere) had attained upper-middle-class income levels. They had extensive job security, pensions, long paid vacations, and comprehensive unemployment insurance or "lifetime employment." Above all, they had achieved political power. . . . Thirty-five years later, in 1990, industrial workers and their unions were in retreat. They had become marginal in numbers. Whereas industrial workers who make or move things had accounted for two-fifths of the American work force in the 1950s, they accounted for less than one-fifth in the early 1990s—that is, for no more than they had accounted for in 1900, when their meteoric rise began. . . . By the year 2000 or 2010, in every developed free market country, industrial workers will account for no more than an eighth of the work force. Union power has been declining just as fast. . . . The newly emerging dominant group is "knowledge workers." . . . By the end of this century knowledge workers will make up a third or more of the work force in the United States. . . . But for the developed countries, too, the shift to knowledge-based work poses enormous social challenges. Despite the factory, industrial society was still essentially a traditional society in its basic social relationships of production. But the emerging society, the one based on knowl-

edge and knowledge workers, is not. It is the first society in which ordinary people—and that means most people—do not earn their daily bread by the sweat of their brow. It is the first society in which "honest work" does not mean a callused hand. It is also the first society in which not everybody does the same work, as was the case when the huge majority were farmers or, as seemed likely only forty or thirty years ago, were going to be machine operators. This is far more than a social change. It is a change in the human condition.

➤ ◄

The vulnerability of established firms and industries in the mid- and late 1970s was, in retrospect, glaring. From 1969 to 1979, the Dow Jones Industrial average dropped from 876.72 to 844.40, while the Gross Domestic Product (GDP) grew by more than 150 percent, from $982.2 billion to $2.56 trillion. The undervaluing of corporate stock presented the ideal circumstances for what would become a flood of leveraged buyouts, hostile takeovers, mergers, and acquisitions.

At the same time, one of the primary mechanisms used by corporate America to strangle the rise of competitors—its intimate, if not closed, relationship with the nation's banking community—began to fracture in the face of competition. Leading the charge was a new breed of investment banker, the most innovative and controversial of the first generation of whom was Michael Milken of Drexel Burnham. Milken pioneered the sale of high-yield and high-risk junk bonds that became key mechanisms in the reorganization of much of corporate America, providing venture capital for start-ups ranging from Cable News Network (CNN) to MCI.

The change in the corporate culture of American business was dramatic. By the late 1990s, James Annable, former senior vice-president and director of economics for Bank One Corporation, wrote in the *Wall Street Journal*:

> When senior managers were sheltered by limited trade, industry cartelization, inefficient capital markets, and passive shareholders, they typically took the easy road. They sought to satisfy not just shareholders, but all their organization's constituents—workers, vendors, managers, and communities. With respect to

employees, explicit or implicit contracts evolved over time, guaranteeing employment rights, established wage differentials, and the continuation in trends in real compensation growth. Such contracts became the cornerstones of corporate culture. Globalization, deregulation, the threat of corporate takeovers, and the rise of shareholder activism have dramatically changed the comfort levels of senior executives. Most are now convinced that their jobs depend on taking aggressive actions to increase earnings and push up their stock prices. . . . The continuing revision in implicit and explicit employee contracts takes several forms. Employees—often higher wage middle managers and professional workers—are being eliminated outright via outsourcing, improved efficiency, discontinuation of product lines and the use of temporary workers. Non-wage benefits are coming under tighter control.

THE REPUBLICAN PARTY AND RISK

Together, the economic and cultural revolutions put risk, and the management of risk, at the center of the political agenda. The policies of the contemporary Republican Party—from its aggressive foreign policy and its determination to democratize the world to its advocacy of Social Security privatization and cutting off of welfare entitlements—all involve major risks. These policies further assume that such risks can be well managed, not only by government leaders, the private sector, and the military but also by the poor, the elderly, and by people like Ben Martinez.

The Republican Party and its major backers are those Americans most optimistic about the opportunities that the business revolution has opened up and most confident of their ability to calculate and manage risk. The party and its officeholders have been willing to run high deficits on the chance that they will produce revenue-generating economic growth, a "riverboat gamble," as former Republican Senator Howard Baker described Reagan's 1981 tax cut.

Forcing people off welfare is designed to compel them to learn to transact in the economic marketplace—a risky proposition. The 2003 invasion of Iraq—with its possible payoff in terms of driving modernization in Arab countries, reducing terrorism, and potentially improving American access to Mideast oil—is worth the risk of regional chaos, in the Republican view. It is worth the thousands of casualties and many more wounded, as well as the risk of turning millions of radicalized Muslims and their sympathizers—in Europe and across the Islamic countries of Asia—into enemies.

The GOP's tax and social policies provide incentives and rewards for winners who undertake risk—the recipients of capital gains, high-paid CEOs, those who generate large estates—leaving losers to fend for themselves in the conviction that the market is the best teacher. Sometimes the high-risk strategies of the GOP pay off in spades. Newt Gingrich's sustained assault on the House Democratic majority had the hallmark of grandiose fantasy until it delivered the Congress into Republican hands in November 1994. The 1996 welfare reform bill, the Personal Responsibility and Work Opportunity Reconciliation Act of 1996, slashed the welfare rolls; the downside, in terms of violent social disorder, did not materialize. Reagan's high-risk face-off with the air traffic controller's union (PATCO) in 1981 dealt a body blow to trade unionism. So, too, Ronald Reagan's strategy of escalating military spending arguably contributed to the downfall of the Soviet Union, ruptured the communist bloc, and brought an end to the Cold War. Crime rates are down, a result, in the eyes of many Republicans, of conservative bets on tough mandatory sentencing laws and jail time for low-level drug offenders. Conversely, Republicans in Texas recently were willing to risk an about-face, passing legislation mandating treatment rather than prison for first-time drug offenders. "Like so many Nixons going to China, Republican policy makers . . . are rethinking prison policies for non-violent and drug offenders," said the executive director of the Justice Policy Institute. "Instead of cutting spending on schools and hospitals, states can reduce their corrections expenditures while protecting public safety. Texas moving to divert non-violent offenders into treatment instead of incarceration solidifies it as a national trend because Texas is widely viewed as the nation's toughest state when it comes to prison policies."

➤ ◄

In a high-wire act, the American business community and the Bush administration kept the American financial sector afloat in the perilous days after the September 2001 attack that wreaked havoc in New York's financial district. The same business-political alliance brought the Dow Jones industrial average back to 11,000 by May 2006, up nearly 4,000 points since its nadir in 2001—just in time to lend the GOP much-needed support before the 2006 midterm elections.

Other high-risk Republican strategies have bombed: the Watergate burglary, Nixon's failure to produce, between 1969 and 1974, a military victory in Vietnam, Reagan's sale of arms to Iran to finance the Contras in Nicaragua, and the attempted Clinton impeachment all imposed substantial costs on the Republican Party. The outcome and consequences of the war in Iraq remain uncertain. President Bush's risk-management credentials were called into serious question by the release on April 10, 2004, of documents revealing that the president had been specifically warned of terrorist threats a month before the 9/11 attacks. The August 6, 2001, presidential daily security briefing (PDB) was headlined "Bin Ladin Determined to Strike in U.S." and informed the president that surveillance by the FBI "indicates patterns of suspicious activity in this country consistent with preparations for hijackings or other types of attacks, including recent surveillance of federal buildings in New York."

DEMOCRATS MORE RISK AVERSE

The Democratic Party—less confident and less optimistic than the GOP—has become the advocate of risk aversion. As they seek government protection, Democrats support a taxpayer-financed safety net for the elderly, for unmarried mothers, for children, for the disabled, for those out of work, for immigrants, for the poor and the sick—in other words, for those who cannot compete in today's marketplace. The party also offers only reluctant support to unilateral or preemptive, high-risk military engagements and is wary of retaliation and of unintended consequences.

Many Democratic voters make similarly cautious and risk-averse judgments as they support protectionist trade policies. Democratic voters are more sensitive to the possible risks of investment; often having no margin for error, they are more eager to pool risk with public underwriting of social insurance and guaranteed, if smaller, benefits. Core Democratic constituencies are similarly in need of protected enclaves such as those provided by lenient bank-

ruptcy laws, rent control, state subsidized health care,,extended unemployment benefits, family leave, and worker compensation laws.

Upscale social liberals—those higher-income Democrats from
the upper strata of academia and from the nonprofit and professional sector—are often particularly concerned with the risks the
free market poses to ordinary working families. As Elizabeth Warren, a professor at Harvard Law School, writes:

> Over the past generation, an economic transformation has
> taken place in the heart of the middle class family. The once-
> secure family that could count on hard work and fair play to
> keep it safe has been transformed by current economic risk and
> realities. Now a pink slip, a bad diagnosis, or a disappearing
> spouse can catapult a family from solidly middle class to newly
> poor in a few months.
>
> The changes in the basic economic structure of the Ameri-
> can family are staggering. In just one generation, millions of
> mothers have gone to work, so that the typical middle class
> household in America is no longer a one-earner family. . . . In-
> stead, the majority of families with small children now have
> both parents rising at dawn to commute to jobs so that they can
> both pull in paychecks.
>
> . . . Today a fully employed male earns $41,670 per year.
> After adjusting for inflation, that is nearly $800 less than his
> counterpart of a generation ago. The only real increase in
> wages for a family has been the second paycheck added by a
> working mother. With both adults in the workforce full-time,
> the family's combined income is $73,770—a whopping 75 per-
> cent higher than the household income for the family in the
> early 1970s. But increasing family income by sending more
> people into the workforce has an overlooked side effect: family
> risk has risen as well.
>
> Today's families have budgeted to the limits of their new
> two-paycheck status. As a result, they have lost the parachute
> they once had in times of financial setback—a back-up earner
> who could go into the workforce if the primary earner (usually
> Dad) got laid off or was sick. This phenomenon, known as the
> added-worker effect, could buttress the safety net offered by
> unemployment insurance or disability insurance to help fami-
> lies weather bad times. But today, with all workers already
> going—and spending—flat out, there is no one left in reserve
> to step in during the tough times. Any disruption to family for-
> tunes can no longer be made up with extra income from an
> otherwise-stay-at-home partner.

➤ ◁

The House and Senate votes in October 2001 on Bush's plan to invade Iraq demonstrated the divide between the two parties on an issue combining risk and aggression in foreign policy. In the 296 to 133 House vote, a majority of Democrats, 127 out of 209, voted no, compared with only 6 of 229 Republicans. The Senate backed the measure 77 to 23, with only one Republican, Lincoln Chafee of Rhode Island, voting against it, compared with 22 Democrats in opposition.

In the 217 to 215 House vote in support of the Central American Free Trade Agreement (CAFTA), 188 members of the Democratic caucus voted no and 15 voted yes; Republicans supported the treaty by a 202 to 27 margin. Democrats consistently vote by stronger margins than do Republicans to protect Medicaid, Medicare, and other safety net programs and are far less supportive than the GOP of tax cuts that threaten government revenues. Democrats are also firmly on the side of those who would protect the environment in disputes with commercial developers of wilderness areas and natural resources.

There are compelling reasons why each party takes a different attitude toward risk. Democrats far more than Republicans represent those in the bottom third of the income distribution, those with the fewest resources to fall back upon, those without the means to recoup losses, those with the ability to survive should a risk-taking venture fail, those less likely, on average, to have profited from accelerating innovation in the business sector. If, twenty years from now, Social Security has become privatized and a retired President Bush, then in his late eighties, sees the stocks in his private Social Security account go belly-up, he will still have other assets valued (in 2004) at somewhere between $9.63 million and $26.59 million—not to mention the millions more he can expect to make from speeches, books, real estate transactions, and other ventures once he leaves office. Conversely, a voter in the bottom third of the income distribution today would, in all likelihood, see his or her means of subsistence disappear should investments in a privatized Social Security account collapse.

The costs of risk taking are obviously far lower for those with extensive resources—a strongly Republican constituency—than for those without them—a Democratic constituency. In addition, insofar as risk management requires skill, the affluent have the opportunity and resources to learn and to pass on such skills to friends and family members, whereas those of moderate means and the poor have little opportunity, none of the resources, and few friends, family, or other helpers to assist them in acquiring high-level risk-management skills.

CONFIDENT RISK TAKERS AND PARTISAN ALIGNMENT

One of the most Republican demographic groups—affluent white men—is the demographic with the highest number of confident risk takers. Among academic researchers, this phenomenon is known as "the white male effect." A 1992 study reported in the journal *Risk Analysis* found that, in a survey of 1,512 people, men saw less risk than women from each of twenty-five potential health hazards including nuclear waste, pesticides, blood transfusions, radon, and X-rays: "Sizeable differences between risk perceptions of men and women have been documented in dozens of studies. Men tend to judge risks as smaller and less problematic than do women."

In 2000, the journal *Health, Risk & Society* published findings showing that

> the "white male effect" seemed to be caused by about 30 percent of the white male sample that judged risks to be extremely low. When these risk-tolerant white males were compared with the rest of the respondents, they were found to be better educated, had higher household incomes, and were *politically more conservative* [emphasis added]. They also held very different attitudes, characterized by trust in institutions and authorities and by anti-egalitarianism.

This group of risk takers is made up of men inclined toward the Republican Party. Not only are conservative white men risk takers, but they are, on the whole, relatively successful risk managers, as shown by their high incomes and net worth.

There is another group of risk-tolerant males: criminals. These men are majority nonwhite—64 percent of prison inmates in 2001 were members of racial or ethnic minority groups—and have failed to manage risk effectively, as evidenced by their high incarceration rates.

The partisan differences in attitudes toward risk are echoed in the gender gap, or in the differing attitudes of men and women that can be found in polling by the National Election Studies (NES), Voter News Service (VNS), and other organizations. In a test of backing for government safety net programs, NES polls show that women consistently support government intervention by margins of ten to fifteen points more than men when asked to choose between the following alternatives: "Some people feel that the government in Washington should see to it that every person has a job and a good standard of living. . . . Others think the government should just let each person get ahead on their own." In 2004, women were almost evenly split, with 33 percent saying government should make sure people have a good job and a good standard of living, and 36 percent saying people should take responsibility for themselves. Men, however, decisively came down on the side of individual responsibility, 47 to 29.

When Democrats and Republicans were asked the same question, a strong 42 to 25 plurality of Democrats came down on the side of government responsibility, whereas a decisive 61 to 17 majority of Republicans backed individual responsibility. Nearly half, 46 percent, of men and more than half of the Republicans, 55 percent, said government is "too powerful"; only a third of women, 33 percent, shared that view and just 28 percent of Democrats.

The 2004 network exit polls produced a parallel finding: voters were asked, "Should the government do more to solve problems?" Those who answered yes were majority female, 53 to 47, and they backed Kerry, the Democrat, by a 66 to 33 margin. Those who said no were solidly in George W. Bush's camp, 70 to 29, and they were majority male, 57 to 43. On the issue of defense spending, a majority of men, 55 percent, compared with 40 percent of women told NES pollsters in 2004 that money for the military should be increased; among partisans, 68 percent of Republicans backed more money for the Pentagon compared with 31 percent of Democrats.

In times of economic recession, the Democrats' commitment to the safety net and welfare programs has served the party well. The

Great Depression gave the Democrats majority status, and recessions like those in 1953–1954, 1957–1958, 1973–1974, 1981–1982, and 1991–1992 all produced favorable election results for the Democrats. A problem for Democrats, however, is the long tradition in the United States of encouraging and venerating risk, of preference for the private sector (including the nonprofit sector) over the public sector to provide social services, and of a deep commitment to untrammeled individualism and liberty. Under normal economic conditions, Democratic policies on issues of risk and government intervention are to the left of the voting population as a whole.

A strikingly high percentage of young people in the United States today, 63 percent, say there is a "good chance" they will be rich someday. In terms of voters judging their own capacity to manage risk, among all Americans fully 69 percent believe they are "above average" in their overall personality and character, and 86 percent say their intelligence is above average. And it can make such voters angry (tap their "anger points") to be told that the government they view as wasteful, spendthrift, and unwisely redistributive can do a better job of allocating their dollars than they can.

RISK TAKERS AND REPUBLICANS WANT GOVERNMENT TO TREAD LIGHTLY

The advantage the Republican Party derives from Americans' aversion to government regulation and control is substantial. Seymour Martin Lipset, the sociologist and author of *American Exceptionalism: A Double-Edged Sword*, has written about the characteristic American preference for an enhanced sphere of individual freedom of action and a relatively smaller role for the state:

> Not only do we remain the most moralistic of Western societies, we are also the least statist, the least deferential to public authority, and the most involved in voluntary associations and charitable activities. Our social norms can only be strengthened in ways consistent with our commitments to liberty and equality; our civic life can only be renewed in ways that respect our historic commitment to civil society and reservations about the public sector. This is not to say that government has no role to play in reinvigorating citizenship. But to be effective,

government must tread lightly, act as a catalyst rather than an overseer, and maximize respectful collaboration with voluntary associations and local communities.

American exceptionalism—including the characteristic inclination toward individually managed risk—is based on a deeply rooted optimism and self-confidence. The contemporary Democrat tends to stress the more pessimistic prospects of the American economy and the likelihood of failure—as is to be expected for a party that represents the bottom half of the income spectrum. The grim assessment by many Democratic leaders of the damage to American workers from free trade, the party's partiality to increased government social welfare spending, its choice of stringent regulation of private enterprise, its emphasis on the need for downward redistribution and for higher taxes, its focus on the dangers of global warming, species extinction, and environmental degradation, its commitment to what detractors see as a "nanny state"—all militate against the party being viewed by centrist middle-class voters as generating well-being and prosperity. These factors also put the party, to some degree, at odds with the optimistic and can-do American ethic—the ethic Reagan exploited so effectively with his 1984 campaign theme, "It's morning again in America."

STEVE CARR AND BEN MARTINEZ

To return to the story of Steve Carr and Ben Martinez that began this chapter, those who voted Republican in 2004 might imagine that Martinez picked himself up after losing his job at Hertz and successfully started over, participating in the business revolution. After all, there were 1.6 million Hispanic-owned businesses in 2002, and their receipts that year were $226.5 billion. Or—under a Republican scenario—Martinez, rather than being a victim, might have gone on to study automotive repair, as his boss, Steve Carr, did, and secure a better job in a large corporation. Market forces, responding to the need for increasingly well-trained technicians to maintain and repair complex modern cars (such as those in a rental fleet), have created a vast number of proprietary schools that sell training and certification in automotive subspecialties valued by corporations such as Hertz and Avis—online and in physical locations across the country. Training is available in the fields of autotronics, shop management, advanced heating, ventilation, air conditioning and refrigeration, detailing, upholstery, auto body repair, diesel mechanics, motorcycles, and so forth. Graduates of such programs (with instruction available in both English and Spanish) are also valuable to automobile dealerships and other facilities dealing with warranty repairs. The mean hourly wage for this kind of work in 2000 was $18.44.

What happened to Ben Martinez is not known, but many Republican voters—including Latinos—will identify with Steve Carr more than with Martinez, feeling that a business regime of "no excuses" is a core component of success in America's entrepreneurial economy. In this regard, where sympathy for the underdog is a factor, the two parties are genuinely polarized.

In many ways, Elizabeth Warren captures the mindset of the leadership of the Democratic Party: she is empathetic, responsible, and alarmed; she is putting her shoulder to the wheel and fighting for more equitable public policies. She was an important voice during the congressional debate on legislation—backed by the GOP, major banks, and the credit card industry—reducing bankruptcy protection for ordinary people who fall into debt. Warren produced scholarly research and data showing that

> one million men and women each year are turning to bankruptcy in the aftermath of a serious medical problem—and three-quarters of them have health insurance.
>
> A family with children is nearly three times more likely to file for bankruptcy than an individual or couple with no children.
>
> More children now live through their parents' bankruptcy than through their parents' divorce. . . . A family driven to bankruptcy by the increased costs of caring for an elderly parent with Alzheimer's disease is treated the same as someone who maxed out his credit cards at a casino. A person who had a heart attack is treated the same as someone who had a spending spree at the shopping mall. A mother who works two jobs and who cannot manage the prescription drugs needed for a child with diabetes is treated the same as someone who charged a bunch of credit cards with only a vague intent to repay. . . . If Congress is determined to sort the good from the bad, then

begin by sorting those who have been laid low by medical debts, those who lost their jobs, those whose breadwinners have been called to active duty and sent to Iraq, those who are caring for elderly parents and sick children from those few who overspend on frivolous purchases. . . . Overwhelmingly, American families file for bankruptcy because they have been driven there—largely by medical and economic catastrophe—not because they want to go there.

Warren's plea was to no avail, and stringent bankruptcy legislation, adding new burdens for those Warren described, passed. Why should Elizabeth Warren's well-intentioned crusade to spare lives already damaged, if not ruined, by catastrophic bad luck have broad political implications? Because hard luck stories, to some extent, have become associated with the Democratic Party, and in much of "red" America the Democratic Party is viewed as a coalition of "losers." To some extent, it has become a liability for the Democrats to be sensitive to the real dilemmas, the hardship, and the suffering of the bottom half of the social order in a country that worships optimism and success—and a country that can be angered by the demands of the poor.

The next chapter will explore the strengths and weaknesses of the Democratic Party at this critical point.

7

The Democrats:
Two Sets of Problems—
Ideological and Structural

The strongest evidence of the problems of the Democratic Party lies in the rejection of the party's candidates by a decisive majority of white voters. In 2004, Kerry lost to Bush among white voters with annual household incomes of $30,000 to $75,000 by a landslide twenty-two percentage points. This population includes a majority of the white American working class. Among whites making more than $75,000, Bush's margin was almost identical to his working- and middle-class margins, twenty-three points.

For many middle-income voters, the economy offers little or no job security; their health care coverage, if they have any at all, can be cut off without warning; the cost of housing has skyrocketed along with the price of energy and gasoline; there is widespread dissatisfaction with the public schools; and most families are having a difficult or impossible time piecing together the money to send their children to college or to some form of technical training. The political question is: Where will these Americans go when they enter the voting booth? Will they swing toward the Democrats or move toward the GOP?

THE CONFLATION OF RACE,
IMMIGRATION, AND VALUES

Issues having to do with race—and now with immigration as well— are entangled in these economic matters and are exploited by

Republicans to generate polarization. Race and immigration combine with other sociocultural matters to recruit very large white majorities to the GOP. These developments propel domestic politics to the right and make the formation of a populist, class-based, biracial center-left voting coalition difficult—the subject of my earlier book, *Chain Reaction: The Impact of Race, Rights, and Taxes on American Politics.*

Problems facing the Democratic Party have evolved, I argued,

> in complex ways, from one of the major struggles of the twentieth century: the struggle between so-called traditional values and a competing set of insurgent values. Traditional values generally have been seen to revolve around commitments to the larger community—to the family, to parental responsibility, to country, to the work ethic, to sexual restraint, to self-control, to rules, duty, authority, and a stable social order. The competing set of insurgent values, the focus of rights-oriented political ideologies, of the rights revolution, and of the civil-rights movement, has been largely concerned with the rights of the individual—with freedom from oppression, from confinement, from hierarchy, from authority, from stricture, from repression, from rigid rule-making, and from the status quo.
>
> On a level essentially ignored by liberal elites—but a level, nonetheless, of stark reality to key voters—the values debate has become conflated with racial politics. Among Democrats and liberals the stigmatization of racism in the 1960s had the unintended and paradoxical consequence of stigmatizing the allegiance of many voters to a whole range of fundamental moral values. In the late 1960s and early 1970s the raising of the "traditional values" banner over such issues as law and order, the family, sexual conduct, joblessness, welfare fraud, and patriotism was seen by liberals and blacks—with some accuracy—as an appeal to racist, narrow-minded, repressive, or xenophobic instincts, designed to marshal support for reactionary social policies. The conflation by the political right of values with attempts to resist racial integration, to exclude women from public life, and to discredit the extension of constitutional rights to minorities fueled an often bitter resistance by the left and by blacks to the whole values package.
>
> The result was that liberal Democrats often barred from consideration what are in fact legitimate issues for political discourse, issues of fundamental social and moral concern which must be forthrightly addressed by any national candidate or party. This stigmatization as "racist" or as "in bad faith" of

open discussion of values-charged-matters—ranging from crime to sexual responsibility to welfare dependency to drug abuse to standards of social obligation—has for more than two decades created a values barrier between Democratic liberals and much of the electorate. Insofar as many voters feel that their cherished policies and practices have been routed, the values barrier has been a major factor in fracturing a once deeply felt loyalty to a liberal economic agenda.

HAVE AMERICANS BEEN DUPED?

Many Democrats and liberals reject the idea of a "values barrier"—with or without its racial implications—and are convinced that Americans have been duped into voting against their own economic interests by a sophisticated Republican Party waving red-flag cultural issues before the electorate, an argument made most forcefully by Thomas Frank in *What's the Matter with Kansas*:

> What we are observing, then, is a populist movement [Republican conservatism] that has done irreversible harm to the material interests of the common people it professes to love so tenderly—a form of class animosity that rages against a shadowy "elite" while enthroning a new aristocracy of bankers, brokers, and corporate thieves. . . . But on closer inspection the country we have inhabited for the last three decades seems more like a panorama of madness and delusion worthy of Hieronymus Bosch: of sturdy patriots reciting the Pledge while they resolutely strangle their own life chances; of small farmers proudly voting themselves off the land; of devoted family men carefully seeing to it that their children will never be able to afford college or proper health care; of hardened blue-collar workers in Midwestern burgs cheering as they deliver up a landslide for a candidate whose policies will end their way of life, will transform their region into a "rust belt," will strike people like them blows from which they will never recover.

In Frank's view, "it is precisely because the Democrats won't take up that battle and won't talk that old language of economic populism that Republicans are able to get away with this kind of hallucinatory class world that they live in."

What's the Matter with Kansas provided comfort to many of those on the left who remain convinced of the underlying validity of their beliefs and of their stands on issues—the book remained on the *New York Times* best-seller list for more than four months. Frank is one of the leaders of a chorus of liberal Democrats who has echoed this theme in recent decades. In 1986, pollster Stan Greenberg argued, "To regain the initiative and the minds of the American people, we need to recapture Democratic themes: populism, the middle class, government, family, pride and economic opportunity. . . . The American public, including the potential Democratic electorate, is profoundly populist."

In 2005, David Sirota, one of the Democratic Party's young shining lights, argued that populism "is the path Karl Rove fears. He knows his GOP is vulnerable to Democrats who finally follow leaders who have translated a populist economic agenda into powerful cultural and values messages." These assertions are made despite the evidence of the failure of populist appeals, such as those made by Gore in 2000 ("the people against the powerful") or in primary contests—Howard Dean in 2004 ("the Democratic wing of the Democratic Party"), John Edwards in 2004 ("Today, under George W. Bush, there are two Americas, not one: One America that does the work, another that reaps the reward"), Representative Richard A. Gephardt in 1988 and 2004, Senator Tom Harkin in 1992, or Jesse Jackson in 1984 and 1988.

While Clinton won only 43 percent of the vote in 1992 (Perot's disproportionately white 19 percent delivered the election to the Democrats) and only 49.2 percent in 1996 (with Perot again a spoiler at 8.4 percent of the vote), the Arkansas governor "had spent his entire political career," as Earl and Merle Black point out, "learning how to bob and weave liberal and conservative themes in order to create and maintain a successful biracial coalition." The only successful Democratic presidential candidates in the past four decades have been two southern governors experienced in assembling just such coalitions.

GOP NOW WINS WHITE VOTERS AT THE CONGRESSIONAL LEVEL

The shifting pattern of voting over the past forty years, with Republicans making gains among once-Democratic white voters, is not restricted to presidential contests. A study by the National Committee for an Effective Congress (NCEC) of the eighty-eight congressional districts that shifted from Democratic to Republican from 1994 to 2000 showed that fifty-nine, or two-thirds of the total, had average incomes below the national norm. In sixty-eight, or nearly three-quarters, of these eighty-eight districts that the GOP picked up, the percentage of residents with college degrees was below the national average. In direct contrast to the Republican shifts, 63 percent, or twenty-nine of forty-six, of seats that went from the GOP to the Democratic Party had higher than average national incomes.

THE DEMOCRATIC PARTY IS NOT A POPULIST ORGANIZATION

The Democratic Party, then, faces two sets of problems. One set is *ideological*—to do with issues that include values, race, immigration, the use of force, wealth generation, the broader topic of rights, and so on. The other set of problems is *structural* and includes (but is not limited to) the distribution of voters across states and districts, intra-party class divisions, straight-ticket voting, gerrymandering, the electoral college, voter turnout, party organization, candidate recruitment, campaign staff, sources of money and its regulation, and so on. The two sets of problems are inextricably linked.

One reason the Democratic Party has had so much difficulty making a credible populist appeal to the electorate in recent years, for example, is that structurally it is not a populist organization; it is dominated by a well-educated, culturally liberal, relatively affluent white elite presiding over a Democratic Party rank and file that is 46 percent minority—Black, Hispanic, Native American, and Asian American. From Nancy Pelosi (daughter and sister of Baltimore mayors, 2004 assets between $25 million and $102 million) to Harold Ickes (son of FDR's secretary of the interior, Sidwell Friends School, Stanford, and Columbia Law), Howard Dean (Park Avenue, St. Georges, Yale), George Soros (Hungarian currency speculator, net worth $7.2 billion), Ellen Malcolm (an heiress to the IBM fortune), Jane Fonda (the record-breaking contributor to a liberal nonprofit in 2000 with a gift of $12.3 million), John Kerry (net worth estimated at $163,626,399, St. Paul's, Yale, Skull and Bones), Al Gore (St Albans, Harvard, son of a U.S. senator), and Hillary Clinton (former first lady, Wellesley, Yale Law), the Democratic leadership class is from a markedly different and more privileged background than many of the citizens whose votes it seeks.

DEMOCRATIC PARTY STRUCTURAL STRENGTHS

On the structural front, the Democratic Party is no longer mired far behind the Republicans in the battle for money. After years of facing a better financed Republican Party, Democrats have since 2004 been the beneficiaries of a massive influx of money—much of it via the Internet—from culturally, racially, and socially liberal donors, large and small. The presidential campaign of John F. Kerry nearly matched the Bush re-election bid, $249.8 million to $274.6 million, and the DNC, which had been consistently beaten by more than a two-to-one margin in the past, raised $311.5 million, nearly 80 percent of the RNC's $392.4 million. Just two years earlier, in 2001–2002, the DNC had raised less than half the amount raised by the RNC, $93.4 million to $213 million.

The most striking development in 2004 was the surge in small contributions to Democrats through online credit card donations. The amount of money raised in donations of $200 or less rose for Democratic presidential candidates from $11 million in 2000 to $127 million in 2004, an eleven-fold increase, while for Republican presidential candidates, contributions of $200 or less rose from $43 million to $78 million—not quite doubling. In 2004, then, the Democrats eliminated what had been one of their major financial liabilities: their weakness in small-donor fundraising.

The Internet Benefits Democrats

Democrats and liberals in 2004 matched their adversaries in the effective use of the most important technological advance in recent years: the Internet. In many cases, Democrats and liberals were ahead of Republicans and conservatives in the use of the Web as a vehicle for partisan recruitment and intra-party debate, for cost-effective low-dollar fundraising, for political communication, and for the mobilization of activists and of voters. For a party and ideology that have been outgunned by conservatives and the GOP in such crucial past developments as direct mail, opposition research, effective use of CSPAN, talk radio, the formation of think tanks and leadership institutes, and the creation of post-television political party machines, Democratic success in capitalizing on the Web is no small achievement. It has proved crucial to the survival of the party as a competitive force and prevented the 2004 elections from turning into a full-scale Democratic disaster.

The Internet has been, preeminently, a new tool for Democratic fundraising. The formation, since 2003, of Web-based communications networks has facilitated liberal online communities. As of this writing, the liberal blog Daily Kos by Markos Moulitsas Kuniga has consistently been the political Web site receiving the most "hits" from Internet users. Many politically oriented blogs provide "donation" buttons leading to candidates' home pages and to a credit card form, making contributing to campaigns instantaneous and virtually effortless. This has been particularly important for the left, which has lacked the organizing venues—mega-churches and "family values" groups, for example—that have offered fundraising opportunities to the right.

Of the top ten political Web sites in 2005, as measured by Technorati—which tracks links between Web sites—seven were on the left (Daily Kos, The Huffington Post, Crooks and Liars, Think Progress, Talking Points Memo, Eschaton, MyDD, and AMERICAblog), and three were on the right (Michelle Malkin, Instapundit, and Hugh Hewitt). A similar pattern favoring the left emerged in the daily Web site viewing count conducted by TheTruthLaidBear, which found that the top two political sites as of early 2006 were both liberal, Daily Kos and Eschaton. A 2005 study published by the New Democrat Network (NDN) found that "the 98 most trafficked progressive blogs totaled an amazing 15,181,649 page views per week, an average of over two million daily page views. . . . By way of comparison, the top one-hundred and fifty conservative blogs had less than ten million page views per week during this period, and just over one million unique visits a day."

The success of progressives on the Web was widely heralded. It was crucial to the early success of Dean's presidential campaign and to the breaking of Democratic fundraising records by Kerry. In the August 4, 2003, issue of the *Nation*, Andrew Boyd wrote enthusiastically, "Whatever else it has done, the Internet has helped to level the playing field between an entrenched government and corporate and media power, and an insurgent citizenry. The future might indeed be up for grabs." In March of that year, Moveon.com's Eli Pariser told the *New York Times*: "We don't think a month in advance. . . . We can capture the energy of the moment better at the moment."

In actual practice, however, the Republican Party in 2004 was more successful than the Democratic Party in locating and mobilizing its base voters and its prospective voters who needed to be registered and turned out on election day. The media focused on the success of the Dean campaign, Moveon, Meetup, Daily Kos, myriad progressive blogs, and other institutions on the left in tapping into new constituencies of supporters and donors, as well as on the colorful role of such figures as Joe Trippi, Pariser, Ben Brandzel, Tom Matzzie, Jerome Armstrong, and Zack Exley in "turning politics into the sports page." But at the polls in 2004, the GOP's more mundane and businesslike pursuit of voter lists, consumer databases, conservative and religious organization membership lists, and other data mining techniques—the work of people like Matt Dowd and Alex Gage—all carefully tested and modified in the elections of 2002 and 2003, paid off in victory.

"Like many observers, I was taken in by early reports of unprecedented turnouts, envisaging armies of young Howard 'Deaniac' disciples and newly registered Hispanic citizens leading the charge for John Kerry. But this turnout proved far more varied than initially thought, reflecting stronger Republican than Democratic organizing efforts," wrote demographer William Frey in the *Financial Times*.

An Increase in the Number of Seculars and Hispanics

There are a number of long-range demographic trends suggesting that some liberal (blue) constituencies are growing while certain key constituencies of conservative (red) America are declining. The fastest growing "religious" group is decisively pro-Democratic: seculars, nonbelievers, agnostics, and those for whom religion has little or no relevance. Those who never, or almost never, attend religious services voted for Kerry over Bush by 62 to 36. From 1970 to 2004, the percentage of voters who say they never attend services has nearly tripled from 12 to 35 percent. There are, however, substantial costs to this demographic gain: the Democratic Party has become increasingly identified as irreligious or even anti-religious in a country where a decisive majority of voters say they believe in God.

The Hispanic share of the electorate, a Democratic-majority constituency, has been growing extremely rapidly, more than doubling from 3.7 percent of the electorate in 1992 to 8 percent in 2004, only twelve years later. While this growth should benefit the Democrats, the Republican Party has in recent years been increasing its minority share of the Hispanic vote. In 2004, the Hispanic vote was Democratic by only a 53 to 44 margin, the lowest Democratic percentage since exit polling began in 1972. Almost all Republican gains among Hispanics have been among the growing Latino evangelical Protestant community, as opposed to among the Hispanic Catholic electorate.

Immigration Splits the GOP

Republicans have been divided on immigration policy, with one wing of the party eager to court Hispanics and another concerned with border security and keeping out or sending home undocumented "aliens." Divisions appear within Democratic ranks as well, but at this writing, the Republican Party—with one faction adamant in its demands for border fencing, repatriation, zero tolerance, and denial of amnesty—faces the danger of losing the roughly 10 percent gain the party picked up in 2004 among Hispanic voters.

In terms of splitting the GOP electorate and the Republican Party leadership, immigration is among the most potent issues. In 2008, Republicans face the prospect not only of fractured unity on immigration policy but also the possibility of an explicitly anti-immigration candidate running for the presidential nomination, perhaps Colorado Representative Tom Tancredo—a man Karl Rove told to never "darken the door of the White House" again. Tancredo's outspoken criticism of lax border enforcement has made him increasingly influential on Capitol Hill, meaning that his potential to splinter his own party is substantial. And Tancredo is willing to exploit his status: "My ability to get anything done around here is based around my ability to make this into a national issue. My megaphone is pointed at the ear of America."

The intensity of conflict within Republican ranks—a division that undercuts any advantage the GOP might have had—can be seen in the divided opinion on this topic. One side of the Republican debate was captured by journalist John Judis in his 2006 *New Republic* article "Border War." Judis argues that the most divisive aspects of the immigration struggle have to do not with border security but with assimilation:

> Leaders of the movement to restrict immigration usually began by expressing concerns that illegal immigration was undermining the rule of law and allowing terrorists to sneak across the border—concerns they seem to believe are most likely to win over a national audience. But they invariably became most animated, and most candid, when talking about what they see as the unwillingness of Mexican immigrants—legal or illegal—to assimilate into American culture. . . . That's what bothers [former Arizona House Majority Whip Randy] Graf. . . . "We are talking about assimilation," says the congressional candidate. . . . "I don't have any problem about anyone who wants to salute our flag and learn our language and be a citizen. What got me into the whole issue was that I was standing in line in a Safeway, and this woman was ahead of me, and she had an infant, and was pregnant, and her mother was with her. She was paying for groceries in food stamps. . . . I found it odd that an entire family could be here on welfare and not speak any English. On welfare!" . . . [Russell] Pearce, [chairman of the Arizona House Appropriations Committee] . . . lives in the Phoenix suburb of Mesa. Last fall, he complained, . . . "It's not the Mesa I was raised in. They have turned it into a Third World country," he said. By "they," Pearce means Latinos in general. On his website, he warns, "Over 800,000 Americans fled California last year because LA became a clone of Mexico City." Pearce, like Connie and Graf, envisages a cultural conflict between the white America he grew up in and an invading army of dark-skinned, Spanish-speaking immigrants from south of the border.

Senator John McCain captures the other side of the Republican debate on immigration. In his March 2006 remarks on the Senate floor, McCain argued:

> There are over 11 million people in this country illegally. They harvest our crops, tend our gardens, work in our restaurants, care for our children, clean our homes. They came as others before them came, to grasp the lowest rung of the American ladder of opportunity, to work the jobs others won't, and by virtue of their own industry and desire, to rise and build better lives for their families and a better America. That is our history. . . . We are not a tribe. We are not an ethnic conclave.
>
> We are a nation of immigrants, and that distinction has been essential to our greatness. . . . They came to grasp the lowest rung of the ladder, and they intend to rise. Let them rise. Let them rise. Let us take care to protect our country from harm, but let us not mistake the strengths of our greatness for weaknesses.
>
> We are blessed, bountiful, beautiful America—the land of hope and opportunity—the land of the immigrant's dreams. Long may she remain so.

Democrats Benefit from Decline in Rural Population

Rural voters, currently a reliable Republican constituency—voting for Bush over Kerry by 59 to 40 in 2004—make up a declining fraction of the electorate, an advantage for Democrats. During the 1990s, rural communities had the slowest growth rate, 7.3 percent, compared with 16.5 percent in suburbs, 11.7 percent in exurbia (the communities on the outskirts of traditional metropolitan areas), and a 9.8 percent growth rate in central cities, according to demographer William Frey. There are conflicting partisan trends in the suburbs and exurbia. Democrats have made striking gains in the nation's oldest and most affluent counties, winning sixteen of the twenty-five counties with the highest per capita incomes in 2004 (see Table 1). Before the 1990s, these were Republican suburban strongholds, the often upscale suburbs in the first or inner ring surrounding such cities as Philadelphia, New York, Detroit, San Francisco, and Los Angeles. As these areas have trended Democratic, the Republicans have been gaining strength

Table 1. Demographic Characteristics and Voting Patterns of Suburban
Counties in 2000 and 2004 Elections

Suburb Type	Number	Population (in millions)	% Growth from 1990 to 2000	% White	Bush-Kerry Percentage Spread	Bush-Gore Percentage Spread
Inner suburbs	41	39.9	69.8	5.4	41–59	41–56
Mature suburbs	66	48.7	74.2	11.6	48–52	45–52
Emerging suburbs	146	32.7	88.8	29.6	57–43	53–44
Exurbs	147	5.6	92.4	20.7	62–38	58–40

in the rapidly growing, recently rural, exurban communities, many
located twenty-five to fifty miles from the central cities. Demographers now refer to four kinds of counties or political jurisdictions; going from most to least Democratic, they are: (1) core
cities, (2) traditional suburbia, (3) exurbia, and (4) rural-small
town America.

Sexual Demographics: Privacy and Autonomy Now Are Cherished Rights

Much less noticed are trends in sexual behavior and changing sexual
norms, all of which have political consequences and many of which
would appear to favor Democrats. As noted in chapter 4, Tom W.
Smith of the National Opinion Research Center (NORC) at the
University of Chicago has found that the percentage of women reporting that they were virgins at marriage has dropped steadily,
reaching just 20 percent (or one out of five) for those who turned
twenty between 1963 and 1972, just when the sexual revolution
began to take off. For many of these women and their descendants,
sexual autonomy is now a right that they are prepared to defend
should it come under assault in the political arena. Many women
and, importantly, many men now see the collection of rights that
fall under the rubric of post-1960s sexual and personal freedom as
essential.

While Republicans have demonstrated no greater commitment
at an individual level to traditional rules of sexual morality, the party
legislatively supports a return to the rules of sexual conduct extant
prior to the pill. In the 1996 welfare reform bill, for example, the

Republican Congress included abstinence education grants that could only be awarded to a program that

> has as its exclusive purpose, teaching the social, psychological, and health gains to be realized by abstaining from sexual activity; Teaches abstinence from sexual activity outside marriage as the expected standard for all school age children; Teaches that abstinence from sexual activity is the only certain way to avoid out-of-wedlock pregnancy, sexually transmitted diseases, and other associated health problems; Teaches that a mutually faithful monogamous relationship in context of marriage is the expected standard of human sexual activity; Teaches that sexual activity outside of the context of marriage is likely to have harmful psychological and physical effects.

In addition, the GOP has declined to waver from its efforts to make abortion illegal, or at least increasingly difficult to obtain, and is making substantial efforts to keep the so-called morning-after pill ("Plan B") out of the hands of consumers. Much of this effort is alienating moderate voters and has arguably cost the GOP more than it needed to, as pro-life voters have little political choice other than to decline to vote at all.

Race

The salience of race—an obstacle to a progressive alliance for the past four decades—has been diminished as an overt political issue by the success of the now large black middle class, by 1996 welfare reform legislation, by a reduction in government-sponsored affirmative action programs, by plummeting crime rates, by the distance in time from the race riots of the 1960s, by lessened attention to the urban "underclass," and by the highly visible Republican embrace of diversity—the Republican rhetoric of "compassionate conservatism" and the appointments of Colin Powell, Condoleeza Rice, and others to high-profile positions. Nonetheless, the lowered visibility of racial conflict does not mean that race has disappeared as an issue benefiting the GOP. Race is still the driving cause of white disaffiliation from the Democratic Party, and race is an issue that—when it spontaneously arises in the course of events—conservatives often can and do choose to inflame.

Gun Rights

Finally, Democrats have made it a point to support Second Amendment rights, reducing the visibility of gun control, declaring allegiance to sportsmen, and fielding a number of candidates who are firearms enthusiasts. At the same time, growing numbers of sportsmen and sportsmen's organizations have become increasingly wary of Republican pro-development environmental policies—the commercialization of the wilderness, building, logging, mining, drilling, and so on.

➤ ◁

In terms of Democratic advantages, then, a number of trends seems to suggest that forty years of Republican-conservative domination of the national political agenda may come to an end. John Judis and Ruy Teixeira made a persuasive argument—based on demographic evidence—for upcoming progressive victories in their 2002 book *The Emerging Democratic Majority*. The argument here, however, will emphasize a number of different factors.

TRENDS WORKING AGAINST THE DEMOCRATS

The parties are not static; political parties receive new information from the marketplace in every election cycle and have the opportunity to make adjustments. Like all institutions that must respond to market feedback, the parties vary substantially in their ability to react to new information effectively. In recent decades, the GOP has proven more agile in responding to the electorate, and trends operating to the detriment of Democrats continue to be powerful.

Geography and Demographics

One important trend involves shifts in the voting pattern of the nation's generally smaller but fastest growing counties—with populations fueled by, among other things, white flight—where the Republican Party has experienced remarkable success. In these exurban counties, many located just outside the beltways of large metropolitan areas, Bush won in 2004, often by large margins, capturing ninety-seven of the one hundred counties with the highest growth rates.

The closeness of the contest for the suburban vote can be seen in the election patterns in the counties of the fifty largest metropolitan areas, demonstrated in a study by the Metropolitan Institute at Virginia Tech (Table 1). The Virginia Tech report found that Gore and Kerry did well in the older, close-in suburbs where the population is concentrated and 30.2 percent minority. Bush did well in the more numerous but smaller, fast-growing counties, which are 92.4 percent white.

Gore in 2000 won the aggregation of suburban voters by a 1.7 million margin, and Kerry won in 2004 by only 500,000, a difference that is accounted for by Bush's better performance almost everywhere in 2004 compared with 2000. The short-term trend lines are not promising for the Democratic Party.

GOP Voters Are Distributed Efficiently

A second structural disadvantage for Democrats is that voters are increasingly casting straight-party ballots, a phenomenon that has combined with the geographic distribution of voters to give the Republican Party a strong, built-in advantage in the competition for control of the House and Senate.

An examination of presidential voting in House districts by University of California–San Diego political scientist Gary Jacobson shows how "inefficiently" Democratic voters are distributed compared to Republicans. With rare exceptions (such as the Democratic presidential landslide of 1964), 47 to 53 percent of all House districts have cast Republican presidential majorities by 2 percent or larger margins. In contrast, 32 to 39 percent of House districts have cast 2 percent or larger Democratic majorities, and the remaining districts, ranging from 8 to 19 percent, have had very close elections at the presidential level. Consequently, Republicans have had a consistent advantage in House contests since at least 1952, the earliest election in Jacobson's study: substantially more districts cast Republican presidential majorities than cast Democratic majorities.

Much of this outcome results because Democratic voters are often concentrated in a relatively small number of minority and urban districts, districts that cast huge Democratic majorities of 60 percent or more in presidential elections, whereas Republican voters are spread out more thinly but more efficiently across more districts that, in turn, vote for GOP presidential candidates by narrower margins.

Until 1994, Democrats were able to consistently prevent this built-in advantage from becoming decisive by capitalizing on the willingness of voters to split their tickets, especially in the South and in other conservative areas, when the Democratic candidate separated himself from the presidential wing of the party. By 1994, however, millions of voters in conservative-leaning districts, especially in the South, had ended ticket-splitting practices and voted for Republican House (and Senate) candidates, as they had voted Republican in presidential contests.

The Republican takeover of the House in 1994 coincided with a marked increase in party-line voting, a trend that has accelerated ever since. Consequently, with a majority of House districts casting majorities for Republican presidential candidates, it will be much tougher for Democrats to regain their past majorities because they face an electorate inclined to vote Republican from the top to the bottom of their ballots. Even if the Democrats do win back the House, they will face a tough fight retaining it every election year, because many Democratic incumbents will represent electorates inclined to vote for Republicans.

In many respects, Jacobson points out, the same pattern of polarized voting benefits the Republican Party in the battle for control of the Senate. In 2004, twenty states voted for Kerry, and thirty voted for Bush. Insofar as the voters in these states are inclined to vote straight-Republican or straight-Democratic tickets, the Republicans have the edge in the battle to hold the Senate and to take it back should they lose it.

Jacobson and political scientist Thomas Mann of the Brookings Institution have both noted that gerrymandering of congressional districts worked to the advantage of the Republican Party in the elections following the 1990 and 2000 censuses. Mann points out that the post-2000 round of redistricting "had a significant partisan and competitive impact. Republicans, already enjoying a more efficient distribution of voters across congressional districts, saw their partisan advantage grow from 228 to 240 in the new districts, in spite of the fact that their presidential candidate lost the popular vote in the 2000 election."

Political scientists William Galston of the University of Maryland and Pietro Nivola of Brookings point to the more efficient distribution of Republican votes as another structural advantage for the GOP in state legislature and governor contests. In the pro-Republican red states, they point out, the Republican advantage is only modest when measured by the percentage of identifiers with each party—enough to win, but not wasteful. In contrast, Democrats in blue states have many more partisans—a fifteen-point advantage—than they need.

Democratic Liabilities: Unwilling to Stay the Course

Structurally, Democrats have, over the past forty years, had problems sustaining institutions and have lacked continuous investment in party-building enterprises. In 2003–2004, Democratic donors led by financier George Soros and insurance magnate Peter Lewis contributed a total of $132 million to create Americans Coming Together (ACT). Their goal was to create a permanent institution with headquarters in every battleground state to turn out Democratic voters. When ACT and its sister organization, the $59.4 million Media Fund, failed to produce a Democratic presidential victory, however, Soros and Lewis quickly pulled the plug, forcing the closure of both ACT and the Media Fund and effectively writing off nearly $200 million as a failed gamble.

The story of ACT stands in sharp contrast to the creation of the Heritage Foundation. In 1973, thirty years before ACT, Paul Weyrich and Edwin Feulner Jr., backed by Joseph Coors and Richard M. Scaife, created the conservative Heritage to act as a counterweight to the then-dominant liberal ideological presence in the nation's capital. Success did not follow quickly—if anything the setbacks were more severe than those suffered by Democrats in the course of Kerry's 2004 defeat. In 1974, a year after Heritage was established, the Republican Party was crushed in the wake of Watergate. Two years later, in 1976, the Republican Party lost the White House. Coors and Scaife, the two conservative donors—

early counterparts to Soros and Lewis—did not abandon Heritage after the debacles of 1974 and 1976. Instead, Coors and Scaife, along with a growing number of other conservative donors, stuck with Heritage through thick and thin. By the time Ronald Reagan was elected in 1980, Heritage had become the premier think tank on the right in Washington, exercising significant policy influence on the Reagan administration.

Democrats and liberals have shown little interest in maintaining and sustaining institutions designed to produce majorities in Congress and to win the White House. A 2005 study commissioned for a new liberal nonprofit group made up of wealthy donors, the Democracy Alliance, highlighted many of the infrastructural and financial differences between institutions on the left and right, including the lack on the Democratic side of coordination and concentration of resources:

> Conservatives systematically invest in non-electoral, social, religious and cultural networks to wage a "permanent campaign" that continuously dialogues with people around conservative values outside of election season and then inspires them to make conservative electoral choices. Progressive capacity concentrates efforts on the eve of elections, while conservatives work to create conservative culture and work to produce conservative voters year-round.

Conservative donors tend to give unrestricted contributions with long-term commitments for money in future years, whereas "progressives suffer from a boom and bust syndrome and a pattern of project-specific grant-making rather than long-term support for infrastructure and expansion."

At the level of the political parties, control of the DNC has changed hands repeatedly with little or no attempt to develop a trained staff, failing to build a permanent field infrastructure, and lagging behind in the dogged work of designing and building the tools of politics—voter lists, direct mail lists, email lists, and donor lists. In contrast, there are Republicans who have simultaneously built the party—computer specialist Tom Hoeffler, coalition-builder Tony Feather, lawyer Benjamin Ginsberg, get-out-the-vote specialist Maria Cimeno, direct mail entrepreneur Wyatt Stewart—and gone on to use their experience to establish private sector careers, all the while maintaining a deep commitment to the GOP itself. There are no Democratic counterparts.

Perhaps of most importance is the difference in the link between the party and the network of allied interest groups on each side of the aisle. Conservatives and the Republican Party were unified by the shared goal of ending their minority status and taking the reins of power. For Grover Norquist, president of Americans for Tax Reform, Feulner of the Heritage Foundation, Weyrich of the Free Congress Foundation, former Moral Majority president Jerry Falwell, Pat Robertson of the Christian Broadcast Network, Dirk Van Dongen, president of the National Association of Wholesale Distributors, John Engler, president of the National Association of Manufacturers, and a host of others in charge of organizations on the right side of the spectrum, the Republican Party is their political arm, an integral part of their public lives, and crucial to their ability to press policy and legislative agendas.

"What is to be done?" wrote Paul Weyrich, chairman and CEO of the Free Congress Foundation on November 21, 2005, in the nineteenth of his ongoing series of emailed articles on the topic of "The Next Conservatism":

> Most Liberal Republicans have been in Washington long enough to chair either committee or subcommittee. The Leadership should get the Republican Conference in both Houses to adopt a legislative agenda. Senators and Congressmen would be told in advance that the agenda would include party discipline votes. If a Senator or Congressman would not vote for the GOP agenda he or she could not chair a committee or subcommittee. . . . If [liberal Republicans] were to defect, so be it. If it meant that because of defections the Democrats would control Congress, well and good. Then at least the situation would be clarified, Liberals in one party, Conservatives in the other.

Weyrich's argument is subject to debate, but what is striking about it is that he conceives of an ideal world in which his conservatism and the Republican Party are one and the same, in which conservatives "could do the real work for which they were elected free of political blackmail by Liberal Republicans." Weyrich and others on the right are often deeply critical of the Republican Party, but they are critical because they hold a deep, even passionate, proprietary interest in it.

In contrast, the mainstay organizations of the left were created when liberals and Democrats were in power. Their function was to influence sympathetic decision makers who controlled both branches of Congress for many decades, not to wrest power from adversaries. Virtually every leader of the liberal network is a Democrat. But Ralph Neas of People for the American Way, Nan Aron of the Alliance for Justice, and Wade Henderson of the Leadership Conference on Civil Rights all see themselves and the goals of their respective organizations as separate and distinct from the Democratic Party. On the left, this separation applies almost across the board to include the NAACP, the ACLU, Common Cause, the American Association of University Women, the Children's Defense Fund, NARAL Pro-Choice America, the Human Rights Fund, the National Organization of Women, and so on.

Upscale and Downscale Democrats: The Difficulty of Maintaining a Left Populist Coalition

Another dimension of the Democrats' structural dilemma stems from the party's growing dependence on the votes of upscale social liberals to replace the defecting white working- and middle-class voters. Take, for example, Montgomery and Bucks counties to the north of Philadelphia. Montgomery ($61,919 median household income compared with $41,994 nationally, 41.7 percent of those over age twenty-five with college degrees compared to 24.4 percent nationally) and Bucks ($59,727 household income, 31.2 percent with college degrees) have moved decisively toward the Democratic Party. Counties like these—New York's Westchester, Suffolk, and Nassau; California's Marin, San Mateo, Santa Cruz, and Monterey; Washington's King, Thurston, and Jefferson counties—have become the most important source of new Democratic voters. Of the nation's twenty-five most affluent counties, as measured by per capita income, sixteen voted for Kerry.

These affluent, college-educated voters, many of them with jobs in the professions, are drawn to the Democratic Party not because of economic populism. Instead, these voters are, in the main, social liberals. They adamantly dislike the religious right and any notion of externally imposed, repressive morality. They generally believe that abortion is an issue to be decided by the pregnant woman and, perhaps, her doctor. Religion is not a significant factor in the lives of many of these voters, who are often nonbelievers.

Andrew Kohut, president of the Pew Research Center, has found that these voters differ from other Democratic groups in that 90 percent of upscale Democrats believe that "relying too much on military force to defeat terrorism creates hatred that leads to more terrorism," compared to 51 percent of all voters; 88 percent are worried that the government is too involved in moral issues, compared with 51 percent of the whole electorate. Just under half, 49 percent, have a college degree or higher, 43 percent seldom or never go to religious services, and 41 percent have incomes of $75,000 or more. They are the least likely to have a gun (23 percent) or to attend Bible study or prayer meetings (12 percent).

The problem facing advocates of Democratic populism is that the party has become economically and ideologically bifurcated. At the top, the ascendant wing of the party is not populist; it is elitist. It is affluent, well educated, urban, secular, and on the most controversial social issues of abortion and gay marriage very liberal. Not only are these upscale voters the growing and dominant force in the Democratic Party but their values prevail in party debates and in the writing of the Democratic platform.

At this elite level, the Democratic Party is the party of the liberal side of the sexual, civil rights, and women's rights revolutions. While African American voters are generally liberal on most of these issues—or at least not animated to vote for the GOP because of them—the white working- and middle-class voters that Democratic populists would like to bring back into the party's fold are often not on the same side as the liberal warriors in these matters. Instead, many of the white centrist voters see liberal culture as a threat to the traditions that hold their families and communities together. Many are strongly opposed to gay marriage and believe that there is a Christian moral code that sets a standard for everyone, even though few, including themselves, maintain this standard.

The Democratic Party can no longer be described as the bottom-up coalition it was from the start of the Great Depression through the end of the 1960s. The New Deal coalition provided the base for Franklin Roosevelt to conduct his 1936 re-election campaign as a populist assault on "economic royalists," the

> small group [that] had concentrated into their own hands an almost complete control over other people's property, other people's money, other people's labor—other people's lives. For too many of us life was no longer free; liberty no longer real; men could no longer follow the pursuit of happiness. Against economic tyranny such as this, the American citizen could appeal only to the organized power of Government.

Twelve years later, Harry S. Truman was able to bring his presidency back from the brink of defeat with an equally strong appeal. "The people know that the Democratic Party is the people's party, and the Republican Party is the party of special interest, and it always has been and always will be," Truman told delegates at the 1948 Democratic convention. "In 1932 we were attacking the citadel of special privilege and greed. We were fighting to drive the moneychangers from the temple. Today, in 1948, we are now the defenders of the stronghold of democracy and of equal opportunity, the haven of the ordinary people of this land and not of the favored classes or the powerful few."

Al Gore's rhetoric failed to resonate, however, when he told convention delegates in 2000 that "as President, I'll stand up to them, and I'll stand up for you. . . . I want you to know this: I've taken on the powerful forces. And that's the difference in this election. They're for the powerful, and we're for the people." Similarly, Kerry's declared commitment to regular working Americans did not produce a groundswell of support from middle-class white voters struggling to make ends meet:

> Let me tell you what we won't do: we won't raise taxes on the middle class. You've heard a lot of false charges about this in recent months. So let me say straight out what I will do as President: I will cut middle-class taxes. I will reduce the tax burden on small business. And I will roll back the tax cuts for the wealthiest individuals who make over $200,000 a year, so we can invest in job creation, health care and education.

Instead, they voted by overwhelming margins against Kerry.

The Democrats Are Still the Party of the Poorest Voters

At the same time, the Democratic Party continues to be the party of the poorest voters from the bottom third of the income distribution, white, black, and Hispanic. In an analysis of class-based voting over the space of more than half a century, Princeton political scientist Larry M. Bartels found that, "while it is generally true that Democratic presidential candidates have lost support among white voters, . . . those losses have been entirely (and roughly equally) concentrated in the middle- and upper-income groups, and have been partially offset by increasing support for Democratic candidates among low-income white voters."

It is inaccurate, however, to describe those whites in the bottom third of the income distribution as working class and as the basis for a vital left populism. Fewer than half of those in this tier, 45 percent, work at all, compared with 80 percent of those in the top third. A more accurate portrayal would be to describe such voters as socially and economically "subdominant" (whether temporarily or permanently), as the term was used in chapter 1. More than half, 59 percent, of the bottom third have never married or are divorced, widowed, or separated compared with just 20 percent of the top third. And of the 55 percent of those in the bottom third who are unemployed, most are students, retired, or (often single) homemakers compared with 20 percent of the top third.

The Resurgence of Class-based Voting

While losing support overall among middle-income and upscale whites, Democrats have made significant gains in smaller demographic categories, according to National Election Studies (NES) data. Among whites with jobs in the professions, whose support for Democratic presidential and House candidates ranged from the low to mid-40 percent level between the 1960s and the early 1990s, Democratic support shot up to 56 percent in 2004.

Similarly, among very high-income whites, those in the ninety-sixth to one hundredth percentiles whose support for Democrats ranged from the low 20 to the mid-30 percent level between the mid-1960s and the early 1990s, Democratic voting rose to 46 percent in

2004. These are the elite Democratic whites who dominate the party's agenda-setting processes.

New Deal, class-based voting remained strong through the election of 1948 that pitted Harry Truman against Thomas Dewey. In that contest, the bottom third of the electorate voted Democratic by a 62 to 38 margin, while the top 5 percent voted Republican by a 68 to 32 margin. The Eisenhower years of the 1950s, however, saw a sudden muting of class-based voting that continued into the early 1970s. From 1952 to 1972, there was virtually no "class" voting among white voters, if class is defined by dividing the electorate into thirds based on income. Bartels reports:

> Averaging over this period, Democratic presidential candidates garnered 46 percent of the votes of whites in the bottom third of the income distribution, 47 percent of those in the middle third, and 42 percent of those in the upper third [or just a four-point difference between the upper and bottom thirds]. In only one of these six elections, 1964, did the gap in Democratic support between upper-income whites and lower-income whites exceed six percent.

Starting in the mid-1970s and continuing through the 2004 election, there has been a resurgence of class-based voting, both among all voters and among whites. Bartels found that from 1976 to 2004, Democratic margins among white voters in the bottom third of the income distribution increased five points, from 46 to 51 percent, while Democratic voting among those in the top third fell by five points, from 42 to 37 percent. What had been a very modest four-point difference, 46 to 42, between voting patterns of the bottom and top thirds of white Democratic voters in the years from 1952 to 1972 became a much more substantial fourteen-point difference, 51 to 37, in the years since 1972.

The Uneasy Alliance between the Top and Bottom of the Democratic Coalition

As noted earlier, there are now two major factions within the Democratic coalition: the largely white, well-educated, professional class, and much of the bottom third of the socioeconomic ladder made up of lowest-income whites, blacks, and Hispanics. The bottom third constituency essentially does not participate fully—if at all—in the industrial or postindustrial economy and places a heavy emphasis on redistributive government tax and spending policies. Some in this constituency see a strong link between a belief in God and morality, many are opposed to homosexual rights, few in this income group work for gun control, and while there may be only weak support for the war in Iraq, there is little active opposition. The upscale wing of the Democratic Party supports liberal economic policies, but its core motivating issues overwhelmingly involve social, sexual, and personal rights and freedoms, including abortion and gay rights, hostility to firearms, grave reservations about, or frank opposition to, the war in Iraq (although the party has been split on this), and an intense animosity to the Christian conservative movement.

The contemporary Democratic coalition does not provide the foundation for a populist party. Populism of the left or right requires a strong *majority* base of hard-working men and women who believe, with justification, that they are inadequately rewarded for their efforts, that they are personally demeaned, that they are deprived of their rights, and that their values are not honored by society. Insofar as the bottom third of the American income distribution, which provides high margins of support for Democratic candidates, is made up of many people who do not work (fewer than half of this third, 45 percent according to NES data, work at all); and insofar as another third of the party is made up of relatively affluent, well-educated members of the middle to upper-middle class; and insofar as the party leadership elite is disproportionately privileged, powerful, and wealthy, the catalytic brew of shared resentments and justified outrage that fuel effective populism are, at present, lacking.

Democratic dependence on the lowest-income voters carries a further structural liability: voter registration and turnout levels are lowest in this group. The 2004 NES survey found that twice as many of those in the bottom third as those in all other income brackets were not registered to vote. Furthermore, according to NES figures, more than twice as many of those in the bottom third—including those who were registered—reported they did not vote compared with those surveyed who were in the middle and top thirds of the income distribution.

Insufficient Attention to the Goal of Winning

The problems of the Democratic coalition would not be as serious if the interests of all the constituent groups were managed in such a way that none dominated and if attention were focused on the goal of winning general elections. In practice, however, the social-issue left overwhelmingly sets the agenda of the Democratic Party. There are, for example, few litmus tests more important for a Democratic presidential candidate than full commitment to abortion rights. This became strikingly apparent in the early debate within the Democratic left over prospective presidential candidates for the 2004 election. Studs Terkel suggested in the May 6, 2002, edition of the *Nation* that the ideal presidential candidate for progressives in 2004 would be Congressman Dennis Kucinich, a Cleveland Democrat who, Terkel argued, could "win back the blue-collar Reagan Democrats. . . . We'd have an honest-to-God working class President for the first time in our history."

A few days later, fellow *Nation* writer Katha Pollitt attacked both Terkel and Kucinich: the Ohio congressman was anti-abortion. "Abortion is not just another item on the list. It goes straight to the soul. It is about whether society sees you as fully human or as a vessel for whom no plan or hope or possibility or circumstance, however desperate, matters more than being a nest for that 'itty bitty zygote.'" Kucinich quickly abandoned his opposition to abortion. "I would be a pro-choice president," Kucinich told reporters in Cedar Rapids, Iowa, on February 16, 2003, but had his candidacy developed, the issue would have sapped his support among women and dogged him to the end—as it would for any Democratic candidate who failed to embrace abortion.

Coalition Management: Concrete Programs Breed Conflict for Democrats

Calls for the establishment of a new and vital center-left coalition by analysts such as Tom Frank, Stan Greenberg, and David Sirota allow for the benefits—but skirt the costs—of the contemporary "postmaterialist," rights-based progressive agenda. University of Michigan political scientist Ronald Inglehart has characterized the difference between the postmaterialist needs of the affluent—involving "quality of life" issues such as the right to self-potentiation, the environment, peace, personal fulfillment, freedom of speech, giving people more say in important political decisions, and women's rights such as abortion—on the one hand, and material needs important to the economically deprived, such as food, shelter, physical safety, wages, and job security, on the other. These needs sit uneasily together in a single political coalition such as that attempted by contemporary Democrats.

On another level, many of the new Republican voters see dangers in the concrete programs of contemporary Democratic liberalism. They view them as genuine threats to their schools, their children, their status in the workplace, their own educational opportunities, and the moral environment. Most progressive Democratic theorists have not yet begun, or have only just begun, to map out these costs and to search for ways to mitigate them.

Two well-intentioned liberal policies are good examples: the distribution of condoms to high school students and instruction in condom use, and the adoption of sex education programs that explore not only traditional reproductive matters but gay and lesbian sex and transgender issues. Culturally liberal proponents of condom distribution and of wide-ranging sex education see such policies as necessary and beneficial in a society where premarital sex is commonplace and where the refusal of parents to accept this reality can result not only in unwanted pregnancies but also in AIDS and other life-threatening conditions. Convinced of the legitimacy of their advocacy, proponents of such programs fail to understand just how extensively they violate the moral convictions of many traditional parents, who believe heart and soul that it is their right to apply their convictions to the upbringing of their children. For such parents, advanced sex education and condom distribution represent an intolerable intrusion by the government into matters best left to the family and the church. For these parents, contemporary sex education curricula suggest that the school is promoting sexual intercourse for young teenagers, and worse.

In 1991, two years after African American Democrat David Dinkins was elected mayor, the New York School Board approved condom distribution in high schools and, by a one-vote margin, rejected an "opt-out" amendment that would have allowed parents to make their children ineligible. Staten Island board member Michael

Petrides declared: "There's no way in this city and in these United States someone is going to tell my son he can have a condom when I say he can't." "If parents want to put a condom next to a box of Wheaties and send their children off to school, that's fine," Msgr. John G. Woolsey, representing the Roman Catholic Archdiocese of New York, said. "But for those parents who find it totally abhorrent, please vote to opt out."

Dinkins supported the condom distribution program and opposed the opt-out amendment. The condom issue was just one in a number of matters in Dinkins' failed re-election bid that shared a common theme in the minds of many voters: disorder. Under a liberal Democrat, the city was descending into disorder—homeless men begging on subways and applying squeegees to car windows and demanding payment, rising rates of crime, a school system in disarray, and a palpable sense of squalor and decay. Since then, New York, an overwhelmingly Democratic city, has elected and re-elected Republican mayors four times.

Even Montgomery County, Maryland—a bastion of socially liberal, affluent voters who backed Kerry over Bush by a 66 to 33 margin, where more than half the adult population has a college degree, and where the 2002 median household income was $80,978—faced massive parental pressure when it announced adoption of a new sex education curriculum. The program taught that "sexual orientation is not a choice," that "gender identity [is] a person's internal sense of knowing whether you are male or female," that "sex play with friends of the same gender is not uncommon among early adolescents," and that "same-sex parents" are one of many different types of families. The course featured, in addition, a video demonstration of proper condom use. To proponents, and to many culturally progressive parents, the teaching material addressed the contemporary realities of life. The proposal produced an unexpected firestorm of protest, however, from parents with more traditional views, again tapping a popular conviction that liberal mores were bringing dangerous levels of disorder into the community. On May 23, 2005, six months after the controversy began, the Montgomery School Board voted 7 to 1 to abandon the program.

Structural Conflicts Are Built into the Democrats' Biracial Coalition

Sex education is a volatile and politically polarizing matter, but perhaps the issue most threatening to the essential Democratic project of forging a biracial voting coalition is affirmative action. The NAACP in 2005, for example, attacked efforts by well-known affirmative action opponent Ward Connerly to amend the Michigan state constitution in such a way as to prohibit "discrimination" against whites. The proposed amendment declared that all agencies of the state, including the university system, "shall not discriminate against, or grant preferential treatment to, any individual or group on the basis of race, sex, color, ethnicity, or national origin in the operation of public employment, public education, or public contracting." The NAACP contended that "the consequences of the [amendment] campaign are broad and will irreparably harm the ability of all Michigan residents to enjoy a fair chance in education and employment."

From a white perspective, a policy giving preferential treatment to minorities will "irreparably harm the ability" of some white residents "to enjoy . . . education and employment." From a black perspective, without affirmative action protection, the deck is stacked against African Americans. These are zero-sum competitions; with only a finite number of spaces in the magnet school, in the university, or in the police academy, and a limited number of public contracts to be let, for every winner there will be a loser.

For Democratic candidates, these issues are often viewed as best glossed over. When John Kerry was asked about affirmative action during one of the 2004 debates, he evaded the tough issues:

> The fact is that in too many parts of our country, we still have discrimination. And affirmative action is not just something that applies to people of color. Some people have a mistaken view of it in America. It also is with respect to women, it's with respect to other efforts to try to reach out and be inclusive in our country. I think that we have a long way to go, regrettably. If you look at what's happened—we've made progress, I want to say that at the same time.

Similarly, Kweisi Mfume, former NAACP president and a 2006 Senate candidate in Maryland, praised affirmative action policies, saying, "Americans of all races should have every reason to believe that their government will work to ensure a level playing field for all people in the areas of commerce, employment and education."

The basic function of affirmative action is to tilt the playing field so that the descendants of those who were historically denied equality of opportunity now have a better chance to win jobs, promotions, or admission to college. Insofar as African American needs determine the position of the Democratic Party on affirmative action, their white adversaries are losers in this zero-sum competition—and are virtually guaranteed to express their opposition in the privacy of the voting booth.

Lack of Credible Solutions

Many progressive Democrats have argued that the party can trump Republican exploitation of racial and cultural wedge issues by stressing bottom-line economic matters and by shifting the debate to domestic social programs. The difficulty for Democrats on this front is their lack of credible policies. In two critical areas—coping with the forces of globalization and making substantial improvements in education—there is nothing that can now be described as successful Democratic policy.

In the case of globalization, the Democratic Party and its major constituent groups have not found a solution to the problems of the broad swath of lower-income earners most vulnerable to hypercompetition—to the consequences of exacerbated market forces and open borders and their impact on American wages, job security, and labor-management relations. "If you don't believe that [globalization] changes the average wages in America, then you believe in the tooth fairy," liberal economist and Nobel Laureate Paul Samuelson wrote in 2004. He might have added that many Democrats continue to believe just that.

Republicans and proponents of free trade have a set of policies that attempt, rightly or wrongly, to deal with the reality of international market forces, contending that over the long haul the substantial costs of globalization will be more than balanced by the benefits of expanding both the worldwide market for American goods and the number of countries providing cheap imports for U.S. consumers. Republican voters—more affluent, better educated on average than Democratic voters, and dominant (as the word was used in chapter 1)—are far better positioned to ride out and profit from the economic storm. In contrast, key liberal and Democratic critics of fair trade have less in the way of protection or fallback to offer their less-skilled, less-protected, and relentlessly squeezed constituents.

On November 23, 2005, after General Motors announced that it was closing twelve production facilities and laying off 30,000 workers, AFL-CIO president John Sweeney countered with a statement that disregarded the brutal economic pressures bearing down on the American auto industry—pressures that include the health care, pension, and other costs for employees and retirees that help to make GM cars uncompetitive: "Instead of relying on layoffs to turn the company around, General Motors should acknowledge that its workers are among its greatest assets and have improved product quality and productivity, boosting strong gains in critical areas. GM should focus its restructuring efforts on improving products for consumers and boosting sales, not downsizing the very workers who make the company run."

Among labor intellectuals, Jeff Faux, founder of the Economic Policy Institute, has become a leading critic of free trade policies. In his most recent book, *The Global Class War*, Faux' proposals are extremely optimistic—even utopian. Faux argues for the conversion of the United States, Canada, and Mexico into a trade bloc with a "continental bill of rights" enforceable across national borders and the creation of a "North American Congress" financed by "unions, foundations and enlightened business groups." Initially, this congress would be an informal group, but over time it would gain "a formal role in the emerging continental political systems of all three nations." Once in place, the congress "could establish the right of the citizens of one country to attempt to influence the important policies of the two other North American countries." This congress would represent "the interests of the cross-border working class majority" against the democratically elected governments of each country, which are controlled by "big money" or what Faux calls the "corporate-supported Party of Davos." Although Faux has a strong track record as an advocate for labor, and although Democrats need innovative ideas to deal with global competition, cross-border alliances such as the one he suggests seem far in the future. There is no guarantee that Faux' proposal would work in the near term, and as such, it offers only slender hope for the current dilemmas of the Democratic Party.

Faux' ideas compete within the Democratic policy universe with the economic views of those most important to the economic successes of the Clinton years: Robert Rubin, Alan Greenspan, and Larry Summers—all supporters of the North American Free Trade Agreement pushed through by the Clinton administration in 1993 over the bitter objections of organized labor. This triumvirate presided over the longest period of economic expansion in American history, overseeing a roughly 37 percent increase in the U.S. gross domestic product, 13 million new jobs, and a rise in the GDP for the private sector of approximately 41 percent. In the years 1992–2000, wages went up, median household income rose to $38,000 (then an all-time high), the overall poverty rate dropped to 12.7 percent (an historic achievement), and unemployment was at its lowest point in three decades. The net worth—the value of real estate, stocks, bonds, and other assets—of the median family increased dramatically, to some extent a rebuke to protectionists and antagonists of the corporate sector.

Notwithstanding the extensive suffering of American workers who have been downsized, outsourced, and in genuine pain, Democrats have been hurt at the polls by the widespread perception that the anti-centrist left wing of the party has an inadequate understanding of modern postindustrial economies and of how competition, markets, tax and monetary policy, incentives, and regulation interact with government initiatives to foster or hinder the generation of wealth. This implication has hurt parties of the left everywhere and creates a stiff challenge for the American progressive movement.

Education Poses Serious Political Hurdles for Democrats

In the case of education, Democrats have lost their historic advantage and have ceded ground to Republicans and to the No Child Left Behind Act. Democrats are trapped between competing constituencies—parents of ethnic and racial minority students, parents of white students (in the places where these are a distinct constituency), and unionized teachers. Too often, policy alternatives that are acceptable to the National Education Association (NEA) and to the American Federation of Teachers (AFT) have defined the boundaries of the debate. Vouchers, teacher testing, merit pay, tenure, and performance standards have been either barred from consideration or so modified and amended as to be entirely ineffectual. Some Democrats are cognizant of these problems and offer ideas (an end to easy tenure, the elimination of empty credentialing, the admission to the teacher pool of more able jobseekers, longer schooldays, Saturday classes, sophisticated proficiency assessments, and so on), but implementing such reform means introducing hypercompetition to the safe harbor of primary and secondary school teaching and thus threatens key support to Democrats from the AFT and NEA.

As the school-aged population continues to grow and as record levels of total elementary and secondary enrollment are predicted, these issues hold significance that extends beyond the realm of education. "Through education, Democrats reach for their own deepest aspiration: a country where birth doesn't dictate destiny. . . . [If] Democrats evade questions of culture and institutions, . . . if Democrats cannot speak powerfully to an issue that speaks so powerfully to them, they cannot expect to prevail on tougher ideological terrain," argues Robert Gordon, vice-president of the liberal Center for American Progress.

Gordon points out that drawing a new population of teachers into the pool is critical: "[A]s talented women have moved on to other professions, teacher quality has declined. Education majors score below national averages on standardized tests. . . . Teacher quality is lowest in the poorest schools, where good teachers are needed most. . . . [Pupils in such schools] are twice as likely to be taught by teachers who lack even a minor in the relevant subject." Again, the answer for many white parents has been to move to the distant suburbs and vote Republican.

At the same time, the Democratic resistance to innovation in public education—to the experimental use of vouchers, for example, which is supported by many minority parents—continues to subject poor students to the worst education and does little to motivate minority voters from dysfunctional school districts to head to the polls. The failure of Democrats on this score points to the glaring deficiencies of the party as it struggles to help its African American constituency.

In Washington DC, an unwavering Democratic stronghold, the educational levels of black and Latino students are among the lowest of any city or state, with close to two-thirds lacking even basic math or reading skills. In the nation at large, even as the ability to read and understand complicated information is increasingly important in the competitive workplace, the National Assessment of Educational Progress' (NAEP) long-term trend reading assessments reveal that only half of all white seventeen-year-olds, less than one-quarter of Latino seventeen-year-olds, and less than one-fifth of African American seventeen-year-olds can read and understand "complicated information." By age seventeen, only about one in seventeen seventeen-year-olds can read and gain information from specialized text, for example, the science section in the local newspaper.

The NAEP data show that in 2000, of Hispanic fourth-grade students:

- 58 percent were below the reading achievement basic level,
- 26 percent were within the basic level range,
- 13 percent were within the proficient level range, and
- 3 percent were within the advanced level range.

For black fourth-grade students in 2000:

- 63 percent were below the reading achievement basic level,
- 25 percent were within the basic level range,
- 10 percent were within the proficient level range, and
- 2 percent were within the advanced level range.

Figures such as these illustrate with clarity some of the many difficulties facing Democrats as they grapple with education issues and as they struggle to assemble a multiracial, multiethnic alliance capable of grasping and holding political power.

Deaf

Democratic pollsters have been documenting Democratic liabilities for more than two decades. In 1985, the DNC paid $250,000 for thirty-three focus groups and a survey of 5,000 voters that found that key white working- and lower middle-class Democratic constituencies were convinced that

> their party is not helping them. Instead it is helping the blacks, Hispanics and the poor. . . . These voters view gays and feminists as outside the orbit of acceptable social life. These groups represent, in their view, a social underclass. . . . White urban ethnics feel threatened by an economic underclass that absorbs their taxes and even locks them out of the job, in the case of affirmative action. They also fear a social underclass that threatens to violate or corrupt their children.

That same year, Democratic pollster Stan Greenberg, who worked for Bill Clinton in 1992, Al Gore in 2000, and John Kerry in 2004, found that, among working-class whites in suburban Detroit, "[t]he special status of blacks is perceived by almost all of these individuals as a serious obstacle to their personal advancement. Indeed, discrimination against whites has become a well-assimilated and ready explanation for their status, vulnerability and failures."

Greenberg has repeatedly documented the difficulties facing his party. In a post-election study in November-December 2000, Greenberg, who was an architect of Gore's populist theme, "Standing up for the people, not the powerful," concluded that the theme had failed. The election results showed, he said, that "we lost it downscale and gained it upscale." In a presentation of his findings, Greenberg said: "Progressives need to ask: What is the character of a progressive movement without the aspiration to represent working-class voters?" Among white voters without college degrees—a crucial populist constituency—the Republican Party was viewed significantly more favorably than the Democratic Party. This was especially true of white men without college degrees. Among these men, 54 percent described their views of the GOP as "warm" and 27 percent as "cool." Their views of the Democratic Party were 38 percent warm and 41 percent cool, a sixteen-point spread on Democrats and fourteen points on the GOP for a combined thirty percentage point difference.

After the 2004 election, the Democracy Corps, a group founded by Greenberg, James Carville, and Bob Shrum, conducted a series of focus groups that once more reached a similar conclusion:

> Regardless of voters' attitudes on the role of religion in public life or their position on touchstone issues such as abortion and gay marriage or even their personal religious faith, they all see Republicans as a party with a clear and consistent position on cultural issues and an abiding respect for the importance of faith and traditional social norms. Democrats' lack of a consistent stance on cultural issues leaves a vacuum that is clearly being filled by voices on the right. Most referred to Democrats as "liberal" on issues of morality, but some even go so far as to label them "immoral," "morally bankrupt," or even "antireligious." Rather than being tied to specific issues, these beliefs are fueled by a perception of Democrats as "too politically correct," "caring too much about the rights of a few rather than the rights of the many." While there are clear racial overtones to these feelings among some voters, these attitudes were most powerfully captured in symbolic issues such as display of the Ten Commandments in public buildings, removing God from the Pledge of Allegiance, or outlawing public manger displays at Christmastime. On each of these symbolic cases, there was a broad perception that Republicans were on the side of American tradition, Judeo-Christian values, and the forgotten majority, while Democrats would stand up and fight for a subversive minority seeking to erode the moral foundation of our country.

When, in turn, Democrats look to see who in their party has won, especially in general election contests with large numbers of conservative voters, a relatively clear pattern emerges. The two Democrats who won the presidency since 1968, Jimmy Carter and Bill Clinton, ran as moderates, each maintaining some independence from the traditionally liberal social agenda, both Southern Baptists supporting the death penalty, and both conveying certain cultural values through the cadence and rhetoric of southern vernacular.

Mark Warner and Tim Kaine, the current and past Democratic governors of Virginia, have staked out similar stands separating themselves from Democratic orthodoxy, as have Montana Governor Brian Schweitzer, Wyoming Governor Dave Freudenthal, Oklahoma Governor Brad Henry, Arizona Governor Janet Napolitano, and Kansas Governor Kathleen Sebelius, all Democrats and all of whom had favorability ratings of 55 percent or more as of late 2005. (Hillary Clinton has also made efforts in this direction, most notably calling abortion a "sad, even tragic choice" and one that should be "rare.") On issues of national security, however, all of these officeholders lack credible experience, thus playing to another Democratic vulnerability.

➤ ◄

A huge vacuum exists in contemporary American politics. The potential for filling this empty space is the subject of the concluding chapter.

8
Conclusion: Three-Quarters or Half a Party

There is a growing vacuum in America, a space going unfilled despite the built-in competitive nature of the political system encouraging the major political players to take over any unoccupied territory. The Republican Party has been able to eke out repeated, if slim, victories, capitalizing on the weakness of its adversary. Corruption, hubris, the costs of such externally generated catastrophes as Hurricane Katrina, government incompetence, and excessive risk-taking—as in the Iraq War—may take the GOP down in individual elections, but the party has exceptional recuperative powers, resourceful allies, and a profound distaste for defeat.

The Republican Party and the conservative movement have been unrelenting in their drive to control national policy and debate, but no one could argue that the GOP has captured a solid majority of the electorate. There has been no permanent conservative realignment. The protective stance of Republicans toward the rich and the dominant, and the acquiescence to a morally and intellectually repressive social agenda, are too much at odds with the American egalitarian ethic to achieve the overwhelming strength of the Democratic coalition of the New Deal era, of the Republican Party in the years that followed the Civil War, or of the strength of the party after the election of 1896. Instead, Americans are offered what amounts to a choice between three-quarters of a political party—the Republicans—and half a party—the Democrats—not only in terms of the structural and organizational weaknesses of each party but also in terms of their polarized ideologies.

Each party now bears the costs and benefits of its own fundamental philosophical principles. Core GOP ideology revolves around the virtues of competition, whereas the Democrats' core philosophy revolves around the virtues of cooperation. The virtues of cooperation have become increasingly hard to sell to the top half of the income distribution in a country as driven by consumption, the acquisition of resources and status, and the tradition of individualism as is the United States. This is even more true when the bottom half of the distribution is heavily minority and when the left coalition is committed to values frequently antagonistic to those of moderates and conservatives—attitudes toward the distribution of wealth, equality, the women's movement, codes of sexual conduct, religion, the business ethos, education, multiculturalism, and the rights of the unborn.

Michael Tomasky of the *American Prospect* articulates well the fundamental ideological orientation of the left coalition:

> For many years—during their years of dominance and success, the period of the New Deal up through the first part of the Great Society—the Democrats practiced a brand of liberalism quite different from today's. Yes, it certainly sought to expand both rights and prosperity. But it did something more: *That liberalism was built around the idea—the philosophical principle—that citizens should be called upon to look beyond their own self-interest and work for a greater common interest.*
>
> This, historically, is the moral basis of liberal governance—not justice, not equality, not rights, not diversity, not government, and not even prosperity or opportunity. *Liberal governance is about demanding of citizens that they balance self-interest with common interest.* Any rank-and-file liberal is a liberal because she or he somehow or another, through reading or experience or both, came to believe in this principle. And every leading Democrat became a Democrat because on some level, she or he believes this, too. [emphases added]

Amy Sullivan, in the *Washington Monthly*, has written hopefully that

> learning to speak to and appeal to religious constituencies is not simply a matter of political calculation, but a quality Americans demand from their leaders. Even people who aren't terribly religious know moral vision when they see it—agnostic liberals

tear up when they see video clips of Martin Luther King Jr. holding forth on the National Mall—and they respond to faith when it's sincere and tied to a politics in which they believe. A president who can talk about his personal faith and explain how it connects to his policy initiatives enjoys both the tactical advantage of attracting the "swing faithful" and the moral stature to excite and inspire all those, religious or not, who are already predisposed to support him on the issues. To become America's majority party again, the Democrats will have to get religion.

Compare Tomasky's vision—and Sullivan's—with that of an investment firm, Agora Financial, which offers a worldview that, despite its flamboyant language, puts forward ideas strikingly similar to those articulated publicly and privately by key Republican leaders and voters. Agora's hyperbolic sales pitch echoes the vision and fears of many of today's American business leaders, Republican officeholders, policy makers, conservative voters, and Christians who flock to the "prosperity gospel":

Americans are headed for a whole new war. . . . Young versus old, rich versus poor, boomers versus Generation X, . . . father against son, mother against daughter, . . . locked in a material and ideological struggle bad enough to make the 1960s look like a piñata party. . . . Every penny you've ever saved, borrowed, or invested is in danger. Brace yourself as income taxes triple, . . . real estate implodes, . . . and Washington slashes Social Security and Medicare payouts in half. . . . [We will] *show you how to . . . triple your money at the height of this crisis . . . [and how to] protect yourself* [from a] . . . "Suburbistan." . . . This is not a bombed-out quarter in Baghdad. You won't find it in Kabul. Instead, it's right here in America, . . . abandoned buildings, shells of their former selves, . . . elderly with nothing left, crushed by broken promises, . . . a shortage of hospital beds and medical care, . . . family wealth in ruins, . . . lawless "no go" zones where even the cops don't dare to tread. . . . . This isn't the kind of war in which shots are fired. . . . But when it's done, . . . money, wealth, and the American dream [will] virtually vaporize overnight! Literally billions of dollars will disappear from "rich" retirement accounts. . . . The mall isn't closing; it's just closed. Permanently. The escalator doesn't hum. In the food court, you'll find no cheese fries, no chicken, no Chinese food. There's only a Motor Vehicle Administration office open, clinging to a corner in this dying Mecca to capitalism. . . . In

2008, the leading-edge boomers—born in 1946—turn 62. . . . The "boomer bomb" [is coming] . . . when 77 million ex-hippie, disco-dancing, "Me Decade" Americans start traipsing into retirement. . . . Imagine a fiscal gut punch that . . . doubles your federal income taxes, . . . hikes your state taxes by at least 20%, . . . slashes your monthly social security benefits by half, . . . eliminates half of your annual Medicare benefits, . . . erases half of every military pension check. . . . Good-paying, white-collar, "Ward Cleaver" jobs disappear. . . . Soaring health care expenses go unpaid. . . . Property prices plunge in the wake of panic selling. . . . Rampant price inflation sends the cost of food and energy soaring. . . . Police, fire, and highway crews shut down services. . . . Countless schools close. . . . City and state governments default on their bonds. . . . One "safe" pension fund after another goes the way of Enron. . . . There is no way for American investors to avoid this event. They can only choose *how to protect themselves* from the outcome. . . . Dozens of high-profile companies will fail, unable to carry staggering health care and pension obligations running to the billions of dollars. General Motors and Ford are just the first in a long line to issue similar warnings to the stock market. . . . The irony is, *in the middle of the same rough times, a few investors will discover several enormous opportunities to get filthy rich.* . . . Provided you know how to look at this, you've also got in your lap one of the greatest investment opportunities of all time! . . . With 77 million babies born between 1946 and 1964, our beloved boomers have long been the pot-bellied pig in the python. . . . We already have 10 times more people over age 65 than we did at the start of the last century. And today, the fastest-growing age group in America is the group over age 85! . . . By mid-century, we'll have an estimated 323% more people over 85 than we have now. And America alone will have 600,000 people living over the age of 100. . . . And every extra year of life—especially at that age—will cost a fortune. . . . [And] America has a baby shortage. What happened? Birth control. Women in the workforce. Plunging wages and consuming careers. . . . In 1980, 10% of American women ended their childbearing years without giving birth. Today, nearly twice as many—19%—will never have children. . . . So by 2030, the number of over-65 Americans doubles. . . . Each member of our shrinking younger generation has to cover a bigger and bigger chunk of the bill. . . . When the bulk of the 77 million baby boomers starts having financial trouble, it's not just the boomers who suffer, . . . but everyone else who depends on the boomer trends . . . will also get burned. . . . [Look at] how little America's biggest generation has socked away. Do houses count as savings? . . . Unless you're double-mortgaged to the hilt, as many Americans are, . . . you need a pension or 401(k), running principally on valuable and well-paying stocks or other investments. . . . Most boomer households are barely invested at all. . . . The total picture is a lot more grim than even the politicians have painted—at a time when as much as 56% of America's older population could not live without full Social Security payments and government medical care. *It all adds up to an epic battle for future wealth.* [emphases added]

There is little—indeed no—common ground between To-masky's cooperative progressive vision, or Sullivan's view, and the hypercompetitive outlook represented by Agora—quoted at length because it reveals so vividly the gulf between the Democratic conception of "a greater common interest" and the alternative Republican framework of individual responsibility and self-insurance against illness, aging, and bad luck, as well as the right (or obligation) to seize the opportunity to profit. As the Agora prospective states, "in the middle of the same rough times, a few investors will discover several enormous opportunities to get filthy rich." Ronald Reagan captured a similar dimension of conservative ideology in his remarks at a Republican congressional dinner saluting him in 1982: "We're the party that wants to see an America in which people can still get rich."

The investment firm's rhetoric is designed to sell a product, but it captures some of the ideological thrust of the Bush administration's officially stated goal to "replace the empty promises of the current [Social Security] system with real assets of ownership." The view of the Bush administration is that

Medicare is not financially secure for the retirement of the Baby Boom. The 77 million Americans who will be in Medicare by 2030 are counting on Medicare's promised benefits. Yet Medicare's fund for hospital insurance will face cash flow deficits beginning in 2016, and Medicare's fund for its other benefits will likely require a doubling of beneficiary premiums and of Medicare's claims on general revenues to remain solvent over the next 10 years. Medicare's bifurcated accounting disguises the true fiscal health of Medicare and makes it difficult to plan ahead.

The Bush administration's focus on Social Security privatization, on health care savings accounts—designed to turn patients into cost-conscious "shoppers"—on an "ownership society," on school vouchers, and on building an "investor class" all speak to the yawning ideological gap between the beliefs of the contemporary Democratic and Republican coalitions. They emphasize the parties' radically polarized conceptions of the role of government and of what constitutes America's "common dream."

Politics functions as a market, and the political marketplace is now significantly out of balance—it is in disequilibrium. If political parties were corporations, the political market would be viewed as territory ripe for takeover or for the entry of an outside competitor.

The current circumstances of Democrats and Republicans reflect a larger failure of the country's two-party system to represent effectively the competing interests of its citizenry. The American political system has gone through similar crises in the past, and it has consistently repaired itself. The country is at such a moment once again. Once again the system will be tested.

Notes

Chapter 1 ➤ Democratic Party Weaknesses Have Magnified Republican Party Advantages

p. 1   *identify with the dominant*: "The existence of a minority in a society implies the existence of a corresponding dominant group with higher social status and greater privileges. Minority status carries with it the exclusion from full participation in the life of the society" (Louis Wirth, "Morale and Minority Groups," *American Journal of Sociology* 47, no. 3 [1941]: 415–433). Marvin Harris states:

> The relationship of super-ordination and sub-ordination which characterizes the majority vis-à-vis the minority . . . [means] differential control over the economic, political, and ideological mechanisms of social stratification. In brief, the basic model for a majority-minority situation is commonly understood to be that in which a dominant social subgroup prevents or restrains a lower ranking subgroup from achieving comparable status. ("Caste, Class, and Minority," *Social Forces* 37, no. 3 [1959]: 248–254)

p. 1   *presidential election were white*: CNN.com, Election Results, 2004, available online at http://www.cnn.com/ELECTION/2004/pages/results/states/US/P/00/epolls.0.html (accessed January 2006).

p. 2   *of the disadvantaged swells*: Earl and Merle Black remark on the essential skill possessed by southern Democrats to "create and maintain a successful biracial coalition." Earl Black and Merle Black, *The Rise of Southern Republicans* (Cambridge: Harvard University Press, 2002), p. 27. See also Michael Lind, *Made in Texas: George W. Bush and the Southern Takeover of American Politics* (New York: Basic Books, 2003).

p. 3   *whole damn thing*: "Sick of government," interview with author, January 2006. Source requests anonymity.

p. 3   *executive branches of government*: National Conference of State Legislatures, available online at http://www.ncsl.org (accessed May 2006).

p. 4   *set the national agenda*: David C. Leege, Kenneth D. Wald, Brian S. Krueger, Paul D. Mueller, Politics of Cultural Differences: Social Change and Voter Mobilization Strategies in the Post–New Deal Period (Princeton: Princeton University Press, 2002), pp. 6, 12.

p. 5   *Southern Baptist Convention*: "The country's largest Protestant denomination, the Southern Baptist Convention, which has received considerable attention for its positions that wives should submit to the leadership of their husbands, and on the inerrancy of Scripture, showed a 7 percent increase between 1994 and 2005, to 16,439,000 members" (Bob Reeves, "Keeping the Faith?" *Lincoln Journal Star* [Nebraska], August 20, 2005, p. C1).

p. 5   *right-leaning Catholic communities*: Evangelicals are defined here as Christians who believe in the inerrancy of the Bible, who see Jesus as their personal savior, and who proselytize others.

p. 5   *goals of economic efficiency*: Conservative Philanthropy, The Strategic Philanthropy of Conservative Foundations, Media Transparency, available online at http://www.mediatransparency.org/conservativephilanthropy.php (accessed May 2006). John S. Saloma, *Ominous Politics: The New Conservative Labyrinth* (New York: Hill and Wang ,1984).

p. 7   *power in the White House*: Dana Milbank and Justin Blum, "Document Says Oil Chiefs Met with Cheney Task Force," *Washington Post*, November 16, 2005, p. A01. Dana Priest, "CIA Holds Terror Suspects in Secret Prisons; Debate Is Growing within Agency about Legality and Morality of Overseas System Set Up after 9/11," *Washington Post*, November 2, 2005, p. A01.

p. 7   *and "Super Rangers"*: Thomas B. Edsall, Sarah Cohen, and James V. Grimaldi, "Pioneers Fill War Chest, Then Capitalize," *Washington Post*, May 16, 2004, p. A01. James V. Grimaldi and Thomas B. Edsall, "Fundraiser Denies Link between Money, Access; EPA Rule on Hazardous Waste Favored Ohio Businessman Who Is a Big GOP Donor," *Washington Post*, May 17, 2004, p. A01. James V. Grimaldi and Thomas B. Edsall, "Across Federal Spectrum," *Washington Post*, May 17, 2004, p. A09. Thomas B. Edsall, James V. Grimaldi, and Alice R. Crites, "Redefining Democratic Fundraising; Kerry Has Amassed Record Sums from Disparate Groups Opposed to Bush," *Washington Post*, July 24, 2004, p. A01.

p. 9   *segregation forever*: "The 1963 Inaugural Address of Governor George C. Wallace," January 14, 1963, Montgomery, Alabama, Alabama Department of Archives and History, available online at http://www.archives.state.al.us/govs_list/inauguralspeech.html (accessed May 2006).

p. 10   *the most of it*: Ibid. On June 27, 2005, the U.S. Supreme Court ruled unconstitutional the display of the Ten Commandments in two Kentucky courthouses. The decision reignited the anger of many voters—particularly in the South—toward what they view as intrusive federal courts restricting religious expression. *McCreary County vs. ACLU*, available online at http://www.aclu.org/404/index.php (accessed May 2006).

p. 12   *act preemptively*: The National Security Strategy of the United States of America, Section V, "Prevent Our Enemies from Threatening Us, Our Allies, and Our Friends with Weapons of Mass Destruction," issued September 2002, available online at http://www.Whitehouse.gov/nsc/nss5.html (accessed May 2006).

p. 14   *after the 1968 election*: Byron E. Shafer, *Quiet Revolution: The Struggle for the Democratic Party and the Shaping of Post-Reform Politics* (New York: Russell Sage Foundation, 1983).

p. 14   *women to the Democratic Party*: John R. Petrocik and Karen Kaufmann, "The Changing Politics of American Men: Understanding the Sources of the Gender Gap," *American Journal of Political Science* 43, no. 3 (July 1999): 864–887.

p. 14   *an eight-point drop*: Mark Gersh, "Swing Voters," *Blueprint Magazine* (DLC), July 25, 2004, available online at http://www.dlc.org/ndol_ci.cfm?contentid=252802&kaid=127&subid=900056 (accessed May 2006); and 2004 exit poll data, available at CNN Web site, http://www.cnn.com/ELECTION/2004/pages/results/states/US/P/00/epolls.0.html (accessed May 2006).

p. 14   *men favoring regulation*: Benjamin I. Page and Robert Y. Shapiro, *The Rational Public* (Chicago: University of Chicago Press, 1992), pp. 295–296. Also, according to 2004 NES data, men were twice as supportive of increased military spending as women; data available online at http://www.umich.edu/~nes/ (accessed May 2006).

p. 15   *genuinely hospitable to men*: Sociologist Andrew Hacker puts the gender gap in more global terms, especially, but not only, among women identified with feminist goals:

> What has changed . . . is the readiness of women to subsume themselves or limit their ambitions to make life more congenial for men. Few are willing to sustain the former complementarity that required them to play a subordinate role. More broadly, they expect full equality, not just legally and in the economic arena, but in the holistic sense of being perceived as an integral human being. As hardly needs recounting, women are now entering spheres that were once dominated by men. And as more of them are revealing their talents, they are competing against men, a circumstance that was never contemplated in the past. Concurrently, today's high rate of divorce may be evidence of a growing estrangement, which transcends the difficulties of individual couples. Developments like these have begun to undermine what was once accepted as the affinity of the sexes. (*Mismatch: The Growing Gulf between Women and Men* [New York: Scribner, 2003], pp. 4–5)

p. 15   *critical mass of voters*: "But despite their fundraising success, Democrats simply did not spend their money as effectively as Bush. That is the conclusion of an extensive examination of campaign fundraising and spending data provided by the Federal Election Commission, the Internal Revenue Service and interviews with officials of the two campaigns and the independent groups allied with them" (Thomas B. Edsall and James V. Grimaldi, "On Nov. 2, GOP Got More Bang for Its Billion, Analysis Shows," *Washington Post*, December 30, 2004, p. A1).

p. 15   *only a few examples*: As examples: "Most of the NCC's largest denominations have suffered deep membership declines for 35 years or more. The NCC's critics say it has moved from being mainline to sideline, more renowned for its reflexively left-leaning politics than fostering genuine Christian unity. Fewer than one in three American church members now belong to an NCC denomination" (available online at http://www.adherents.com/largecom/prot_lib.html [accessed May 2006]). "The financially struggling National Council of Churches, despite painting a recovery picture early this year, finished the fiscal year with a deficit of $1.75 million and will take another hard look in mid-November at its future. . . . The United Methodist Church and other mainline denominations completed a $2 million rescue of the NCC late last year" (John Dart, "New NCC Dollar Woes," *Christian Century*, October 24, 2001, vol. 118, no. 29, p. 11). "Conservative Protestant denominations grew, while mainstream Protestant denominations declined" (available online at http://www.pbs.org/fmc/book/pdf/ch6.pdf [accessed May 2006]).

p. 16   *defeat of Republican candidates*: Conservative ideologues delight in fulminating against major philanthropies that have channeled funds to the left, notably Rockefeller, Ford, and Carnegie:

> Foundation-supported poverty advocates fought to make welfare a right—and generations have grown up fatherless and dependent. Foundation-funded minority advocates fought for racial separatism and a vast system of quotas—and American society remains perpetually riven by the issue of race. On most campuses today, a foundation-endowed multicultural circus has driven out the very idea of a common culture, deriding it as a relic of American imperialism. Foundation-backed advocates for various "victim" groups use the courts to bend government policy to their will, thwarting the democratic process.

And poor communities across the country often find their traditional values undermined by foundation-sent "community activists" bearing the latest fashions in diversity and "enlightened" sexuality. (Heather MacDonald, *City Journal* [Autumn 1996], available online at http://www.city-journal.org/html/6_4_a1.html [accessed May 2006]).

p. 16   *two major factions*: See Thomas B. Edsall, "The Old and New Democratic Parties," in *Varieties of Progressivism*, edited by Peter Berkowitz (Stanford, CA: Hoover Press, 2004), pp. 31–55. See also Berkowitz introduction for an overview.

p. 17   *National Center for Health Statistics*: Brady E. Hamilton, Stephanie J. Ventura, Joyce A. Martin, and Paul D. Sutton, "Preliminary Births for 2004," CDC, National Center for Health Statistics, Division of Vital Statistics, Table 1, see especially column on "Percent of births to unmarried mothers"; available online at http://www.cdc.gov/nchs/products/pubs/pubd/hestats/prelim_births/prelim_births04.htm (accessed May 2006).

p. 17   *basic necessities of life*: Pew Research Center, "Beyond Red vs. Blue," May 10, 2005, available online at http://people-press.org/reports/display.php3?ReportID=242 (accessed May 2006).

p. 17   *or on parole*: In March 2001, the White House Office of National Drug Control Policy reported:

In 1999, approximately 6.3 million adults—3.1% of the nation's adult population—were under correctional supervision (that is, incarceration, probation, or parole). Additionally, 98,913 juveniles (9% of whom were drug offenders) were incarcerated in public or private juvenile facilities for nonstatus offenses. Drug offenders accounted for 21% (236,800) of the State prison population in 1998, up from 6% (19,000) in 1980, and 59% (55,984) of the Federal prison population in 1998, up from 25% (4,749) in 1980. Also, in 1998, an estimated 26% (152,000) of all inmates under local supervision were incarcerated for drug offenses. This increase in the drug offender prison population mirrors the steady increase in arrests for drug offenses. The Federal Bureau of Investigation (FBI) reported 580,900 arrests for drug offenses (5.6% of all arrests) in 1980. The number of arrests peaked at 1,559,100 (10.4% of all arrests) in 1997. In 1999, there were 1,532,200 drug arrests, which accounted for 10.9% of all arrests. ("Drug Treatment in the Criminal Justice System," Executive Office of the President, Office of National Drug Control Policy, March 2001, available online at http://www.Whitehousedrugpolicy.gov/publications/factsht/treatment/#6 (accessed May 2006).

p. 17   *$159 billion in 1999*: "In 1999 the Federal government alone spent 27 billion dollars on the justice system. State governments spent $57 billion on criminal and civil justice in 1999. Local governments contributed the most (51%) to the criminal and civil justice system" (U.S. Department of Justice, Bureau of Justice Statistics, available online at http://www.ojp.usdoj.gov/bjs/abstract/jeeus99.htm [accessed May 2006]).

p. 17   *numbers of this group*: "United States HIV and AIDS Statistics Summary," available online at http://www.avert.org/statsum.htm (accessed May 2006); "HIV and Aids in the USA," available online at http://www.avert.org/aids-usa.htm (accessed May 2006).

p. 18   *teachers, and therapists*: Definition of professionals, State of Wisconsin, Department of Procurement, "Professionals: Occupations," available online at http://vendornet.state.wi.us/vendornet/contract/defs.asp (accessed May 2006).

p. 18   *some postgraduate education*: The Pew Research Center for the People and the Press, "Beyond Red vs. Blue," May 10, 2005, available online at http://people-press.org/reports/display.php3?ReportID=242 (accessed May 2006). For more information on Pew typology groups see: http://people-press.org/reports/display.php3?PageID=950 (accessed May 2006).

p. 18   *to have good values*: Pew Research Center, "Beyond Red vs. Blue," May 10, 2005, available online at http://people-press.org/reports/display.php3?ReportID=242 (accessed May 2006).

p. 19   *Pledge of Allegiance*: For "post-materialist" values, see Ronald Inglehart, *Silent Revolution: Changing Values and Political Styles among Western Publics* (Princeton: Princeton University Press, 1977); and *Culture Shift in Advanced Industrial Society* (Princeton: Princeton University Press, 1990).

p. 19   *up for adoption*: Michael Stephens, interview with the author, Alpharetta, Georgia, January 11, 2006.

p. 20   *"personal responsibility"*: The Pew Research Center for the People and the Press, "Beyond Red vs. Blue," May 10, 2005, available online at http://people-press.org/reports/display.php3?ReportID=242 (accessed May 2006). Thomas B. Edsall, "In Calif., War Becomes Litmus Test; Two Areas Reflect Deep Divide," *Washington Post*, April 13, 2003, p. A01. George Lakoff, *Moral Politics* (Chicago: University of Chicago Press, 1996), pp. 163–169.

p. 20   *burden on the child*: Retired policeman (did not give name), interview with the author, Alpharetta, Georgia, January 11, 2006.

p. 21   *that's how I feel*: David Loudenflager, interview with the author, Alpharetta, Georgia, January 11, 2006.

p. 21   *communities and families safe*: Thomas B. Edsall, "GOP Touts War as Campaign Issue; Bush Adviser Infuriates Democrats with Strategy Outlined at RNC Meeting," *Washington Post*, January 19, 2002, p. A02.

p. 22   *trying to kill it*: Transcript of Rove's speech as released by the Republican National Committee by email, January 20, 2006.

p. 23   *State of the Union address*: Bush 2006 State of the Union Address, available online at http://www.whitehouse.gov/stateoftheunion/2006/index.html (accessed May 2006).

p. 23   *of a different nature*: Transcript of the Rumsfeld briefing, available at the Department of Defense Web site, http://www.defenselink.mil/transcripts/2006/tr20060201-12403.html (accessed May 2006).

p. 23   *be a long war*: Josh White and Ann Scott Tyson, "Rumsfeld Offers Strategies for Current War; Pentagon to Release 20-Year Plan Today," *Washington Post*, February 3, 2006, p. A8.

p. 24   *opposing the war in Iraq*: Sixty-one percent of Democratic voters favored an immediate withdrawal of troops from Iraq, compared with 18 percent of Republicans, according to a Quinnipiac University poll of 1,230 voters surveyed November 28 to December 4, 2005, available online at http://www.bloomberg.com/apps/news?pid=10000087&sid=acX6_Shl20ZE&refer=top_world_news (accessed May 2006). Democratic senators supported the 2003 U.S. invasion of Iraq 29 to 21.

p. 24   *Trade Adjustment Assistance programs*: Much has been written about these developments. For an brief overview, see "The Challenges of the New Financial Economy: The Efforts of the IMF to Reduce the Risk of Financial Crises," Statement by Flemming Larsen, Director, IMF Office in Europe to the Joint Meeting of the Commission des Finances of the French National Assembly and the Haut Conseil de la Coopération Internationale, Paris, November 15, 2001:

> [Recent years have seen] an end to the government—controlled systems that prevailed from the end of WWII until the 1970s or 1980s—and in some cases much longer. The government-controlled financial

systems were highly regulated and designed to steer financial resources toward politically favored sectors and objectives. While these
systems occasionally were subject to crises—sometimes forcing a
country to devalue—they often appeared to be quite stable. However,
this stability came at a considerable price in the form of a lack of competition, high costs of financial intermediation, and inefficient or outright wasteful allocation of scarce financial resources. . . . If the benefits of a market-based financial system are so obvious, why were the
regulations put in place to start with? Why did not governments liber-
alize earlier? Here it is useful to recall that the government-controlled
financial systems had been put in place as a reaction to perceived
shortcomings of the liberal economic system that prevailed during the
gold standard period prior to WWI. These shortcomings included
economic instability and widespread social problems. Together with
the establishment of social safety nets and the active use of macroeco-
nomic policies for stabilization purposes, the government-controlled
financial systems were also a response to the banking failures and the
economic crises during the Great Depression. The implicit distrust in
market forces played a key role in economic strategies adopted after
WWII and remained prevalent throughout the industrial countries
for several decades. Greater faith in markets has been gradually restored since the early 1970s when a search for new policies was
prompted by an abrupt slowdown in economic growth, a sharp rise in
unemployment, and a surge in inflation. (available online at http://
www.imf.org/external/np/speeches/2001/111501.htm [accessed May
2006])

p. 24   *creating new wealth*: Morris Fiorina, with Samuel J. Abrams and Jeremy
C. Pope, *Culture War? The Myth of a Polarized America* (New York: Pearson Longman, 2005). Fiorina et al. remark that, as Clinton moved the Democratic Party
closer to the center on economic issues, the salience of cultural issues increased (p.
87).

p. 25   *low-wage global competition*: "Ford to Cut 30000 Jobs in North America,"
http://www.msnbc.msn.com/id/10946664 (accessed June 2006); "Delphi Demand:
Brutal Cuts," available online at http://www.detnews.com/2005/autoinsider/
0510/07/A01-340904.htm (accessed June 2006); "GM to Cut 30000 Jobs," available online at http://www.nytimes.com/2005/11/21/business/21cnd-gm.html
?ex=1290229200&en=e9078ee2aa73f1b6&ei=5088&partner=rssnyt&emc=rss
(accessed May 2006). For more on hypercompetition, see chapters 5 and 6.

p. 25   *a driving one*: David Wessel, "To a Seer It's Clear: Budget Will Buckle
under Health Costs," *Wall Street Journal*, January 12, 2006, p. A2.

p. 26   *to 26.8 percent*: Carmen DeNavas-Walt, Bernadette D. Proctor, and
Cheryl Hill Lee, "Income, Poverty, and Health Insurance Coverage in the United
States: 2004," U.S. Census Bureau, Current Population Reports (Washington,
DC: U.S. Government Printing Office, 2005), pp. 60–229.

p. 26   *to 7.4 percent*: David Cay Johnston, "Richest Are Leaving Even the Rich
Far Behind," *New York Times*, June 5, 2005, p. A1.

p. 27   *cannot be infringed*: "2004 Republican Party Platform: A Safer World and
a More Hopeful America," available online at http://www.gop.com/media/
2004platform.pdf (accessed May 2006).

p. 27   *nonsexual intimate relationships*: "Who Is Right about Homosexuality?
Conservative Christians, or Others?" updated January 6, 2002, available online at
http://www.religioustolerance.org/hom_rite.htm (accessed May 2006); and

"Reparative and Similar Therapies," updated December 4, 2003, available online at http://www.religioustolerance.org/hom_exod.htm (accessed May 2006).

p. 28 *freedom of private behavior*: Alan Wolfe, *One Nation After All: What Middle-Class Americans Really Think about God, Country, Family, Racism, Welfare, Immigration, Homosexuality, Work, the Right, the Left, and Each Other* (New York: Viking, 1998), pp. 72–84. Alan Wolfe, *Moral Freedom: The Impossible Idea That Defines the Way We Live Now* (New York: W. W. Norton, 2001).

p. 28 *field of human sexuality*: Pew Research Center for the People and the Press, "Less Opposition to Gay Marriage, Adoption and Military Service," March 22, 2006. Summary of findings: "Public acceptance of homosexuality has increased in a number of ways in recent years, though it remains a deeply divisive issue. Half of Americans (51%) continue to oppose legalizing gay marriage, but this number has declined significantly from 63% in February 2004, when opposition spiked following the Massachusetts Supreme Court decision and remained high throughout the 2004 election season. . . . The poll also finds less opposition to gays serving openly in the military and a greater public willingness to allow gays to adopt children. A 60% majority now favors allowing gays and lesbians to serve openly in the military, up from 52% in 1994, and 46% support gay adoption, up from 38% in 1999." Available online at http://people-press.org/reports/display.php3?ReportID =273 (accessed June 3, 2006). For an example of scientific research, see Hans A. Hofmann, "Functional genomics of neural and behavioral plasticity," *Journal of Neurobiology* 54, no. 1 (2003): 272–282, published online December 16, 2002, http://www3.interscience.wiley.com/cgi-bin/abstract/101526012/ABSTRACT ?CRETRY=1&SRETRY=0 (accessed May 2006).

p. 28 *than are older Americans*: "Young People More Supportive of Gay Marriage," The Pew Forum on Religion and Public Life, available online at http://pewforum.org/docs/index.php?DocID=39#2 (accessed May 2006).

p. 30 *concept of "compassionate conservatism"*: Marvin Olasky, *Compassionate Conservatism: What It Is, What It Does, and How It Can Transform America* (New York: The Free Press, 2000). Marvin Olasky, *The Tragedy of American Compassion* (Washington, DC: Regnery, 1992).

p. 31 *'don't kill me'*: "A Memorial to Karla Faye Tucker Brown," *Talk* magazine clip, available online at http://www.geocities.com/RainForest/Canopy/2525/karlamain.html (accessed May 2006).

p. 31 *no ifs, ands or buts*: American Political Network, Inc., The Hotline, "Health Care: GOP Group Wants Total Defeat of Clinton Plan," December 2, 1993, available online at http://nationaljournal.com/cgi-bin/ifetch4?ENG +HOTLINE+7-hot0195+1177391-REVERSE+0+0+47353+F+1+1+1+kristol +AND+PD%2f12%2f01%2f1993%2d%3e12%2f03%2f1993 (accessed May 2006).

p. 32 *influence public opinion*: All survey data on the political views of reporters and, to a slightly lesser extent, editors show a strong tilt to the Democratic Party. In addition, reporters support abortion rights, affirmative action, gay rights, and privacy rights in much higher percentages than the general public. The Media Research Center has compiled this data, available online at http://www.mediaresearch .org/biasbasics/welcome.asp#how (accessed May 2006).

p. 32 *over the past ten years*: Regnery bestsellers, available online at http://www .regnery.com/bestsellers.html (accessed May 2006).

p. 32 *minimal exceptions—been identical*: Thomas B. Edsall, "In Bush's Policies, Business Wins," *Washington Post*, February 8, 2004, p. A04.

p. 33 *Clinton and his wife*: On the Paula Jones and Whitewater cases, see "The Givers: Lynde and Harry Bradley Foundation," available online at http://www .pfaw.org/pfaw/general/default.aspx?oid=2065&print=yes&units=all (accessed

May 2006); "The Men Who Kept Paula Jones Lawsuit Going," Salon Newsreal, available online at http://salon.com/news/1998/04/cov_02news.html (accessed May 2006); *Time's* Jay Branegan on the Paula Jones Suit, 4/01/98," available online at http://www.time.com/time/community/transcripts/chattr040198.html (accessed May 2006).

p. 34   *student loan programs*: Congressional Budget Office, cost estimate, S. 1932, "Deficit Reduction Act of 2005, Conference Agreement, as Amended and Passed by the Senate on December 21, 2005," January 27, 2006, available online at http://www.cbo.gov/ftpdocs/70xx/doc7028/s1932conf.pdf (accessed May 2006).

p. 34   *Center on Budget and Policy Priorities*: Jason DeParle, "Liberal Hopes Ebb in Post-Storm Poverty Debate," *New York Times*, October 11, 2005, p. 1.

p. 35   *New Deal realignment*: Clerk of the House of Representatives, "Political Divisions of the House of Representatives (1789 to Present)," available online at http://clerk.house.gov/histHigh/Congressional_History/partyDiv.html (accessed May 2006).

p. 35   *Democratic advantage in 1933*: Ibid.

p. 37   *comfort books for liberals*: Matt Bai, "The Excluded Middle," Book Review, *New York Times*, December 11, 2005, p. 18.

p. 37   *as unmarried people*: L. A. Lillard and L. J. Waite, "The Decision to Marry and the Work and Earning Careers of Spouses," presented at the Second Annual Social Security Retirement Research Consortium Conference, Washington, DC, May 2000. Hyunbae Chun and Injae Lee, "Why Do Married Men Earn More: Productivity or Marriage Selection?" *Economic Inquiry* 39, no. 2 (April 2001): 307–319. Chun and Lee study summarized in *Business Week*, "Why Married Men Earn More":

> What explains the so-called marriage premium—the fact that married men tend to earn more than single men of similar backgrounds and educations? . . . In a new study in the journal *Economic Inquiry*, Hyunbae Chun, of Queens College in New York, and Injae Lee, of New York University, . . . [a]nalyzing 1999 survey data covering nearly 2,700 men, . . . find that married men earn an average of 12.4% more per hour than never-married men, after adjusting for age, work experience, education. . . . [I]t appears related to the state of being married—and specifically to the likelihood that wives shoulder household tasks. Chun and Lee report that the wage gap declines as wives put in more hours working outside the home. While married men whose wives aren't employed earn about 31% more per hour than never-married men, for example, men married to women with a full-time job earn only 3.4% more. (September 17, 2001, available online at http://www.businessweek.com/magazine/content/01_38/c3749028.htm #B3749030 [accessed May 2006])

Also see Hal R. Varian, "Analyzing the Marriage Gap, *New York Times*, July 29, 2004, available online at http://www.sims.berkeley.edu/~hal/people/hal/NYTimes/2004-07-29.html (accessed May 2006).

p. 37   *26 percent more than single men*: Panel Study of Income Dynamics, Center for the Study of Aging, "Grow Old with Me," RAND Corporation, available online at http://www.rand.org/publications/RB/RB5011/ (accessed May 2006).

p. 38   *particularly for women*: Carol S. Aneshensel and Jo C. Phelan, eds., *Handbook of the Sociology of Mental Health* (New York: Kluwer Academic/Plenum Publishers, 1999), p. 237.

p. 40   *many of them inland*: See, William H. Frey, "Metropolitan Magnets for Domestic and International Migration," Brookings Institution Center on Urban and Metropolitan Policy, October 2003; William H. Frey, "Metro Magnets for Minorities and Whites: Melting Pots, the New Sunbelt, and the Heartland," Research Report 02-496, Population Studies Center, University of Michigan, Ann Arbor, February 2002; and William H. Frey, "Emerging Demographic Balkanization: Toward One America or Two," Research Report 97-410, Population Studies Center, University of Michigan, Ann Arbor, 1997; references to all papers available at http://www.frey-demographer.org/reports.html (accessed May 2006).

p. 40   *ramifications of this movement*: Sam Roberts, "Come October Baby Will Make 300 Million or So," *New York Times*, January 13, 2006, p. A1.

p. 40   *likely to vote Democratic*: Voter News Service exit poll data, 2000–2004, available online at http://www.cnn.com/ELECTION/2004/pages/results/states/US/P/00/epolls.0.html (accessed May 2006).

p. 43   *in 1964 by Barry Goldwater*: "Two Rode Together," review of *Before the Storm: Barry Goldwater and the Unmaking of the American Consensus, The Economist*, April 26, 2001, available online at http://www.economist.com/books/displayStory .cfm?Story_ID=587301&tranMode=none (accessed May 2006).

p. 43   *both key institutions*: Interview by the author with Stephen Moore, March 2004.

p. 44   *why would you be a Democrat*: Interview by the author with Grover Norquist, June 2003.

p. 44   *Franklin D. Roosevelt's New Deal*: "The GOP Generation, a Special Report on Election 2004," prepared by Rasmussen Reports, December 10, 2004. This study can be purchased for $25 from Rasmussen Reports at http://www .rasmussenreports.com/GOP%20Generation%202004%20Edition.htm (accessed May 2006).

p. 44   *55 to 45 percent*: John Zogby, "Investors for Bush: How Social Security Reform Can Bring about a Republican Realignment," *Wall Street Journal*, Tuesday, March 15, 2005, WSJ.com, available online at http://www.opinionjournal.com/editorial/feature.html?id=110006425 (accessed May 2006).

p. 45   *key court cases*: In *Gratz v. Bollinger*, June 23, 2003, a Republican-appointed majority on the Supreme Court invalidated the University of Michigan's affirmative action program for undergraduate admission because the undergraduate school used a point system based in part on race (Linda Greenhouse, *New York Times*, June 24, 2003, p. A1). President Bush had asked the Court to declare the university's policy unconstitutional. In *Hopwood v. Texas*, a Republican-appointed Supreme Court majority declined to review a 5th U.S. Circuit Court of Appeals decision holding that colleges and universities could not use race in deciding which applicants to accept. "In a decision that reverberated through higher education nationwide yesterday, a federal appeals court ruled that public universities may not justify affirmative action programs based on the benefits of racial diversity. The 5th U.S. Circuit Court of Appeals decision issued late Monday struck down an admissions policy at the University of Texas law school giving preference to blacks and Hispanics as a violation of the Constitution's equal protection guarantee" (Joan Biskupic, "Texas Diversity Policy Overturned: U.S. Appeals Court Rules Campus Admissions Plan Unconstitutional," *Washington Post*, March 20, 1996, p. A1).

p. 47   *firm's Web site*: The Livingston Group, www.livingstongroupdc.com/.

p. 47   *law as of 2004*: Urban Institute, Brookings Institution, Tax Policy Center, Microsimulation Model, available online at http://taxpolicycenter.org/TaxModel/tmdb/TMTemplate.cfm?DocID=740&topic2ID=60&topic3ID=66 &DocTypeID=7 (accessed May 2006).

p. 48   *the top quintile, $3,623*: Ibid.

Chapter 2 ➤ Anger Points: Polarization as a Republican Strategy

p. 50   *designed explicitly to appeal*: The Dowd memo details are from an interview with Matt Dowd by the author, May 17, 2005, Washington, DC.

p. 50   *his own "compassionate conservatism"*: Marvin Olasky, "What Is Compassionate Conservatism and Can It Transform America?" Heritage Foundation Lecture #676, July 24, 2000, available online at http://www.heritage.org/Research/PoliticalPhilosophy/hl676.cfm (accessed May 2006). "Mr. Olasky and his followers believe that poverty is not caused by a lack of money, but by a lack of moral values on behalf of the poor. As such, they see welfare as a poor alternative to religion" (Toronto *Globe & Mail*, January 13, 2001, available at http://www.commondreams.org/headlines01/0113-02.htm [accessed May 2006]).

> President Bush and Karl Rove have the vision, one they've promoted since Bush was governor: compassionate conservatism, a vision of rich and poor, and of Whites, Blacks and Hispanics, working together in communities and developing their own plans from the bottom up. Liberals often respond condescendingly to that vision, saying it's a nice thought but maintaining their belief that a strong government hand is needed. They have what Thomas Sowell termed "the vision of the anointed." They see themselves as saviors of the poor but have become oppressors. The compassionate conservative vision, though, emphasizes faith-based and community initiatives rather than bureaucratic ones. (Marvin Olasky, "Karl Rove Time," November 13, 2002, Townhall.com, available online at http://www.townhall.com/opinion/columns/marvinolasky/2002/11/13/164893.html [accessed May 2006])

p. 51   *platform of 1956 or 1960*: Thomas B. Edsall, "Bush Abandons 'Southern Strategy'; Campaign Avoids Use of Polarizing Issues Employed by GOP since Nixon's Time," *Washington Post*, August 6, 2000, p. A19.

p. 51   *backs of the poor*: Ron Fournier, "Bush Criticizes GOP-led Congress on Spending Priorities," Associated Press, September 30, 1999.

p. 51   *we're all God's children*: Alison Mitchell, "The 2000 Campaign: The Texas Governor; Bush Talks to Gays and Calls It Beneficial," *New York Times*, April 14, 2000, p. 26A.

p. 52   *percentage of true swing voters*: Matt Dowd interview with the author, May 17, 2005, Washington, DC.

p. 52   *as angry as conservatives do*: Hal Malchow, of Malchow, Schlackman & Hoppy, quoted in Richard A. Viguerie and David Franke, *America's Right Turn* (Chicago: Bonus Books, 2004), p. 160.

p. 52   *classic fuck you gesture*: Karl Rove interview with the author, June 30, 1997.

p. 54   *total population in 2050*: U.S. Census Bureau, "Census Bureau Projects Tripling of Hispanic and Asian Population in 50 Years; Non-Hispanic Whites May Drop to Half of Total Population," March 18, 2004, available online at http://www.census.gov/Press-Release/www/releases/archives/population/001720.html (accessed May 2006).

p. 55   *calling upon God*: Partial transcript of comments from the Thursday, September 13, 2001, edition of the *700 Club*, available online at http://www.sacred-texts.com/ame/911/700club.htm (accessed May 2006).

p. 56   *breadth of the redistributive state*: The phrase "wing-tip Republicans" was coined by Mark Gauvreau Judge, "Right-Wingtips," *The American Spectator*, January 4, 2006, available online at http://www.spectator.org/dsp_article.asp?art_id=9208 (accessed May 2006).

p. 56   *steer American politics*: Thomas Byrne Edsall and Mary D. Edsall, *Chain Reaction: The Impact of Race, Rights and Taxes on American Politics* (New York: Norton, 1991); ". . . chain reaction, a point of political combustion reached as a linked series of highly charged issues collide" (p. 4).

p. 57   *patrons of the Stonewall bar*: "After Stonewall," PBS special, aired June 23, 1999, http://www.afterstonewall.com/press_as.html (accessed May 2006). Nicholas C. Edsall, *Toward Stonewall: Homosexuality and Society in the Modern Western World* (Charlottesville: University Press of Virginia, 2003), pp. 259–260.

p. 57   *fragmented and shunned community*: "After Stonewall: From the Riots to the Millennium," available online at http://www.afterstonewall.com/press_as.html (accessed May 2006).

p. 57   *in at least one state*: Evelyn Nieves, "Gay Rights Groups Map Common Agenda: Priorities Include Right to Marry, Ending Restrictions on Military Service," *Washington Post*, January 17, 2005, p. A03.

p. 57   *$21 billion for HIV and AIDS*: Centers for Disease Control and Prevention, HIV/AIDS Surveillance Report 2004, vol. 16, reported by Avert.org, available online at http://www.avert.org/statsum.htm; "HIV and AIDS in the USA," available online at http://www.avert.org/aids-usa.htm; "President's Emergency Plan for AIDS Relief," available online at http://www.avert.org/pepfar.htm (all sites accessed May 2006).

p. 58   *as neighbors and equals*: Adam Lisberg, "Dean Signs Civil Unions into Law," *Burlington Free Press* (Burlington, VT), April 27, 2000, p. 01A.

p. 58   *dignity as free persons*: Legal Information Institute, Supreme Court of the United States, *Lawrence et al. v. Texas*, No. 02-102, argued March 26, 2003, decided June 26, 2003, available online at http://supct.law.cornell.edu/supct/html/02-102 .ZS.html (accessed May 2006).

p. 58   *seven or younger*: Michael Paulson, "Abuse Study Says 4% of Priests in US Accused Figure Is Higher Than Church Officials Expected," *Boston Globe*, Spotlight Investigation, February 17, 2004.

p. 58   *grievous form of evil*: "Pope Denounces 'Evil' Sex Priests," BBC News, March, 21, 2002, available online at http://news.bbc.co.uk/1/hi/world/europe/1885380.stm (accessed May 2006).

p. 59   *lowest levels since the mid-1990s*: Susan Page, "Americans Less Tolerant on Gay Issues," *USA Today*, July 29, 2003, p. 1A.

p. 59   *sine qua non of marriage*: The Massachusetts Court System, *Hillary Goodridge & Others v. Department of Public Health & Another*, SJC-08860, November 18, 2003, available online at http://www.mass.gov/courts/courtsandjudges/courts/supremejudicialcourt/goodridge.html (accessed May 2006).

p. 59   *licenses issued in the state*: Charisse Jones, "Gay Marriage Debate Still Fierce One Year Later," *USA Today*, May 16, 2005, available online at http://www.usatoday.com/news/nation/2005-05-16-gay-marriage_x.htm (accessed May 2006).

p. 60   *as husband and wife*: "Bush's Remarks on Marriage Amendment." *New York Times*, February 25, 2004, p. 18.

p. 60   *stance on gun control*: Pew Research Center for the People and the Press, "Gay Marriage a Voting Issue, but Mostly for Opponents," February 27, 2004, available online at http://people-press.org/reports/display.php3?ReportID=204 (accessed May 2006).

p. 60   *voters age 65 and older*: Ibid.

p. 61   *for the gay marriage ban*: Daniel A. Smith, "Was Rove Right? The Partisan Wedge and Turnout Effects of Issue 1, Ohio's 2004 Ballot Initiative to Ban Gay Marriage," University of Florida, available online at http://www.clas.ufl.edu/users/pjwoods/smithbrownbag.pdf (accessed May 2006).

p. 61   *function as political "brand names"*: Matt Levendusky, "Sorting in the U.S. Mass Electorate," Department of Political Science, Stanford University,

September 26, 2005, presented at the annual meeting of the Midwest Political Science Association.

p. 62   *to my friends and neighbors*: Matt Dowd interview with the author, May 17, 2005, Washington, DC.

p. 62   *shapes attitudes toward policy issues*: Thomas M. Carsey and Geoffrey C. Layman, "Changing Sides or Changing Minds? Party Identification and Policy Preferences in the American Electorate,"*American Journal of Political Science* 50, no. 2 (2006): 464–477.

p. 63   *opposite of what the commission*: "The Separate Realities of Bush and Kerry Supporters," October 21, 2004, principal investigator, Steven Kull, Program on International Policy Attitudes, a joint program of the Center on Policy Attitudes and the Center for International and Security Studies at the University of Maryland, available online at http://zzpat.tripod.com/cvb/pipa.html (accessed May 2006).

p. 63   *William Frey's two Americas*: See William H. Frey, "Metropolitan Magnets for Domestic and International Migration," Brookings Institution Center on Urban & Metropolitan Policy, October 2003; William H. Frey, "Metro Magnets for Minorities and Whites: Melting Pots, The New Sunbelt, and The Heartland," PSC Research Report No. 02-496, Population Studies Center, University of Michigan, February 2002; and William H. Frey, "Emerging Demographic Balkanization: Toward One America or Two," PSC Research Report 97-410, Population Studies Center, University of Michigan, 1997, references to all papers available online at http://www.frey-demographer.org/reports.html (accessed May 2006).

p. 64   *America that are distinctively red*: Ross Douthat and Reihan Salam, "The Party of Sam's Club," *Weekly Standard*, November 14, 2005, available online at http://www.weeklystandard.com/Content/Public/Articles/000/000/006/312korit.asp?ZoomFont=YES (accessed May 2006).

p. 65   *National Election Studies surveys*: National Election Studies, data available online at http://www.umich.edu/~nes/nesguide/gd-index.htm#9 (accessed May 2006).

p. 66   *giant 2004 energy bill*: Thomas B. Edsall, "2 Bills Would Benefit Top Bush Fundraisers: Executives' Companies Could Get Billions," *Washington Post*, November 22, 2003, p. A1.

p. 66   *Jewish vote in 2004*: Jewish voters made up 3 percent of the total vote in 2004, and of that percentage, 25 percent went to Bush, up over 6 percent from 2000 according to CNN poll data, available online at http://www.cnn.com/ELECTION/2004/pages/results/states/US/P/00/epolls.0.html (accessed May 2006).

p. 66   *opposed to the war in Iraq*: American Jewish Committee, "2005 Annual Survey of American Jewish Opinion—War on Terrorism and Iraq," December 20, 2005, available online at http://www.ajc.org/site/apps/nl/content3.asp?c=ijITI2PHKoG&b=846741&ct=1740355 (accessed May 2006).

p. 66   *investment banks and brokerage houses*: "Rubin, Greenspan & Summers, The Committee to Save the World," *Time* (cover), February 15, 1999.

p. 67   *and they are stupid*: Papers of Dwight David Eisenhower, Volume 15: *The Presidency: The Middle Way*, Part VI: "Crises Abroad, Party Problems at Home; September 1954 to December 1954," Chapter 13: "A New Phase of Political Experience," Document #1147, November 8, 1954, to Edgar Newton Eisenhower, Series EM, AWF, Name Series, Category: Personal and confidential, available online at http://www.eisenhowermemorial.org/presidential-papers/first-term/documents/1147.cfm (accessed May 2006).

p. 68   *self-described "liberals"*: In 2004, the National Election Studies survey found that 23 percent of voters were liberal and 39 percent were conservative, data available online at http://www.umich.edu/~nes/nesguide/toptable/tab3_1.htm (accessed December 17, 2005).

p. 68   *"The Politics of Polarization"*: William Galston and Elaine Kamarck, "The Politics of Polarization," published online by Third Way, A Strategy Center for Progressives at http://www.third-way.com/news/pop.htm (accessed December 17, 2005).

p. 70   *the American Conservative Union*: American Conservative Union (ACU) ratings, available online at http://www.acuratings.org/statedelegation.asp?state=az (accessed May 2006).

p. 71   *attack on Kerry's war record*: David C. Leege, Kenneth D. Wald, Brian S. Krueger, and Paul D. Mueller, *Politics of Cultural Differences: Social Change and Voter Mobilization Strategies in the Post-New Deal Period* (Princeton: Princeton University Press, 2002), p. 9.

p. 71   *available resources to 50 percent*: Matt Dowd interview with author, May 17, 2005, Washington, DC.

p. 73   *media usage patterns*: Scarborough Research web site, http://www .scarborough.com/index.php (accessed May 2006).

p. 75   *CBS Evening News is cost-effective*: Data provided by Will Feltus of National Media Inc., based on research conducted for the Bush-Cheney 2004 campaign.

p. 76   *176 million individuals*: Acxiom Corporation web site, http://www .acxiom.com/ (accessed May 2006).

p. 77   *United Automobile Workers Union*: Information about Gage's company, TargetPoint, is based on interviews by the author with Gage, Brent Seaborn, and Michael Myers of TargetPoint on December 12, 2004, September 12, 2005, and October 26, 2005. The interviewees also provided samples of their research work.

p. 77   *in their message delivery*: Terry McAuliffe interview with author, July 27, 2004.

Chapter 3 ➤ Polarization as a Republican Strategy: Christians to the Right, Media to the Left

p. 78   *religious traditionalists of all faiths*: The term "evangelical" is used throughout to refer to fundamentalist, Pentecostal, evangelical, and charismatic Protestant Christians, many of whom identify themselves as "born again," believe in the literal truth of the Bible, and aim to convert others. See chapter 1, note p. 262.

p. 78   *61.2 percent, of GOP voters*: Bush administration policy has been as useful in turning out the conservative Catholic vote as it has been in mobilizing evangelicals. In 2004, Catholic turnout was up 6 percent, with such voters providing over 12 percent of the overall Republican vote. See Patrick Basham, "The Pope, the President, and the Changing Catholic Voter," April 15, 2005, available online at http://www.cato.org/pub_display.php?pub_id=3737 (accessed May 2006).

p. 79   *and social welfare programs*: "Religious Mobilization in the 2004 Presidential Election," by James L. Guth of Furman University, Lyman A. Kellstedt of Wheaton College, Corwin E. Smidt of Calvin College, and John C. Green of the University of Akron and the Pew Forum on Religion and Public Life, delivered at the annual meeting of the American Political Science Association, Washington, DC, September 1–4, 2005.

p. 79   *packaging key cultural/racial*: David C. Leege, Kenneth D. Wald, Brian S. Krueger, Paul D. Mueller, *Politics of Cultural Differences: Social Change and Voter Mobilization Strategies in the Post–New Deal Period* (Princeton: Princeton University Press, 2002), pp. 6, 12.

p. 79   *78 percent to 10 percent*: John C. Green, "The American Religious Landscape and Political Attitudes: A Baseline for 2004," available at the Web site of the

Pew Forum on Religion & Public Life, http://pewforum.org/publications/surveys/green-full.pdf (accessed May 2006).

p. 79   *casualties as acceptable*: Gary C. Jacobson, *A Divider, Not a Uniter: George W. Bush and the American People* (New York: Pearson Longman, 2006), chapter 8.

p. 80   *galvanize the cultural left*: Debra Chasnoff, "Bluster over 'Buster,'" *Washington Post*, February 4, 2005, p. A17; "Education Chief Rips PBS for Gay Character," MSNBC "Politics," http://www.msnbc.msn.com/id/6869976/ (accessed June 2006).

p. 81   *remember taking a life*: These and many, many other examples can be found in the press releases of the Department of Health and Human Services at http://www.hhs.gov/news/press/.

p. 82   *Church of Scientology*: Thomas B. Edsall, "Robertson Joins Liberals in Faulting Bush's 'Faith-Based' Plan," *Washington Post*, February 22, 2001, p. A5.

p. 82   *Operation Blessing International*: "Robertson Charity Wins 'Faith-Based' Grant," *Washington Post*, October 3, 2002.

p. 83   *human face on the party*: Thomas B. Edsall and Alan Cooperman, "GOP Using Faith Initiative to Woo Voters; Office's Officials Have Appeared with Republican Candidates in Tight Races," *Washington Post*, September 15, 2002, p. A5.

p. 83   *democratic public life*: Independent Women's Forum, press release, "IWF Awarded Grant to Support Iraqi Women," September 28, 2004, available online at http://www.iwf.org/iraq/iraq_detail.asp?ArticleID=677 (accessed May 2006).

p. 83   *forms of sex trafficking*: Concerned Women for America, press release, "CWA Awarded Anti-Trafficking Grant," September 29, 2005, available online at http://www.cwfa.org/articledisplay.asp?id=9068&department=MEDIA &categoryid=freedom (accessed May 2006).

p. 83   *maintain their religious integrity*: Richard B. Schmitt, "Justice Unit Puts Its Focus on Faith—A Little-known Civil Rights Office Has Been Busily Defending Religious Groups," *Los Angeles Times*, March 7, 2005.

p. 84   *entity was funded by government*: National Public Radio, *All Things Considered*, October 4, 2005, "Judge Rules Use of Religion in Hiring Decisions Is OK," reporter Barbara Bradley Hagerty, host Michele Norris.

p. 84   *build bridges to the middle*: Thomas B. Edsall, "Grants Flow to Bush Allies on Social Issues: Federal Programs Direct at Least $157 Million," *Washington Post*, March 22, 2006, p. A01.

p. 84   *people are drawn to that*: Ronnie Floyd, interview with author, November 5, 2005.

p. 84   *third of the Republican electorate*: In 2004, self-identified white, evangelical, and born-again Christians cast 78 percent of their votes for Bush. Extrapolating from that, they made up 33.6 percent of Bush voters, according to exit poll data available at CNN, http://www.cnn.com/ELECTION/2004/pages/results/states/US/P/00/epolls.0.html (accessed May 2006).

p. 85   *leadership by redeemed wives*: Council on Biblical Manhood and Womanhood (CBMW), "Danvers Statement," December 1987, published in final form by the CBMW in Wheaton, Illinois, November 1988, available online at http://www.cbmw.org/about/danvers.php#rationale (accessed May 2006); Donald Wildmon's American Family Association (AFA) online, http://www.afa.net/family/articles.asp; "Paying the Price for Free Sex," AFA Journal, January 2001, available online at http://www.afa.net/journal/january/familye.asp (accessed May 2006).

p. 85   *democratization of perversion*: Recent episode titles on reality soap opera *The Maury Show*, for example, are "SECRET Sex Videos . . . Ruined Lives! Caught on Tape!" "I Think I Got Our Babysitter Pregnant . . . Don't Divorce Me!" and "I'll Prove My Baby Is Your 14th Child!" Chip Crews, "Paternity Ward," *Washington Post*, March 28, 2006, p. C1.

p. 85   *Queer Eye for the Straight Guy*: Laura Grindstaff, "Trashy or Transgressive? 'Reality TV' and the Politics of Social Control," available online at http://

proxy.arts.uci.edu/~nideffer/Tvc/section3/11.Tvc.v9.sect3.Grindstaff.html   (accessed May 2006).

p. 85   *important part of daily life*: Thomas Byrne Edsall, "Blue Movie," *Atlantic Monthly*, vol. 291, January/February 2003, p. 36.

p. 86   *intended plan for healthy families*: Richard Land, "Salt Action Alert—Abstinence Education," available online at http://www.faithandfamily.com/CC/article/0,,PTID314166percent7CCHID600894percent7CCIID1991920,00.html (accessed May 2006).

p. 86   *change your belief systems*: Richard Land, "An Affair of the Mind," 2003 radio show, *Richard Land Live!*, available online at http://www.pastors.com/article .asp?ArtID=2973 (accessed May 2006).

p. 86   *societal approval of homosexual behavior*: Richard Land, "Keep the Faith: A Deviance from God's Norm," available online at http://www.beliefnet.com/story/125/story_12582_1.html (accessed May 2006).

p. 86   *they can't answer it*: Richard Land, "Keep the Faith: Symptom of Moral Crisis," available online at http://www.beliefnet.com/story/145/story_14583_1 .html (accessed May 2006).

p. 87   *virgins when they married*: Tom W. Smith, "American Sexual Behavior: Trends, Socio-Demographic Differences, and Risk Behavior," National Opinion Research Center, University of Chicago, GSS Topical Report No. 25, updated December 1998, available online at http://www.norc.uchicago.edu/online/sex.pdf (accessed May 2006).

p. 87   *by most reliable estimates*: "Sexual Behavior and Selected Health Measures: Men and Women 15–44 Years of Age, United States, 2002," Advance Data from Vital and Health Statistics, National Center for Health Statistics (NCHS), Centers for Disease Control, available online at http://www.cdc.gov/nchs/products/pubs/pubd/ad/361-370/ad362.htm (accessed May 2006): "In response to a question that asked, 'Do you think of yourself as heterosexual, homosexual, bisexual, or something else?' 90 percent of men 18–44 years of age responded that they think of themselves as heterosexual, 2.3 percent of men answered homosexual, 1.8 percent bisexual, 3.9 percent "something else," and 1.8 percent did not answer the question (figure 8). Percents for women were similar. These findings are similar to data collected in 1992 by Laumann et al."

p. 87   *above the national average*: David Crary, "Bible Belt Leads U.S. in Divorces," Associated Press online, https://www.nexis.com/research/home?_key =1107612362&_session=11dd3b86-777f-11d9-a904-8a0c5904aa77.1 .3285065162.50037.percent20.0.0&_state=&wchp=dGLbVzb-zSkBz&_md5 =46fd1d1622acb73ae384f377d2f44b30 (accessed May 2006).

p. 88   *Louisville, Kentucky, 28.8*: Table 1-22. "Number of Births to Unmarried Women by Race . . . Metropolitan Areas of the United States: 2000" Metropolitan Statistical Areas (MSAs), Vital Statistics of the United States, 2000, vol. 1: *Natality*, National Center for Health Statistics, available online at http://www.cdc.gov/nchs/data/statab/t001x22.pdf (accessed May 2006).

p. 88   *disintegrating American family*: Focus on the Family, Evangelical Council for Financial Accountability, available online at http://ecfa.org/ContentEngine .aspx?PageType=Control&PageName=MemberProfile&MemberID=5152   (accessed May 2006).

p. 90   *This is the big one*: Dr. Dobson's Newsletter, September 2003, "Marriage on the Ropes," available online at http://www.family.org/docstudy/newsletters/a0027590.cfm (accessed May 2006).

p. 90   *It is not*: From "Congregation for the Doctrine of the Faith, Letter to the Bishops of the Catholic Church on the Pastoral Care of Homosexual Persons," given at Rome, October 1, 1986, by Joseph Cardinal Ratzinger, Prefect, available   online   at   http://www.vatican.va/roman_curia/congregations/cfaith/

documents/rc_con_cfaith_doc_19861001_homosexual-persons_en.html (accessed May 2006).

p. 91 *accepting such a culture*: Cardinal Dionigi Tettamanzi, Archbishop of Genoa, "Christian Anthropology and Homosexuality" appeared in the March 12, 1997, issue of *L'Osservatore Romano*, published by the Vatican, available online at http://www.catholicculture.org/docs/doc_view.cfm?recnum=165 (accessed May 2006).

p. 91 *grew by 11 percent*: John C. Green, Corwin E. Smidt, James L. Guth, and Lyman A. Kellstedt, "The American Religious Landscape and the 2004 Presidential Vote: Increased Polarization," The Pew Forum on Religion & Public Life, February 3, 2005, available online at http://pewforum.org/docs/print.php?DocID =64 (accessed May 28, 2006).

p. 92 *child waiting to be born*: FDCH Political Transcripts, "President George W. Bush Delivers Remarks at Center for the Pope," March 22, 2001, available on Lexis-Nexis at https://www.nexis.com/research/home?_key=1089425853&_session=-4dc0a0b0-d217-11d8-8d90-8a0c59acaa77.1.3266878653.50037.%20.0 .0&_state=&wchp=dGLbVtz-zSkBB&_md5=1083c79f541d784a7861e70ecb41f324 (accessed May 2006).

p. 92 *a group of Catholic bishops*: Thomas B. Edsall, "Bush Aims to Strengthen Catholic Base: Republicans Seeking Solid Majorities among All White Religious Voters," *Washington Post*, April 16, 2001, p. A02.

p. 93 *abortion is a foundational issue*: David D. Kirkpatrick and Laurie Goodstein, "Group of Bishops Using Influence to Oppose Kerry," *New York Times*, October 12, 2004.

p. 93 *during a typical month*: "More People Use Christian Media Than Attend Church," available online at http://www.barna.org/FlexPage.aspx?Page =BarnaUpdate&BarnaUpdateID=184 (accessed May 2006).

p. 93 *membership is now one-third Latino*: Gregory Rodriguez, "It's Latino Immigrants Who Can Save the Catholic Church," *Los Angeles Times*, April 7, 2003, available online at http://www.newamerica.net/index.cfm?pg=article&DocID=807 (accessed May 2006).

p. 93 *32 percent in the West*: "Megachurches Today," Summary of data from the Faith Communities Today Project, Hartford Seminary, available online at http://hirr.hartsem.edu/org/faith_megachurches_FACTsummary.html (accessed May 2006); "Largest Religious Groups in the United States of America," available online at http://www.adherents.com/rel_USA.html#religions (accessed May 2006).

p. 94 *80,000 names on its rolls*: Event Transcript, Rick Warren, Senior Pastor and Founder, Saddleback Church, Orange County, California, "Myths of the Modern Mega-Church," The Pew Forum on Religion and Public Life, Key West, Florida, May 23, 2005, available online at http://pewforum.org/events/index .php?EventID=80 (accessed May 2006).

p. 94 *tax forms and in buying houses*: William C. Symonds, with Brian Grow and John Cady, "Earthly Empires: How Evangelical Churches Are Borrowing from the Business Playbook," *BusinessWeek*, May 23, 2005, available online at http://www .businessweek.com/magazine/content/05_21/b3934001_mz001.htm (accessed May 2006). Luisa Kroll, "Christian Capitalism: Megachurches, Megabusiness," Forbes.com, September 17, 2003, available online at http://www.forbes.com/ 2003/09/17/cz_lk_0917megachurch.html (accessed May 2006). "Churches as Businesses, Jesus, CEO," The Economist.com, December 20, 2005, available online at http://www.economist.com/world/na/displaystory.cfm?story_id=5323597&no_na _tran=1 (accessed May 2006).

p. 94 *60 million copies since 1995*: William C. Symonds, with Brian Grow and John Cady, "Earthly Empires: How Evangelical Churches Are Borrowing from the Business Playbook," *BusinessWeek*, May 23, 2005, available online at http://www

.businessweek.com/magazine/content/05_21/b3934001_mz001.htm (accessed May 2006).

p. 94 *with considerable justification*: Event Transcript, Rick Warren, Senior Pastor and Founder, Saddleback Church, Orange County, California, "Myths of the Modern Mega-Church," The Pew Forum on Religion and Public Life, Key West, Florida, May 23, 2005, available online at http://pewforum.org/events/index.php ?EventID=80 (accessed May 2006).

p. 95 *ever give it to him*: Ralph Blumenthal, "A Preacher's Credo: Eliminate the Negative, Accentuate Prosperity," *New York Times*, March 30, 2006, p. B1.

p. 95 *service to people*: Transcript of the Floyd sermon provided to the author by Americans United for Separation of Church and State.

p. 96 *The Meaning of a Man*: First Baptist Church of Springdale web site, http://www.fbcs.net.

p. 96 *rate of most private schools*: Council for Christian Colleges & Universities, http://www.cccu.org/news/newsID.396,parentNav.Archives/news_past_detail.asp.

p. 96 *according to advocacy organizations*: The National Home Education Research Institute, http://www.nheri.org/modules.php?name=Content&pa =showpage&pid=21.

p. 97 *"practical apprenticeship methodology"*: For an insightful article on Patrick Henry College and its students, see Hanna Rosin, "God and Country: A College That Trains Young Christians to Be Politicians," *The New Yorker*, June 27, 2005. Also see Patrick Henry College web site, http://www.phc.edu/; and David D. Kirkpatrick, "College for the Home-Schooled Is Shaping Leaders for the Right," *New York Times*, March 8, 2004, p. A1.

p. 97 *established by our Founding Fathers*: Information about Generation Joshua is available at the organization's web site, http://www.generationjoshua.org/dnn/ Default.aspx?tabid=1.

p. 98 *take over the South*: Richard A. Viguerie and David Franke, *America's Right Turn: How Conservatives Used New and Alternative Media to Take Power* (Chicago and Los Angeles: Bonus Books, 2004), p. 150.

p. 98 *divide on authentic lines*: Robert S. McElvaine, "GOP 'Values?' Read Their Lip-Service: Polarization of Americans, a Staple since Nixon, Looks Really Shabby on Columbus Day," *Los Angeles Times*, October 12, 1992, p. B7.

p. 98 *far the larger half*: William H. Freivogel, "Civil Rights Controversial Candidates Bring Racial Issues into Sharp Focus," *St. Louis Post-Dispatch*, February 28, 1992, p. 1B.

p. 98 *enemy whenever you can*: David Horowitz, *The Art of Political War* (Dallas: Spence Publishing Company, 2000) pp. 10–11.

p. 100 *represent the views of America*: Vice President Spiro Agnew, "On the National Media," a speech delivered at Des Moines, Iowa, November 13, 1969, available on the Southern Methodist University Web site, http://faculty.smu.edu/ dsimon/Change-Agnew.html (accessed May 2006).

p. 100 *tapped into a political goldmine*: William Safire, then a speechwriter for President Nixon, was the author of "nattering nabobs of negativism," according to *The Washingtonian*, March 1985, p. 11, and the *Washington Post*, August 27, 1987, p. C4.

p. 101 *capitalize on such findings*: According to Media Matters for America:

In addition to being funded by the Scaife and Olin foundations, when Lichter's Center for Media and Public Affairs (CMPA) launched in 1985, it sent out fund-raising letters with endorsements from conservatives including then-President Ronald Reagan; future Republican presidential candidate Pat Buchanan; attorney general under Reagan (and staunch anti-choice advocate) Ed Meese; and Christian Coalition founder Pat Robertson—according to a 1998 report by national media watch group Fairness & Accuracy in Reporting (FAIR). Nonetheless, CMPA's website announces that it "is a nonpartisan research and educational organization which conducts scientific studies of the *news* and *entertainment media* [CMPA's emphasis]." Lichter currently serves as a "media analyst" for FOX News Channel and also co-hosts a weekly radio show, *What's the Story*, with conservative *Weekly Standard* executive editor Fred Barnes, who cited Lichter's polls on *Special Report with Brit Hume* on May 24. *What's the Story* is nationally syndicated by Radio America, whose "mission is to produce and syndicate quality radio programs reflecting a commitment to traditional American values, limited government and the free market." (available online at http://mediamatters.org/items/200405280002 [accessed May 2006])

p. 101 *backed by conservative foundation money*: "Krauthammer and Barnes Misrepresented Pew Journalists Survey," Media Matters for America, May 28, 2004, available online at http://mediamatters.org/items/200405280002 (accessed May 2006).

p. 101 *leaned to the GOP*: American Society of Newspaper Editors, "The Newspaper Journalists of the '90's," October 31, 1997, available online at http://www.asne.org/kiosk/reports/97reports/journalists90s/journalists.html (accessed May 2006).

p. 102 *important role in their lives*: Eric Black, "Q: Are Journalists Liberal? A: Yes, Researchers Have Repeatedly Found That Journalists Tend to Hold Liberal Views and Vote for Democrats. What They Haven't Found Is Why, or How Much These Personal Views Affect Political Coverage," *Minneapolis Star Tribune*, August 18, 1996, p. 21A.

p. 102 *ultimately as Rush Limbaugh*: Richard A. Viguerie and David Franke, America's Right Turn: How Conservatives Used New and Alternative Media to Take Power (Chicago and Los Angeles: Bonus Books, 2004), pp. 178–179.

p. 102 *get in and get out*: Ibid., p. 179.

p. 103 *as of July 2005*: Chris Bowers and Matthew Stoller, "Emergence of the Progressive Blogosphere: A New Force in American Politics," The New Politics Institute, New Democrat Network, www.newpolitics.net.

p. 104 *whole different mindset*: Richard A. Viguerie and David Franke, America's Right Turn: How Conservatives Used New and Alternative Media to Take Power (Chicago and Los Angeles: Bonus Books, 2004), pp. 198–199.

p. 104 *some semblance of objectivity*: Ibid., p. 179.

p. 104 *most-trafficked progressive blogs*: Chris Bowers and Matthew Stoller, "Emergence of the Progressive Blogosphere: A New Force in American Politics," The New Politics Institute, New Democrat Network, www.newpolitics.net, and Joe Garofoli, "Top Dems Convene, Drawn by Bay Blog," *San Francisco Chronicle*, June 9, 2006, p. A1.

p. 105 *hostile to good reporting*: Michael Massing, "The End of News?" *New York Review of Books*, December 5, 2005, available online at http://www.nybooks.com/articles/18516 (accessed May 2006).

p. 105 *are on the fringe*: Michelle Cottle, appearing on CNN's *Reliable Sources*, "Battle over Terri Schiavo: Are Journalists Paying Enough Attention to Religion?" aired March 27, 2005, available online at http://transcripts.cnn.com/TRANSCRIPTS/0503/27/rs.01.html (accessed May 2006).

Chapter 4 ➤ The Republican Party Weds Corporate America

p. 106 *without a hitch*: Thomas B. Edsall and Jeffrey H. Birnbaum, "Industry Advocates Play Key Convention Roles: Republican Party Grants Unusual Access," *Washington Post*, September 1, 2004, p. A21.

p. 107 *beliefs of our party*: Ibid.

p. 109 *methyl tertiary butyl ether (MTBE) waiver*: Thomas B. Edsall and Justin Blum, "Rep. Barton Faces Energy Challenge: New Panel Chairman and Industry Ally Will Be Man behind Major Legislation," *Washington Post*, April 14, 2005, p. A 25: "MTBE (methyl tertiary butyl ether) is a gasoline additive that is the subject of groundwater-pollution litigation nationwide. Barton and DeLay have been the leading defenders of MTBE producers, insisting they be protected from product-defect lawsuits."

p. 109 *Anglo-Saxon blood aristocracies*: Glen Justice, "Once at Arm's Length, Wall Street Is Bush's Biggest Donor," *New York Times*, October 23, 2003, p. A1.

p. 110 *independent oilmen and ranchers*: Saul Friedman, "Texas Ranchers Have Key Role in Goldwater's Campaign," *Houston Chronicle*, July 26, 1964; Warren Berry, "Goldwater Meets Money Men First," *Denver Post*, July 17, 1964; "Oil Millionaires Support Goldwater," radio program transcript reprinted in the *Madison (Wisconsin) Capitol Times*, August 3, 1964. References originally found in Mary C. Brennan, *Turning Right in the Sixties* (Chapel Hill: University of North Carolina Press, 1995), p. 171, and confirmed by author. See also, Thomas B. Edsall, "Corporate Chiefs Put Heart into Contributions to GOP," *Washington Post*, August 29, 1986, p. A1; Thomas B. Edsall, "Independent Oil's Political Prospectors Drill a Lot of Dry Wells," *Washington Post*, November 17, 1982, p. A6; Thomas B. Edsall, "New Power Network: Independent Oil Fuels the Right," *Washington Post*, October 9, 1982, p. A1; Thomas B. Edsall and Edward Walsh, "Tax Battle on Hill Is Heating Up: Bidding War Escalates for Tax Votes on Hill; Democrats Weigh New Breaks for Estates, Oil Profits," *Washington Post*, July 16, 1981, p. A1.

p. 110 *and their top executives*: Information on early soft money contribution sources are available at the PoliticalMoneyLine Web site, http://www.fecinfo.com/, and at the Center for Responsive Politics, http://www.opensecrets.org/.

p. 111 *greatly facilitated the merger*: Thomas B. Edsall, Sarah Cohen, and James V. Grimaldi, "Pioneers Fill War Chest, Then Capitalize," *Washington Post*, May 16, 2004, p. A01.

p. 112 *by individuals, corporations, and unions*: For interesting discussions of campaign finance reform, see Franklin Foer, "Will McCain Feingold Breed Democratic Fratricide? Petty Cash," *New Republic*, May 29, 2002, available online at http://www.tnr.com/doc.mhtml?i=20020603&s=foer060302 (accessed May 2006); and John Judis, "Putting Liberty First: The Case against Democracy," *Foreign Affairs*, May/June 2003, available online at http://www.foreignaffairs.org/20030501fareviewessay11224/john-b-judis/putting-liberty-first-the-case-against-democracy.html (accessed May 2006).

p. 114 *fifth place at $5.9 million*: "Shift of Sources of GOP Campaign Money from Sunbelt to North," Center for Responsive Politics, available online at http://www.opensecrets.org/presidential/index.asp (accessed May 2006).

p. 115 *gave $309,150*: Lists of Pioneers and Rangers from 2000 and 2004 can be found at the Public Citizen Web site, http://www.Whitehouseforsale.org/. Detailed listings of the geographic sources of contributions and of the major employers of donors can be found at the Web site maintained by Citizens for Responsive Politics, http://www.opensecrets.org/.

p. 115 *American International Group, $276,000*: David Donnelly, "Tax Breaks for Donors," Campaign Money Watch, available online at http://www.campaignmoney.org/spotlight/sis04_15_04.htm (accessed May 2006).

p. 115 *on behalf of investors*: "Cut in Dividend, Capital Gains Taxes Will Spur Economic Growth as Equity Investing Becomes More Attractive to Investors: Securities Industry Praises President, Congressional Leaders for Historic Achievement on Tax-Cut Package," Securities Industry Association statement, May 22, 2003, available online at http://www.sia.com/press/2003_press_releases/html/pr_praise_president.html (accessed May 2006).

p. 117 *on the NRCC Web site*: The fundraising events list for the National Republican Campaign Committee (NRCC) is constantly updated, and past events removed. The list can be found online at http://www.nrcc.org/nrcc_contents/events/events/ (accessed May 2006).

p. 117 *annual tax break of $22,335*: William G. Gale and Peter R. Orszag, "Bush Administration Tax Policy: Distributional Effects," Tax Notes, September 27, 2004, available online at http://www.taxpolicycenter.org/publications/template.cfm?PubID=1000689 (accessed May 2006):

> In particular, all of the measures indicate that high-income households benefit at the expense of other households, who lose in aggregate. About 80 percent of households would be worse off under the tax cuts plus proportional financing than they would be without the tax cuts, including a majority in every quintile. The percentage of tax units with a tax cut rises with income. The top quintile is the only group to receive a net tax cut, but even in the top quintile, almost two-thirds of all households in the 80th to 99th percentile face net tax increases. Both of the measures that gave anomalous results when financing was ignored—the percentage change in federal taxes and the share of income tax paid—now show that households in the bottom 80 percent of the income distribution are worse off on average, while those in the top quintile are better off.

p. 117 *most other developed countries*: Gary Burtless and Christopher Jencks, "American Inequality and Its Consequences," March 5, 2003, pp. 18–19, available online at http://www.brookingsinstitution.org/dybdocroot/GS/Events/americaninequality.pdf (accessed May 2006). Samuel Bowles, Herbert Gintis, and Melissa Osborne Groves, *Unequal Chances* (Princeton, NJ: Princeton University Press, 2005). Lawrence Mishel, Jared Bernstein, and Sylvia Allegretto, *The State of Working America, 2004/2005* (Ithaca, NY: Cornell University Press, 2005), p. 48: "[Between 1995 and 2000, B]lack family income growth surpassed that of whites by 0.8 percent a year (2.9 percent versus 2.1 percent) while Hispanic family income grew more than twice as fast as white income during the five-year interval (4.6 percent). . . . However, when the labor market weakened in 2001, these growth rates sharply reversed course, especially compared to that of the median white family. Black families lost 1.5 percent a year between 2000 and 2003, three times the annual decline for white families, and the gap between white and Hispanic incomes grew even faster."

p. 118 *public utilities to corporate acquisition*: Susan Milligan, "Bush Signs $14.5 Billion Energy Bill: Says Fuel Production Increases Will Lessen Foreign Dependence," *Boston Globe*, August 9, 2005, available online at http://www.boston.com/news/nation/washington/articles/2005/08/09/bush_signs_145_billion_energy_bill/ (accessed May 2006).

p. 118 *should not be underestimated*: Thomas B. Edsall, "Conservatives Join Forces for Bush Plans: Social Security, Tort Limits Spur Alliance," *Washington Post*, February 13, 2005, p. A4, available online at http://www.washingtonpost.com/wp-dyn/articles/A19782-2005Feb12.html (accessed May 2006).

p. 118 *crucially important by American business*: American Tort Reform Association, available online at http://www.atra.org/wrap/files.cgi/7963_howtortreform .html (accessed May 2006).

p. 118 *donate to Democratic candidates*: Center for Responsive Politics, "Lawyers/ Law Firms: Long-Term Contribution Trends," available online at http://www .opensecrets.org/industries/indus.asp?cycle=2006&ind=K01 (accessed May 2006).

p. 119 *tort litigation have greatly increased*: Thomas F. Burke, "Lawyers, Lawsuits, and Legal Rights: The Battle over Litigation in American Society," California Series in Law, Politics, and Society, 2002, available online at http://www .ucpress.edu/books/pages/9231/9231.intro.html (accessed May 2006).

p. 120 *litigation have continued to grow*: Ibid.

p. 121 *underperforming schools or districts*: Walter Olson, "Regulation through Litigation," PointofLaw.com, Web site of the Manhattan Institute and American Enterprise Institute, August 30, 2005, available online at http://www.pointoflaw .com/regulation/overview.php (accessed May 2006).

p. 121 *defamation,' and much more*: Walter Olson, "Harassment and Sex Discrimination Law," available online at http://walterolson.com/categories/women .html (accessed May 2006). See also Olson, "Employment Law," available online at http://www.pointoflaw.com/employmentlaw/ (accessed May 2006).

p. 121 *Texas governor in 1994*: PoliticalMoneyLine, summary and detailed information on lobbying expenditures for each six-month reporting period, available online at http://www.fecinfo.com/cgi-win/lp_summary.exe?DoFn (accessed May 2006).

p. 121 *restructuring of lawsuit rules*: Thomas B. Edsall, "Conservatives Join Forces for Bush Plans: Social Security, Tort Limits Spur Alliance," *Washington Post*, February 13, 2005, p. A4, available online at http://www.washingtonpost.com/wp-dyn/articles/A19782-2005Feb12.html (accessed May 2006).

p. 122 *issue of lawsuit reform*: 2005 lobbying data from PoliticalMoneyLine, "Available Large $ Expenditure Year End 2005 Lobby Filers," available online at http://www.fecinfo.com/ (accessed May 2006).

p. 122 *advanced by class action litigation*: Walter K. Olson, *The Litigation Explosion: What Happened When America Unleashed the Lawsuit* (New York: Truman Talley Books/St. Martins, 1991); and Walter K. Olson, *The Rule of Lawyers: How the New Litigation Elite Threatens America's Rule of Law* (New York: Truman Talley Books/St. Martin's, 2003); Philip K. Howard, *The Death of Common Sense: How Law Is Suffocating America* (New York: Random House, 1994).

p. 123 *the small business owners*: "President's Remarks at Ask President Bush Event,"Albuquerque, New Mexico, August 11, 2004, available online at http://www .whitehouse.gov/news/releases/2004/08/20040811-6.html (accessed May 2006).

p. 123 *can't go into the courthouse*: Sheila Jackson Lee, Reuters, October 27, 2005, available online at http://my.aol.com/news/news_story.psp?type=1&cat =0700&id=20051027191700002264944 (accessed May 2006).

p. 124 *1992 total of 10,771*: Amy Saltzman, "Suppose They Sue? Why Companies Shouldn't Fret So Much about Bias Cases," *US News*, September 22, 1997, available online at http://www.manhattan-institute.org/html/_us_news-suppose .htm (accessed May 2006).

p. 124 *discrimination and sexual stereotypes*: For lawsuits, see "Court Cases in the News," available online at http://www.workplacefairness.org/index.php?page =courtcases (accessed May 2006).

The last decade has seen an explosion of employment discrimination class action lawsuits that have been resolved through record breaking settlements. The best known of these cases is the $176 million settlement involving Texaco, one that came on the heels of the much publicized discovery of tape-recorded meetings that seemingly indicated the use of explicit racial epithets by management-level employees. There have also been substantial settlements involving Coca-Cola ($192 million), Home Depot ($104 million), Shoney's ($105 million), Publix Markets ($81 million), and State Farm Insurance Co. ($157 million). A recently filed sex discrimination suit against Wal-Mart appears poised to set a new record. (Michael Selmi, "The Price of Discrimination: The Nature of Class Action Employment Discrimination Litigation and Its Effects," *University of Texas Law Review* 81, no. 5 [April 2003], available online at http://www.utexas.edu/law/journals/tlr/abstracts/81/81-5.pdf [accessed May 2006])

See also, Costco Class Web site, https://genderclassactionagainstcostco.com/costco94.pl?wsi=0&websys_id=&websys_screen=public_faqs_index (accessed May 2006). For the Smith Barney suit, see "Sex Discrimination in the American Workplace: Still a Fact of Life," National Women's Law Center, available online at http://www.nwlc.org/details.cfm?id=316&section=employment (accessed May 2006). For Borgata Babes, see Gaming News, "Borgata Hit with Lawsuit," January 31, 2006, available online at http://www.casinocitytimes.com/news/article.cfm?contentID=156234 (accessed May 2006).

p. 125 *by the Microsoft juggernaut*: "There have been quite a number of assaults on Microsoft, but most were motivated by economic interests and weren't widely supported by the public. The biggest lawsuits targeting Microsoft have generally been organized by companies that were plowed under by the Microsoft juggernaut. They posed a formidable threat when several state attorney generals rallied behind them. . . . Microsoft has been resorting to increasingly desperate measures to ward off the Linux menace, which it officially considers its second biggest threat" ("Linux: The Penguin That Ate Microsoft," available online at http://www.freedomware.us/stars/linux/ [accessed January 2006]).

p. 125 *problems over all these years*: Trent Lott quote, Thomas B. Edsall, "Lott Decried for Part of Salute to Thurmond: GOP Senate Leader Hails Colleague's Run as Segregationist," *Washington Post*, December 7, 2002, p. A06.

p. 126 *the suit got $22 million*: John F. Harris and William Branigin, "Bush Signs Class-Action Changes into Law," *Washington Post*, February 18, 2005, available online at http://www.washingtonpost.com/wp-dyn/articles/A35084-2005Feb18.html (accessed May 2006).

p. 126 *Department of Homeland Security*: Liability legislation information supplied to the author by Ginny Smith, Communications Director, U.S. Chamber Institute for Legal Reform, February 13, 2006.

p. 127 *And we will do it*: "Senator Frist Addresses Lincoln-Reagan Day Dinner," Hampstead, New Hampshire, February 3, 2006, available on the Volunteer Political Action Committee Web site, http://www.volpac.org/index.cfm?FuseAction=Speeches.Detail&Speech_id=25&Month=2&Year=2006 (accessed May 2006).

p. 128 *returned to the contributors*: Thomas B. Edsall, "Breakfast with the Senate Finance Chairman—for $10,000," *Washington Post*, February 3, 1987, p. A1; and Thomas B. Edsall, "Bentsen Decides to Disband His $10,000 Breakfast Club," *Washington Post*, February 7, 1987, p. A1.

p. 128 *coming from trial lawyer firms*: The Web site PoliticalMoneyLine tracks campaign contributions and provides information on these and other fundraising committees. Its Web site is http://www.fecinfo.com/.

p. 129 *53 percent of the vote*: Information on lobbyists, their clients, and annual fees can be found on a Web site maintained by the U.S. Senate, http://sopr.senate.gov/cgi-win/m_opr_viewer.exe?DoFn=0.

p. 131 *by the mainstream media*: Articles by Stephen Burd in the *Chronicle of Higher Education*: "Selling Out Higher-Education Policy? Led by Sallie Mae and the Apollo Group, the Loan Industry and For-Profit Colleges Use Political Donations to Try to Get Their Way on Capitol Hill," July 30, 2004, available online at http://chronicle.com/free/v50/i47/47a01601.htm (accessed May 28, 2006); "Ways & Means: Lawmaker Tells Loan-Industry Officials He Is on Their Side," December 16, 2005, available online at http://chronicle.com/temp/reprint.php?id =29kcp57g8f221b0bwwdgxzrt7sfx64y8 (accessed May 28, 2006); "Boehner's Candidacy for Leadership Post Throws Spotlight on His Ties to Student-Loan Industry," January 13, 2006, available online at http://chronicle.com/temp/reprint .php?id=yt9g0l1dggqq1ssjmmq9nvdmk78fclhb (accessed May 28, 2006).

p. 131 *lucrative relationship between Republicans and business*: Three watchdog organizations, The Center for Public Integrity, The Center for Responsive Politics, and PoliticalMoneyLine do an excellent job of keeping track of campaign finance, lobbying, and other potential avenues of political corruption. The Abramoff scandal, which began with the publication of Susan Schmidt's story in the *Washington Post* in February 2004, revealed a pattern of campaign contributions, privately paid trips for members of Congress and their staffs to resorts here and abroad, and numerous other benefits financed by Abramoff and his clients, including Indian tribes operating gambling casinos. The scandal, at this writing, threatens to produce a number of indictments or derailed careers of elected officials, other lobbyists, Republican operatives, and present and former congressional staffers. See Susan Schmidt, "A Jackpot from Indian Gaming Tribes: Lobbying, PR Firms Paid $45 Million over 3 Years," *Washington Post*, February 22, 2004, p. A1. Susan Schmidt, James Grimaldi, and R. Jeffery Smith, as well as editor Jeff Leen of the *Washington Post* have, between 2004 and 2006, produced exceptional coverage of the Jack Abramoff lobbying scandal and all of its ramifications. Regarding print media reporting on lobbying, Peter Stone of *National Journal* and Brody Mullins, who moved in 2005 from *Roll Call* to the *Wall Street Journal*, vigorously cover the intersection of money and politics in Washington.

p. 132 *this far without your assistance*: Kate Ackley and Tory Newmyer, "K Street Files: Packed House," *Roll Call*, April 18, 2005, available online at http://www .rollcall.com/issues/50_100/kfiles/8875-1.html (accessed May 2006).

p. 132 *whip the vote on the outside*: Thomas B. Edsall, "House Majority Whip Exerts Influence by Way of K Street," *Washington Post*, May 17, 2005, p. A19.

p. 134 *China was temporarily suspended*: Jonathan Weisman, "Conferees Agree on Corporate Tax Bill," *Washington Post*, October 7, 2004, p. A05; and "Estimated Budget Effects of the Conference Agreement for H.R. 4520, the 'American Jobs Creation Act of 2004,' Fiscal Years 2005–2014," Joint Committee on Taxation, October 7, 2004, JCX-69-04, available online at http://www.house.gov/jct/x-69-04 .pdf (accessed May 2006).

p. 134 *second half of 2004*: See the lobby disclosure site at the U.S. Senate Web site, http://sopr.senate.gov/cgi-win/m_opr_viewer.exe?DoFn=3&CLI=GENERAL %20ELECTRIC%20CO&CLIQUAL==&sequence=0 (accessed May 2006).

p. 135 *just a nice little hint*: Hedrick Smith, "The People and the Power Game," 1996, available online at http://www.hedricksmith.com/PBSDoc/ thePeopleAndThePowerGame.shtml (accessed May 2006).

p. 135 *The word is out*: David Maraniss and Michael Weisskopf, "Speaker and His Directors Make the Cash Flow Right," *Washington Post*, November 27, 1995, p. A1.

p. 136 *see that I carried on*: Hedrick Smith, "The People and the Power Game," 1996, available online at http://www.hedricksmith.com/PBSDoc/ thePeopleAndThePowerGame.shtml (accessed May 2006).

p. 136 *GOP freshmen backed DeLay*: Michael Weisskopf and David Maraniss. "Forging an Alliance for Deregulation," *Washington Post*, March 12, 1995, p. A1.

p. 136 *"Boehner can rely on K Street Cabinet"*: Jonathan E. Kaplan, "Boehner Can Rely on K Street Cabinet," *The Hill*, October 6, 2005, available online at http://www.hillnews.com/thehill/export/TheHill/News/Frontpage/100605/boehner.html (accessed May 2006).

p. 137 *business where we can*: Brody Mullins, "Hoyer's Own 'K St. Project,'" *Roll Call*, May 21, 2003, available online at http://www.rollcall.com/issues/48_94/vested/1644-1.html (accessed May 2006).

p. 137 *opposed both bills*: Alexander Bolton, "Dems' Downtown Help against Bush," *The Hill*, February 17, 2005, available online at http://www.hillnews.com/thehill/export/TheHill/News/Frontpage/021705/downtown.html (accessed May 2006).

p. 139 *"vote for George Bush"*: Chris LaCivita quote, Institute of Politics, Harvard University, ed., *Campaign for President: The Managers Look at 2004* (Lanham, MD: Rowman & Littlefield, 2006), pp. 215–218.

p. 139 *which Kerry never won back*: "John O'Neill," *The American Enterprise On-Line*, April/May 2005, available online at http://www.taemag.com/issues/articleid.18461/article_detail.asp (accessed May 2006).

p. 140 *prohibited by federal election law*" Dana Milbank and Thomas B. Edsall, "Bush-Cheney Lawyer Advised Anti-Kerry Vets," *Washington Post*, August 25, 2004, p. A1.

p. 140 *exempt from combat duty*: Interview with Bob Dole, CNN *Late Edition with Wolf Blitzer*, aired August 22, 2004, available online at http://transcripts.cnn.com/TRANSCRIPTS/0408/22/le.00.html (accessed May 2006). "Vietnam War Veteran John Kerry's Testimony before the Senate Foreign Relations Committee, April 22, 1971," available online at http://www.richmond.edu/~ebolt/history398/JohnKerryTestimony.html (accessed May 2006):

> I would like to talk, representing all those veterans, and say that several months ago in Detroit, we had an investigation at which over 150 honorably discharged and many very highly decorated veterans testified to war crimes committed in Southeast Asia, not isolated incidents but crimes committed on a day-to-day basis with the full awareness of officers at all levels of command. . . .
>
> They told the stories at times they had personally raped, cut off ears, cut off heads, taped wires from portable telephones to human genitals and turned up the power, cut off limbs, blown up bodies, randomly shot at civilians, razed villages in fashion reminiscent of Genghis Khan, shot cattle and dogs for fun, poisoned food stocks, and generally ravaged the countryside of South Vietnam in addition to the normal ravage of war, and the normal and very particular ravaging which is done by the applied bombing power of this country.
>
> We call this investigation the "Winter Soldier Investigation." The term "Winter Soldier" is a play on words of Thomas Paine in 1776 when he spoke of the Sunshine Patriot and summertime soldiers who deserted at Valley Forge because the going was rough.
>
> We who have come here to Washington have come here because we feel we have to be winter soldiers now. We could come back to this country; we could be quiet; we could hold our silence; we could not tell what went on in Vietnam, but we feel because of what threatens this country, the fact that the crimes threaten it, not reds, and not redcoats but the crimes which we are committing that threaten it, that we have to speak out.

p. 141 *revoke Senator Kerry's awards*: "Request for Investigation, Determination and Final Disposition of Awards Granted to Lieutenant (junior grade) John Forbes

Kerry, USNR," complaint filed by Judicial Watch, August 17, 2004, available online at http://www.judicialwatch.org/archive/2004/kerryawards.htm (accessed May 2006). Vice-Admiral R. A. Route, the navy inspector general, conducted the review of Kerry's Vietnam War military service awards at the request of Judicial Watch. He found no evidence that the medals had been awarded improperly. In October 2004, Secretary of the Navy Gordon England wrote to Judicial Watch supporting Route's finding. The letters can be viewed on the Judicial Watch Web site, http://www.judicialwatch.org/3848.shtml (accessed May 2006).

p. 141 *The Dick Cavett Show*: Transcript of O'Neill-Kerry debate on ABC's June 30, 1971, broadcast of *The Dick Cavett Show*, available online at http://horse.he.net/~swiftpow/index.php?topic=KerryONeill (accessed May 2006).

p. 141 *activist's popular appeal*: Michael Dobbs, "After Decades, Renewed War on Old Conflict," *Washington Post*, August 28, 2004, p. A01.

p. 141 *discussing these questions"* Ken Mehlman quote, Institute of Politics, Harvard University, ed., *Campaign for President: The Managers Look at 2004* (Lanham, MD: Rowman & Littlefield, 2006), p. 191.

p. 142 *and a Rhodes Scholar*: "Presidential Medal of Freedom Recipient General Wesley K. Clark," available online at http://www.medaloffreedom.com/WesleyClark.htm (accessed May 2006).

p. 142 *Wes won't get my vote*: Transcript, *Meet the Press*, NBC News, December 14, 2003, available online at http://msnbc.msn.com/id/3476052/ (accessed May 2006):

> MR. RUSSERT: I want to give you a chance to respond to some of the comments some of your fellow military men have said about you, because it has received a lot of coverage in the newspapers and on television. This was a question posed to Hugh Shelton, who was the chairman of the Joint Chiefs of Staff under President Clinton: "What do you think of General Wesley Clark and would you support him as a presidential candidate?" "I've known Wes for a long time. I'll tell you the reason he came out of Europe early had to do with integrity and character issues, things that are very near and dear to my heart. . . . I'll just say Wes won't get my vote." Tommy Franks, who led the effort in Iraq, said this: Would you make a good president? He said, "Absolutely not." Norman Schwarzkopf added, "I do know that Clark's always been viewed as being very, very ambitious. I mean, he was fired as a NATO commander, and when Hugh Shelton said he was fired because of matters of character and integrity, that is a very, very damning statement, which says if that's the case, he's not the right man for president as far as I'm concerned." What is General Shelton referring to? Why were you given the ax as NATO commander?
>
> GEN. CLARK: Well, I don't know what he's referring to. At the time, he told me I was being replaced so that Joe Ralston could take my position. I think what we had here was a policy disagreement that Hugh Shelton let become personal. I'm sorry he did. He did not appreciate, and I don't think the others in the Pentagon did either, what was going on in the Balkans. They had a strategy that called for us to be prepared to fight in Iraq or Korea. There wasn't supposed to be any trouble in Europe. And when I began to warn of it, it wasn't well-received.

p. 142 *as far as I'm concerned*: Roger Simon, "Who Let the Dogs Out," *US News and World Report*, November 24, 2003, available online at http://www.usnews.com/usnews/issue/031124/usnews/24notes_2.htm (accessed May 2006).

p. 142 *Secretary of Defense William Cohen*: Bradley Graham and Dana Priest, "Pentagon to Replace NATO Commander: Gen. Wesley K. Clark Will Leave as NATO's Commander in April after a Series of Disputes with the Pentagon," *Washington Post*, July 28, 1999, p. A1, available online at http://www.washingtonpost .com/wp-srv/inatl/longterm/balkans/stories/clark072899.htm (accessed May 2006).

p. 142 *the Cohen Group*: The Cohen Group, 1200 19th Street, NW, Suite 400, Washington, DC 20036, Web site available at http://www.cohengroup.net/team .html (accessed May 2006).

p. 143 *I approve this message*: The "Wolves" ad was reminiscent of the Reagan thirty-second "Bear" commercial, which pictured a wandering grizzly bear and made a case for Reagan's extraordinary military buildup: "There is a bear in the woods. For some people the bear is easy to see. Others don't see it at all. Some people say the bear is tame. Others say it's vicious and dangerous. Since no one can really be sure who is right, isn't it smart to be as strong as the bear? If there is a bear." "Creating Reagan's Image," "Bear" ad text, available online at http://medialit.med .sc.edu/reagansimage.htm (accessed May 2006). The "Wolves" ad text is available online at http://www.factcheck.org/article291.html (accessed May 2006).

p. 144 *topped all competitors*: Brian McCabe quote, Institute of Politics, Harvard University, ed., *Campaign for President: The Managers Look at 2004* (Lanham, MD: Rowman & Littlefield, 2006), pp. 218–221.

p. 144 *the content of this message*: Progress for America Voter Fund, "Ashley" ad, Political Advertising Resource Center (PARC), available online at http://www .umdparc.org/AdAnalysisAshleysStory.htm (accessed May 2006).

p. 145 *decriminalization of marijuana*: David S. Broder, "Wealthy Benefactors Stoke Campaigns for Medical Marijuana," *Washington Post*, October 20, 1998, p. A5. Joel Stein, "The New Politics of Pot: Can It Go Legit? How the People Who Brought You Medical Marijuana Have Set Their Sights on Lifting the Ban for Everyone," *Time*, October 27, 2002, available online at http://www.time.com/ time/covers/1101021104/story.html (accessed May 2006).

p. 145 *to motivate Republican donors*: Donors to the Democratic Party have been greeted in parts of the conservative universe with persistent anti-Semitism. For example, the online journal *The American Thinker* notes that "in the 2004 campaign four Jews—George Soros, Peter Lewis, Steven Bing and Herbert Sandler—gave over $80 million to Democratic 527 groups. This level of political giving by a few individuals has never happened before in the history of the country" (available online at http://www.americanthinker.com/articles.php?article_id=4272&search =peter [accessed May 2006]).

p. 145 *$2 million each*: Republican donors, Center for Responsive Politics, available online at http://www.opensecrets.org/527s/527indivs.asp?cycle=2004 (accessed May 2006).

p. 145 *from 2000 through 2004*: Al Kamen, "Money Talks, Arnall Walks," *Washington Post*, February 13, 2006, p. A19, available online at http://www .washingtonpost.com/wp-dyn/content/article/2006/02/12/AR2006021201079 .html (accessed May 2006).

p. 146 *John F. Kerry was close behind*: PoliticalMoneyLine Web site, http://www .fecinfo.com/cgi-win/pml1_sql_PRESIDENTIAL.exe?DoFn=2004 (accessed May 2006).

p. 147 *"move on" to other issues*: For liberal media critiques of MoveOn, see Chris Suellentrop, "Feel-Good Politics: The Therapeutic Activism of MoveOn .org," *Slate*, December 8, 2004, available online at http://www.slate.com/id/ 2110819/ (accessed May 2006); and Peter Beinart, "An Argument for a New Liberalism. A Fighting Faith," *New Republic*, December 2, 2004, available online at http://www.tnr.com/doc.mhtml?i=20041213&s=beinart121304&c=2 (accessed May 2006).

p. 147 *"managing customized Linux platforms"*: Lawrence Lessig, Lessigblog, "Interview with Joe Trippi," August 19, 2003, available online at http://www.lessig .org/blog/archives/001428.shtml (accessed May 2006); Noam Scheiber, "Joe Trippi Reinvents Campaigning," *New Republic*, November 10, 2003, p. 18.

p. 147 *comprehensive trusted computing ecosystem*: Wave Systems Corp., http:// www.cbronline.com/companyprofile.asp?guid=7F38AF3A-76B9-4003-9E17- 6FCC9E4E5F53&CType=Background (accessed May 2006).

p. 147 *doctors, neurosurgeons, psychiatrists, professors*: Noam Scheiber, "Joe Trippi Reinvents Campaigning," *New Republic*, November 10, 2003, p. 18.

p. 147 *everybody in a presidential campaign*: Lawrence Lessig, Lessigblog, "Interview with Joe Trippi," August 19, 2003, available online at http://www.lessig.org/ blog/archives/001428.shtml (accessed May 2006).

p. 147 *credit card donation capabilities*: Trippi in the Lessig interview (ibid.) describes events of early 2002:

> . . . a little twist of fate, or maybe destiny. A guy named Matt Gross came wandering into my office one day. He told me he had just driven from Utah because he cared so much about Howard Dean. He had decided to drive to Burlington without calling first, looking for a job. He managed to maneuver past the receptionist's desk and stuck his head in long enough to scream out, "I wrote for the myDD blog .com"! I immediately said, "You're hired!" And I think about 48 hours later he had this really ugly blog up that was on Blogspot. He was going to run back to Utah and get all his belongings and come back, but I said he had a job on the condition that he got a blog up before he left. And so in 3 or 4 hours, he created what was then the "Call to Action" blog. It was cute and ugly at the same time, but I think it was the first blog of a presidential campaign. . . . In the early days, there were many things that we had to get going. To get the blog going needed somebody like Matt. It needed somebody who was going to be able to care for it every day and make sure it happened while people like me and the governor were running around Iowa. Until Matt showed up, we just didn't have that person.

p. 147 *raised through the Internet*: The Dean fundraising figure was calculated by the author from data on the Federal Election Commission Web site, http://query .nictusa.com/cgi-bin/dcdev/forms/C00378125/109872/ (accessed May 2006).

p. 147 *generating grassroots political interest*: "As Election Nears, Web's Grass Roots Still Growing," CNET News.com, October 27, 2004, available online at http://news.com.com/As+election+nears%2C+Webs+grass+roots+still+growing +-+page+2/2100-1028_3-5428950-2.html?tag=st.num (accessed May 2006).

p. 148 *providing high-tech skills*: Scott Duke Harris, "Scott Duke Harris Last Wrote for the Magazine about Vote-Swapping on the Internet," *Los Angeles Times*, February 29, 2004, Part I, p. 22:

> When terrorists struck on U.S. soil, Eli Pariser was a 20-year-old college graduate working for a nonprofit that advised philanthropists. The son of 1960s antiwar protesters, Pariser soon launched an online petition that was the modern equivalent of a daffodil stuck in gun barrels. His website urged a "restrained" response to terrorism. Soon he had more than 100,000 signatures in the U.S. and nearly a half million worldwide. Wes Boyd was impressed; MoveOn members also were wary of military response. In early 2002, Boyd hired Pariser as campaigns director.

Joseph Menn, "The Race to the White House; Internet Upstart Turns Insider; Zack Exley, 34, Has Gone from Running a Website Dedicated to Mocking Bush to Running Kerry's Official Online Organizing Effort," *Los Angeles Times*, May 30, 2004, p. A24:

> "I wanted to work on longer-term, bigger-picture change," he said. "I had the feeling that the Internet, which was still very new then, could be used for grass-roots organizing, and I wanted to experiment."
>
> In December 1998, he poked around and saw that the Bush campaign had registered GeorgeWBush.com but not GWBush.com, and he bought two-year rights to that site for $70.
>
> Exley got in touch with a loosely organized group of anticorporate activists and pranksters called RTMark (pronounced "art-mark"), and he asked them to develop content for the Bush site.
>
> After the Bush campaign filed a complaint with the Federal Election Commission, claiming that GWBush.com was subject to financial disclosure rules, hundreds of thousands of Internet users visited the site.
>
> Exley took back editorial control and posted fake campaign statements under such headlines as "George II: Restoring the Throne to its Rightful Heir." He also sold anti-Bush bumper stickers and posters through the website.
>
> What really got the Bush campaign's goat, however, were the phony pictures of Bush using drugs.
>
> The FEC ultimately dismissed the Bush campaign's complaint after deciding the issues at stake were too low a priority. The pictures remained on the site, which was no longer being updated as of last week.
>
> All the attention spurred Exley to pursue more Internet activism.
>
> In the fall of 2000, he mused on another website about the possibility that Democratic nominee Al Gore would win the popular vote—yet lose in the electoral college. He urged voters to protest if that were to happen.
>
> Few noticed his prediction until after the election, when it came true.
>
> Overwhelmed with e-mail from potential protesters, Exley set up a system for distributing messages free to subscribers on eGroups, an electronic bulletin board system later bought by Yahoo. Thousands turned out for marches around the country, grabbing media time for the issue—and for Exley himself.
>
> "Without the Internet, there would have been no way for a single person to propose a day of protests, and for word of it to spread to so many people," he wrote in the December 2000 issue of *Mother Jones* magazine. It would have required "acres of rented telemarketing space, thousands of volunteers and countless phone lines."
>
> Exley began trading ideas with Berkeley-based MoveOn.org, which had grown out of an Internet petition to Congress calling for an end to the impeachment hearings on President Clinton.
>
> MoveOn hired Exley as organizing director early last year. Its staffers credit him with leading the group's "virtual primary," in which members voted electronically to demonstrate support for the various Democratic candidates.

Thomas B. Edsall, James V. Grimaldi, and Alice R. Crites, "Redefining Democratic Fundraising; Kerry Has Amassed Record Sums from Disparate Groups Opposed to Bush," *Washington Post*, July 24, 2004, p. A1: "As great as the impact of major donors has been the role of the Internet. Even before Kerry won in Iowa, his campaign was moving to capitalize on the technology that helped Dean to his early lead. Josh Ross, a Silicon Valley executive, was brought in to restructure Kerry's Web site."

p. 148 *trying to call me*: Thomas B. Edsall, James V. Grimaldi, and Alice R. Crites, "Redefining Democratic Fundraising; Kerry Has Amassed Record Sums from Disparate Groups Opposed to Bush," *Washington Post*, July 24, 2004, p. A1.

p. 148 *small donations to Bush in 2000*: Campaign Finance Institute, available online at http://www.cfinst.org/pr/pdf/100404_Table3.pdf (accessed May 2006).

p. 149 *ages of forty-five and sixty-four*: "The Dean Activists: Their Profile and Prospects, an In-Depth Look," The Pew Research Center for the People and the Press, April 6, 2005, available online at http://people-press.org/reports/display .php3?ReportID=240 (accessed May 2006).

p. 149 *"just him and the Lord"*: Thomas B. Edsall, James V. Grimaldi, and Alice R. Crites, "Redefining Democratic Fundraising; Kerry Has Amassed Record Sums from Disparate Groups Opposed to Bush," *Washington Post*, July 24, 2004, p. A 1.

p. 150 *nonexistent in the Kerry campaign*: Ibid.

p. 151 *Center for Participation in Democracy*: See WhitehouseForSale.org for list of Kerry fundraisers, http://www.whitehouseforsale.org/demfundraising/bundler _search.cfm (accessed May 28, 2006).

Chapter 5 ≻ The Two Revolutions

p. 155 *within the Catholic Church*: At 24.1 percent of the population in 2001, Catholics are the largest denomination in America, followed by Baptists at 16.3 percent; data available online at http://www.adherents.com/rel_USA.html #religions (accessed May 2006). For Vatican II and the role of Catholics in the sexual revolution, see Leslie Woodcock Tentler, *Catholics and Contraception: An American History* (Ithaca, NY: Cornell University Press, 2004).

p. 155 *the emerging "culture wars"*: For a discussion on how the culture wars are driven by political elites, see Morris Fiorina, with Samuel J. Abrams and Jeremy C. Pope, *Culture War? The Myth of a Polarized America* (New York: Pearson Education, 2005). Fiorina et al. write, "With Bill Clinton the electorate got an admitted adulterer, a confessed marijuana smoker (but not inhaler), and a champion of gay rights. . . . These were pretty clear signals that he was located on the 'progressive' side of the moral dimension." At the same time, the authors argue that "elites are imposing their own agendas on the electorate. . . . The common observation that religiosity is now more closely related to party identification may reflect a repositioning rather than a change in voter attitudes. The Republican party has become closely allied with white evangelicals, while the Democratic party has become more aggressively secular" (pp. 87–88).

p. 156 *equality and sexual liberalization*: Ronald Inglehart and Pippa Norris, *Rising Tide: Gender Equality and Cultural Change around the World* (New York: Cambridge University Press, 2003). Pippa Norris and Ronald Inglehart, "Islam & the West: Testing the 'Clash of Civilizations' Thesis," Harvard University, The John F. Kennedy School of Government, available online at http://ksghome.harvard.edu/ ~pnorris/Acrobat/Clash%20of%20Civilization.pdf (accessed May 2006).

p. 157 *the mechanization of agriculture*: Nicholas Lemann, *The Promised Land: The Great Black Migration and How It Changed America* (New York: A. A. Knopf, 1991). According to author Nicholas Lemann,

> as recently as 1940, 77% of African Americans still lived in the South—49% in the rural South. Between 1910 and 1970, six and a

half million black Americans moved out of the South in two great
waves, five million of them after 1940. The mechanization of agriculture, especially cotton picking, along with discrimination, drove
African Americans off the land and out of the South. At the same time,
the post-WWII economic boom created millions of jobs in northern
and western manufacturing centers like New York, Pittsburgh, Baltimore, Philadelphia, Cleveland, Gary, St. Louis, Los Angeles, Seattle
and Chicago. By 1970, when the migration ended, black America was
only half Southern and less than a quarter rural; "urban" had become
a contemporary euphemism for "black." The black migration was one
of the largest and most rapid mass internal movements of people in
history. . . . In sheer numbers it outranks the migration of any other
ethnic group—Italians or Irish or Jews or Poles—to this country.

See also http://www.newsreel.org/guides/goingui.htm (accessed May 2006).

p. 157 *America's position in the world*: Seymour Martin Lipset, *American Exceptionalism: A Double-Edged Sword* (New York: W W Norton, 1997). "But the
more recent focus of the civil rights movement, with its emphasis on substantive
equality and preferential treatment, explicitly conflicts with the individualistic,
achievement-oriented element in the [American] Creed" (p. 115).

p. 157 *broadening the inequality gap*: The wealth gap has steadily broadened over
the past three decades. According to the Federal Reserve Survey of Consumer Finances released on February 23, 2006, during the period from 2001 to 2004, "median household net worth rose four percent for the richest tenth of Americans and
fell eleven percent for the poorest two-tenths of Americans" (Nell Henderson,
"Growth in Families' Wealth Stalls," *Washington Post*, February 24, 2006, p. D2).

p. 158 *0.3 per 1,000 population*: Population Reference Bureau, "A Century
of Progress in U.S. Infant and Child Survival," AmeriStat, December 2002, available online at http://www.prb.org/AmeristatTemplate.cfm?Section=Mortality1
&template=/ContentManagement/ContentDisplay.cfm&ContentID=7912 (accessed May 2006).

p. 159 *child-raising upon themselves*:

Both the advent of female contraception and the legalization of abortion are analogous to technical change: each has shifted out the frontier of available choices. While the morality of these options generates
heated debate, family planners have viewed female contraception and
abortion as welfare-improving for women: they have made women
free to choose. But technological innovation creates both winners and
losers. A cost-saving innovation almost invariably penalizes producers
who, for whatever reason, fail to adopt it. . . . In the case of female
contraception and abortion, women who want children, and women
who because of indecision or religious conviction have failed to adopt
the new innovations, have lost disproportionately. . . . [I]n the case of
female contraception and abortion, men may have been the beneficiaries. . . . [T]he legalization of abortion and the availability of female
contraception could result in a decline in the competitive position of
women relative to men—especially if they do not use contraception
or abortion. . . . Sexual activity without commitment is increasingly
expected in a premarital relationship, immiserating at least some
women, since their male partners do not have to assume parental responsibility in order to engage in sexual relations. . . . The change in
sexual customs and the subsequent rise in out-of-wedlock births have
been accompanied by a decline in the stigma attached to out-of-

wedlock childbearing. . . . Humpty Dumpty cannot be put back together again. . . . When the cost of abortion is low, or contraceptives
are readily available, potential male partners can easily obtain sexual
satisfaction without making . . . [a promise] to commit to marriage. . . . Nowadays women are freer to chose, but men are affording
themselves the comparable option. . . . The man reasons: "if she is not
willing to obtain an abortion or use contraception, why should I sacri-
fice myself to get married?" . . . [Technology shock] enhanced the
willingness of unmarried women to participate in uncommitted premarital sex by reducing the odds of pregnancy in the first place, . . .
[thus triggering] behavioral shifts . . . [and] giving rise to increased autonomy on the part of women who were willing to avail themselves of
contraception and abortion, but also spurring a period in which single
motherhood and the feminization of poverty began their long and
steady rise. . . . Women who wanted to bear children were immiser-
ized because of their competitive position, and thereby their ability to
bargain for the marriage guarantee deteriorated. Moreover, their
partners' degree of empathy and willingness to bargain after the fact,
may also have declined. . . . The technology shock theory explains the
reduced marriage rates of both educated men with low unemployment
and uneducated men with high unemployment. The technology
shock model also predicts, and our survey results . . . confirm, a decline in intimacy between sexual partners, since relations are likely to
be short term. (George A. Akerlof, Janet L. Yellen, and Michael L.
Katz, "Analysis of Out-of-Wedlock Childbearing in the United
States," *The Quarterly Journal of Economics* 111, no. 2 [May 1996]:
279–313)

p. 159 *ten among African Americans*: Paul Offner, "Reducing Non-Marital
Births," The Brookings Institution, August 2001, available online at http://www
.brookings.edu/es/research/projects/wrb/publications/pb/pb05.htm (accessed May
2006): "Between 1960 and 1999, the non-marital ratio went from 5.3 percent (low
enough to please even the most committed conservative) to 33 percent. . . . The
same pattern holds for African Americans, who are disproportionately represented
on the welfare rolls, and whose non-marital ratio went from 23.3 percent in 1960
to an alarming 69.1 percent in 1999." For a look at the relationship between non-
marital birthrates and the movement to reform welfare, see Jason DeParle, *American Dream: Three Women, Ten Kids, and a Nation's Drive to End Welfare* (New York:
Viking, 2004).

p. 159 *much of the human race*: For a modernist, congratulatory perspective, see
Leonard Steinhorn, *The Greater Generation: In Defense of the Baby Boom Legacy*
(New York: St. Martins Press, 2006).

p. 159 *new financial instruments and institutions*: Jeremy Greenwood, *The Third
Industrial Revolution: Technology, Productivity, and Income Inequality* (Washington
DC: AEI Press, 1997), pp. 2–5, 24–35.

p. 160 *transformation generated new jobs*: Regarding cognitive and behavioral
skills, see Samuel Bowles, Herbert Gintis, Melissa Osborne Groves, eds., *Unequal
Chances: Family Background and Economic Success* (Princeton, NJ: Russell Sage Foundation and Princeton University Press, 2005): "Personality is able to elucidate a
significant mechanism by which families transmit economic status. The inclusion
of personality, controlling for education, tenure, and cognitive performance, is estimated to reduce the unexplained portion of earnings transmission by four percentage points, more than twice that of cognitive performance" (p. 221; see also pp.
7–13, 20–22, 26–27, 69–79, 80–82, 165, 187, 210, 218–221, 230).

p. 160 *more cheaply at a distance*: John D. McKinnon and Peter Wonacott, "Outsourcing Work Looms Large in U.S.—India Ties," *Wall Street Journal*, March 4, 2006, p. A4.

p. 160 *9.1 million in the 1990s*: For immigration by decade, see *2004 Yearbook of Immigration Statistics*, Office of Immigration Statistics, Department of Homeland Security, January 2006, available online at http://uscis.gov/graphics/shared/statistics/yearbook/Yearbook2004.pdf (accessed May 2006). According to the U.S. Census Bureau,

> The nation's foreign-born population numbered 34.2 million in 2004, accounting for 12 percent of the total U.S. population, according to U.S. Census Bureau data released today. The number of foreign-born is 2.3 percent higher than it was in 2003.
>
> Within the foreign-born population, 53 percent were born in Latin America, 25 percent in Asia, 14 percent in Europe and the remaining 8 percent in other regions of the world, such as Africa and Oceania (Australia, New Zealand and all of the island nations in the Pacific).
>
> Second-generation Americans, natives with one or both parents born in a foreign country, numbered 30.4 million, or 11 percent of the total U.S. population. (*U.S. Census Bureau News*, February 22, 2005, available online at http://www.census.gov/Press-Release/www/releases/archives/foreignborn_population/003969.html [accessed May 2006])

p. 160 *estimated by the Census Bureau*: For the Bear Stearns' figure on illegal immigration, see Robert Justich and Betty Ng, "The Underground Labor Force Is Rising to the Surface," Bear Stearns Report, January 3, 2005, available online at http://www.bearstearns.com/bscportal/pdfs/underground.pdf (accessed May 2006).

p. 160 *35.7 million in that year*: Jeffrey S. Passel, "Estimates of the Size and Characteristics of the Undocumented Population," Pew Hispanic Center, March 21, 2005, www.pewhispanic.org. "Report: Demand for Outside Workers Still Strong in United States," MSNBC, US News, March 31, 2005, available online at http://www.msnbc.msn.com/id/7255409/ (accessed May 2006).

p. 160 *forty-one cents an hour in 2005*: The China Labor Watch National Labor Committee in "Wal-Mart Sweatshop Toys Made in China: 'Always Low Prices' Means Rolling Back Respect for Human Rights," under a subhead titled Nominal Wage Increase Wiped Out by Increased Production Quotas, Increased Fees and Fines, stated:

> The Lungcheong factory did, in word, honor a government decreed minimum wage increase in March of 2005, which raised the legal minimum wage from 450 yuan, or $55.49 a month to 574 yuan, or $70.78. (The Lungcheong factory actually raised the rate to just 570 yuan.) Still, this raised the hourly wage from 32 cents to 41 cents, a nominal increase of 27 percent. Though inflation in China is low in relation to many other developing countries, still between early 2002 and October 2005, the compounded inflation rate was 6.5 percent. And there were strikes at the Lungcheong factory in 2003 and 2004 over the low wages. (December 15, 2005, available online at http://www.chinalaborwatch.org/upload/Wal-MartLungcheongReport.pdf [accessed May 2006])

p. 160 *to $8.17 in 2005*: For the U.S. hourly wage, see "Economic Report of the President: 2006 Report Spreadsheet Tables," Table B-47: Hours and earnings in

private nonagricultural industries, 1959–2005, available online at http://www
.gpoaccess.gov/eop/tables06.html (accessed May 2006).

p. 161 *exploded to $665.39 billion*: For data on the trade deficit, see ibid., Table
B-103: U.S. international transactions, 1946–2005.

p. 161 *calculated in constant 1982 dollars*: Ibid., Table B-46: Employees on nonagricultural payrolls, by major industry, 1959–2005; and Table B-47: Hours and
earnings in private nonagricultural industries, 1959–2005.

p. 162 *New Yorkers for Constitutional Freedoms*: Reverend Duane Motley,
Rochester, New York, telephone interview with author, August 2005.

p. 162 *mob and of the jungle*: Barry Goldwater's 1964 Republican Presidential
Nomination Acceptance Speech, Republican National Convention, Cow Palace,
San Francisco, available online at http://www.nationalcenter.org/Goldwater.html
(accessed May 2006).

p. 163 *to 58 percent after 1964*: National Election Studies, breakdown of the
percentage of the two-party vote received by Democratic and Republican candidates, available online at http://www.umich.edu/~nes/nesguide/toptable/tab9a_1
.htm (accessed May 2006).

p. 163 *net benefit for the GOP*: Computations of vote shifts between 1960 and
2004 are by author and based on NES data available online at http://www.umich
.edu/~nes/nesguide/gd-index.htm#9 (accessed May 2006).

p. 163 *drop another atomic bomb*: Interview by author with Carl Djerassi, January
24, 1997.

p. 163 *more than 10 million*: Public Broadcasting System, "The Pill," a timeline
of its development, available online at http://www.pbs.org/wgbh/amex/pill/
timeline/timeline2.html (accessed May 2006).

p. 164 *the trigger on history*: Alvin Toffler: "the book that pulled the trigger on
history"; see http://www.wwnorton.com/catalog/fall01/032257.htm (accessed May
2006).

p. 164 *my children and my home*: Betty Friedan, *The Feminine Mystique* (New
York: Dell Publishing, 1984), p. 32.

p. 164 *any state on account of sex*: See the U.S. Constitution Online, "The Failed
Amendments," available online at http://www.usconstitution.net/constamfail.html
(accessed May 2006).

p. 164 *1972 Final Senate ERA Vote*: 1971 *Congressional Quarterly*, House vote 68
to 9; and 1972 *Congressional Quarterly Almanac*, Senate vote 17 to 8.

p. 165 *1978 Final Senate ERA Vote*: 1978 *Congressional Quarterly Almanac*, Senate vote 64 and House vote 176.

p. 166 *gave them a political basis*: Jo Freeman, "Sex, Race, Religion and Partisan
Realignment," in *We Get What We Vote For . . . Or Do We? The Impact of Elections on
Governing*, edited by Paul Scheele (Westport, CT: Greenwood Publishing Group,
1999), pp. 167–190.

p. 167 *the breakdown of the family*: Tanya Melich, *The Republican War against
Women* (New York: Bantam, 1996), pp. 291–292.

p. 167 *by the pro-life movement*: Alan Cooperman, "Gay Marriage as 'the New
Abortion' Debate Becomes Polarizing as Both Sides Become Better Organized,
Spend Millions," *Washington Post*, July 26, 2004, p. A03.

p. 167 *compromise will diminish*: Ibid.

p. 168 *regular voters to political elites*: Pew Research Center for the People and
the Press, "Beyond Red vs. Blue: Republicans Divided about Role of Government—Democrats by Social and Personal Values," May 10, 2005, available online
at http://people-press.org/reports/display.php3?ReportID=242 (accessed May
2006).

p. 169 *over the past half century*: Tom W. Smith, "American Sexual Behavior:
Trends, Socio-Demographic Differences, and Risk Behavior," National Opinion
Research Center, University of Chicago, GSS Topical Report No. 25, Updated

December 1998, available online at http://www.norc.uchicago.edu/library/sexual
.pdf (accessed May 2006).

p. 170   *during her affair with President Clinton*: Kassorla was among the many advocates of women's new rights to sexual freedom. According to Kassorla, "100 orgasms within two hours [were] not uncommon among women she treat[ed] in sex therapy" (*Time*, April 19, 1982, p. 70). According to the Starr Report, Dr. Kassorla was Monica Lewinsky's therapist at the time of her affair with President Clinton. Dr. Kassorla treated Lewinsky from 1992 to 1997, and Lewinsky gave the Office of Special Counsel permission to interview her. Kassorla informed Starr's staff that "Ms. Lewinsky told her of the sexual relationship with the President. Ms. Lewinsky said she performed oral sex on the President in a room adjacent to the Oval Office, that the President touched Ms. Lewinsky causing her to have orgasms, and that they engaged in fondling and touching of one another. . . . The President was in charge of scheduling their sexual encounters and 'became Lewinsky's life'" (pp. 76, 77). Kassorla, in turn, reported that she "advised Ms. Lewinsky against the relationship, stating that she was an employee having an office romance with a superior and that the relationship would cost Ms. Lewinsky her job." Starr Report, Referral to the United States House of Representatives Pursuant to Title 28, United States Code §595(c), Submitted by the Office of the Independent Counsel, September 9, 1998, "Testimony of Dr, Irene Kassorla", including footnotes 75, 76, and 77, available online at http://www.time.com/time/daily/scandal/starr_report/files/ (accessed May 2006).

p. 170   *Don't you look back*: "Don't Stop," Fleetwood Mac, http://www
.lyricsdepot.com/fleetwood-mac/dont-stop.html (accessed May 28, 2006).

p. 170   *months prior to the revelation*: Howard Kurtz, "A Big Story—But Only Behind the Scenes: Media Fretted over Reporting Dole Affair," *Washington Post*, November 13, 1996, p. D1. See also, "Rep. Hyde's Former Lover Speaks Out," Associated Press, September 17, 1998; Frank Greve and David Hess, "Livingston to Resign, Stunning Congress: Dogged by His Own Sexual Liaisons, He Hoped to Set an Example," *Philadelphia Inquirer*, December 20, 1998, p. A1; Robert Scheer, "Newt Gingrich, Moral Guardian: His Divorce and Six-Year Affair Are a Fitting End to a Decade of Hypocrisy," *Pittsburgh Post-Gazette*, December 30, 1999, p. A27; J. R. Moehringer, "Rep. Barr Inspires Loyalty, Loathing in Home District," *Los Angeles Times*, January 19, 1999, available online at http://www.ferris.edu/ ISAR/Institut/CCC/barrhome.htm (accessed May 2006) (for the claim by Barr's second wife that, while still married to her, he had an affair with the woman who was to become his third wife). Regarding Dan Burton, see *The NewsHour with Jim Lehrer* transcript, September 8, 1998, available online at http://www.pbs.org/ newshour/bb/media/july-dec98/burton_9-8.html (accessed May 2006):

> TERENCE SMITH: In Indiana last week Republican Congressman Dan Burton confessed that he had had an extramarital affair 15 years ago in which he had fathered a child out of wedlock.

> REP. DAN BURTON: This is something that happened a long time ago. And my wife and my family have been aware of this for a long time. I have accepted my responsibilities a long time ago. The boy and the mother and my wife and my family and I have all reached an agreement about this a long time ago.

p. 171   *haven in a heartless world*: Christopher Lasch, *Haven in a Heartless World* (New York: Norton, 1977): "The woman in particular would serve, in a well-worn 19th century phrase, as an 'angel of consolation.' Her mission of mercy extended to her children as well" (p. 5).

p. 171 *major portion of their identity*: Judith Walzer Leavitt, *Brought to Bed: Child-bearing in America, 1750 to 1950* (New York: Oxford University Press, 1986), extracts available online at http://www.cola.wright.edu/PublicHistory/rubicon/childbirth.html (accessed May 2006).

p. 171 *about 2.1 births per woman*: "Fertility of American Women, June 2000: Population Characteristics," U.S. Census Bureau, October 2001, available online at www.census.gov/prod/2001pubs/p20-543rv.pdf (accessed May 2006).

p. 171 *given birth to was 1.9*: Family size data are from the U.S. Census Bureau, "Trend Lines," *Washington Post*, March 8, 2006, p. A2.

p. 172 *participation rate of all men*: Bureau of Labor Statistics, "Women in the Labor Force: A Databook," U.S. Department of Labor, Report 985, May 2005, available online at http://www.bls.gov/cps/wlf-databook-2005.pdf (accessed May 28, 2006).

p. 173 *controversial and burdensome provisions*: David L. Rose, "Twenty-Five Years Later: Where Do We Stand on Equal Employment Opportunity Law Enforcement," *Vanderbilt Law Review* (May 1989): 1,131.

p. 173 *men and women were unlawful*: Jo Freeman, "The Revolution for Women in Law and Public Policy," available online at http://www.jofreeman.com/lawandpolicy/revlaw1.htm (accessed May 2006).

p. 173 *many multimillion dollar awards*:

> AT&T signed a $38 million agreement with the Department of Labor and EEOC, the largest job discrimination settlement in the nation's history. It provided that AT&T and its 24 operating companies make one-time lump-sum payments totaling $15 million to 15,000 workers the EEOC found were victims of "pervasive and systemic" discrimination. An additional $23 million per year was allocated for wage adjustments aimed at elevating women and minority males to equal standing with white males in similar jobs. It also provided for new hiring practices aimed at getting more men as operators and clerks and more women into outside craft jobs, and a broadening of management opportunities. (*The Feminist Chronicles: 1963–1972*, p. 4, available online at http://www.feminist.org/research/chronicles/fc1973a.html [accessed January 2006])

p. 173 *complied with the law*: Hugh Davis Graham, *The Civil Rights Era: Origins and Development of National Policy, 1960–1972* (New York: Oxford University Press, 1990), p. 207; and *The Feminist Chronicles: 1963–1972*, p. 4, available online at http://www.feminist.org/research/chronicles/fc1973a.html (accessed January 2006).

p. 173 *Levy v. Louisiana, 1968*: U.S. Supreme Court, *Levy V. Louisiana*, 391 U.S. 68 (1968), available online at http://www.justia.us/us/391/68/ (accessed May 2006).

> Appellant, on behalf of five illegitimate children, brought this action under a Louisiana statute (La. Civ. Code Art. 2315) for the wrongful death of their mother. The trial court dismissed the suit and the Court of Appeal affirmed, holding that a surviving "child" under the statute did not include an illegitimate child, denial of whose right of recovery was "based on morals and general welfare because it discourages bringing children into the world out of wedlock." The State Supreme Court denied certiorari. Held: The statute as construed to deny a right of recovery under Art. 2315 by illegitimate children creates an invidious discrimination contravening the Equal Protection Clause of the Fourteenth Amendment, since legitimacy or illegitimacy of birth has no relation to the nature of the wrong allegedly inflicted on the mother.

p. 174 *or work in the evening*: Sonia Pressman Fuentes interview, "History of the Equal Employment Opportunity Commission (EEOC)," available online at http://www.utoronto.ca/wjudaism/contemporary/articles/history_eeoc.htm (accessed May 2006).

p. 174 *to Justice William Brennan*: Geoffrey Stone interview with the author, April 6, 1997.

p. 175 *country's civil rights policies*: William Bradford Reynolds, "The Reagan Administration and Civil Rights: Winning the War against Discrimination," *University of Illinois Law Review* 4 (1986): p. 1,014.

p. 175 *"humiliating to the South"*: Lou Cannon, *President Reagan: The Role of a Lifetime* (New York: Simon & Schuster, 1991), p. 520; and Ernest Holsendolph, "Reagan Backs Modified Plan on Rights Bill," *New York Times*, November 13, 1981, p. A21.

p. 176 *Depo-Provera, and the diaphragm*: Ellen Nakashima, "Cut in Birth Control Benefit of Federal Workers Sought," *Washington Post*, April 12, 2001, p. A29.

p. 176 *interest in any given sport*: Department of Education, Office of Civil Rights, "Additional Clarification of Intercollegiate Athletics Policy: Three-Part Test_Part Three," March 17, 2005.

p. 177 *yourself on this scale*: Computed from National Election Studies data on a seven-point scale of responses to the question, "Some people believe that we should spend much less money for defense. Others feel that defense spending should be greatly increased. Where would you place yourself on this scale or haven't you thought much about this?" Available online at http://www.umich.edu/~nes/nesguide/toptable/tab4d_3b.htm (accessed May 2006).

p. 177 *zero ratings were Republicans*: Peace Action Education Fund, "Congressional Voting Record," available online at http://www.peace-action.org/pub/votes/2003VR.pdf (accessed May 2006).

p. 177 *over 20 percentage points*: National Opinion Research Center, "1999 National Gun Policy Survey," available online at http://www.norc.uchicago.edu/online/gunrpt.pdf (accessed May 2006).

p. 178 *a ratio of 68.5 to 1*: National Rifle Association, "2004 Gun Issues," available online at http://www.nrapvf.org/ (accessed May 2006).

p. 179 *safer place in which to live*: The text of Reagan's convention speech is available on the 4President.org Web site at http://www.4president.org/speeches/reagan1980convention.htm (accessed May 2006).

p. 179 *thereby protecting America*: Thomas B. Edsall, "GOP Touts War as Campaign Issue: Bush Adviser Infuriates Democrats with Strategy Outlined at RNC Meeting," *Washington Post*, January 19, 2002.

p. 179 *understanding for our attackers*: A transcript of Rove's remarks is available on the *Washington Post* Web site, http://www.washingtonpost.com/wp-dyn/content/article/2005/06/24/AR2005062400097.html.

p. 179 *the following commercial*: Republican National Committee Web site, http://www.gop.com/News/Read.aspx?ID=5988 (accessed December 11, 2005).

p. 180 *Bureau of Justice Statistics*: Bureau of Justice Statistics, Department of Justice, "Family Violence Statistics Including Statistics on Strangers and Acquaintances," June 2005, available online at http://www.ojp.usdoj.gov/bjs/pub/pdf/fvs06.pdf (accessed May 2006).

p. 181 *women who have lower earnings*: Lee Lillard and Linda Waite, "Marriage, Divorce, and the Work and Earning Careers of Spouses," University of Michigan Retirement Research Center, April 2000, available online at http://www.mrrc.isr.umich.edu/publications/briefs/pdf/ib_003.pdf (accessed May 2006).

p. 181 *just 50 percent of women*: Federal Interagency Forum on Aging-Related Statistics, "Older Americans 2004: Key Indicators of Well-Being," available online at http://www.agingstats.gov/chartbook2004/population.html (accessed May 2006).

p. 181 *more than a month annually*: Bureau of Labor Statistics, "American Time Use Survey," available online at http://www.bls.gov/news.release/atus.toc.htm (accessed May 2006).

p. 181 *oppose both affirmative action*: In 2003, the Pew Center found that white men barely backed 48 to 41 affirmative action when asked a question that made no references to preferential policies, "Do you favor or oppose programs that help blacks, women and other minorities get jobs and education." White women were strongly in favor, 66 to 27. See http://people-press.org/reports/display .php3?ReportID=184 (accessed May 2006).

p. 181 *"hostile workplace environment"*: See *Harris v. Forklift Sys., Inc.*, 510 U.S. 17, 21–22 (1993) and a discussion of the Court decision on the federal Equal Employment Opportunity Commission Web site, http://www.eeoc.gov/policy/docs/ harris.html (accessed May 2006); and *Meritor Sav. Bank, FSB v. Vinson*, 477 U.S. 57, 65 (1986), and EEOC description available online at http://www.eeoc.gov/ abouteeoc/35th/milestones/1986.html (accessed May 2006).

p. 182 *seeing women as "sexual objects"*: David C. Geary, *Male, Female: The Evolution of Human Sex Differences* (Washington DC: American Psychological Association, 1998); Alice H. Eagly, *Sex Differences in Social Behavior: A Social-Role Interpretation* (Hillsdale, NJ: Lawrence Erlbaum Associates, 1987); Carol Gilligan, *In a Different Voice: Psychological Theory and Women's Development* (Cambridge, MA: Harvard University Press, 1993).

p. 183 *employer's sexual advances or favors*: "Sexual Harassment Policy, Definition of Sexual Harassment," available online at http://web2.sunyit.edu/human _resources/sexualharrasment_policy.inc (accessed May 2006).

p. 183 *it will be graded*: Rush Limbaugh, "The Way Things Aren't: Rush Limbaugh Debates Reality," available online at http://www.fair.org/index.php?page =1895 (accessed May 2006).

p. 183 *parlor for the same purpose*: Right Wing News, "The Wendy McElroy Interview by John Hawkins," available online at http://rightwingnews.com/ interviews/mcelroy.php (accessed May 2006).

p. 184 *where their fathers were living*: "Epidemiology of Divorce," *The Future of Children*, Princeton/Brookings, available online at http://www.futureofchildren .org/information2827/information_show.htm?doc_id=75527 (accessed May 2006).

p. 185 *there were 2.8 million matches*: "The Child Support Enforcement Process," available at the *Almanac of Policy Issues* Web site, http://www.policyalmanac.org/ social_welfare/archive/child_support_02.shtml (accessed May 2006).

p. 185 *sex offenders are male*: Lawrence A. Greenfeld, "Sex Offenses and Offenders: An Analysis of Data on Rape and Sexual Assault," Bureau of Justice Statistics, U.S. Department of Justice, NCJ-163392, February 1997, available online at http://www.ojp.usdoj.gov/bjs/abstract/soo.htm (accessed May 2006).

p. 187 *mid-30s throughout these decades*: National Election Studies, available online at http://www.umich.edu/~nes/nesguide/toptable/tab9a_1.htm (accessed May 2006).

p. 187 *55 percent to 39 percent*: Ruy Teixeira, "It's the White Working Class, Stupid," Century Foundation, February 8, 2005, available online at http://www .emergingdemocraticmajorityweblog.com/donkeyrising/archives/001042.php (accessed May 2006).

p. 188 *voter's partisan self-identification*: Information provided by Dick Morris in a series of interviews with the author in 1997. See also Thomas B. Edsall, "Blue Movie," *The Atlantic*, January/February 2003.

p. 189 *has a personal moral responsibility*: William Jefferson Clinton, 1992 Democratic National Convention Acceptance Address, "Our New Covenant," available online at http://www.americanrhetoric.com/speeches/billclinton1992dnc.htm (accessed May 2006).

p. 190 *Republican loyalists Linda Tripp*: Jeff Leen and Gene Weingarten of the *Washington Post* ("Linda's Trip," March 15, 1998) wrote:

> If President Clinton falls, it will be Linda Tripp who largely made it happen. She coolly trapped her young friend Monica Lewinsky into describing, on tape, in occasionally crude detail, what Lewinsky had denied under oath and was evidently prepared to continue denying: that she had a sexual affair with the president. Tripp then carried this information to attorneys representing Paula Corbin Jones and then to investigators for independent counsel Kenneth Starr, effectively baiting a second trap. Armed with Tripp's information, which had still not surfaced publicly, lawyers for the Arkansas woman suing the president for sexual harassment were able to ambush Clinton, obtaining an unambiguous denial, under oath, of a sexual relationship with Lewinsky.

Linda Tripp was a White House employee in the George H. W. Bush administration who "revered President Bush, according to friends," and who

> was appalled at what she saw in the Clinton White House: the messy, unkempt nature of certain members of the staff, the lack of reverence for the institution itself. Jeans. Walkmans. Dirty hair. . . . Tripp served Vince Foster his last meal—a cheeseburger with some M&M's she scooped up and put on his lunch tray—and, by her account to investigators, she was deeply shaken by his suicide on July 20, 1993. It fed her growing disaffection. A person who'd talked to Tripp about the suicide said Tripp felt that Clinton officials acted as though they had a lot to hide: rifling Foster's office, looking for God-knows-what. The whole thing seemed disrespectful to her, almost sordid. Vince Foster's suicide also led to Tripp's fateful first contact with Lucianne Goldberg in early 1994. Goldberg was looking for sources for a possible book about Foster's death, and a mutual friend, conservative commentator Tony Snow, said he knew the woman who served Foster his last meal. . . . On Nov. 29, 1993, Kathleen Willey told Tripp that the president had just made a pass at her inside the Oval Office. (p. F01)

p. 190 *and Lucianne Cummings Goldberg*: Working for the Nixon White House in 1972, Lucianne Cummings Goldberg was "a $1,000-a-week spy planted in the McGovern press corps. Nixon, his White House tapes show, referred to her by her code name, 'Chapman's friend.' But the agent's real name was Lucianne Cummings Goldberg, now back in the news as the book agent behind the taping of former White House aide Monica S. Lewinsky's account of her alleged relationship with President Clinton" (George Lardner Jr., "Goldberg a Veteran at Recording Gossip," *Washington Post*, February 4, 1998, p. A12).

p. 190 *while losing the popular vote*: There are those who argue that the "vast right wing conspiracy" went so far as to illegally tamper with Democratic voting processes in the 2004 election. See Steven F. Freeman, "The Unexplained Exit Poll Discrepancy," Research Report, University of Pennsylvania, Center for Organizational Dynamics, December 29, 2004, available online at http://72.14.203 .104/search?q=cache:F4RCdMBlKxkJ:www.appliedresearch.us/sf/Documents/Ex-itPoll.pdf+stephen+freeman+university+of+pennsylvania&hl=en&gl=us&ct=clnk &cd=2 (accessed May 2006). See also Mark Crispin Miller, *Fooled Again: How the Right Stole the 2004 Election and Why They'll Steal the Next One Too (Unless We Stop Them)* (New York: Basic Books, 2005), and Mark Crispin Miller, "None Dare Call

It Stolen," *Harpers* magazine online, September 7, 2005, available online at http://
www.harpers.org/ExcerptNoneDare.html (accessed May 2006).

p. 190 *60 Minutes televised campaign interview*: As evidence of the many faces of
the women's movement, Tammy Wynette demanded an apology, saying Mrs. Clinton had "offended every true country music fan and every person who has made
it on their own with no one to take them to a White House." Available online at
http://www.cbsnews.com/stories/2003/06/05/entertainment/main557119.shtml
(accessed May 2006).

p. 191 *and Marilyn Jo Jenkins*: For information on Marilyn Jo Jenkins, see John
F. Harris, *The Survivor: Bill Clinton in the White House* (New York: Random House,
2005), p. 294.

> Although senior Democrats are gathering around the Arkansas Gov-
> ernor, they are doing so nervously, fearful of a new scandal. . . . Their
> jitters increased yesterday with news that Playboy magazine is run-
> ning a spread in its next issue on Elizabeth Ward, a former Miss
> America, who was one of five women mentioned in a 1990 Arkansas
> lawsuit alleging they had had affairs with Mr. Clinton. The article ap-
> pears on 7 April, the day of primaries in New York, Wisconsin and
> Kansas. (Rupert Cornwell, "Tsongas Quits Presidential Race," *The
> Independent* [London], March 20, 1992)

Ward Gracen issued a qualified denial:

> A former Miss America, Elizabeth Ward, declines in the May issue of
> Playboy magazine to discuss whether she had had an affair with Gov.
> Bill Clinton of Arkansas. Speculation about the article has circulated
> around the Clinton campaign for months. "Have I slept with this per-
> son," she said in response to a question in the article, which will be on
> newsstands before the April 7 New York primary. "I don't believe that
> is anyone's business." ("Ex-Miss America Avoids Discussing Clinton,"
> *New York Times*, March 28, 1992, p. 9)

p. 191 *rape by Juanita Broaddrick*: Dorothy Rabinowitz, "Juanita Broaddrick
Meets the Press," *Wall Street Journal*, February 19, 1999, editorial page, http://
online.wsj.com/search/full.html (accessed June 2006).

p. 191 *revolutions in the Clinton presidency*: Clinton's "bimbo problems" were legion: on March 13, 1998, Paula Jones' lawyers, as part of their opposition to the
Clinton legal team's February 17 motion for summary judgment, released a statement by Dolly Kyle Browning:

> My name is Dolly Kyle Browning. I am over twenty-one years of age
> and I am fully competent to make this declaration. 1. I have known
> William Jefferson Clinton since I was eleven years old. I call him
> "Billy." We attended high school together. During the period from
> the mid-1970's until January 1992, we had a relationship that included
> sexual relations. The frequency of our contact with each other, and
> the frequency of our sexual encounters, varied over that time period,
> but we did have sexual relations many times during that time period.
> 2. Our relationship ended abruptly in January of 1992 when Billy
> would not return my telephone call. I told his secretary, Linda, that a
> tabloid had the story about me and Billy. I asked her to have him call
> me and he refused. Instead he had my brother, who was, at that time,
> working in the 1992 Clinton presidential campaign, call me from

Billy's New Hampshire apartment or office. My brother said that Billy was afraid to talk to me because everyone thought that I might record the conversation as Gennifer Flowers had done. He said "we" think you should deny the story. He finally said: "if you cooperate with the media we will destroy you." 3. The next time I spoke with Billy was at our high school reunion in 1994. At that reunion he and I had a conversation that lasted approximately 45 minutes. At the reunion, but prior to our conversation, I had avoided contact with Billy. He approached me sometime around midnight. He greeted me, saying "how are you?" I responded: "You are such an ass-hole, I can't believe you'd even bother to ask!" ("*Jones v. Clinton*, Overview," *Washington Post*, March 13, 1998, available online at http://www.washingtonpost .com/wp-srv/politics/special/pjones/docs/browning031398.htm [accessed May 2006])

p. 191 *Conservative Political Action Conference*: "Former Arkansas State Worker Says Clinton Made 1991 Proposition," Associated Press, February 11, 1994.

p. 192 *margin of 79 to 21*: "Battleground Polling Data," January 25, 1996, conducted by Celinda Lake and Ed Goeas, available online at http://aladinrc.wrlc.org/handle/1961/2000 (accessed May 2006).

p. 192 *between Lewinsky and Clinton*: "Sex & the Starr Report: Was the Report More Explicit Than Necessary to Serve Prosecutorial Goals?" University of Missouri–Kansas City School of Law Web site, http://www.law.umkc.edu/faculty/projects/ftrials/clinton/starrreport.html (accessed May 2006).

p. 192 *ran to 336 pages*: Kenneth Starr, *The Starr Report: The Official Report of the Independent Counsel's Investigation of the President* (Prima Lifestyles, 1998).

p. 192 *actually shares our values*: Paul M. Weyrich, "Letter to Conservatives," February 16, 1999, available online at http://www.nationalcenter.org/Weyrich299 .html (accessed May 2006).

p. 192 *popular with the electorate*: Clinton's advantage on economic issues was substantial:

Bill Clinton has presided over the longest period of economic expansion in American history—whether by design or default, whether by strategic appointments to critical government agencies or by caving in to the private sector, whether by fine-tuning fiscal policy or by getting out of the way. During the years of the Clinton administration, the U.S. gross domestic product has increased roughly 37 percent after adjusting for inflation, 13 million new jobs have been created, and the GDP for the private sector alone has risen approximately 41 percent. Wages are up, median household income at $38,000 a year has reached an all-time high, the overall poverty rate is down to 12.7 percent (a historic achievement), and unemployment is at its lowest point in three decades. The net worth—the value of real estate, stocks, bonds, and other assets—of the typical (median) family has increased dramatically. At the same time, while the largest budget deficit of the twentieth century was $290.4 billion in 1992, the U.S. government was running a $9.5-billion surplus in 1999. (Thomas B. Edsall, "A Man for This Season," *American Prospect*, February 28, 2000, available online at http://www.prospect.org/web/page.ww?section=root&name =ViewPrint&articleId=5615 [accessed May 2006])

p. 193 *of the two-party vote*: Robert G. Kaiser, "Is This Any Way to Pick a Winner? To Researchers, Election Is All Over but the Voting," *Washington Post*, May 26, 2000.

p. 193 *backed Bush 62 to 33*: "Exit Poll Results—Election 2000," Voter News Service via CNN.com, available online at http://www.udel.edu/poscir/road/course/exitpollsindex.html (accessed May 2006). Morris Fiorina, with Samuel J. Abrams and Jeremy C. Pope, *Culture War? The Myth of a Polarized America* (New York: Pearson Education, 2005), pp. 88–89. "Despite Clinton's generally high job approval ratings, his personal ratings were always significantly lower and dropped further during his scandal-ridden administration. And a new item on the 2000 National Election Study survey asked respondents whether since 1992 the country's moral climate had gotten better, worse, or stayed the same. Only 5 percent said it had gotten better, and 45 percent said it had gotten worse."

Chapter 6 ≻ The Business Revolution: An Enormous Expansion in the Role of Market Forces

p. 194 *best workers was Ben Martinez*: Martinez is a pseudonym, anonymity requested.

p. 194 *corporation lays stuff down*: Three interviews by the author with Steve Carr, Hertz manager, Reno, Nevada, airport, 1997.

p. 195 *virtually every sector of the economy*: For a fine overview of the 1970s and the "financialization" of American life, see David Harvey, *A Brief History of Neoliberalism* (New York: Oxford University Press, 2005), pp. 1–38.

p. 195 *"the manic logic of capitalism"*: William Greider, *One World, Ready or Not: The Manic Logic of Capitalism* (New York: Simon & Schuster, 1997).

p. 195 *local knowledge to act effectively*: Barun S. Mitra, "Hayek's Road to Freedom, a Centenary That May Hold the Key to the Next Millennium: A Tribute to Friedrich A. von Hayek on his Birth Centenary—May 8, 1999," Liberty Institute, available online at http://www.angelfire.com/mi/libertyinstitute/hayek1.html (accessed May 2006).

p. 195 *exposed to such concepts*: The Nobel Memorial Prize in Economics, information available online at http://cepa.newschool.edu/het/schools/nobel.htm (accessed May 2006). Anna J. Schwartz, "'Who Is Milton? What Is He?' Reflections on Two Lucky People: Milton and Rose D. Friedman, Memoirs," Federal Reserve Bank of Minneapolis, September 1998, available online at http://minneapolisfed.org/pubs/region/98-09/anna.cfm (accessed May 2006).

p. 195 *the 1930s, become dominant*: F. A. Hayek, *Socialism and War : Essays, Documents, Reviews (The Collected Works of F. A. Hayek)*, edited by Bruce Caldwell (Chicago: University of Chicago Press, 1997), p. 222.

p. 196 *any consumer in the world*: Robert Kuttner, *Everything for Sale: The Virtues and Limits of Markets* (Chicago: University of Chicago Press, 1996), reviewed by Marcia Stepanek in "Rethinking Capitalism," *Salon*, February 10, 1997, available online at http://archive.salon.com/feb97/news/news970210.html (accessed May 2006).

p. 196 *settled in for the long haul*: Joseph Nocera, *A Piece of the Action: How the Middle Class Joined the Money Class* (New York: Simon & Schuster, 1994), pp. 10, 11, and throughout. Nocera names a fourth factor, pointing to inflation in the 1970s as key: "Finally, inflation altered forever the relationship of the middle class to its money. Here is when old behaviors were abandoned and new financial habits acquired. . . . Looking back, it almost seems as though . . . everything that had previously taken place in the money revolution had been leading up to this point. Most certainly, everything that happened afterward flowed from it" (p. 168). Also see Christopher Lehmann-Haupt, "Once, a Penny Saved; Now, a Dollar Charged," *New York Times*, October 10, 1994.

p. 197 *leisure activities, and dreams fulfilled*: This success contrasts with what Franklin Roosevelt saw in 1937 when he delivered his Second Inaugural Address

(January 20, 1937, available online at http://www.britannica.com/eb/article-9116956?hook=809200 [accessed May 2006]):

> But here is the challenge to our democracy: In this nation I see tens of millions of its citizens—a substantial part of its whole population—who at this very moment are denied the greater part of what the very lowest standards of today call the necessities of life.
>
> I see millions of families trying to live on incomes so meager that the pall of family disaster hangs over them day by day.
>
> I see millions whose daily lives in city and on farm continue under conditions labeled indecent by a so-called polite society half a century ago.
>
> I see millions denied education, recreation, and the opportunity to better their lot and the lot of their children.
>
> I see millions lacking the means to buy the products of farm and factory and by their poverty denying work and productiveness to many other millions.
>
> I see one-third of a nation ill-housed, ill-clad, ill-nourished.

p. 197 *increase in 2001 drug spending*: "Prescription Drug Expenditures in 2001," The National Institute for Health Care Management Research and Educational Foundation, available online at http://72.14.203.104/search?q=cache:YnmqRZgZUhwJ:www.nihcm.org/spending2001.pdf+best+selling+drugs&hl=en&gl=us&ct=clnk&cd=61 (accessed May 2006).

p. 198 *in terms of velocity and scale*: "The Information Revolution," *Annals of the American Academy of Political and Social Science* 412 (March 1974): (entire issue). See also, James Fallows, "Wake Up America!" *New York Review of Books* 37, no. 3 (March 1, 1990), available online at http://www.nybooks.com/articles/3718 (accessed May 2006).

p. 198 *of Harvard Business School*: Interview with Thomas McCraw by the author, April 19, 1997.

p. 199 *change in the human condition*: Peter Drucker, *The Atlantic Monthly*, November, 1994, available online at http://www.theatlantic.com/politics/ecbig/soctrans.htm (accessed May 2006).

p. 199 *$982.2 billion to $2.56 trillion*: *The Economic Report of the President* (Washington DC: U.S. Government Printing Office, 1997), Table B-93, p. 406, and Table B-10, p. 312.

p. 200 *coming under tighter control*: James Annable, *Wall Street Journal*, April 28, 1997, p. A-18.

p. 200 *described Reagan's 1981 tax cut*: Howard Baker quote in Daniel Shaviro, "Contemporary U.S Tax Policy," posted online January 14, 2005, available online at http://www.aei.org/publications/pubID.21813,filter.all/pub_detail.asp (accessed May 2006).

p. 201 *it comes to prison policies*: Justice Policy Institute, "Texas Sentencing Reforms Reflect National Trend: States Emphasizing Treatment over Incarceration for Low Level Offenders," available online at http://www.justicepolicy.org/article.php?id=216 (accessed May 2006). The quote is from executive director of the Justice Policy Institute, Vincent Schiraldi.

p. 202 *federal buildings in New York*: Dana Milbank and Walter Pincus, "Declassified Memo Said Al Qaeda Was in U.S.: Aug. 6 Report to President Warned of Hijacking," *Washington Post*, April 11, 2004, p. A1.

p. 203 *otherwise-stay-at-home partner*: Elizabeth Warren, "Rewriting the Rules: Families, Money and Risk," The Privatization of Risk, Social Science Research Council, October 21, 2005, available online at http://privatizationofrisk.ssrc.org/

Warren/ (accessed May 2006). Amelia Warren Tyagi and Elizabeth Warren, *The Two Income Trap: Why Middle-Class Mothers and Fathers Are Going Broke* (New York: Basic Books, 2003).

p. 204 *and natural resources*: Americans for Democratic Action puts out an annual vote tabulation for members of the House and Senate that clearly demonstrates the partisan differences on issues from the environment to taxes to domestic social programs. Those reports can be found at http://www.adaction.org/ under "Publications."

p. 205 *less problematic than do women*: James Flynn, Paul Slovic, and C. K. Mertz, "Gender, Race, and Perception of Environmental Health Risks," *Risk Analysis* 14, no. 6 (1994): 1001–1008.

p. 205 *authorities and by anti-egalitarianism*: Melissa L. Finucane, Paul Slovic, C. K. Mertz, James Flynn, and Theresa A. Satterfield, "Gender, Race, and Perceived Risk: The 'White Male' Effect," *Health, Risk & Society* 2 (November 2, 2000).

p. 206 *members of racial or ethnic minority groups*: U.S. Department of Justice, Bureau of Justice Statistics, "Criminal Offenders Statistics," available online at http://www.ojp.usdoj.gov/bjs/crimoff.htm#findings (accessed May 2006).

p. 206 *individual responsibility, 47 to 29*: National Election Studies, University of Michigan, specific questions and responses can be found at http://www.umich.edu/~nes/nesguide/toptable/tab4a_4b.htm (accessed May 2006).

p. 206 *just 28 percent of Democrats*: Ibid.

p. 206 *majority male, 57 to 43*: Exit poll data provided to the *Washington Post* by survey sponsors, a consortium of news organizations that includes ABC, CBS, NBC, FOX, CNN, and the Associated Press.

p. 206 *31 percent of Democrats*: National Election Studies, University of Michigan, available online at http://www.umich.edu/~nes/nesguide/gd-index.htm#4 (accessed May 2006).

p. 207 *favorable election results for the Democrats*: National Bureau of Economic Research, "Business Cycle Expansions and Contractions," available online at http://www.nber.org/cycles/ (accessed May 2006).

p. 207 *they will be rich someday*: Richard Morin, "What Teens Really Think: A Poll of Washington Area Kids Gives Us a Piece of Their Minds," *Washington Post*, October 23, 2005, p. W14, a telephone survey conducted August 3–8, 2005, among a nationally representative sample of 570 respondents fourteen to eighteen years of age.

p. 207 *their intelligence is above average*: *Washington Post* survey conducted November 4–8, 2005, of 1033 adults aged eighteen and over.

p. 208 *voluntary associations and local communities*: Seymour Martin Lipset, "An Exceptional Nation," *Blueprint Magazine*, Democratic Leadership Council, April 1, 1999, available online at http://www.dlc.org/ndol_ci.cfm?kaid=115&subid=172&contentid=1447 (accessed May 2006).

p. 208 *"It's morning again in America"*: "It's Morning Again in America," 1984 campaign television ad for Ronald Reagan.

p. 208 *year were $226.5 billion*: U.S. Census Bureau News, press release, July 28, 2005, available online at http://www.census.gov/Press-Release/www/releases/archives/business_ownership/005477.html (accessed May 2006).

p. 209 *work in 2000 was $18.44*: John E. Buckley, "Rankings of Full-time Occupations, by Earnings, 2000," Department of Labor, Bureau of Labor Statistics, available online at http://www.bls.gov/ncs/ocs/sp/ncar0002.pdf (accessed May 2006).

p. 210 *they want to go there*: U.S. Congress, Senate Committee on the Judiciary, Hearings on "Bankruptcy Reform," Testimony of Professor Elizabeth Warren, Professor of Law, Harvard Law School, February 10, 2005, available online at http://judiciary.senate.gov/testimony.cfm?id=1381&wit_id=3996 (accessed May 2006).

Chapter 7 ➤ The Democrats: Two Sets of Problems— Ideological and Structural

p. 211 *working- and middle-class margins*: "Unrequited Love: Middle Class Voters Reject Democrats at the Ballot Box," a study by Third Way, a Democratic strategy and think tank, available online at http://www.third-way.com/ (accessed May 2006).

p. 212 *white majorities to the GOP*: Polarization works both ways. According to Morris Fiorina, writing about polarization of the media,

> the *Boston Herald* reported Clinton adviser Paul Begala as saying, on November 18, 2000, that "tens of millions of good people in Middle America voted Republican. But if you look closely at that map you see a more complex picture. You see the state where James Byrd was lynch-dragged behind a pickup truck until his body came apart—it's red. You see the state where Matthew Shepard was crucified on a split-rail fence for the crime of being gay—it's red. You see the state where right-wing extremists blew up a federal office building and murdered scores of federal employees—it's red." (Morris Fiorina, "Politics: What Culture Wars?" *Hoover Digest* 4 [Fall 2004], available online at http://www.hooverdigest.org/044/fiorina.html [accessed May 2006])

p. 212 *the subject of my earlier book*: Thomas B. Edsall with Mary D. Edsall, *Chain Reaction: The Impact of Race, Rights, and Taxes on American Politics* (New York: Norton, 1991).

p. 213 *loyalty to a liberal economic agenda*: Thomas Byrne Edsall with Mary D. Edsall, "When the Official Subject Is Presidential Politics, Taxes, Welfare, Crime, Rights, or Values, . . . the Real Subject Is Race," *Atlantic*, May 1991, available online to subscribers at http://www.theatlantic.com/politics/race/edsall.htm.

p. 213 *they will never recover*: See the official Thomas Frank Web site, http://www.tcfrank.com/ (accessed June 3, 2006).

p. 213 *world that they live in*: Interview with Frank, available online at http://www.buzzflash.com/interviews/04/08/int04045.html (accessed June 3, 2006).

p. 214 *is profoundly populist*: "Contesting Democratic Ideas," a 1986 paper by Stanley Greenberg, available online at http://www.greenbergresearch.com/publications/reports/r_contestingdemocratic_0486.pdf (accessed May 2006).

p. 214 *powerful cultural and values messages*: David J. Sirota, "The Democrats' Da Vinci Code," *American Prospect*, posted December 8, 2004, available online at http://www.prospect.org/web/page.ww?section=root&name=ViewWeb&articleId=8917 (accessed May 2006).

p. 214 *maintain a successful biracial coalition*: For an analysis of the Perot vote and his disproportionate wins among key GOP constituencies, see footnote 1 in chapter 1. Earl Black and Merle Black, *The Rise of Southern Republicans* (Cambridge, MA: Harvard University Press, 2002), p. 27.

p. 215 *higher than average national incomes*: Thomas B. Edsall, "Voter Values Determine Political Affiliation," *Washington Post*, March 26, 2001, p. A1.

p. 215 *Native American, and Asian American*: The figures on minority voters in Democratic Party were computed by the author from National Election Studies (NES) 2004 data available online at http://www.umich.edu/~nes/nesguide/gd-index.htm#9 (accessed May 2006).

p. 215 *between $25 million and $102 million*: Zachary Coile, "Bay Lawmakers among Wealthiest: Feinstein and Pelosi Continue to Top the List of the Richest Members of Congress," *San Francisco Chronicle*, June 26, 2004, available online at http://www.sfgate.com/cgi-bin/article.cgi?f=/c/a/2004/06/26/BAG7B7CDMQ1 .DTL (accessed May 2006).

p. 215 *George Soros*: On George Soros, see James V. Grimaldi and Thomas B. Edsall, "Super Rich Step into Political Vacuum: McCain-Feingold Paved Way for 527s," *Washington Post*, October 17, 2004, p. A1, available online at http://www .fairelections.us/article.php?id=257 (accessed May 2006).

p. 215 *Ellen Malcolm*: Glen Justice, "For '04 Democratic Campaigns, She's Queen of the Hat-Passers," *New York Times*, May 13, 2004, available online at http://www.nytimes.com/2004/05/13/politics/campaign/13MALC.html?ex =1144382400&en=d408329277e590bc&ei=5070 (accessed May 2006).

p. 215 *Jane Fonda*: Regarding Jane Fonda, see Thomas B. Edsall, "Fundraising Doubles the Pace of 2000," *Washington Post*, August 21, 2004, p. A1.

p. 216 *John Kerry*: Sean Loughlin and Robert Yoon, "Millionaires Populate U.S. Senate: Kerry, Rockefeller, Kohl among the Wealthiest," CNN Washington Bureau, June 13, 2003, available online at http://www.cnn.com/2003/ALLPOLITICS/06/13/senators.finances/ (accessed May 2006).

p. 216 *socially liberal donors, large and small*: "The new small donors, who played a much bigger role in 2004 than in the past, are polarized on ideological, cultural and economic issues in much the same way that large givers are, according to a survey by the Institute for Politics, Democracy & the Internet at George Washington University of all donors, both those using the Internet and those who did not" (Thomas B. Edsall, "Rise in Online Fundraising Changed Face of Campaign Donors: Small Contributors Found to Be Polarized but More Representative of Middle Class," *Washington Post*, March 6, 2006, p. A3).

p. 216 *$93.4 million to $213 million*: For financial data on both presidential candidate and political party fundraising, see PoliticalMoneyLine at http://www .fecinfo.com/ (accessed May 2006).

p. 216 *their weakness in small-donor fundraising*: For detailed charts and data on campaign finance trends, go to the Campaign Finance Institute's Web site at: http://www.campaignfinanceinstitute.org/ (accessed May 2006).

p. 217 *and Hugh Hewitt*: http://www.technorati.com/pop/blogs/ (accessed March 26, 2006).

p. 217 *Daily Kos and Eschaton*: http://truthlaidbear.com/TrafficRanking.php ?start=1 (accessed March 26, 2006).

p. 217 *unique visits a day*: "NPI's Blogosphere Report," New Democrat Network, New Politics Institute, August 10, 2005, available online at http://www.ndn .org/issueadvocacy/commentary/ (accessed May 2006). The standing of individual blogs in the pecking order is quickly transformed, but the general principles appear to hold.

p. 218 *might indeed be up for grabs*: Andrew Boyd, "The Web Rewires the Movement: Articles; Grassroots Organizing Power of the Net," *Nation*, August 4, 2003.

p. 218 *better at the moment*: George Packer, "Smart-Mobbing the War," *New York Times*, March 9, 2003.

p. 218 *politics into the sports page*: Kos' first entry was as follows: "I am progressive. I am liberal. I make no apologies. I believe government has an obligation to create an even playing field for all of this country's citizens and immigrants alike. I am not a socialist. I do not seek enforced equality. However, there has to be equality of opportunity, and the private sector, left to its own devices, will never achieve this goal" (quoted in Matt Stoller, "A Beginning of the Dean/Clark Campaigns," available online at http://www.bopnews.com/archives/000133.html [accessed May 2006]).

p. 218 *William Frey in the Financial Times*: William H. Frey, "The Democrats Must Woo a New Demographic," *Financial Times*, November 4, 2004.

p. 219 *tripled from 12 to 35 percent*: National Election Studies, available online at http://www.umich.edu/~nes/nesguide/toptable/tab1b_5b.htm (accessed May 2006).

p. 219 *say they believe in God*: "Social and Religious Characteristics of the Electorate," National Election Studies, available online at http://www.umich.edu/~nes/nesguide/gd-index.htm#1 (accessed May 2006).

p. 219 *Hispanic Catholic electorate*: Pew Hispanic Center, http://pewhispanic .org/.

p. 220 *pointed at the ear of America*: Shailagh Murray and T. R. Reid, "Tuning In to Anger on Immigration: Rep. Tancredo's Profile Grows with Push to Secure U.S. Borders," *Washington Post*, March 31, 2006, p. A1.

p. 220 *from south of the border*: John B. Judis, "Border War," *New Republic*, January 16, 2006, p. 15.

p. 221 *Long may she remain so*: "McCain Statement on Border Security and Immigration Reform Legislation," March 30, 2006, available online at http://mccain .senate.gov/index.cfm?fuseaction=NewsCenter.ViewPressRelease&Content_id =1686 (accessed May 2006).

p. 222 *sexual revolution began to take off*: Tom W. Smith, "American Sexual Behavior: Trends, Socio-Demographic Differences, and Risk Behavior," National Opinion Research Center, University of Chicago, GSS Topical Report No. 25, December 1998, available online at http://www.norc.uchicago.edu/library/sexual .pdf (accessed May 2006). Andrew Hacker also notes in his book *Mismatch* (New York: Scribner, 2003) that, on average, the length of time between the arrival of women at sexual maturity and the time at which women marry and/or bear children has lengthened considerably in recent years, suggesting much greater scope for premarital sexual activity: "The National Center for Health Statistics also has figures going back to 1970, which show that 72.9 percent of women college graduates began having children before they reached thirty. Now only 35.7 percent are giving birth that early" (p. 70).

p. 223 *harmful psychological and physical effects*: "Fact Sheet: Section 510 State Abstinence Education Program, History and Purpose," Department of Health and Human Services, Administration for Children &Families, available online at http:// www.acf.dhhs.gov/programs/fysb/content/abstinence/factsheet.htm (accessed May 2006).

p. 223 *do choose to inflame*: For example, in April 2006, African American Representative Cynthia McKinney of Georgia was not recognized by a security guard at the entrance to the Capitol. Ms. McKinney ignored the order of the guard to halt, and an altercation ensued. Republicans delighted in transmitting this story to the media and supporters, "eagerly working to keep the story alive" (see "Mckinney v. the World," April 5, 2006, available online at http://www.tnr.com/blog/theplank [accessed May 2006]). The Independent Womens' Forum, a popular conservative women's organization posted a typical set of right-wing comments on its Web site:

> Rep. Cynthia McKinney, the Democratic congresswoman from Georgia who evidently thinks that wearing her member-of-Congress ID pin makes her look fat, gave a press conference this morning in her home town of Atlanta to explain why she allegedly plunged her cell phone into the chest of a Capitol Police officer who dared to accost her as she swept past the security checkpoint that's mandatory in the House Office Building for folks who aren't wearing their member-of-Congress ID pins. And there, well, did our Cynthia ever play that race card! Michelle Malkin has the pix. "Our sister was set up! Set up!" lamented one McKinney supporter, echoing the words of former Washington, D.C., Mayor Marion Barry when he was caught smok-

ing crack in a hotel room in 1989. Come again? How can you be "set up" in an incident like that? Did Dennis Hassler steal McKinney's pin? Did McKinney think she was reaching into her purse for a pack of Kleenex, except that someone had substituted a cell phone?

And Neil Boortz, a conservative talk show host made the following transparently racist comments on air:

> BOORTZ: For instance, or for goodness sakes, jump in and I'm gonna say—I'm gonna start out with something controversial. I saw Cynthia McKinney's new hair-do. . . . She looks like a ghetto slut. . . . It's just—it's hideous. . . . It just flies away from her head in every conceivable direction. It looks like an explosion in a Brillo pad factory. It's just hideous. To me, that hairstyle just shows contempt for—no, it's not an Afro. I mean, no, it just shows contempt for the position that she holds and the body that she serves in. . . . She looks like Tina Turner peeing on an electric fence. . . . She looks like a shih tzu.

Boortz posted similar comments on his Web site:

> It doesn't look like the latest Cynthia McKinney mess is going to go away any time soon. Today's *Atlanta Journal-Constitution* is reporting that the Capitol Hill police have notified the federal prosecutor's office in Washington that they are going to seek an arrest warrant for McKinney next week. OK, now I've seen Cynthia McKinney's new hairstyle. There is just no other way to say this. It's just hideous. She looks like ghetto trash. Get a braider over there . . . quick! Nobody with a modicum of self-respect would go around looking like that. (March 31, 2006, available online at http://mediamatters.org/items/200603310005 [accessed May 2006])

p. 225 *counties with the highest growth rates*: Ronald Brownstein and Richard Rainey, "GOP Plants Flag on New Voting Frontier: Bush's Huge Victory in the Fast-Growing Areas beyond the Suburbs Alters the Political Map," *Los Angeles Times*, November 22, 2004.

p. 225 *promising for the Democratic Party*: Robert E. Lang and Thomas W. Sanchez, "The New Metro Politics: Interpreting Recent Presidential Elections Using a County-based Regional Typology," Metropolitan Institute at Virginia Tech, available online at http://www.mi.vt.edu/uploads/NationalElectionReport.pdf (accessed May 2006). Table compiled by the author from data presented by Lang and Sanchez.

p. 226 *back should they lose it*: Interview with Gary Jacobson, March 20, 2006. Unpublished charts and graphs in the form of a PowerPoint presentation made at a Brookings/Hoover conference on "Red and Blue Nation? Causes, Consequences and Correction of America's Polarized Politics," The Brookings Institution, Washington DC, March 13–14, 2006, supplied to the author by Jacobson.

p. 227 *popular vote in the 2000 election*: Thomas E. Mann, "Partisan Polarization: Is Gerrymandering at All Responsible?" paper delivered at the Brookings/Hoover conference on "Red and Blue Nation? Causes, Consequences and Correction of America's Polarized Politics," The Brookings Institution, Washington DC, March 13–14, 2006.

p. 227 *than they need*: William A. Galston and Pietro Nivola, "Delineating the Problem," paper presented at the Brookings/Hoover conference on polarization, Washington DC, March 13–14, 2006.

p. 228 *conservative voters year-round*: Joanne B. Wright, "Civic Engagement Sector Analysis," *Democracy Alliance*, Fall 2005, p. 1.

p. 228 *long-term support for infrastructure and expansion*: Ibid.

p. 229 *Conservatives in the other*: Paul M. Weyrich, "A Leadership Lacking Spirit," posted November 28, 2005, available online at http://www.enterstageright.com/archive/articles/1205/1205replead.htm (accessed May 2006).

p. 229 *political blackmail by Liberal Republicans*: Ibid.

p. 230 *sixteen voted for Kerry*: Department of Commerce, Bureau of Economic Analysis, http://www.bea.gov/. See also, Wikipedia, The Free Encyclopedia, "Highest Income Counties in the United States," http://en.wikipedia.org/wiki/Richest_counties_in_the_United_States.

p. 231 *attend Bible study or prayer meetings*: "Beyond Red vs. Blue: Republicans Divided about Role of Government—Democrats by Social and Personal Values," Pew Research Center for the People and the Press, released May 10, 2005, available online at http://people-press.org/reports/display.php3?ReportID=242 (accessed May 2006).

p. 232 *organized power of Government*: Franklin D. Roosevelt's address to the Democratic National Convention, June 27, 1936, available at The Miller Center of Public Affairs, University of Virginia, http://millercenter.virginia.edu/scripps/diglibrary/prezspeeches/roosevelt/fdr_1936_0627.html (accessed May 2006).

p. 232 *favored classes or the powerful few*: Truman's Democratic convention acceptance speech, July 15, 1948, available on the Public Broadcasting System's Web site, http://www.pbs.org/newshour/character/links/truman_speech.html (accessed May 2006).

p. 232 *and we're for the people*: Al Gore's convention acceptance speech, August 17, 2000, available on the Public Broadcasting System's Web site, http://www.pbs.org/newshour/election2000/demconvention/gore.html (accessed May 2006).

p. 232 *job creation, health care and education*: John F. Kerry's speech to the 2004 Democratic National Convention, July 29, 2004, The American Presidency Project, University of California, Santa Barbara, available online at http://www.presidency.ucsb.edu/shownomination.php?convid=20 (accessed May 2006).

p. 233 *among low-income white voters*: Larry M. Bartels, "What's the Matter with What's the Matter with Kansas?" Department of Politics, Woodrow Wilson School of Public and International Affairs, Princeton University, paper delivered at the American Political Science Association meeting August 25, 2005, Washington DC.

p. 233 *20 percent of the top third*: Data on whites in the bottom third of the income distribution supplied by David Howell of the staff of National Election Studies (NES), University of Michigan, November 30, 2005.

p. 234 *party's agenda-setting processes*: National Election Studies, "Party Identification 3-Point Scale 1952–2004," available online at http://www.umich.edu/~nes/nesguide/toptable/tab2a_2.htm (accessed May 2006).

p. 234 *by a 68 to 32 margin*: National Election Studies, "Presidential Vote 2 Major Parties 1948–2004," available online at http://www.umich.edu/~nes/nesguide/toptable/tab9a_1.htm (accessed May 2006).

p. 234 *lower-income whites exceed six percent*: Larry M. Bartels, "What's the Matter with What's the Matter with Kansas?" Department of Politics, Woodrow Wilson School of Public and International Affairs, Princeton University, available online at http://www.princeton.edu/~bartels/kansas.pdf (accessed May 2006).

p. 234 *in the years since 1972*: Ibid.

p. 235 *according to NES data*: Only 45 percent of those of voting age in the bottom third of the income distribution work, compared to 80 percent of those in the top third. Data on whites in the bottom third of the income distribution supplied to the author by David Howell of the staff of National Election Studies (NES), University of Michigan, November 30, 2005.

p. 235 *top thirds of the income distribution*: National Election Studies, "Political Involvement and Participation in Politics," available online at http://www.umich.edu/~nes/nesguide/gd-index.htm#6 (accessed May 2006).

p. 236 *first time in our history*: Studs Terkel, "Kucinich Is the One," *Nation*, May 6, 2002.

p. 236 *'itty bitty zygote'*: Katha Pollitt, "Regressive Progressive?" *Nation*, May 27, 2002.

p. 236 *who failed to embrace abortion*: Thomas Beaumont, "Kucinich Changes to Pro-choice," *Des Moines Register*, February 27, 2003.

p. 237 *attempted by contemporary Democrats*: For postmaterialist values, see Ronald Inglehart, *Silent Revolution: Changing Values and Political Styles among Western Publics* (Princeton, NJ: Princeton University Press, 1977); and *Culture Shift in Advanced Industrial Society* (Princeton, NJ: Princeton University Press, 1990).

p. 237 *search for ways to mitigate them*: Todd Gitlin in *The Twilight of Common Dreams* (New York: Metropolitan Books, 1995) wrote about the havoc wreaked on the left by battles over diversity, identity politics, and multiculturalism in the 1980s and 1990s. The lack of cohesion Gitlin describes continues today even as those particular battles have subsided. Gitlin refers to

> collections of interest groups . . . [lacking] a vocabulary for the common good, . . . vulnerable to centrifugal tendencies. . . . Democrats could not agree on a common story. They did not march onward together toward an extension of rights; . . . they did not march onward together, period. . . . They lacked even terms of unification. . . . They didn't add up. They were . . . less than the sum of their parts. . . . Their incapacity was a chapter in a longer ordeal: the breakdown of the idea of a common Left. (pp. 82–83)

p. 238 *when I say he can't*: Nick Chiles, "4–3 Vote Defeats Opt-out Plan," *Newsday*, September 12, 1991, p. 6.

p. 238 *please vote to opt out*: Dennis Hevesi, "Board Rejects 'Opt out' Plan on Condoms," *New York Times*, September 12, 1991, p. B1.

p. 238 *median household income was $80,978*: U.S. Census 2002 national demographic data for the nation, states, and counties, available online at http://factfinder.census.gov/servlet/ADPGeoSearchByListServlet?_lang=en&_ts=142353118294 (accessed May 2006).

p. 238 *7 to 1 to abandon the program*: Lori Aratani, "Md. Board Restarts Overhaul of Sex Ed: Citizens Panel to Help Mold Program," *Washington Post*, May 24, 2005, p. B3.

p. 239 *public education, or public contracting*: Michigan Civil Rights Initiative, an anti-affirmative action drive supported by Ward Connerly, American Civil Rights Coalition Chairman, available online at http://www.michigancivilrights.org/index.htm (accessed May 2006).

p. 239 *fair chance in education and employment*: "NAACP Passes Michigan Affirmative Action Resolution during 96th Annual Convention: Affirmative Action IS Necessary for Realizing Democracy in Our Nation," NAACP press release, July 14, 2005, available online at http://www.naacp.org/news/2005/2005-07-14.html (accessed May 2006).

p. 239 *say that at the same time*: Commission on Presidential Debates, transcript of the third debate in Tempe, Arizona, October 13, 2004, available online at http://www.debates.org/pages/trans2004d.html (accessed May 2006).

p. 240 *commerce, employment and education*: "NAACP Applauds Bush's Affirmative Action Defense," NAACP press release, August 11, 2001, available online at http://www.naacp.org/news/2001/2001-08-11.html (accessed May 2006).

p. 240 *continue to believe just that*: Paul A. Samuelson, "Where Ricardo and Mill Rebut and Confirm Arguments of Mainstream Economists Supporting Globalization," *Journal of Economic Perspectives* 18, no. 3 (Summer 2004): 135–146.

p. 241 *who make the company run*: "Statement by AFL-CIO President John Sweeney on GM's Layoff Announcement," AFL-CIO press release, November 23, 2005.

p. 241 *Party of Davos*: Jeff Faux, *The Global Class War: How America's Bipartisan Elite Lost Our Future—and What It Will Take to Win It Back* (Hoboken, NJ: John Wiley & Sons, 2006).

p. 242 *antagonists of the corporate sector*: Thomas B. Edsall, "A Man for This Season," *American Prospect*, February 28, 2000, available online at http://www.prospect.org/web/page.ww?section=root&name=ViewPrint&articleId=5615 (accessed May 2006).

p. 243 *beyond the realm of education*: The National Center for Education Statistics (NCES) forecast, available online at http://nces.ed.gov/programs/digest/d04/ (accessed May 2006).

p. 243 *minor in the relevant subject*: Robert Gordon, "What Democrats Need to Say about Education," *New Republic*, May 30, 2005, available online at http://www.tnr.com/doc.mhtml?pt=aQv7Q66Pcy65XAVIyW2UIX%3D%3D (accessed May 2006).

p. 244 *to head to the polls*: Diana Jean Schemo, "Federal Program in Vouchers Draws Strong Minority Support," *New York Times*, April 6, 2006, p. A1. The dire condition of public education and the failures of the Democratic Party on this score are reflected in some grim statistics:

> Although performance on assessments of mathematics and science achievement by the National Assessment of Educational Progress (NAEP) has improved since the 1970s, few students are attaining levels deemed Proficient or Advanced by a national panel of experts, and the performance of U.S. students continues to rank substantially below that of students in a number of other, mostly Asian, countries. This cross-national achievement gap appears to widen as students progress through school. ("Elementary and Secondary Education: How Well Do Our Students Perform in Mathematics and Science?" available online at http://nsf.gov/statistics/seind02/c1/c1s1.htm [accessed May 2006])

p. 244 *basic math or reading skills*: Diana Jean Schemo, "Federal Program in Vouchers Draws Strong Minority Support," *New York Times*, April 6, 2006, p. A1.

p. 244 *science section in the local newspaper*: National Institute for Literacy (NIFL), National Assessment of Educational Progress (NAEP), "Reading Scores," available online at http://www.nifl.gov/nifl/facts/NAEP.html (accessed May 2006).

p. 244 *NAEP data show that in 2000*: Ibid.

p. 245 *violate or corrupt their children*: Milton Kotler and Nelson Rosenbaum, "Strengthening the Democratic Party through Strategic Marketing: Voters and Donors," a confidential report for the Democratic National Committee, CRG Research Institute, 1985.

p. 245 *vulnerability and failures*: Stanley B. Greenberg, "Report on Democratic Defection," The Analysis Group, April 15, 1985, pp. 13–18.

p. 246 *thirty percentage point difference*: Thomas B. Edsall, "Values Voters Determine Political Affiliation," *Washington Post*, March 26, 2001, p. A1.

p. 246 *moral foundation of our country*: "The Cultural Divide & the Challenge of Winning Back Rural & Red State Voters," Democracy Corps, August 9, 2005, available online at www.democracycorps.com (accessed September 2005).

p. 247 *as of late 2005*: Ibid.

p. 247 *one that should be "rare"*: "Remarks by Senator Hillary Rodham Clinton to the NYS Family Planning Providers," January 24, 2005, available online at http://clinton.senate.gov/~clinton/speeches/2005125A05.html (accessed May 2006).

Chapter 8 ➤ Conclusion: Three-Quarters or Half a Party

p. 249 *she or he believes this, too*: Michael Tomasky, "Party in Search of a Notion," *American Prospect*, April 18, 2006, available online at http://www.prospect.org/web/page.ww?section=root&name=ViewWeb&articleId=11424   (accessed May 2006).

p. 250 *Democrats will have to get religion*: Amy Sullivan, "Do the Democrats Have a Prayer? To Win in '04 the Next Nominee Will Need to Get Religion," *Washington Monthly*, June 2003, available online at http://www.washingtonmonthly.com/features/2003/0306.sullivan.html (accessed May 2006).

p. 250 *flock to the "prosperity gospel"*: The *Christian Sentinal* reported as follows on the prosperity gospel:

> [T]he Church of Laodicea has a new star on the rise in the world of positive motivational Christianity. It's Joel Osteen, pastor of Lakewood Church in Houston. The younger Osteen lives the life of prosperity that he preaches. A 2001 Real Estate Guide (http://north-valley.com/realestate_board/messages/157.html) valued his home at $1,265,500. His sermon titles give clues as to the focus of Osteen's ministry:
>
>> Enlarge Your Vision
>> Holding onto Your Dreams
>> Financial Prosperity
>> How Valuable You Are in God's Eyes
>> Overcoming the Greatest Hindrance to Healing
>> Developing Miracle-working Faith
>> Faith to Change Your World
>> Believe God for the Greater Works
>> Do All You Can Do to Make Your Dreams Come True
>> Living a Life of Excellence
>> Developing Your Potential
>
> . . . Now with his super-star celebrity status Osteen is moving Lakewood Church into the Compaq Center, the 18,000-seat arena where Houston's basketball team has played. They have entered into a lease and are busy remodeling the entire center which they will rename "the Lakewood International Center." A fund-raising campaign to raise the $70 million dollars for the improvements is asking supporters to sponsor a seat for $2500 each. (Available online at http://cultlink.com/ar/osteen.htm [accessed May 2006])

p. 252 *an epic battle for future wealth*: Agora Financial, "Welcome to Strategic Investment," available online at http://www.agorafinancial.com/THE_PUBS/DRI/ (accessed May 2006).

p. 252 *people can still get rich*: President Ronald Reagan, remarks at a Republican congressional dinner saluting him, Washington DC, May 4, 1982, Public Papers of the Presidents of the United States: Ronald Reagan, 1982, p. 558, available online at http://www.bartleby.com/73/1384.html (accessed May 2006).

p. 252 *with real assets of ownership*: The White House, President George W. Bush, "Strengthening Social Security," available online at http://www.whitehouse .gov/infocus/social-security/ (accessed May 2006).

p. 252 *makes it difficult to plan ahead*: The White House, President George W. Bush, "Fact Sheet: Strengthening Medicare," January 2002, available online at http://www.whitehouse.gov/news/releases/2002/01/20020128-14.html (accessed May 2006).

p. 253 *on building an "investor class"*: Compare to the Agora quote this statement of Bush administration policy from the White House Web site ("Strengthening Social Security," http://www.whitehouse.gov/infocus/social-security/ [accessed May 2006]):

> President Bush has discussed the importance of Social Security and the need to fix the Social Security system for future generations of Americans. . . . [Social Security] needs to be fixed for younger workers—our children and grandchildren. The government has made promises it cannot afford to pay for with the current pay-as-you-go system.
>
> * In 1950, there were 16 workers to support every one beneficiary of Social Security.
>
> * Today, there are only 3.3 workers supporting every Social Security beneficiary.
>
> * In 2008—just three short years from now—baby boomers will begin to retire. And over the next few decades, people will be living longer and benefits are scheduled to increase dramatically. By the time today's youngest workers turn 65, there will only be 2 workers supporting each beneficiary.
>
> * Under the current system, today's 30-year-old worker will face a 27% benefit cut when he or she reaches normal retirement age.
>
> If we do not act to fix Social Security now, the only solutions will be dramatically higher taxes, massive new borrowing or sudden and severe cuts in Social Security benefits or other government programs.
>
> * Just 13 years from now, in 2017, the government will begin to pay out more in Social Security benefits than it collects in payroll taxes—and shortfalls then will grow larger with each passing year.
>
> * By the year 2027, the government will somehow have to come up with an extra $200 billion a year to keep the system afloat.
>
> * By 2033, the annual shortfall will be more than $300 billion a year.
>
> * By 2041, when workers in their mid-20s begin to retire, the system will be bankrupt—unless we act now to save it.
>
> To keep the promise of Social Security alive for our children and grandchildren, we need to fix Social Security now once and for all. We can not pretend the problem doesn't exist. The fact is Social Security will go broke when our young workers get ready to retire. Every year we wait the problem becomes worse for our children.
>
> President Bush has pledged to work with Congress to find the most effective combination of reforms. He will listen to any good idea that does not include raising payroll taxes.
>
> * Fixing Social Security permanently requires a candid review of the options.

- Over the years, many people from both parties have offered suggestions such as limiting benefits for wealthy retirees, indexing benefits to prices, instead of wages; increasing the retirement age; or changing the benefit formula to create disincentives for early retirement. All of these options are on the table.

As we fix Social Security, we must make it a better deal for our younger workers by allowing them to put part of their payroll taxes in personal retirement accounts.

- Personal accounts would be entirely voluntary.

- The money would go into a conservative mix of bond and stock funds that would have the opportunity to earn a higher rate of return than anything the current system could provide.

- A young person who earns an average of $35,000 a year over his or her career would have nearly a quarter million dollars saved in his or her own account upon retirement.

- That savings would provide a nest egg to supplement that worker's traditional Social Security check, or to pass on to his or her children.

- Best of all, it would replace the empty promises of the current system with real assets of ownership.

Index